D1616366

HORSE JOURNAL™
GUIDE TO EQUINE **SUPPLEMENTS** AND
NUTRACEUTICALS

HORSE JOURNAL™
GUIDE TO EQUINE **SUPPLEMENTS**
AND **NUTRACEUTICALS**

Eleanor M. Kellon, V.M.D.

THE LYONS PRESS
Guilford, Connecticut
An Imprint of The Globe Pequot Press

The content of this book has been distilled from articles published in *Horse Journal*. In many cases, the testing methodology and other details have been omitted or condensed to concentrate on the results and recommendations.

Prices noted in the text were accurate at the time the articles were published in *Horse Journal* and are provided in this book to convey price ranges as well as relative prices. All prices are subject to change without notice by manufacturers and retailers.

To buy books in quantity for corporate use or incentives, call **(800) 962–0973** or e-mail **premiums@GlobePequot.com**.

The Lyons Press is an imprint of The Globe Pequot Press.

Text design by Casey Shain

Library of Congress Cataloging-in-Publication Data is available on file.

ISBN 978-1-59921-178-7

Printed in the United States of America

10 9 8 7 6 5 4 3 2 1

CONTENTS

Foreword by Cynthia Foley..vi

Introduction: The Shift to Preventive and Natural Healthcare
   and the Emerging Field of Natural Health Products vii

1. Does Your Horse Need a Vitamin and Mineral Supplement? 1

2. Anti-Inflammatories 17

3. Antioxidants 22

4. Appetite Stimulation 30

5. Blood Builders 37

6. Building Strong Bones 45

7. Calming and Stress Reduction Additives 49

8. Cushing's Disease 63

9. Digestive-Tract Aids 75

10. Electrolytes 105

11. Feeding Pregnant, Lactating, and Growing Horses 116

12. Feeding Senior Horses 136

13. Hoof Support 145

14. Immune-System Support 151

15. Joint Support 166

16. Laminitis/Insulin Resistance 187

17. Muscle Support 198

18. Obesity..220

19. Performance...230

20. Respiratory Aids...237

21. Skin and Coat Supplements...258

22. Weight-Gain Strategies 268

Index 277

About the Author 291

FOREWORD

Since 1994, *Horse Journal*'s field trials, product recommendations and down-to-earth philosophy on training, nutrition, and horse care have earned the respect of both its readers and the publishing world in general. Never before had a horse magazine honestly and openly shared opinions about the quality of specific product brands. We don't buckle under pressure from advertising dollars or from the influence of a professional organization with its own ax to grind. In fact, we accept no advertising, making us accountable to no one except our readers. We're proud of what we do, and we're happy to tell you that much of it can be directly attributed to one of our strongest assets: Dr. Eleanor Kellon.

I've had the privilege of working professionally with Eleanor for more than two decades, and during that time she has become one of my oldest and dearest friends. I've known few people who can combine strength, integrity and compassion as gracefully as Eleanor. A *magna cum laude* graduate of the University of Pennsylvania Veterinary School and a former accomplished hunter-jumper rider, Eleanor has an incredible ability to analyze a problem thoroughly and look deeply for causes and solutions. To Eleanor, there is no such thing as a hopeless case.

Through her work in her own practice and in field trials for *Horse Journal*, Eleanor has vast experience with both conventional and unconventional therapies. She knows what works and what doesn't—and will tell you exactly why. Woe to the manufacturer that dares to challenge her. Eleanor is a fiery, fully armed opponent, exposing products that lack the ingredients needed to get the job done.

—CYNTHIA FOLEY,
Editor-in-Chief, *Horse Journal*

INTRODUCTION

The Shift to Preventive and Natural Healthcare and the Emerging Field of Natural Health Products

The adage, "You are what you eat" couldn't be more true. Life begins when a single cell, the egg, receives a complementary copy of DNA from a single cell, the spermatozoa. The stage is now set for the creation of a new horse. All the instructions and blueprints are contained in the fertilized egg, but to "build" the horse requires raw materials. Everything used to make the horse comes from the mare's diet, through her bloodstream, and after birth from the horse's diet. Fats, carbohydrates, proteins, vitamins, and minerals cannot be manufactured out of thin air. Cars run better on quality gasoline, houses made of the most durable materials last longer, and horses constructed and maintained on high-quality diets with the correct nutrients in adequate amounts are stronger and healthier.

Nothing could be more natural than feeding horses healthful foods as a first step in keeping them healthy. This sounds simple enough, and there is indeed a lot we can learn by studying the details of the natural diet horses consumed as they were evolving, but domestication makes it impossible to duplicate those conditions. Unless your horses are roaming freely over hundreds of acres of land with the same diversity of plant species as were available to their ancestors, you are not really keeping your horses "naturally." Further complicating matters is the fact that different breeds have different requirements and tolerances for the types of things we commonly feed domestic horses, such as simple carbohydrate-rich grains. What is good and natural for a pony would starve the modern, selectively bred Thoroughbred; and what is good and natural for the Thoroughbred would rapidly produce obesity—and likely laminitis—in a pony.

"Natural" has become a catchword, synonymous with better and safer for many people. Whether it's a feeding plan, a

Defining Natural Health Care

Natural means different things to different people—from basically turning the horse out on grass and letting nature take its course, to incorporating a host of natural supplements into the horse's diet in hopes of avoiding the use of any drug or manmade chemical whatsoever. For the purposes of this book, the natural approach will encompass:

- Feeding the horse calories of a type and amount suitable to maintain normal body weight for the breed and level of work

- Guaranteeing correct and balanced intake of key vital minerals and vitamins, with supplementation geared to the individual horse's needs and what is already in the diet

- Using supplemental nutrients and nutraceuticals to support normal growth and assist the horse in dealing with stresses, injuries, or illnesses

- Exploring the use of nutraceuticals and herbals as alternatives to drugs.

    Long story short, the goal is not to deprive the horse of the benefits of modern medicine and science, but to use the information science has provided us to make our horses as healthy, sound, and strong as possible. We won't be able to prevent every illness or injury, but when one occurs we want to be sure to give the appropriate nutritional support and not rely completely on drugs.

general supplement, or a nutritional or herbal supplement designed to address a specific concern, there is a high demand for anything labeled natural. However, the fact remains that horses are living longer and healthier lives thanks in large part to advances in deworming, drugs like antibiotics, effective vaccines, and advances in nutrition. Some of our most effective "natural" alternatives, like joint nutraceuticals, are not at all natural ingredients in a horse's diet. We also have science to thank for our knowledge and understanding of the potential health benefits of the vitamins, minerals, and nutraceuticals.

A positive outgrowth of the emphasis on "natural" has been a realization of the power of a healthful diet and appropriate supplements to prevent disease and equip the horse with a strong body to fight off threats and heal insults without always having to rely on drugs after the damage has been done. This, to me, is at the heart of what a natural approach to health means and is in keeping with *Horse Journal*'s basic premise of "back to the basics." There is also a rapidly growing body

"Natural" is a buzz word in horse care these days, but not really attainable.

of knowledge giving important insights into how naturally occurring substances can be supplemented to help the horse's own body defend against disease, meet the challenges of exercise, and heal injuries. Our goal at *Horse Journal* has always been to take a hard look at the claims made for naturally based products, explain the rationale behind them, test for ourselves what the effects may be, and share this information with our readers so that they can make informed decisions based on more than just the claim that a product is natural.

Caveat Emptor

"Let the buyer beware" is another founding cornerstone of *Horse Journal* and certainly applies to the arena of nutritional supplements and nutraceuticals.

Basic dietary supplements are those that contain the nutrients recognized to be essential in the diet. This includes carbohydrates, fats, protein, calcium, phosphorus, magnesium, sodium, chloride, potassium, iron, copper, zinc, manganese, and selenium, as well as some basic vitamins. Supplements containing these ingredients are regulated as feeds. AAFCO, the Association of American Feed Control Officials, has established definitions for these ingredients and forms that are considered appropriate in supplements. Their recommendations are not laws, just suggestions for uniformity between individual states. The FDA is involved to the extent of monitoring for contaminants, establishing a list of safe additives, and regulating medicated feeds. FDA decrees for the most part are laws, but again are directed at only the basic nutrients known to be required for life.

So where do nutraceuticals like glucosamine, chondroitin, or even bioflavonoids fit in? They don't. In fact, anything that is not on the list of basic nutrients required for life is technically illegal to sell for animal use. Their method of manufacture, potency, safety, and efficacy are not regulated in any way. Even with human supplements, confusion reigns.

Dr. Stephen DeFelice coined the term "nutraceuticals" in 1989, but it lacks a clear definition—except for the obvious, as a cross between a nutrient and a drug. Dr. DeFelice described a nutraceutical as "a food (or part of a food) that provides medical or health benefits, including the prevention and/or treatment of a disease." The problem with this is that it is precisely the same definition that the FDA uses for a drug. A variety of different approaches to defining nutraceuticals versus dietary supplements have been proposed, including that dietary supplements are meant only to complement the diet, while nutraceuticals also have the power to influence disease states. The problem here is that all essential nutrients have the capacity to influence disease states. Vitamin E given to a healthy horse is a dietary supplement, but if given to a vitamin E–deficient horse with neurological disease, it becomes a nutraceutical! Small wonder that regulatory officials are having a difficult time deciding exactly what is and is not a nutraceutical and how they should be regulated. The current situation with human supplements is that they are being allowed as long as there are no obvious safety issues. Claims that they prevent, mitigate, or treat diseases are not supposed to be made, but this is largely ignored.

A huge number of nutraceuticals have made their way into the equine marketplace. The most familiar, and undoubtedly biggest sellers, are joint nutraceuticals—primarily glucosamine, chondroitin, hyaluronic acid, and various natural sources of these substances, such as Perna mussel or shark cartilage. Also addressing joint issues are such things as Ester-C and hydrolyzed collagen. Another big chunk of the market goes to alternative pain- and inflammation-relieving substances, such as MSM and a host of herbs, including devil's claw and white willow. Other popular categories are muscle building, performance enhancement, and attitude-adjusting supplements. Coat- and hoof-improving supplements are extremely good sellers, but focus on ingredients that fall more properly into the dietary supplement rather than nutraceutical category, although the line between the two remains very vague.

With the vast array of products to choose from, without guarantees as to potency, safety, or effectiveness, the horse owner can use some help. It has been the goal of *Horse Journal* over the years to provide just that.

Horse Journal *Field Trials*

A *Horse Journal* supplement investigation begins with a scientific search into the nature of the problem—e.g., What are the most common causes of poor hoof quality? We condense this information for the readers so that they have a basic education in what aspects might be involved, particularly relating to their individual situations. Products in our trials are primarily chosen based on the claims the manufacturers make for them. We want to be sure to use products that readers may be likely to buy based on advertising claims. If our research has led us to believe that other products that may not be specifically labeled for the problem in question could be helpful, we may include those as well. For example, nutritional deficiencies that result in hoof-quality issues are also commonly involved with skin or coat problems. All products are evaluated under real-life conditions, to mimic as closely as possible the results our readers are likely to see. However, *Horse Journal* field trials go a step beyond the testimonials you may see on a supplement manufacturer's Web site. Any changes in diet, supplementation, drug use, exercise, or general management that could potentially influence the results are not allowed. Participating horses are carefully screened to make sure they are appropriate for the field trial. Finally, a specific set of observations is used to compare the responses. These are kept as objective and factual as possible—e.g., a lameness grade would be used to evaluate the response to joint nutraceuticals or alternative pain relievers. Because of this standard and the fact that *Horse Journal* does not accept advertising so is not catering to advertising clients, the results of *Horse Journal* product trials carry a good bit of weight with both owners and manufacturers. *Horse Journal* results have strongly influenced many product lines, and it's common to see *Horse Journal* findings quoted by manufacturers. 🐎

Does Your Horse Need a Vitamin and Mineral Supplement?

Your horse, like every living thing, relies on vitamins and minerals for a variety of body functions and would die without them. So, yes, your horse needs vitamins and minerals. However, that doesn't necessarily mean you need to supplement them above and beyond what's in his current diet.

Whether or not your horse needs a supplement depends on two things—the levels already present in his diet and what his needs are. If needs are being met by diet, he doesn't need more. It's that simple. More is not better. At best, more is a waste but harmless; at worst, more is toxic.

The Basics of Vitamins

Common sense alone tells us that the horse evolved as a species by being able to survive on the nutrients available to him. The horse's ancestors changed from browsers to grazers (grass eaters) around 18 million years ago. Grass is a horse's natural food, and a healthy horse with an adequate supply of fresh, live grass generally doesn't need additional vitamins. Even in winter, a pastured horse's diet isn't as devoid of live material as you might think. Dormant (not dead) grasses still contain active vitamins, and the diet is supplemented by browsing on the tightly closed buds and more tender distal ends of shrubs and trees. Even so, vitamins are not as available as during periods of active grass growth.

B Vitamins and the Gut

A valid argument against routine supplementation of B vitamins is that the organisms in the horse's intestinal tract synthesize them, and this is a built-in source of Bs for the horse, above and beyond what is in the diet. However, this probably only applies to vitamins whose concentration increases in the small intestine. This includes riboflavin, niacin, pantothenic acid, and pyridoxine. With thiamine and biotin, the levels available in the small intestine compared to what is present in the diet aren't as different, making those two vitamins potentially more important in the diet.

Thiamine is actually one of the better studied B vitamins in horses, and the only one where the last National Research Council recommendations recognized that diet may not be an adequate source for performance horses. Similarly, the number of horses with hoof quality problems that respond to biotin supplementation suggests this vitamin may often be in short supply too.

What's Up with Niacin?

Niacin is probably the B vitamin least likely to be deficient. Sources include the diet and synthesis by intestinal flora in the small intestine, and the liver can also manufacture niacin from the amino acid tryptophan. Despite this, niacin is often the B vitamin that is most heavily supplemented in equine products. It's not at all clear what the reason behind the emphasis on niacin might be, but high doses of niacin in people often cause a "niacin flush," with vasodilation and odd skin sensations that a horse could find agitating, making him appear energized. Niacin in the form of nicotinamide rather than nicotinic acid (synonym for niacin) is less likely to cause this reaction.

Vitamin E—The Achilles Heel

Except for the ability to store some E in the liver, the horse has fewer built in protections against vitamin E deficiency than any other vitamin, and it shows. More naturally occurring equine deficiency problems have been found for vitamin E than all other vitamins combined. They range from life-threatening muscular and neurological damage to impaired immune responses.

Vitamins with the highest potential for toxicity are the fat-soluble vitamins: A, D, and K. The horse is protected from A toxicity under natural circumstances by his ability to limit how much of the abundant beta-carotene—the vitamin A precursor in plants—is actually converted to vitamin A. There are no "active" forms of vitamin D in the diet, so natural safety from that poisoning is also provided through regulation of how much inactive vitamin D from plants (also produced in the skin) will be converted to active D. An identical situation exists for vitamin K, where K3 is the active form, but the horse absorbs either K1 (from plants) or K2 (from intestinal bacteria), which the body must then "activate" to K3.

The other vitamins are absorbed in an active form. Vitamin E has little, if any, toxicity, and the horse will absorb E in direct proportion to how much is present in the diet. Vitamin C and the B vitamins are also relatively nontoxic and will be absorbed in proportion to what is present in the diet. Horses on good pasture have much higher levels of these vitamins in their blood than stabled, unsupplemented horses. However, full-blown deficiencies of vitamin C or the Bs do not occur in horses. With vitamin C, the horse is protected because he's able to synthesize at least enough to prevent full-blown scurvy. All foods contain some B vitamins (albeit in low levels), and synthesis of Bs by bacteria in the lower portions of the small intestine is another source. In addition, research in other species has found that absorption of Bs can be increased by activation of special carrier proteins on the intestinal lining cells. This leaves vitamin E, which is a must for any horse not on fresh pasture grasses.

Supplementing Vitamins

A healthy horse on good pasture doesn't need supplemental vitamins, except for E if the horse is working very hard. Vitamins B12, D, and K probably never require supplementation regardless of the diet. Vitamin A should be given as a supplement with caution, and only to horses being fed hay that is a year old or older. That leaves just the B vitamins and vitamins C and E for horses on hay-based diets.

It's a common misconception that horses chew wood because they have dietary deficiencies.

Quitt is a Farnam supplement that targets nutritional deficiencies, which might cause wood chewing.

Estimated Daily B Requirements for an 1,100-lb. Horse

Although brewer's yeast is a concentrated source of B vitamins, because it is fed in small amounts, it's really only a significant source for niacin and pantothenic acid, and even these are fairly low.

Vitamin	NRC	Possible Performance Needs	Good Natural Sources
Thiamine	About 30 mg/day for maintenance, 50 mg/day for performance.	50 to 100 mg/day 500 to 1000 mg/day used for calming	Fresh grass Brewer's yeast* Wheat products
Riboflavin	About 20 mg/day.	40 to 60 mg/day	Fresh grass Brewer's yeast* Alfalfa meal
Niacin	No recommendation. Can by synthesized from tryptophan in the tissues.	50 to 100 mg/day	Fresh grass Alfalfa meal Molasses Peas Beet pulp Brewer's grains All seeds, grains, and brans Whey
Pantothenic Acid	No recommendation. No overt deficiencies found with intakes as low as 2 mg/day (not exercising).	50 to 100 mg/day	Fresh grass Brewer's yeast* Alfalfa meal Molasses Seeds Peas Brans Whey
Pyridoxine	No recommendation.	100 to 200 mg/day	Fresh grass Seeds Brans Brewer's yeast*
Biotin	No recommendation.	5 to 20 mg/day	Fresh grass Moderate levels in seeds and whole grains Brewer's yeast*
Folic acid	No recommendation.	10 to 20 mg/day	Fresh grass Brewer's yeast* Brans Flaxseeds
B12 Cyanocobalamin	No recommendation. Dietary requirement of healthy adults at maintenance likely to be low to nonexistent.	0 to less than 1 mg/day	Only milk or whey. (Plant-eating animals obtain the B12 they need by absorbing vitamins synthesized by organisms in their intestinal tract.)

While it's likely that working horses would benefit from some supplementation of C and B vitamins when they are on hay-and-grain diets, precisely how much is largely a matter of guesswork. The vitamin supplements comparison chart lists some guidelines for amounts to supplement for horses in moderate or heavy work (racing, endurance, upper-level eventing) and compares some multi-vitamin and mineral supplements.

Requirements for vitamin C and the B vitamins may be increased in a variety of situations, including:

- Injury or surgery
- Antibiotic use
- Heavy exercise
- Allergies
- Bowel problems, especially involving the small intestine
- Liver disease
- Lung disease

It is probably prudent to supplement B vitamins at the same level as suggested for moderate exercise in these groups. Because B vitamins have a shorter shelf life than minerals, it's best to supplement them separately. See the chart for best bets for B vitamin supplements.

Since there is absolutely no dietary requirement for vitamin C in the horse, no guidelines for supplementation exist, and little work has been done to suggest what levels might be appropriate for optimizing health or to support the ill or injured horse. However, supplementation in the neighborhood of 5 to 10 grams of vitamin C daily is reasonable. Note: High levels of C can cause diarrhea.

Vitamin E supplementation should be used with every horse, except inactive horses on pasture. Feed 1,000 IU per day of synthetic vitamin E to inactive horses or those in light work, 2,000 IU per day for harder-working horses. Horses with infections and diseases of the nervous or muscular systems or lungs may benefit from more. For best absorption, vitamin E supplements should be given with a meal that contains some fat, or provided in a fat-based supplement such as Uckele's Liquid

Vitamin Supplements Comparison of Products

Vitamin	Requirement for Moderate work	Requirement for Heavy work	Accel 2 oz.	Vita Plus 2 oz.	Dynamite 2 oz.	Maxum 2 oz.	Pennwoods Equine Supreme 4 oz.	Grand Vite 2 oz.	Mega Cell 2 oz.	Equi-Shine 2 oz.	Augment Ultra 2 oz.
Biotin	0 to 20 mg	0 to 20 mg	1 mg	None	0.025 mg	0.03 mg	0.015 mg	1.5 mg	1 mg	1.25 mg	5 mg
B12	None	None	3 mg	0.025 mg	0.275 mg	0.08 mg	None	0.15 mg	0.28 mg	0.07 mg	0.3 mg
Folic acid	0 to 10 mg	0 to 20 mg	10 mg	None	18.75 mg	3 mg	0.016 mg	60 mg	10 mg	5 mg	10 mg
Niacin	0 to 50 mg	0 to 100 mg	63 mg	16 mg	563 mg	125 mg	15.7 mg	125 mg	62 mg	75 mg	25 mg
Pantothenic Acid	0 to 100 mg	0 to 200 mg	25 mg	8 mg	75 mg	25 mg	1.6 mg	42 mg	26 mg	100 mg	10 mg
Pyridoxine	0 to 75 mg	0 to 150 mg	No guarantee	0.625 mg	20 mg	No guarantee	None	18 mg	32 mg	10 mg	No guarantee
Riboflavin	0 to 20 mg	0 to 40 mg	125 mg	3 mg	175 mg	56 mg	1 mg	50 mg	126 mg	25 mg	20 mg
Thiamine	50 to 150 mg	150 to 250 mg	28 mg	2 mg	13.75 mg	28 mg	0.8 mg	48 mg	28 mg	50 mg	30 mg
Vitamin A	0 to 20,000 IU	0 to 20,000 IU	12,500 IU	3,125 IU	59,375 IU	32,000 IU	75,398 IU	22,500 IU	13,750 IU	70,000 IU	15,000 IU
Vitamin C	0 to 7 grams	0 to 7 grams	0.492 grams	None	0.3 grams	None	No guarantee	1.5 grams	0.68 grams	None	None
Vitamin D	None	None	2,500 IU	313 IU	9,375 IU	3,200 IU	875 IU D2, 113 IU D3	2,660 IU	2,750 IU	8,125 IU	1,500 IU
Vitamin E	500 to 2,000 IU	2,000 to 4,000 IU	500 IU	3 IU	87 IU	150 IU	149 IU	500 IU	550 IU	750 IU	300 IU
Vitamin K	None	None	0.5 mg	None	None	2 mg	No guarantee	None	0.5 mg	None	None

Select II 3 oz.	DAC Racing 2 oz.	Sport Horse 6 oz.	Triple Crown 12 2 lb.	Platinum Performance 132g.	TDI 10 2 lbs.	Nutri++ 2 oz.	Formula 707 2 oz.	HS-35 8 oz.	Performance Plus 1.6 oz.
5 mg	0.2 mg	1 mg	2.8 mg	2.5 mg	0.4 mg	0.2 mg	None	0.085 mg	1.6 mg
0.3 mg	None	1 mg	No guarantee	0.044 mg	No guarantee	0.475 mg	0.375 mg	0.010 mg	32 mg
35 mg	30 mg	15 mg	No guarantee	2.5 mg	No guarantee	9.4 mg	1.25 mg	0.6 mg	160 mg
125 mg	175 mg	975 mg	No guarantee	13 mg	No guarantee	50 mg	250 mg	16.5 mg	160 mg
90 mg	None	206 mg	No guarantee	22 mg	No guarantee	50 mg	30 mg	10 mg	160 mg
10 mg	11 mg	206 mg	No guarantee	13 mg	No guarantee	125 mg	6.25 mg	1.85 mg	200 mg
50 mg	None	202 mg	No guarantee	11 mg	40 mg	75 mg	40 mg	2.75 mg	400 mg
40 mg	None	225 mg	No guarantee	13.2 mg	50 mg	91.9 mg	15 mg	1.95 mg	160 mg
50,000 IU	5,000 IU	35,900 IU	72,000 IU	2,500 IU	30,000 IU	62,500 IU	50,000 IU	27,500 IU	12,000 IU
0.03 grams	0.0125 grams	0.94 grams	0.54 grams	0.250 grams	None	0.188 grams	0.003 grams	None	1.6 grams
4,000 IU	500 IU	7,500 IU	10,000 IU	500 IU	7,500 IU	3,125 IU	8,750 IU	5,500 IU	2,000 IU
150 IU	875 IU	1,500 IU	2,000 IU	250 IU	1,000 IU	1,250 IU	40 IU	650 IU	1,280 IU
8 mg	4.4 mg	41.25 mg	No guarantee	1.1 mg	None	9.4 mg	None	1 mg	.002 mg

E-50 (www.uckele.com). Natural vitamin E products are also available, but their price generally exceeds the relatively modest (36%) increase in biological activity of the natural vitamin. There is also a "water-soluble" vitamin E product for horses, which is actually vitamin E complexed with microscopic amounts of fat to avoid the need to offer fat in the meal at the time E is fed. However, once again the price exceeds the advantage in improved absorption.

Basics of Mineral Needs

When you hear "mineral," you probably think bone and calcium. Bone is indeed the most mineral-dense tissue in the horse's body, but it takes more than calcium to build strong, healthy bone, and minerals have many other jobs to do. Electrolytes are minerals in a free, electrically charged (ionized) form. They are critical in regulating the amount of water inside and outside the cells and in the function of nerves and muscle. Minerals are also critical as antioxidants and for enzyme function, as well as for binding oxygen; constructing skin, hair, hooves, tendons, ligaments, and cartilage; and absorbing nutrients. Maintaining the correct balance of each mineral both inside and outside the body cells is essential to normal functioning and repair.

The horse is equipped with a variety of mechanisms for dealing with short supplies of minerals (release from storage in the bone or tissues, increased intestinal absorption), or excesses (secretion in urine or bile, storage in bone, liver, or kidney). However, the horse cannot manufacture minerals out of thin air and can only deal with so much excess before toxicity occurs. While some essential minerals can be toxic when excessive (iron, selenium, iodine), in many cases toxicity occurs not as a direct effect, but because high levels of one mineral will crowd out other essential minerals, creating deficiencies. Picture minerals inside the intestinal tract as balls in a lottery machine, all competing for the same chute. If you have nine black balls for every white ball, it's not difficult to predict what color is likely to hit the chute. Because of this competition effect, maintaining

Mineral Ratios

Since many minerals can compete with each other for absorption, it's very important to have minerals present in the correct amounts, ratios, and balance. For example, a ratio of 2:1 for calcium:phosphorus means twice as much calcium as phosphorus in the diet.

- **Ca:P ratio:** The target ratio is between 2:1 and 1.2:1. A calcium:phosphorus ratio lower than 1.2:1, also often referred to as an inverted Ca:P ratio (less than 1:1), puts the horse at risk for a serious nutritional bone disease called nutritional secondary hyperparathyroidism. This is definitely a situation you want to avoid.

  Otherwise, Ca:P ratios as high as 6:1 are tolerated by adults, at least over short periods of time, because horses adjust the amount of calcium they absorb and slow down release of calcium from bone stores. If you must settle for less than ideal ratios, go a little high.

- **Ca:Mg ratio:** Controversy exists about the correct Ca:Mg ratio in equine diets. Estimates range from 3:1 to 2:1, with some researchers reporting muscle weakness or poor performance at the higher ratios. Magnesium is an important mineral that has been a bit of a stepchild in equine nutrition, and we agree with the nutritionists who strongly feel the current recommendations are too low for horses in work. The most common symptoms of suboptimal intake in performance horses are nervousness, sensitivity to sound and touch, and muscular symptoms ranging from twitching to increased muscle tone ("hard" muscles) to muscle cramps, with weakness in extreme cases. A ratio of 2:1 is therefore suggested.

  However, as is true of minerals across the board, individual horses seem to vary quite a bit in their sensitivity to magnesium intakes.

The current recommendation of a Ca:Mg ratio of 3:1 works just fine for some horses. The 2:1 ratio is considered ideal for several other monogastric (one stomach) species. Low and/ or inverted Ca:Mg ratios should be avoided too, as this can lead to bone changes.

- **Cu:Fe ratio:** The listed copper:iron ratio of 1:4 corresponds to NRC recommended minimum intakes for those minerals. In reality, much lower ratios are often encountered. The effect of high long-term intakes of iron on copper status in horses is unknown. However, adequate intake of copper is necessary for normal handling of iron.

- **Cu:Zn and Cu:Mn:** Excesses of any trace mineral—Cu, copper; Zn, zinc; Mn, manganese—have the potential to interfere with absorption of the others. The closer you can get to ideal, the better. Since copper takes many "hits" in terms of competing minerals, and copper absorption can also be negatively affected by high sulfur in the diet, if you have to choose between copper being slightly high versus low, it's usually best to err a little on the high side. The impact of other trace minerals on selenium has not been specifically studied in horses, but in other species high intakes of sulfur or copper can depress selenium absorption. Under conditions of high intakes of these minerals, increasing selenium may also be wise—or you can check blood selenium levels periodically. Most people are wary of selenium because they have heard it can be toxic, but safety concerns are not an issue until the horse is received from 10 to 25 times more than current common supplement intakes.

  Commonly suggested ratios of Cu:Zn:Mn are from 1:3:3 to 1:5:5.

mineral intakes in the correct balance is just as important as the total amounts of the individual minerals. In fact, higher intakes can be tolerated without toxicity if the minerals are in correct balance.

Supplementing Minerals

There is a huge array of mineral or vitamin/mineral supplements for horses on the market, with a variety of claims. Many are formulated along the lines of an equine "One a Day," providing

vitamins and minerals in correct balances, but varying widely in how much they provide—some fall way below the actual daily requirements, some are higher. Others claim to target specific equine groups (e.g., mares and foals, performance horses), while still others claim superiority because they are mined from this or that source. The bottom line is simply that the best supplement for your horse is the one that fills the gaps and balances your specific diet.

SmartPak Equine's service makes it easy for boarding barns to meet the individual horse's supplement needs.

Your horse's major source of minerals is hay or grass. Even if you are feeding a mineral-fortified feed, unless you offer very large amounts of it, hay or grass is still your horse's major source of minerals. The first step in establishing a good mineral program for your horse is to balance and fortify the minerals present in the hay or grass.

There is a huge variation in mineral levels between plant and grass types. While manufacturers often specify a supplement as appropriate for alfalfa or grass hays, the truth is that no set formula supplement can correctly balance all grass hays. There is simply way too much variation among them.

If your hay always comes from the same source, or you store a several months' supply, at a cost of between $25 and $40 for a complete mineral analysis, it's well worth the investment to have the hay analyzed so that you know exactly what you have. If that isn't feasible, your local agricultural extension agent or the forage experts at your state university will provide information on what deficiencies are common in your area. A consultation with an equine nutritional professional—

Take Math out of Hay Analysis

Your hay analysis will come back showing mineral levels either as a percentage or ppm = mg/kg of hay = mg/2.2 lbs. of hay (22 lbs. of hay = 10 kg). Do your figuring using 22 lbs. of hay, then scale up or down depending on how much you actually feed.

To convert the percentage to grams/day, multiply the number x 100. For example, if calcium is 0.52%, 22 lbs. will provide 52 grams.

For ppm conversions to mg, multiply the result in ppm by 10. Example: If copper is 7 ppm, that's 70 mg in 22 lbs. of hay.

Always use the "as fed" column numbers. Sodium and potassium can be ignored. There's never a significant amount of sodium, and potassium is always adequate, if not several times more than needed. Once you have your numbers, compare these to the target amounts and ratios.

Dairy One

```
FORAGE TESTING LABORATORY          -------------------- ---- ---- --------
DAIRY ONE, INC.                    |Sample Description  |Farm|Code| Sample
730 WARREN ROAD                    |GRASS HAY           |    |103 | 8589070
ITHACA, NEW YORK 14850             -------------------- ---- ---- --------
607-257-1272   (fax 607-257-1350)  |
                                   ----------------------------------------
-------- -------- -------- -- -- ----|         Analysis Results
|Sampled | Recvd  |Printed |ST|CO|Farm|---------------------------------------
|        |04/29/05|05/04/05|  |  |    || Components          |As Fed|  DM
-------- -------- -------- -- -- ----|---------------------------------------
                                   |% Moisture            | 5.5 |
                                   |% Dry Matter          |94.5 |
                                   |% Crude Protein       | 4.2 | 4.5
                                   |% Adjusted Crude Protein| 4.2 | 4.5
                                   |% Acid Detergent Fiber|41.9 |44.3
                                   |% Neutral Detergent Fiber|68.0 |72.0
------------------------------------|% NFC                 |16.4 |17.3
         ENERGY TABLE - NRC 2001   |% NSC                 |11.4 |12.0
Body Wt = 1350 Fat% = 3.7 Tprot% = 3.1|% Starch            | 1.3 | 1.4
------------------------------------|% Sugar               |10.1 |10.7
           NEL      NEL             |% TDN                 |52   |55
Milk, Lb Mcal/Lb  Mcal/Kg  Milk, Kg|NEL, (Mcal/Lb)        | .38 | .41
-------- -------  -------  --------|NEM, (Mcal/Lb)         | .44 | .47
Dry       0.53     1.17    Dry      |NEG, (Mcal/Lb)        | .21 | .22
40        0.51     1.12    18       |Relative Feed Value   |     |70
60        0.49     1.07    27       |% Calcium             | .14 | .15
80        0.46     1.01    36       |% Phosphorus          | .17 | .18
100       0.43     0.94    45       |% Magnesium           | .09 | .09
120+      0.39     0.87    54+      |% Potassium           |1.66 |1.76
------------------------------------|% Sodium              | .010| .010
NEM3X     0.50     1.10             |PPM Iron              |89   |94
NEG3X     0.25     0.54             |PPM Zinc              |18   |19
ME1X      0.88     1.95             |PPM Copper            | 9   | 9
DE1X      1.08     2.37             |PPM Manganese         |53   |56
TDN1X,%      55                     |PPM Molybdenum        | .1  | .1
------------------------------------|Horse TDN, %          |36   |38
                                    Horse DE, Mcal/lb      | .72 | .76
```

Major versus Trace Minerals

Major minerals are called major not because they're the most important, but because they're needed in the largest amounts. The major minerals are calcium, phosphorus, and magnesium and are required in gram (g) amounts.

Trace minerals are so named because they are required in smaller amounts, in milligrams (mg). The traces we're discussing are iron, copper, zinc, manganese, and selenium.

Cobalt and iodine are two trace minerals that don't usually show up on a hay analysis but are at low levels in many hays. If you're using a concentrated mineral supplement, fed at 4 oz./day, look for at least 30 ppm of iodine and 15 ppm of cobalt.

veterinarian or PhD—is another option. Free diet-analysis services offered by feed or supplement companies are appealing, but they're not likely to offer optimal solutions. Feed or supplement manufacturers are going to recommend something from their product line. Although there are exceptions, the odds of them telling you another approach is best are about as likely as a Ford dealership employee telling you that you really need a Dodge! The biggest concern is that they will concentrate on total daily intakes of the individual minerals, but largely ignore mineral balances. Take a look at the charts comparing a variety of supplements and how well they balance three different types of hay. You'll see that many can cover most or even all of the bases if you look only at the levels of individual minerals, but when it comes to keeping minerals in correct balance to each other, they don't perform as well.

The following chapters will deal with specific situations and how nutrition can have an impact. However, you'll notice a recurrent theme: Many of the commonly encountered health or behavior problems are rooted in, or at least feature a strong component of, nutrition. In many situations, if you go back to the basics of balancing your base diet and making sure it is adequate, there will be no need for special supplements. 🐎

Chart Information

The calculations for the products in the chart are the resulting nutritional intakes obtained when you combine that particular hay with the listed dose for the individual supplement. For example, in Hay Number 1, Accel is listed as having 16.3 g of calcium. The product itself does not contain this amount of calcium. The amount listed is reached when you feed both the Hay Number 1 and 2 oz. of Accel.

For individual minerals, our evaluations mean:
• OK = at, above or no more than 0.25 g (Ca, Mg, P) or 10 mg (Cu, Mg, Z) below adequate
• Low = below the adequate level
• High = 10X or more above the adequate level. Note: This ceiling may be too high for iron, detailed information in horses is not available. Iron deficiency of dietary cause has never been found in an adult horse.

For ratios, our evaluations mean:
• OK = ideal ratio, or not more than 0.5 deviation from ideal
• High = first mineral in the ratio is too high compared to the second
• Low = first mineral in the ratio too low compared to the second
On our sample hays, the numbers are from actual analyses.
Mineral abbreviations used in chart are:

Ca – calcium	Fe – iron	Mn – manganese	g – grams
P – phosphorus	Cu – copper	Se – selenium	mg – milligrams
Mg – magnesium	Z – zinc		

Hay Number 1: West Coast Mixed Grass Hay

Mineral	Target Levels	Hay #1 22 lbs.	Accel 2 oz.	Vita-Plus 2 oz.	Dynamite Plus 1.5 oz.	Maxum 2 oz.	Pennwoods Equine Supreme Blue 4 oz.	Grand Vite 2 oz.	Mega Cell 1 oz.	Equi-Shine 4 oz.	Augment Ultra 2 oz.	Select II 3 oz.
Ca (g)	20	14 Low	16.3 Low	15.6 Low	15.15 Low	16.3 Low	27.6 OK	14.28 Low	15.4 Low	23.4 OK	16.7 Low	22.4 OK
P (g)	14	17 OK	18.9 OK	17.85 OK	17.43 OK	18.6 OK	13.8 OK	17.25 OK	17.9 OK	21.5 OK	18.8 OK	22.2 OK
Mg (g)	10	9 Low	9.85 OK	9.25 Low	9.29 Low	9.23 Low	15.8 OK	9.57 Low	9.625 Low	9.45 Low	9.56 Low	9.7 Low
Fe (mg)	400	890 OK	1,212.5 OK	1,090 OK	919 OK	1,590 OK	1,220 OK	1,005 OK	996 OK	1,162.6 OK	1,050 OK	1,440 OK
Cu (mg)	150	90 Low	115 OK	98 Low	92.2 Low	150 OK	195 OK	165 OK	103 Low	203.6 OK	140 OK	240 OK
Z (mg)	450	180 Low	225 Low	220 Low	191.7 Low	430 Low	600 OK	380 Low	234 Low	520.8 OK	330 Low	530 OK
Mn (mg)	400	530 OK	592.5 OK	550 OK	536.3 OK	690 OK	869 OK	764 OK	631 OK	725.4 OK	630 OK	790 OK
Se (mg)	2	0.1 Low	0.6 Low	0.8 Low	0.19 Low	2 OK	2.1 OK	1.1 Low	0.35 Low	2.0 OK	0.5 Low	2.5 OK
Ca:P	1.2:1 to 2:1	Low	Low	Low	Low	Low	OK	Low	Low	Low	Low	Low
Ca:Mg	2:1	Low	Low	OK	OK	OK	OK	Low	Low	High	OK	OK
Cu:Fe	1:4	Low	Low	Low	Low	Low	Low	Low	Low	Low	Low	Low
Cu:Z	1:3	High	Low	High	High	OK	OK	High	High	High	High	High
Cu:Mn	1:3 to 1:2.5	Low	Low	Low	Low	Low	Low	Low	Low	Low	Low	OK

Mineral	Target Levels	Hay #1 22 lbs.	Direct Action (DAC) 2 oz.	Equi-Base 4 oz.	Triple Crown 12	LinPro 4 oz.	Platinum Performance Equine 4.65 oz.	TDI-10 2 lbs.	Gro N' Win 1 lb.	Formula 707 2 oz.	HS-35 8 oz.	Performance Plus 1.6 oz.
Ca (g)	20	14 Low	19.1 Low	35.6 OK	36.7 OK	15.57 Low	14.53 Low	43.5 OK	29.9 OK	16.6 Low	24.2 OK	15 Low
P (g)	14	17 OK	20.1 OK	25.8 OK	22.4 OK	17.42 OK	18.05 OK	39.5 OK	23.8 OK	19.6 OK	20.4 OK	18 OK
Mg (g)	10	9 Low	9 Low	10.1 OK	19.2 OK	11 OK	9.54 Low	10.8 OK	10.8 OK	9.45 Low	9.68 Low	9.5 Low
Fe (mg)	400	890 OK	1,002 OK	1,299 OK	1,230 OK	Unknown	1,154 OK	1,880 OK	1,162 OK	1,031 OK	1,396.9 OK	1,390 OK
Cu (mg)	150	90 Low	109.3 Low	242 OK	217.1 OK	146.8 OK	103 Low	338 OK	180 OK	99.6 Low	171.8 OK	190 OK
Z (mg)	450	180 Low	236.4 Low	611 OK	588.6 OK	407.2 Low	205 Low	855 OK	361 Low	230.8 Low	452.8 OK	680 OK
Mn (mg)	400	530 OK	592.5 OK	848 OK	793.3 OK	Unknown	543 OK	1,115 OK	639 OK	575 OK	744.8 OK	570 OK
Se (mg)	2	0.1 Low	0.6 Low	1.55 Low	1.64 Low	0.12 Low	0.35 Low	1.72 Low	0.8 Low	0.1 Low	1.4 Low	0.6 Low
Ca:P	1.2:1 to 2:1	Low	Low	OK	OK	Low	Low	Low	Low	Low	Low	Low
Ca:Mg	2:1	Low	OK	High	OK	High	OK	High	High	Low	High	OK
Cu:Fe	1:4	Low	Low	Low	Low	Unknown	Low	Low	Low	Low	Low	Low
Cu:Z	1:3	High	High	High	OK	OK	High	High	High	High	High	Low
Cu:Mn	1:3 to 1:2.5	Low	Low	Low	Low	Unknown	Low	OK	Low	Low	Low	OK

ACCEL, $19/5 lbs. www.vitaflex.com, 800-848-2359; DYNAMITE PLUS, $25.50/5 lbs., www.dynamite.mystateusa.com, 800-697-7434; VITA-PLUS, $13/3 lbs. www. farnamhorse.com, 800-234-2269; MAXUM, $9.50/2.5 lbs. www.farnamhorse.com, 800-234-2269; PENNWOODS EQUINE SUPREME BLUE, $16/8 lbs. www.pennwoods. com, 800-255-3066; GRAND VITE, $24/5 lbs. www.grandmeadows.com, 800-255-2962; MEGA CELL, $17.50/5 lbs. www.unitedvetequine.com, 800-328-6652; EQUI-

Hay Number 2: Texas Bermudagrass

Mineral	Target Levels	Hay #2 22 lbs.	Accel 2 oz.	Vita-Plus 2 oz.	Dynamite Plus 1.5 oz.	Maxum 2 oz.	Pennwoods Equine Supreme Blue 4 oz.	Grand Vite 2 oz.	Mega Cell 1 oz.	Equi-Shine 4 oz.	Augment Ultra 2 oz.	Select II 3 oz.
Ca (g)	20	41 OK	43.3 OK	42.6 OK	42.15 OK	42.3 OK	54.6 OK	41.28 OK	42.4 OK	50.4 OK	43.7 OK	49.4 OK
P (g)	14	9 Low	10.9 Low	9.85 Low	9.43 Low	10.6 Low	15.8 OK	9.25 Low	9.936 Low	13.5 Low	10.8 OK	14.2 OK
Mg (g)	10	17 OK	17.85 OK	17.25 OK	17.29 OK	17.23 OK	23.8 OK	17.57 OK	17.625 OK	17.45 OK	17.56 OK	17.7 OK
Fe (mg)	400	300 Low	622.5 OK	500 OK	329 Low	900 OK	630 OK	415 OK	406 OK	572.6 OK	460 OK	850 OK
Cu (mg)	150	40 Low	65 Low	48 Low	42.2 Low	100 Low	145 OK	115 Low	53 Low	153.6 OK	90 Low	190 OK
Z (mg)	450	40 Low	115 Low	80 Low	51.7 Low	290 Low	460 OK	240 Low	94 Low	380.4 Low	190 Low	390 Low
Mn (mg)	400	120 Low	182.5 Low	140 Low	126.3 Low	280 Low	459 OK	354 Low	151 Low	415.4 OK	320 Low	380 Low
Se (mg)	2	1.5 Low	2 OK	1.52 Low	1.59 Low	3.4 OK	3.5 OK	2.5 OK	1.75 Low	3.4 OK	1.9 Low	3.9 OK
Ca:P	1.2:1 to 2:1	High	Low	High	High	High	Low	High	High	High	High	High
Ca:Mg	2:1	High	Low	High	High	High	OK	High	High	High	High	High
Cu:Fe	1:4	Low	Low	Low	Low	Low	Low	OK	Low	OK	Low	Low
Cu:Z	1:3	High	High	High	High	OK	OK	High	Low	High	High	High
Cu:Mn	1:3 to 1:2.5	OK	OK	OK	OK	OK	OK	OK	OK	OK	Low	High

Mineral	Target Levels	Hay #2 22 lbs.	Direct Action (DAC) 2 oz.	Equi-Base 4 oz.	Triple Crown 12	LinPro 4 oz.	Platinum Performance Equine 4.65 oz.	TDI-10 2 lbs.	Gro N' Win 1 lb.	Formula 707 2 oz.	HS-35 8 oz.	Performance Plus 1.6 oz.
Ca (g)	20	41 OK	46.1 OK	62.6 OK	63.7 OK	42.57 OK	41.53 OK	70.5 OK	56.9 OK	43.6 OK	51.2 OK	42 OK
P (g)	14	9 Low	12.1 Low	17.8 OK	14.4 OK	9.42 Low	10.05 OK	31.5 OK	15.8 OK	11.6 Low	12.4 Low	10 Low
Mg (g)	10	17 OK	17 OK	18.1 OK	27.2 OK	19 OK	17.54 OK	18.8 OK	18.8 OK	17.45 OK	17.68 OK	17.5 OK
Fe (mg)	400	300 Low	412.8 OK	709 OK	640.5 OK	Unknown	564 OK	1290 OK	572 OK	441 OK	606.9 OK	800 OK
Cu (mg)	150	40 Low	59.3 Low	192 OK	167.1 OK	96.8 Low	53 Low	288 OK	130 Low	49.6 Low	121.8 Low	140 OK
Z (mg)	450	40 Low	96.4 Low	41 OK	448.6 OK	267.2 Low	65 Low	715 OK	221 Low	90.8 Low	312.8 Low	540 OK
Mn (mg)	400	120 Low	182.5 Low	438 OK	383.3 Low	Unknown	133 Low	705 OK	229 Low	165 Low	314.8 Low	140 Low
Se (mg)	2	1.5 Low	2 OK	2.95 OK	3.04 OK	1.52 Low	1.52 Low	3.12 OK	2.2 OK	1.5 Low	2.8 OK	2 OK
Ca:P	1.2:1 to 2:1	High	High	High	High	High	High	High	High	High	High	High
Ca:Mg	2:1	High	High	High	OK	Low	High	High	High	OK	High	Low
Cu:Fe	1:4	Low	Low	OK	OK	Unknown	Low	Low	OK	Low	Low	Low
Cu:Z	1:3	High	High	High	High	OK	High	High	High	High	High	Low
Cu:Mn	1:3 to 1:2.5	OK	OK	High	High	Unknown	High	High	High	OK	High	High

SHINE, $10/6 lbs. www.equishine.com, 800-639-0249; AUGMENT ULTRA, $41.95/10 lbs. www.adeptusnutrition.com, 866-233-7887; SELECT II, $19.95/5.66 lbs. www.selectthebest.com, 800-648-0950; DIRECT ACTION (DAC), $20/5 lbs. www.feeddac.com, 800-921-9121, EQUI-BASE, $15.50/10 lbs. www.uckele.com, 800-248-0330; TRIPLE CROWN 12% SUPPLEMENT, $40/50 lbs. www.triplecrownfeed.com, 800-451-9916; LINPRO, $27.50/5 lbs. www.foxdenequine.com, 540-942-4500; PLATINUM

Hay Number 3: New York Timothy

Mineral	Target Levels	Hay #3 22 lbs.	Accel 2 oz.	Vita-Plus 2 oz.	Dynamite Plus 1.5 oz.	Maxum 2 oz.	Pennwoods Equine Supreme Blue 4 oz.	Grand Vite 2 oz.	Mega Cell 1 oz.	Equi-Shine 4 oz.	Augment Ultra 2 oz.	Select II 3 oz.
Ca (g)	20	54 OK	56.3 OK	55.6 OK	55.15 OK	56.3 OK	69.6 OK	54.28 OK	55.4 OK	53.4 OK	56.7 OK	62.4 OK
P (g)	14	19 OK	20.9 OK	19.85 OK	19.43 OK	20.6 OK	25.8 OK	19.25 OK	19.936 OK	23.5 OK	20.8 OK	24.2 OK
Mg (g)	10	15 OK	15.85 OK	15.25 OK	15.29 OK	15.23 OK	21.8 OK	15.57 OK	15.625 OK	15.45 OK	15.56 OK	15.7 OK
Fe (mg)	400	4100 High	4422.5 High	4300 High	4120 High	4700 High	4430 High	4215 High	4206 High	4372.6 High	4260 High	4650 High
Cu (mg)	150	70 Low	95 Low	78 Low	72.2 Low	130 OK	175 OK	145 OK	83 Low	183.6 OK	120 OK	210 OK
Z (mg)	450	140 Low	215 Low	180 Low	151.7 Low	390 Low	660 OK	340 Low	194 Low	480.8 OK	290 Low	490 OK
Mn (mg)	400	480 OK	542.5 OK	500 OK	486.3 OK	640 OK	2.75 OK	514 OK	511 OK	775.5 OK	240 Low	740 OK
Se (mg)	2	.75 Low	1.25 Low	.77 Low	.79 Low	2.65 OK	3.9 OK	1.75 Low	1 Low	3.4 OK	1.15 Low	3.15 OK
Ca:P	1.2:1 to 2:1	High	Low	High	High	High	High	High	High	OK	High	High
Ca:Mg	2:1	High	Low	High	High	High	High	High	High	High	High	High
Cu:Fe	1:4	Low	Low	Low	Low	Low	Low	Low	Low	High	Low	Low
Cu:Z	1:3	High	High	High	High	OK	Low	High	High	OK	High	High
Cu:Mn	1:3 to 1:2.5	Low	Low	Low	Low	Low	Low	Low	Low	Low	High	Low

Mineral	Target Levels	Hay #3 22 lbs.	Direct Action (DAC) 2 oz.	Equi-Base 4 oz.	Triple Crown 12	LinPro 4 oz.	Platinum Performance Equine 4.65 oz.	TDI-10 2 lbs.	Gro N' Win 1 lb.	Formula 707 2 oz.	HS-35 8 oz.	Performance Plus 1.6 oz.
Ca (g)	20	54 OK	59.1 OK	75.6 OK	76.7 OK	55.57 OK	54.53 OK	83.5 OK	69.9 OK	56.6 OK	64.2 OK	55 OK
P (g)	14	19 OK	22.1 OK	27.8 OK	24.4 OK	9.42 Low	20.05 OK	41.5 OK	25.8 OK	21.6 OK	22.4 OK	20 OK
Mg (g)	10	15 OK	15 OK	16.1 OK	25.2 OK	17 OK	15.54 OK	16.8 OK	16.8 OK	15.45 OK	15.68 OK	19.5 OK
Fe (mg)	400	4100 High	4212.8 High	4509 High	4440.5 High	Unknown	4364 High	5090 High	4372 High	4241 High	4406.9 High	4600 High
Cu (mg)	150	70 Low	89.3 Low	222 OK	197.1 OK	126.8 Low	83 Low	318 OK	160 OK	79.6 Low	151.8 OK	170 OK
Z (mg)	450	140 Low	196.4 Low	571 OK	548.6 OK	367.2 OK	165 Low	815 OK	321 Low	190.8 Low	412.8 OK	640 OK
Mn (mg)	400	480 OK	542.5 OK	798 OK	743.3 OK	Unknown	493 OK	1065 OK	589 OK	525 OK	694.8 OK	520 OK
Se (mg)	2	.75 Low	1.25 Low	2.2 OK	2.29 OK	.77 Low	1 Low	2.37 OK	2.2 OK	.75 Low	2.05 OK	2 OK
Ca:P	1.2:1 to 2:1	High	High	High	OK	High	High	OK	High	High	High	High
Ca:Mg	2:1	High	High	High	OK	High	High	High	High	High	High	High
Cu:Fe	1:4	Low	Low	Low	Low	Unknown	Low	Low	Low	Low	Low	Low
Cu:Z	1:3	High	High	OK	OK	OK	High	High	High	High	Low	Low
Cu:Mn	1:3 to 1:2.5	Low	Low	Low	Low	Unknown	Low	OK	Low	Low	Low	OK

PERFORMANCE EQUINE, $50/10 lbs. www.platinumperformance.com 800-553-2400; TDI-10, na/$50 lbs. www.tdihorsefeeds.com 800-457-7577; GRO N' WIN, NA/1 lb. www.buckeyenutrition.com,, 330-828-2251; FORMULA 707, $27.95/ 12 lbs. www.johnewing.com, 800-525-8601; HS-35, $35/50 lbs. www.equinesidekick.com 888-875-2425; PERFORMANCE PLUS, $27/5 lbs. www.multivetusa.com 800-356-8776.

Anti-Inflammatories

Drugs like phenylbutazone (bute) and flunixin (Banamine) do a great job of controlling pain. Unfortunately, these drugs come with side effects, and in many horses aren't appropriate for long-term use. Intestinal tract ulceration, kidney damage, and even interference with healing are risks of long-term use. For long-term pain control, many people are turning to over-the-counter products with herbal or nutritionally based ingredients.

Use Caution

As difficult as it is to stand by when the horse is in pain, we need to remember pain is also a warning system. When people have injuries, they can be told what they can and can't do during the healing phases, to avoid reinjury or worsening the damage. We don't have that option with horses; pain is the only way they'll know to protect an area.

Horses with serious problems like fractures, bowed tendons, torn ligaments, or laminitis need that pain input. Control pain to the point that the horse is eating, drinking, urinating, and passing manure normally but still aware enough of the problem to avoid normal weight-bearing.

Although we had no adverse reactions in our trials, it's important to remember that the words "natural" and "over-the-counter" don't mean 100% safe. Individual sensitivity or allergic response to any herbal is always possible. Devil's claw can cause some stomach upset in a small percentage of human users and may do the same in horses.

Hard-working horses are bound to have an assortment of aches and pains.

Caution is particularly indicated in horses known to have ulcers and those prone to going off their feed, although the risk is still much less than with NSAIDs (non-steroidal anti-inflammatory drugs) like bute.

Plant antioxidants, including bioflavonoids, herbs like curcumin, and salicylate-containing plants, can all influence clotting mechanisms. This is often of benefit in inflammatory conditions and not likely to cause any bleeding problems, but if the horse needs surgery, care should be taken to inform your veterinarian that you use these. They can also affect clotting when drugs like heparin, Warfarin, or aspirin are used.

There's still no magic-bullet pill or miracle-in-a-syringe. Over-the-counter pain products are part of a comprehensive plan to keep your horse comfortable.

- Never treat horses with severe acute pain without having a diagnosis first or getting your veterinarian's approval. Influencing the level of pain may make diagnosis more difficult or lead to the horse injuring itself further.

- Don't count on herbal alternatives to control severe pain and inflammation. A few days of a prescription medication is usually appropriate in these situations. Once the acute situation is controlled, you may be able to switch. Discuss this with your vet.

- Try joint nutraceuticals before reaching for a pain product.

- Don't use pain products as a short-cut substitute for local therapy. Intensive cold treatments and wrapping work great for acute inflammation. Aged, stiff joints, tendons, and ligaments benefit from the use of warming liniments, wraps, and sweats.

- With chronic sources of pain, make sure your horse's trimming, shoeing, and exercise schedules

Injuries are an inevitable fact of life with horses that work hard and play hard.

Nutritional anti-inflammatory support can be very beneficial for hard-working horses in sports that do not allow drugs.

It's Not Witchcraft

Herbs are rapidly moving out of the realm of witch-craft and medicine-man lore as science turns to the study of the natural remedies of many cultures. For example, chamomile, long a favorite in poultices, has been found to have activity similar to anti-inflammatory cox-2 inhibitor drugs (e.g. phenylbutazone, flunixine), and devil's claw appears to work by the same mechanism as aspirin.

are appropriate. Consider use of support boots for lower-leg problems.

• Know your horse's baseline level of pain and stiffness and never use a pain product to allow you to work the horse harder on a painful day.

Bottom Line

We tried some of these products under a variety of conditions, from acute injuries and wounds to chronic arthritis pain. The test-horse candidates with chronic-pain problems, from retirees to active performance horses, were required to have a baseline level of discomfort that could be quantified on the standard lameness scale to minimize chances that the natural waxing and waning of symptoms that often occurs in these horses could interfere with our interpretation of the responses.

A variety of ingredients may appear in products that are said to target pain. Devil's claw, which has shown an effectiveness level similar to many prescription drugs in both human trials and laboratory studies, is a common ingredient. Also popular are plants with naturally occurring salicylates (aspirin family), like meadowsweet and white willow. Cat's claw, turmeric, boswellia, yucca, and curcumin have also been found to have anti-inflammatory activity, as do bioflavonoids and other plant based antioxidants.

Liquid supplements are often easier to get into the horse.

Supplements That Help Combat Pain

Product	Price	Comments
Anti-Inflammatory Formula Earth Lodge Herbals www.earthlodgeherbals.com 860-237-8801	$33/lb.	Fragrant, appealing blend of high-quality dried herbs with anti-inflammatory and mild circulation supporting effects. Palatability excellent. Didn't pack enough punch even at higher dosing for active performance horses but good results in stiff seniors with chronic low-grade arthritic problems. More overall freedom of movement, reduction of up to 1 lameness grade. Effects evident after about 2 weeks.
B-L Solution and Paste Equine America www.equineamerica.com 800-838-7524	$14/qt.,	Includes vitamin B12, devil's claw, yucca. Excellent control of pain, swelling, and stiffness. We find it equivalent to 1 to 2 grams of phenylbutazone in acute conditions. Improvements of 1 to 2 lameness grades in chronic conditions. Rapid onset of activity, within 24 hours. Palatable. Thick golden liquid or tan paste (3-dose syringe). Base very sweet, avoid use in insulin resistant laminitic horses.
Blue Stallion Cross Relief JM Saddler www.jmsaddler.com 800-627-2807	$17.95	Liquid. Contains yucca, devil's claw, boswellia, and B12. At high dose (1 oz. or higher), pain relief judged equivalent to that of 1 to 1.5 grams of phenylbutazone, with improvements of up to 1 degree on lameness scale. Palatability good. Fairly sweet.
Cipex Equine Science www.herbs4horses.com 800-479-3537	$23.75/3 lbs.	Pelleted blend of anti-inflammatory and circulation supporting herbs, including hawthorn, nettle, willow, meadowsweet. Mild improvements of 0.5 to 1 lameness grade seen in most of our test horses with arthritis problems, equivalent to low dose (1 gram) phenylbutazone. Onset of improvement slow, 3 to 5 days. Could be a good choice for long-term support of horses with low-grade navicular and postlaminitis problems. Palatability fair to good.
Complete Horse Minerals and Electrolytes with Glucosamine and Noni Life Nutrients USA www.lifenutrientsusa.com 435-652-8006	$26.95/qt.	Glucosamine, noni, chelated minerals, humic shale. No improvement noted with this supplement except for one aged horse with generalized stiffness that appeared to move a bit freer when on it for 30 days and deteriorated again to become more stiff when it was stopped. Palatability excellent. Odorless clear liquid.
DC-Y MedVet Pharmaceuticals www.medvetpharm.com 800-366-8986	$27.95/2 lbs.	Coarse powder. High-dose devil's claw, yucca, boswellia and other anti-inflammatory herbs with grape seed. At 0.5 oz. twice a day, good response in terms of pain, judged equivalent to 1.5 to possibly 2 grams of phenylbutazone. Warm-up times decreased. Takes about 48 hours to reach full effect. Palatability good.
Devil's Claw Plus Uckele www.uckele.com 800-248-0330	$31.30/2 lbs.	Coarse powder. High-dose devil's claw and yucca, with boswellia, turmeric, other plant and nutritional anti-inflammatory and antioxidant ingredients. At 0.5 oz twice a day, very good response in terms of pain, judged equivalent to 1.5 to possibly 2 grams of phenylbutazone. Warm-up times decreased. Takes about 48 hours to reach full effect. Palatability good.
Free Bute Cavalor www.farmvet.com 888-837-3626	$99.99/90 tablets	Base of devil's claw and Perna, with a variety of plant-based antioxidant/anti-inflammatory ingredients, water-soluble-vitamins, chondroitin. Dosed a.m. (2 tabs) and p.m. (3 tabs), may double initially. Control of pain and swelling with acute injuries judged equivalent to low dose (1 to 1.5 grams) phenylbutazone. Improvement of 1 to 2 lameness grades in chronic conditions. About 48 hours to full effect. Palatability good, crushed or whole and mixed into feed. Scored tablets.
Herbal Bute Equine Science www.herbs4horses.com 800-479-3537	$23.75/3 lbs.	Pelleted. Blend of devil's claw, cat's claw, white willow, and meadowsweet. We saw little effect at the 1 oz/day dose even after two weeks of constant use. Doubling the dose led to modest improvements of 0.5 to 1 lameness grade in majority of test horses, judged equivalent to effect of about 1 gram of phenylbutazone. Palatability fair.
Pain X Uckele www.uckele.com 800-248-0330	$28.45/8 oz.	Combination of two amino acids used in the treatment of chronic pain. Phenylalanine is believed to help activate the body's own intrinsic pain relief systems (e.g. endorphins). 75 to 100% complete relief of chronic pain noted for most test horses, within the first 24 to 36 hours. Effective in two horses at half the suggested feeding rate. Palatability excellent.
Pain Management Platinum Performance www.platinumperformance.com 800-553-2400	$36/0.25 lb.	Contains two anti-inflammatory/antioxidant herbal ingredients, phellodendron amurense extract and boswellia, as well as magnesium citrate. Improvements of 1 to 2 lameness grades noted with chronic conditions, after five to 10 days of use. For horses with mild arthritic stiffness, this meant much more freedom of movement and no need for long warm-ups. Too slow-acting for acute problems. Palatability fair.

Product	Price	Comments
Phyto-Quench Uckele www.uckele.com 800-248-0330	$61.70/4 lbs.	Blend of high-potency plant and nutritional antioxidants, capsaicin, boswellia, curcumin and circulation-supporting ingredients. Distinctively spicy aroma. Can double dose for severe problems. Can work for both acute and chronic problems, arthritic joints, injuries and wounds. Good control of pain and swelling within 12 to 24 hours. Open wounds showed good perfusion and healing. Good choice for laminitis pain. Palatability varies. Either they like it or they don't.
Releaf Hilton Herbs www.hiltonherbs.com www.chamisaridge.com 800-743-3188	$31.95/500 ml	Liquid. Combination of natural salicylate-containing herbs meadowsweet and white willow, with devil's claw, in a base of apple-cider vinegar and honey (both organic). Pleasant aroma and excellent palatability. Worked to reduce fever within a few hours in a horse that developed a viral infection during the trial, provided fairly good but short-lived pain relief for a horse with acute laminitis. Only fair results with joint pain at the recommended doses, average 0.5 degree improvement in lameness scale.
S.O.D. and Boswellia Naturvet www.naturvet.com 888-628-8783	$33.95/lb.	Faint apple aroma. Blend of S.O.D. (antioxidant enzyme) and boswellia. The rationale behind these ingredients is sound (although bioavailability of oral S.O.D. is still controversial), but no observable effects were noted in our field trial. Palatable.
Inflamma-Saver Figuerola Laboratories www.figuerola-laboratories.com 800-219-1147	$44.99/lb.	Blend of 100% plant/herb-derived anti-inflammatory and antioxidant extracts, including aspirin-like precursors, boswellia, ginger, curcumin, and others. Double to triple dosing was required for observable effect in fresh injuries or acute flare-ups of chronic problems. Onset slow, 2 to 3 days. With chronic problems in young, actively performing animals there was some effect, roughly equivalent to 1 gram of phenylbutazone, at the high doses and again after a delay of 2 to 3 days. Greater response was seen in older animals, particularly when the horse had pain/stiffness/disability that frequently required bute for control. Downside is poor palatability.

In our trial, devil's claw products once again emerged as the most potent and reliable in terms of reduction of pain in both acute and chronic problems, as well as control of swelling. Most rapid results, and at the best price, were obtained with B-L Solution, which contains devil's claw, vitamin B12, and yucca.

The powdered devil's claw products DC-Y and Devil's Claw Plus were effective, but took a bit longer to reach full effects.

A standout in the chronic pain category was Pain X. This product works differently from the others by influencing pain perception in the brain. Chronic arthritis pain and stiffness doesn't always have a large inflammatory component. The Pain X helped these horses when joint nutraceuticals and anti-inflammatory pain supplements weren't enough. 🐎

Antioxidants

It's unlikely that you haven't heard the word "antioxidants." You probably know they're beneficial to health, but you may not fully understand why.

As you remember from grammar-school science, every tissue in the body uses oxygen to burn the calories in foods. Oxygen, in the form of hydrogen peroxide inside the body, is also a first-line immune defense against invading organisms, even cancer cells.

However, waste products are generated when oxygen is used, and these are called "free radicals." Free radicals are also produced when drugs and/or toxins are broken down, and they enter the horse directly from pollution in air, soil, and water.

Free radicals are harmful. They're electrically unstable, missing an electron, and work to combine with anything in the general neighborhood to regain electrical neutrality. In the process, these free radicals can cause damage to normal cellular walls, DNA, and fats.

Your horse's body limits free-radical damage with antioxidants. Antioxidant enzymes manufactured by the body can instantly neutralize free radicals. The liver also quenches free radicals using proteins that contain sulfur groups.

Antioxidants are vital to a normal immune system, but they don't stimulate it. They provide the nutrients needed to protect white blood cells and surrounding normal cells from damage by enzymes, peroxide, and oxygen-free radicals that are released when the immune system is activated.

The horse's best source of antioxidants is fresh grass.

Boosting Antioxidants

You can help boost your horse's defenses against free radicals by ensuring he has an adequate dietary intake of some specific vitamins and minerals, especially vitamin E, selenium, and vitamin C. These nutrients neutralize free radicals directly and work to keep the antioxidant enzyme systems in an active state.

Other nutrients important in your horse's antioxidant ammunition include the trace minerals copper, zinc, and manganese. These are critical to antioxidant defenses because they're essential cofactors for the antioxidant enzyme systems. The B vitamins—especially B6, B12, and folic acid—are required for antioxidant proteins and enzymes from other amino acids, but most equine diets include adequate levels.

Your horse can also boost his free-radical destroying capacity by consuming foods that have high concentrations of both these basic antioxidant nutrients and preformed, plant-based substances that have antioxidant capacity. These include plant polyphenols, like the familiar bioflavonoids hesperidin, rutin, quercetin, and resveratrol.

We've had good results in past trials using supplements based on grapeseed and/or bioflavonoids, such as hesperidin, in control of respiratory problems. Hesperidin can directly inhibit inflammatory enzyme systems and shares the same functions as vitamin C.

These plant-based antioxidants can have a greater capacity to neutralize free radicals, but they work more slowly and are better as a potent backup system. The antioxidant enzymes and vitamins remain your horse's first line of defense and go to work the most rapidly.

Vitamin E deficiency can lead to significant neurological disease.

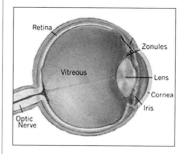

Antioxidants can help protect against age-related changes in the structure of the eye.

Should You Supplement?

It's easy to get caught up in the hype and overdo it. After what you've read, you probably think you need to add antioxidants to your horse's feed (and possibly your own diet). You probably do, but the place to start is by looking at the horse's entire

Regular C or Ester-C

Ester-C is a calcium salt of ascorbic acid that contains key vitamin C metabolites. One of its advantages is that it's nonacidifying, although equine doses make this advantage less of a factor. Blood levels of vitamin C after consumption of Ester-C may be twice as high as with regular vitamin C, although this isn't confirmed in horses. If this were proven in horses, we'd see the advantage to it, as you could use smaller doses. However, we don't know this for certain, and Ester-C is more expensive than regular C. With vitamin C, we'd select the most economical product.

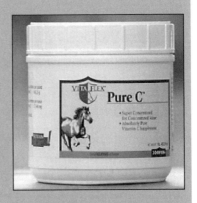

diet and determining if he has adequate dietary intake of the basic antioxidants.

The horse's best source of antioxidant nutrients is fresh grass, so horses that don't have liberal access to grass, including horses pastured over the winter, are likely to benefit from antioxidant supplementation. In addition, horses that are in hard work, fighting infections, have allergies, or are recovering from injuries have increased needs for antioxidants.

We also suggest you consult our list of common symptoms that may be related to inadequate antioxidant defenses. If your horse appears to be battling any of these problems or is at high risk for developing any of them, it's much wiser to ensure an adequate intake now than to wait until the horse gets into trouble.

Once the intake of vitamins A, E, C, the Bs, selenium, copper, zinc, and manganese have been optimized, if the horse con-

Horses without liberal access to grass may benefit from antioxidant supplementation.

Horses Who Need Antioxidant Boosting Have:

- Poor immunity to infections

- Allergies

- Exaggerated inflammatory responses to injury

- Muscular cramping and/or pain

- Poor muscle bulk

- Slow healing

- Tendon/ligament/joint problems not obviously related to intensity of exercise or an injury

tinues to have problems that may be related to poor antioxidant defenses, try further supporting him by using plant antioxidant substances.

Bottom Line

For basic broad-based antioxidant support, our top choices are Vita-Key's Antioxidant Concentrate, Med-Vet's Anti-Ox, and Horse Tech Preox. All three have similar excellent levels of the key basic antioxidant-supporting nutrients and similar costs. Vita-Key has a freshness-control program, including expiration dates and "best if used by" dates.

If you need a product for support of a horse already battling inflammatory problems, like arthritis, we recommend Preox because of its generous levels of the anti-inflammatory omega-3 fatty acid.

Often, however, it's vitamin E, selenium, and vitamin C that your horse lacks, even if receiving other supplements. With the wide variety of supplements available, you can easily supplement exactly the amount you need of each of these three key ingredients.

If you're OK on C (horses on pasture get plenty of C in fresh grasses), but need E and selenium, Uckele's E + Se or the MVP E plus selenium supplement are best buys, but Uckele uses

Estimated Target Intakes of Key Antioxidants

Nutrient	Recommended Level for 1,100-lb. Horse at Maintenance	Recommended Level for 1,100-lb. Stressed Horse
Vitamin C	Horses with pasture, none. No pasture access, 5 to 12 grams/day.	7.5 to 12 grams/day, especially with respiratory or tendon/ligament/joint problems.
Vitamin E	On pasture, 600 IU/day if not exercising; otherwise use stress doses. No pasture, 1,200 IU/day.	With heavy exercise, 2,000 IU/day, higher if the horse is experiencing muscle problems. Much higher doses sometimes recommended for horses with nervous system infections.
Selenium	Minimum of 1 mg/day whether on pasture or hay.	Exercise, infection, allergy, injury may all increase selenium needs. Maintain intake between 2 and 4 mg/day.
B vitamins	For horses without gastrointestinal problems and on diets with good supplemental sources of Bs, such as whole grains, brans, and even fresh grass, supplementation is usually not necessary.	Exercising, older, injured horses and those with digestive tract problems and battling infections may benefit from broad-spectrum B-vitamin support.
Copper, manganese, zinc	NRC minimum estimated requirements will be adequate for horses at maintenance with no health issues: Copper 60 mg; zinc 180 mg; manganese 180 mg. The need to supplement depends on level of intake from hay, pasture, other feeds.	Exercising horses need an intake of 1.5 to twice the NRC minimums. Horses showing any of the symptoms of antioxidant deficiency should have their diet analyzed for both total intake of the individual minerals and to guarantee that there are no imbalances in their ratios, since these minerals may compete with each other for absorption, creating a situation where an excess of one causes deficiencies of the others.

a blend of inorganic and organic selenium sources for improved mineral absorption and gets the nod.

With plain vitamin E, studies show that vitamin E is better absorbed when given with fat/oil, making Liquid E-50 the choice.

While the plant-based antioxidant products have their benefits, you should build your antioxidant program from the bottom up, focusing on the basic vitamins and minerals first. After that, if symptoms persist, move on to adding a more expensive plant-based antioxidant product. In this category, it's either Phyto-Quench or Omega Antioxidant. Both products offer a broad base of potent plant antioxidants and herbal anti-inflammatories to assist in control of both acute and chronic inflammatory states and allergies. 🐎

Grazing horses take in abundant antioxidants from fresh grass, but these are rapidly destroyed by cutting, baling, and storage.

Supplements That Target Antioxidant Ingredients
Selenium, Vitamin E, and Vitamin C Choices

Product	Price	Comments
E + Se, Uckele Animal Health, 800-248-0330, www.uckele.com	$23.70/10 lbs. (15¢/day)	Selenium from both selenite (inorganic) and selenium yeast sources. Dosages appropriate for horse in light to moderate work. Excellent price.
E & Selenium, Vita-Flex, 800-848-2359, www.vita-flex.com	$17.03/4 lbs. (13¢ to 27¢/day)	One oz. is adequate for maintenance when other sources of selenium are available. Use 2+ oz./day for horses in work.
E-5000, Vita-Flex, 800-848-2359, www.vita-flex.com	$31.28/2 lbs. (49¢ to 98¢/day for 2,500 to 5,000 IU of vitamin E)	Concentrated source of vitamin E. Good way to boost E for horses receiving sufficient selenium and those battling muscular or nervous system disease.
Ester-C, Peak Performance Nutrients, 800-366-8986, www.peakperformance nutrients.com	$54.99/1.5 lbs. (41¢ dose)	Blood levels of vitamin C after consumption of Ester-C may be twice as high as with regular vitamin C. Nonacidifying.
Ester-C, MVP, 800-366-8966, www.medvetpharm.com	$46.80/lb. (52¢/dose)	Blood levels of vitamin C after consumption of Ester-C may be twice as high as with regular vitamin C. Nonacidifying.
Liquid E-50, Uckele Animal Health, 800-248-0330, www.uckele.com	$18.95/6 oz. (24¢/day)	Blend of vitamin E from natural sources in a vegetable oil base. Concentrated and absorbable.
NaturVet E-Se NaturVet, 888-628-8783, www.naturvet.com	$14.29/4 lbs. (22¢/oz.)	One-oz. dose adequate for maintenance when other sources of selenium are available. Use 2+ oz./day for horses in work.
Pure C, Vita-Flex, 800-848-2359, www.vita-flex.com	$20.94/lb. (24¢ per 5 gram dose)	Concentrated vitamin C source.
Vit-E-Sel, Select the Best/Richdel, 800-648-0950 www.selectthebest.com	$29.95/5 lbs. (18¢/day at low dose, 36¢/day at low-to-moderate exercise)	Suggested dose most appropriate for inactive horses. Double this for low-to-moderate work.
Vitamin C powder, Uckele, 800-248-0330, www.uckele.com	$9.45/lb. (11¢/day for a 5-gram daily dose).	97% pure vitamin C. Concentrated vitamin C.
Vitamin C 454, MVP, 800-366-8986, www.medvetpharm.com	$16.50/lb. (19¢/day for a 5-gram daily dose)	97% pure vitamin C. Concentrated vitamin C.
Vitamin E 5000, MVP, 800-366-8986, www.medvetpharm.com	$22.95/2 lbs. (26¢/day)	Powder. Concentrated source of vitamin E at an economical price.
Vitamin E and Selenium, Multivet USA, 800-356-8776 www.multivetusa.com	$20/5 lbs. (33¢/day)	Amount/dose appropriate for low- to-moderate exercise.
Vitamin E Concentrate, Peak Performance Nutrients, 800-944-1984, www.peakperformance nutrients.com	$49/lb. (54¢ per 5-gram serving = 2500 IU)	Very concentrated source of powdered vitamin E. Good way to boost E intake for horses already receiving sufficient selenium, and those battling significant muscular or nervous system disease.
Vitamin E plus selenium, MVP, 800-366-8966, www.medvetpharm.com	$14.95/5 lbs. (9¢ to 19¢/day)	At 1 oz./day, appropriate for horses doing light-to-moderate work.
Vitamin E+Se XL, MVP, 800-366-8966, www.med vetpharm.com	$24/5 lbs. (15¢/dose)	The 0.5-oz. dose is appropriate for low-to-moderate exercise. Adjust up or down as needed for activity level and diet.

Broad-Spectrum Antioxidant Choices

Product	Price	Comments
ABC Antioxidant, A.B.C. Helfter, 800-373-5971, www.a-b-c-plus.com	$61.95/2 lbs. (97¢/day)	Nice blend of fat-soluble and water-soluble antioxidants, good choice for horses not receiving whole grain or grass. We'd like to see selenium added, though.
Antioxidant Concentrate, Vita-Key, 800-539-8482, www.vita-key.com	$49.50/5 lbs. (62¢ to $1.24/day)	Full range of all the basic nutrients important to support of antioxidant defenses. Best tried for basic antioxidant support, any problem with an inflammatory or allergic component.
Anti-Ox, Med-Vet Pharmaceuticals Ltd, 800-366-8986, www.med-vetpharm.com	$48.00/5 lbs. (60¢ to $1.20/day)	Full range of all the basic nutrients important to support of antioxidant defenses. Best tried for basic antioxidant support, any problem with an inflammatory or allergic component.
Bioquench, Uckele Animal Health, 800-248-0330, www.uckele.com	$23.70/2 lbs. (74¢/day)	Combination of low-dose basic nutritional antioxidants and high doses of supporting plant-based natural antioxidants. Best tried for control of allergies, chronic respiratory problems, chronic inflammation.
CK Plus Hesperidin Complex, Multivet USA, 800-356-8776, www.multi-vetusa.com	$39/5 lbs. (65¢/day)	Vitamin K, which is not an essential nutrient for horses or an antioxidant, is often found in supplements such as this because horsemen like the idea of feeding the anti-bleeding vitamin to horses that bleed from the lungs during exercise. Good level of vitamin C. Moderate dosage of hesperidin. Best tried for edema related to inflammation, tendon and respiratory problems.
Dr. Benson's E-2000 800-372-3676, www.drbensons.com	$185/10 lbs. ($1.16/day)	Selenium from selenite, although it could be low for many areas. C dose very low, but good levels of E.
E-Se-Mag MVP 800-366-8986, www.medvetpharm.com	$44.80/5 lbs. (28¢-56¢/day)	Very high-potency selenium and vitamin E supplement. Added magnesium makes it a particularly good choice for horses with muscle pain/cramping and for respiratory allergies.
Hesperidin Bioplex, Uckele, 800-248-0330, www.uckele.com	$28.45/2 lbs. (88¢/day)	High-potency C and hesperidin product. Best tried for edema related to inflammation, tendon and respiratory problems.
ImmuAction Vapco 800-523-5614, www.vapco.com	$35.95/1.25 lbs. (92¢/day)	Dose of milk products on the low side. Would likely have to stay at the full loading dose (twice regular dose) for maximum benefit if horse is being worked or stressed.
ImmuSyn Vita-Flex 800-848-2359, www.vita-flex.com	$41.58/lb. ($2.60/day)	Contains GlutaSyn , a milk protein concentrate found in the precursors of glutathione, an antioxidant critical to normal functioning of the skeletal muscle and immune system. We think it's best tried for support of horses under extreme exercise or disease stress, malnutrition, when immune system function is poor and not responding to basic good nutrition, and antioxidant support.
Omega Antioxidant Enreco 800-962-9536 www.enreco.com	$35.00/50 lbs. (11¢/day)	Brans from sorghum (a grain), especially brown sorghum, have been found to have high levels of natural antioxidants of the polyphenol type, same as those found in berries and grapes. The addition of high-quality ground-stabilized flax also provides a good source of the antioxidant omega-3 fatty acids. Best tried as a supplemental source of natural plant antioxidants and omega-3 essential fatty acids for horses without access to fresh grass. Additional antioxidant support for any inflammatory/allergic problem.
Phyto-Quench Uckele Animal Health 800-248-0330 www.uckele.com	$61.70/4 lbs. ($1.25/day)	Broad base of support from anti-inflammatory herbs, circulation-enhancing herbs, and plant-based antioxidants. Best tried for acute and chronic inflammatory and allergic conditions of all types. Alternative to NSAIDs for active laminitis.
Preox HorseTech 800-831-3309, www.horsetech.com	$49.95/5 lbs. (62¢ to $1.24/day)	Full range of all the basic nutrients important to support of antioxidant defenses with the added plus of anti-inflammatory omega-3 fatty acids from flaxseed. Best tried as basic antioxidant support, any problem with an inflammatory or allergic component.
Selon-E with Magnesium Vapco 800-523-5614, www.vapco.com	$37.50/5 lbs. (21¢-42¢/day)	Good choice for horses with muscle problems or lung allergies. Slightly higher E, but half as much selenium, as MVP's E-Se-Mag.
S.O.D & Boswellia NaturVet 888-628-8783 www.naturvet.com	$54.38/lb. ($1.33/scoop)	S.O.D. is superoxide dismutase, an enzyme naturally present in the body that can neutralize free radicals. There is considerable debate as to whether this substance can be absorbed intact, but recent work suggests that many enzymes once thought to be destroyed by the digestive process can be absorbed. Boswellia is a directly anti-inflammatory herb, not truly an antioxidant. Effect is highly dosage dependent. Excellent concentration in this product. Best tried for active inflammation.
Vitamin E, Selenium & Zinc Antioxidant Formula, Peak Performance Nutrients, 800-944-1984, www.peakperformance nutrients.com	$39/lb. (86¢/day)	Excellent vitamin E levels and selenium low enough to be compatible with other feeds that may also contain selenium. Inclusion of Ester-C assists with keeping vitamin E in a functional state. However, its high zinc limits its usefulness to diets that have a specific need for high zinc intakes to balance levels of copper and manganese. Best tried for muscular soreness, allergies, poor immune function, nervous system inflammation.

Appetite Stimulation

Usually, there's no question how the saying "eats like a horse" came to be, but if you're dealing with a picky eater, you know how a horse can also be incredibly adamant about not eating. There are many different scenarios where this might occur, with several possible causes. It's important to carefully define the circumstances.

Overfeeding

Many people feed their horses too much of the wrong things and for all the wrong reasons. There is only one reason to feed the horse—to give him the nutrients and calories that he needs to maintain his body tissues in a normal state. If you're fretting over your horse not cleaning up, but the horse is overweight, your horse may be simply full. You've probably been feeding him the equivalent of Thanksgiving dinner every day.

Good Weight, Just Finicky

A healthy horse in good weight that refuses to eat everything he's given is just finicky. There's nothing wrong with his appetite, as long as you're feeding what the horse likes. In other cases, the horse's naturally present sweet tooth, used to select the most nutrition-packed grasses, may have become distorted by feeding sweet feeds. The horse's preferences usually become an issue either when weight gets too high and there's a need to change feeding, or if the owner wants to introduce a new supplement or medication.

This is the easiest type of picky eater to deal with—as long as you stand your ground. These horses are simply not hungry enough to be well motivated to try the new offerings. They can snort in disgust and walk away, but they won't starve themselves. Some tactics to try include:

A healthy horse in good weight that won't eat is probably just finicky.

- Introduce new hays, feeds, or supplements slowly, mixing in small amounts with the regular ration.

- Offer the new items when the horse is most hungry—morning feed, or after having had nothing to eat for at least an hour.

- Few things motivate like competition. Feed the picky eater close to another horse that is obviously interested in what he's getting, or hand feed the new item to another horse with your picky eater standing close by.

- If the problem is with a medication or supplement, start by syringing the whole dose into the horse's mouth before feeding for a day or two, then gradually begin to decrease the amount you syringe in and increase the level added to the feed. The horse is less likely to notice the item in the feed when he already has a taste in his mouth.

- With powders, trying mixing them into a bit of oil before adding to the feed. This cuts both odor and taste.

- Never cave in by removing what the horse doesn't want to eat and replacing it with something he finds more yummy. This only reinforces the pickiness—i.e, the horse has you trained!

- If it's a feed or concentrate switch you're having trouble with, check the label on the old feed for flavorings.

In Work, Getting Picky

A horse in work that previously had a good appetite and starts getting picky about feed or supplements is telling you that something is bothering him. Ulcers usually get blamed and can

Make the Medicine Go Down

As Mary Poppins sang, a spoon full of sugar does help the medicine go down. But, as long as you know the feed is safe, for horses who won't consume supplements, we suggest you use brown sugar instead. You can also add a dab of molasses as flavoring. However, if the horse is insulin resistant or otherwise needs to avoid sugar, try mixing the supplements into a little baby food, then top dress or mix with the feed. Baby-food carrots are always a favorite, but many horses also go for baby peas and baby peaches. Baby foods pack more flavor and more water than the most commonly attempted carrier, applesauce, and are more likely to get the job done.

If your problem is more difficult, try to get the horse to accept a

Brown sugar might help your horse consume his supplements.

change in grains, or feed wet beet pulp instead of grains. If you've tried all the usual additives, carrot juice might do the trick and is available in cans in most large grocery-store chains. You can also get carrot powder from www.herbalcom.com (888-649-3931) for $6.15/lb. Mixing concentrated frozen fruit juices with less than the usual amount of water will also give you a flavor-packed liquid to add to the feed.

A palatable hay is the cornerstone of the diet.

certainly cause this scenario, but any type of physical discomfort, such as muscle, tendon, foot, or joint pain can do it too. It's time to slow down and go over the horse carefully to try to locate the problem.

Can't Eat Enough

A horse that isn't heavily worked or stressed and eats willingly, just not enough to hold a normal weight, may be a hard keeper.

Start with a close look at the diet, getting an accurate weight on the horse and a calorie count. If the horse has unlimited access to good-quality pasture, grain is rarely needed to hold weight, and even a Thoroughbred should do well in the weight department with minimal to no grain. If not, suspect a dental problem, parasitism, or an underlying medical condition and check for these before assuming the horse isn't eating enough.

With hay or hay-and-grain diets, a horse in light-to-moderate work will need the equivalent of 2 to 2.5% of body weight in good-quality hay. That's 20 to 25 lbs./day for a 1,000-lb. horse. If you're feeding grain, calorie count your grain as 1 lb. of grain = 2 lbs. of hay, so a horse getting 5 lbs. of grain and 15 lbs. of hay is getting the equivalent of 25 lbs. of hay. If the horse is getting enough calories, the next question is whether the horse has always had trouble holding weight on this level of feeding, or if it's a change. If a change, look for a physical cause as above. If not, your horse is a hard keeper.

One common mistake with horses like this is to push the grain to them. Yes, it's a more concentrated source of calories, but too much grain can backfire on you. Undigested grain will be fermented in the large bowel, making it more acidic, decreasing the efficiency of fiber digestion, and robbing the horse of some of those fiber calories. There may also be enough discomfort from the increased acidity to decrease appetite. Before loading the horse up with grain, try:

- Free-choice hay at all times.

- Cytozyme's Ration Plus (www.rationplus.com, 800-728-4667) or a high-potency probiotic like Bio-Vet's Equine Generator (www.bio-vet.com, 800-246-8381) for improved fiber digestion.

- Consider some feedings of beet pulp and wheat bran (4 oz. of bran per pound of pulp). This is palatable, packs about the same calories as grains but supports

Regular exercise can rev up appetites.

Appetite and Sick Horses

A serious systemic illness will often knock back a horse's food and water consumption, reducing his appetite at its lowest when his need for quality nutrition is quite high.

If the horse is well enough to go outside, the best choice is grass. Grass is a good source of water (80%), is easy to chew and digest, and has more readily available energy sources than hay and a higher natural vitamin content, including antioxidants. Even if the horse must be stall bound, you may encourage appetite by hand grazing the horse or picking grass for him several times a day.

Sick horses will also usually accept a wet feed. Soak the usual grain mix in warm water for 15 to 20 minutes. A horse that only picks at hay will more readily accept soaked hay cubes. We've also had success using soaked beet pulp, which appears to be well tolerated even if the horse doesn't have beet pulp normally. Adding one or two alfalfa cubes per pound improves palatability.

If he's well enough to go outside, the grass and exercise may help increase his appetite.

One mare with a life-threatening strangles infection had taken in little food or water for three days and was given about a 40% chance of surviving. Intake picked up immediately when she was offered the more liquid beet-pulp diet. Keep meals small—two pounds of dry ingredients to start—and use generous amounts of warm water to yield a final consistency between that of mush or oatmeal and a thick gruel. Add one teaspoon of salt per pound to enhance flavor and help keep his water intake up.

fiber digestion, and "feeds" the beneficial organisms in the large bowel.

- Feed no more than 3 lbs. of grain per feeding.

Taste Tempters

If you have worked with your veterinarian to rule out physical sources of discomfort that can cause poor appetite and still have a horse that simply will not eat enough to hold his weight well or is refusing a medication or supplement that he needs, there are a few things you can try to make meals more appealing.

- CocoSoya oil from Uckele (www.uckele.com, 800-248-0330, $14.95/gallon). This oil has a caramel-like aroma and is so palatable even the barn cats will lick any spills off the bottle. In addition to being inherently appealing, oils have the advantage of masking and dulling any odors or tastes in supplements and medications.

- Carrot or apple juice: These two perennial equine favorites are good first choices for spicing up fare the horse does not find particularly appetizing. Adding cut-up carrot or apple can be tried, but most horses are very good at picking that out and leaving the rest behind. The juices are more evenly mixed. Baby-food carrots, or a homemade puree prepared by putting canned carrots and their juice in a blender, can be a good vehicle for medications as long as the taste is not extremely strong.

- Warm bran mash has a particularly appealing aroma. Try a handful of this mixed thoroughly into the meal.

- A variety of powders with high taste appeal can be found at very reasonable costs from herbal distributors such as Herbalcom (www.herbalcom.com). Things to try include alfalfa powder, dried clover, apple fiber, barley grass powder, anise, peppermint, or spearmint. A tablespoon or so can be mixed in with the meal, or you can mix it in water before adding.

Make Your Own Grass Juice

We know the one thing almost no horse can resist is fresh grass—and grass is cheap. With that in mind, we packed a blender full of fresh grass and clover, added two cups water, and blended it on high until it was a deep green liquid. We then added the mixture and bute to five pounds of sweet feed. Four of the five test horses ate it right

Blend grass and water together to make your own inexpensive flavoring.

down. The fifth ate about half before stopping.

Bagged, chopped hays can be used to mix in supplements, as they're usually very palatable.

- For insulin-resistant horses or those that are simply overweight and need to be taken off sweet and calorie packed foods, there are now treats and flavorings available that are low fat and low carbohydrate but highly palatable. These can be purchased from Skode's Horse Treats (www.skodeshorsetreats.com, 541-659-5831), or Witcheylady Creations and Potions (www.witchey ladycreations.com, witcheylady.c@cox.net). 🐎

5

Blood Builders

Trainers of horses in speed or endurance sports always want the best red-cell counts in their charges. More red cells mean more oxygen-carrying capacity and therefore more strength and stamina. But those trainers usually reach for an iron-containing supplement, not realizing that it's unlikely the horse has a true iron deficiency.

In fact, iron doesn't increase red-cell counts or hemoglobin. It can do more harm than good, even become toxic, since a potential cause of low red-cell counts is oxidative damage during heavy exercise.

When horses show higher red counts in response to a blood-building product, they're most likely responding to the copper or B vitamins the product contains. Vitamin E, vitamin C, selenium, and other trace minerals are also needed for optimal antioxidant control.

A horse may have adequate iron levels but be unable to use them properly due to a lack of adequate copper in the diet. If the horse is diagnosed with anemia and it's related to copper deficiency, the serum iron level will be normal to high and total iron-binding capacity—a measure of how much more iron the blood can hold—will be low. Normal copper serum values are around 100 mcg/dl for an adult horse.

Cobalt is often noted in blood-building supplements. It's an essential mineral for the synthesis of vitamin B12, and horses undoubtedly have minimum requirements for cobalt. The problem is we don't know what they are. "Best guess" estimates are

All the elements of a horse's diet, including grass and the hays made from them, contain an abundance of iron.

Although iron is added to all blood building products, a laboratory confirmed case of iron deficiency anemia has never been documented in a horse.

You'll find many blood-building products on the market.

in the neighborhood of 0.1 ppm, or about 1 to 3 mg/day. However, a cobalt deficiency state has never been recognized in horses. It is assumed their diets are adequate in cobalt, but we believe it wouldn't hurt to supplement 1 to 2 mg/day as insurance.

Horses are rarely iron-deficient or anemic, as they store large amounts of iron in their body tissues. In fact, a case of diet-related iron deficiency anemia has never been found in a horse. Hays and feeds also contain generous levels of iron compared to a horse's needs. Following a large blood loss, which might result in temporary anemia, the vet may decide that iron supplementation for a few weeks might be in order. However, odds are that most horses have plenty of stored iron and would do fine without it.

Older Horses

Older horses can be diagnosed as anemic, but it's really a result of multiple contributing factors. Older horses are usually considerably less active and fit, which decreases their need for oxygen. In fact, to the extent the lower counts are related to their lower activity levels, it isn't truly anemia. If the horse's red-cell counts are only slightly low and parameters such as cell size and cellular hemoglobin concentrations are normal, with the horse in good health otherwise, there's no need to panic.

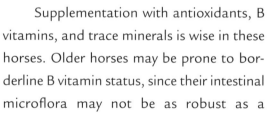

Supplementation with antioxidants, B vitamins, and trace minerals is wise in these horses. Older horses may be prone to borderline B vitamin status, since their intestinal microflora may not be as robust as a younger horse's. The older horse also may not absorb the vitamin B12 as well as younger horses.

Chronic Disease

When a horse is under stress because of a chronic disease, his body often lowers the level of circulating red blood cells. Part of this is caused by a decreased utilization of iron and part by

Blood-Building Nutrients

• **Iron.** Iron is essential, but diet-related deficiencies have not been found in horses, and excess iron is toxic. Skip high-iron supplements, unless blood tests of iron status prove you need it.

• **Copper.** Iron can't be properly utilized and incorporated into red cells with copper deficiency, and low copper is a common problem. Supplement copper with 100 mg/day or use a grain mix with good copper levels (50 to 60 ppm). However, dietary balance is important. Inadequate copper may still be a problem if your hay has high levels of competing minerals like iron, zinc, or manganese. Horses in hard work can have reductions in serum copper as much as 30%

• **Antioxidants.** Although antioxidants aren't directly involved in red-cell production, they do protect the red cells from damage during heavy exercise. We recommend antioxidant supplementation for high-performance horses and older horses when they don't have free access to pasture. Be especially aware that vitamin E (should feed 1,500 to 2,000 IU/day) and vitamin C (should feed 5 to 10 grams per day) are often too low. Vitamin A and its precursors are also important, although vitamin A is plentiful in alfalfa, most supplements, and fortified feeds. Feed 20,000 IU/day of vitamin A and several large carrots for carotenoids.

• **B vitamins.** Vitamin B6, folic acid, and vitamin B12 are especially important for normal hemoglobin and red-cell production. Look for minimums of 50 to 100 mg B6, 4 to 8 mg folic acid and 4,000 to 8,000 mcg (4 to 8 mg) of B12.

Ulcer Watch: Horses on medication that blocks the production of stomach acid—e.g. GastroGard or other generic gastric-blocking drugs—for prolonged periods of time might be at risk for vitamin B12 deficiency, since this complication has been documented in people taking these drugs. Folic-acid deficiency can also be related to some drugs, notably trimethoprim, pyrimethamine, methotrexate, Dilantin, and other anticonvulsants.

Supplements for Anemic Horses

Anemia-Causing Plants

Your horse may become truly anemic if he consumes too much of these plants:
- Onion, onion grass
- Red maple
- Garlic
- Moldy sweet clover hay

Product	Price	Comments
Antioxidant Concentrate Vita-Key, 800-539-8482 www.vita-key.com	$49.50/5 lbs., 62¢/1 oz. per day	A bit lower than we'd like to see for B6 in a one-oz. serving, but otherwise contains all the antioxidants and red-cell nutrients you need, at excellent dosages.
Equi-Cell Select the Best, 800-648-0950 www.selectthebest.com	$15.95/gal., 50¢/day	Vitamins B6 and B12 are lower than we'd like to see, but the folic acid and copper levels are good. Selenium is also good, but vitamin E is low and there's no vitamin C included.
Go Max Farnam, 800-234-2269 www.farnamhorse.com	$18.95/gal., 29¢/day	Includes all the key red-cell nutrients and folic acids, although at lower levels. Because of the economical price, this product is something to consider if you're not sure your already-supplemented diet provides enough nutrients. However, we find the levels too low as stand-alone supplement for an anemic horse.
Hemo-5000 Uckele, 800-248-0330 www.uckele.com	$28.45/80 gram tube, $4.74/dose	For use in horses with anemia that is responsive to vitamin B12.
Horse Honey 2X Uckele, 800-248-0330 www.uckele.com	$14.20/gal., 22¢/day	Liquid. The citric acid in this formula enhances iron absorption from foods. Good folic acid level but otherwise levels are low.
Iron Plus Neogen, 800-477-8201 www.neogen.com	$12.75/gal., 40¢/day at 2 oz./day	Liquid. We'd reserve its use only for veterinarian-confirmed iron deficiency. Copper is low.
Linpro Fox Den Equine, 540-337-5450 www.foxdenequine.com	$25/5 lbs., $1.25/day at 4 oz./day	Pellet, which adds to its palatability. Vitamins A, E, and other natural antioxidants are from flax. Good copper level. High folic acid but no pyridoxine or vitamin B12.
Max Plus Vita-Flex, 800-848-2359 www.vita-flex.com	$51.94/gal., $1.62/2 oz. serving	We find this product contains low levels of ingredients important for red-cell formation, except for folic acid.
Pow'red Performance Cavalor, 888-837-3626 www.cavalor.com	$56.99/3 liters, 95¢/50 ml serving	Would like to see higher levels of vitamins E, B6, and B12 and less iron, but across the board, this supplement is a cut above most equine blood builders. Includes chelated minerals for better absorption.
Power Plus Nutri-Bites Vets Plus, 800-468-3877 www.horsesprefer.com	$15.99/90 tablets, 53¢/day for 1,200-lb. horse (3 tablets)	Tablet. Pluses are that it's heavy on the cobalt and low in iron. However, vitamin B12 is also low.
Pro VM Peak Performance, 800-944-1984 www.peakperformance nutrients.com	$65.99/3.3 lbs., $2.20/day for 50 grams, $1.65/day for 37.5 grams	Would like to see more vitamin B12, but the levels of all other ingredients are excellent even at 37.5 grams/day vs. the recommended 50 grams.
Procell Liquid Multivet USA, 800-356-8776 www.multivetusa.com	$22/gal., 34¢/oz.	Liquid. Folic acid level is good, but otherwise it's low on red-cell supporting nutrients.
Pro-Iron Plus Multivet USA, 800-356-8776 www.multivetusa.com	$45/5 lbs., 75¢/day	All red-cell supporting nutrients at low levels.
Red Cell Farnam, 800-234-2269 www.farnamhorse.com	$14.95/gal., 23¢/day at 1 oz.	Liquid. If you double the serving you get good levels of folic acid and copper, but then you get more iron than you need. Vitamin B6, vitamin B12, and vitamin E are too low. Contains no vitamin C.
Redglo Farnam, 800-234-2269 www.farnamhorse.com	$26.51/gallon, 83¢/2 oz. serving	We advise you not to use this product with any other source of vitamin A, as its level is high. Vitamins E and B vitamin levels fairly low. No copper.

a general slowdown in metabolism that occurs in an effort to help the body deal with the disease challenge. The anemia typically is mild and doesn't respond to supplementation. It corrects itself spontaneously when the disease is adequately treated.

Any horse that suffers a large loss of blood may be anemic, although it takes a significant amount of blood loss. When a sudden, large blood loss occurs, the horse may need a transfusion to avoid damage to critical organs. Otherwise, provision of a high-quality diet with adequate protein and mineral levels, as well as a period of supplementation with B vitamins, is all the horse needs to recover.

Other treatable illness-related causes of anemia include:

- Severe respiratory infections
- Infections of the Babesia, Ehrlichia, or Lyme organisms
- Acute infections of any type, including any severe, systemic bacterial infection and Listeriosis
- Developing antibodies against the body's own red cells, which can be from drugs like penicillin, phenylbutazone, flunixin (Banamine), and ketoprofen
- Autoimmune reactions
- Infections, abscesses containing anaerobic bacteria like Clostridia, or systemic Clostridia infections like colitis and strangles

Bottom Line

You probably don't want to risk supplementing iron, unless blood tests of the horse's iron status prove that the horse needs it.

A number of the products in our chart are good choices for specific situations, such as Pow'red Performance from Cavalor. Our comments are specific for actual blood builders, not as general supplements.

Smart Guide to Blood Building

Who Needs to Be Concerned?

- Trainers of horses in speed and endurance events
- Owners of older horses, especially those losing ground
- Breeders dealing with foals that are heavily parasitized
- Anyone who owns a horse battling a chronic illness
- Those with horses who have lost a large amount of blood

Why Build Blood?

- By increasing the blood's oxygen-carrying capacity, you increase stamina.
- Older horses have weaker digestive systems, necessitating a heavier level of supplementation just to ensure they meet minimum dietary absorption levels.
- Strong blood built through proper nutrition enhances the immune system.

How Do I Build Blood?

- Focus on the B vitamins, antioxidants, and copper. Take a solid look at your horse's current diet to assess if you really need to be supplementing at all. Too much is a waste of money.
- Be careful with iron. While humans can suffer from "iron-poor blood," it's unlikely your fit horse needs dietary iron. Worse, overdoing iron can be toxic.
- Consider contributing factors that cause "weak" blood. Illness, some plants, heavy parasitism in foals, and old age can cause what appears to be anemia. Address the cause of the poor blood rather the symptom.
- Prescription ulcer medications contribute to vitamin B12 deficiency. Vitamin B12 is important for normal hemoglobin and red-cell production. Be sure your horse is consuming 4 to 8 mg of B12, in addition to vitamin B6 and folic acid.

Checking for Iron Deficiency

We think of iron when we hear anemia because it's commonly involved in people, but that's not the case in horses. Before you start pumping your horse full of iron, check his iron status. Serum iron level alone won't tell you anything. You also need total iron binding capacity—a measurement of how saturated the horse's iron-binding protein (transferrin) is, and a serum ferritin. Ferritin is the protein that binds iron in storage form, keeping it from circulating free and causing damage to body tissues.

The only laboratory in the world that can measure equine ferritin is the Comparative Hematology Laboratory at Kansas State University. Its Web site is www.vet.ksu.edu/depts/dmp/service/comp-hemo/index.htm and includes submission forms. You'll need to print out the iron panel request form. Since many vets are not familiar with this testing, they will need to read the sample handling requirements before coming out to test your horse so they are prepared to spin and freeze the blood as required for the test to be accurate.

Interpreting Results:

Serum Iron: Upper normal for most labs is 150 ug/dL. The higher the iron, the more iron your horse has in his diet. Preliminary data shows insulin resistant horses, like insulin resistant people, overabsorb iron. Very high iron intakes will increase any horse's serum iron. Hemolysis (rupture of the red blood cells) will cause a false elevation of this test. Fasting may cause a falsely low reading.

Total Iron Binding Capacity (TIBC): Most horses run in the 250 to 350 ug/dL range. TIBC is an indirect measurement of the level of the protein transferrin, which shuttles iron around in the body. TIBC levels generally parallel serum iron. TIBC itself doesn't tell you too much, but Transferrin Saturation Index (TSI) does. This is calculated by dividing the serum iron by the TIBC result and multiplying by 100, e.g., serum iron 100 divided by TIBC 300 x 100 = 33.3%. Most horses will run in the 30 to 35% range for TSI. When iron overload is developing, TSI rises.

Ferritin: Ferritin is the storage protein for iron. Most horses are in the 100 to 200 mg/ml range, but anemia isn't a concern until ferritins dip down to about 20. The higher the ferritin, the more iron is stored in the body tissues. Primary storage sites are the liver and spleen. Some horses are so heavily loaded with iron that their livers are found to be black on postmortem examinations.

Both falsely high and falsely low readings for ferritin do occur. By "false" we mean the value doesn't truly reflect the horse's iron stores. Pregnancy causes a falsely low test result for ferritin. During pregnancy, the mare's body lowers ferritin production to make sure adequate iron is available to the growing foal.

Infections, inflammation, and malignancy can cause falsely high ferritin readings. It is one of the body's protective mechanisms. Many organisms and cancer cells are highly dependent on iron for their growth and multiplication. By increasing ferritin, the body is trying to keep iron away from them. Iron is also very pro-inflammatory, so the body will sequester more iron to protect itself from runaway inflammation.

If your horse is healthy and you're looking for a supplement to cover all the bases in nutritional support—and therefore be a good "blood builder"—we suggest Vita-Key's Antioxidant Concentrate or Peak Performance Nutrients' Pro VM.

Pro VM is the best if you also need a maintenance dose of glucosamine, plus higher levels of lysine, methionine, and biotin. However, since most horses only need their intakes boosted a bit, we like the levels in Farnam's Go Max, our best buy. 🐎

Building Strong Bones

6

Building strong bone in young horses and maintaining it in adults is a major concern of all horse people. What many don't understand is that there's a lot more to it than just calcium.

It's true that pregnant, lactating, and growing horses need a higher concentration of calcium in their diet. Young horses in training need even more as they go through the process of remodeling their bone to make it stronger. Adults need adequate calcium intake to maintain strong bones. However, if all you are doing is feeding extra alfalfa or a calcium supplement, you may be doing more harm than good.

Formation and maintenance of normal bone can only occur when both calcium and phosphorus in the diet are present in the correct proportions. The ideal ratio is between 1.2 to 2 times as much calcium as phosphorus. In addition to maintaining a correct ratio, you need to ensure that the horse is getting adequate total amounts of both of these minerals. The table on page 48 shows the daily minimum requirement, in grams/day, of a 500 kg (1,100 lb.) horse. Compare that to the daily calorie needs and you'll see that with pregnancy, lactation, and growth the percent change in mineral requirements is higher than for calories. This means that feeding an adult-formula diet to meet calories won't meet the needs of these special circumstances without supplementing minerals.

Inadequate total calcium intake causes joint swelling and risk of developmental bone disease (e.g., physitis, osteochondrosis) in young horses. In adults, it increases the fracture risk

Timothy's calcium:phosphorus ratio makes it a good choice.

and can cause an ill-defined shifting lameness. Excessive calcium changes the character of the bones, but apparently does not produce any symptoms as long as phosphorus intake is adequate. If the total amount of phosphorus being consumed is too low, the consequences are the same as for inadequate calcium. Excessive phosphorus intake and intakes that cause the ratio of calcium to phosphorus to fall below 1.2:1 interfere with calcium absorption and eventually cause deformity and softening of the bones.

Nutrition is critical for development of strong bones in young, rapidly growing horses.

Magnesium, also a major mineral in bone, is not as well studied in horses. In other species, magnesium deficiency causes osteoporosis and loss of bone mineral density. The ideal ratio of calcium to magnesium in other species, and suggested by some authors for horses, is 2:1: That's twice as much calcium as magnesium in the diet.

Both deficiencies and excessive intakes of zinc can cause developmental bone disease in young horses. Bone effects in older horses have not been studied, but in other species (where effects in the young are the same) zinc deficiency leads to impaired ability to remodel and repair bone. Copper deficiency can be a cause of osteochrondrosis, a joint disease that involves the transition zone between cartilage and bone.

Adequate protein, vitamin D, vitamin A, vitamin C, and even calories are also crucial for healthy bone.

What to Do?

First, what not to do. Do not rely on a calcium supplement or a bone supplement to provide everything needed for healthy bone formation, growth, and repair. Calcium and phosphorus are crucial, but they don't provide all the nutrients needed.

For all horses, and especially adults on diets of primarily hay, you really need to have some idea of what the mineral levels are in your hay, which is a major source of minerals. Even when feeding highly supplemented grain mixtures that are correctly balanced and can meet the adult horse's daily mineral needs when feeding only a few pounds a day, there is a very real chance that the mineral profile of your hay may be upsetting the balance of the grain. The same holds true for horses receiving mineral supplements, either without grain or with an unsupplemented grain. Your supplement may be correctly balanced, but when the rest of the diet isn't, it may not work well. The best way to find out what's in your hay is to have it analyzed. Your state university will probably offer this service for a very minimal fee. If your hay changes too frequently to make analysis reasonable, find out where it is grown and place a call to the state agricultural extension agent in that area. They will have average analysis figures available for your hay type, or can tell you where to get them.

See chapter 11 for details on putting together a diet for pregnant, lactating, and growing horses. With horses in work, making sure their base diet is correctly balanced with regard to mineral ratios is the place to start. When increasing calories to keep the horse's weight normal, you will also be increasing mineral intake. As long as the relative proportions of hay and grain do not change, the diet will still be balanced and you will meet the increased needs of exercise. With horses that are still rapidly growing (under the age of 3) and seniors, it's a good idea to make sure they are getting at least 150% of the daily requirements. In young horses, this is to provide some extra insurance against growth spurts. For the older animals, efficiency of digestion and absorption may not be as good as it was in their younger years. 🐎

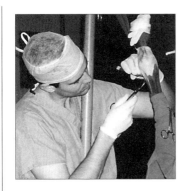

Building strong healthy bones may help prevent future injuries that require surgery.

Changing Calcium, Phosphorus, and Calorie Requirements for a Horse with a Mature Body Weight of 1,100 lbs. (500 kg)

Age and Class	Calcium grams/day	Phosphorus grams/day	Megacalories/day
4-month weanling	39.1	21.7	13.3
6-month weanling	38.6	21.5	15.5
Yearling	37.7	20.9	18.8
2-year-old, not in work	36.7	20.4	18.7
2-year-old, in training	36.7	20.4	21.8
Inactive adult	20	14	15.2 to 18.1
Pregnant, 9 months	36	26.3	19.2
Pregnant, 11 months	36	26.3	21.4
Lactating, 1st month	59.1	38.3	31.7
Lactating, after 3 months	41.7	26.2	29.4

From: National Research Council Nutrient Requirements of Horses, 2007

Calming and Stress Reduction Additives

If you are hoping to find a quick fix tranquilizer alternative that will instantly transform your horse into an automaton, move on. This chapter isn't for you. If you ride a horse that is too strong, too energetic, too eager, or too forward for the job you want done, or for your level of riding expertise, you need a new horse. Both you and the horse will be better off for it. Time, patience, and the help of a professional trainer should all be used in an effort to solve behavior problems before hoping for a fix from a supplement.

That said, there are some horses that just need to quiet down and relax a bit so that they can focus and enjoy their jobs. We don't want anything that influences motor coordination or that makes the horse "doped." We wanted the horse alert, responsive, and eager but able to concentrate.

Situations also arise where nervous vices mysteriously appear or a stall-bound horse gets overly on edge. These horses sometimes need help, but chemical tranquilizers may be overkill. Enter calming supplements.

We did our last trial back in 2002. The horses included:

- Racehorses that were normally high-spirited under routine daily circumstances, but became nervous, agitated, and difficult to control in the paddock before races

- Horses stall-bound for injuries that were overactive, with pacing and stall-walking vices, two of which were flank or side-biting

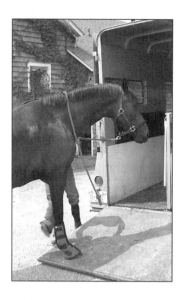

A horse overly anxious about shipping arrives exhausted and may injure himself in the trailer.

- Horses that weren't nervous or hyperactive in general but sensitive to touch and sound and would shy or startle easily when being ridden
- Horses that were overly aggressive in a field situation
- Horses that were otherwise calm and normal, but had irrational "phobias" to shipping or clippers

This chapter reviews those findings, and adds results with a few more products.

Products

Calming is a pretty popular supplement category, and you have many different products to choose from, with a variety of ingredients.

Nutrition-Based Ingredients

Several mineral and vitamin deficiencies or excesses can affect nervous-system function, especially the B vitamins, calcium, and magnesium.

Liberal turnout with plenty of room to run and play is the best way to relieve nervous tension.

Although studies vary as to whether or not thiamine (vitamin B1) "calms" horses, vets have used it intravenously as a non-drug alternative for calming for at least a half century, which may make thiamine the oldest "natural" tranquilizer in modern-day use. Vitamin B6 has a long history of use combating anxiety in humans, especially anxiety, depression, and premenstrual syndrome (PMS).

Magnesium and calcium share many functions in the nervous system. Deficiencies of magnesium are far more common, however, and the blood level of this key ion is not as closely regulated as calcium. Like vitamin B6, in humans magnesium has been used to help symptoms in a wide variety of disorders and is especially helpful for anxiety and PMS. A combination of B vitamins and calcium salts is a common calming intravenous "cocktail" with some vets, and magnesium sulfate delivered intravenously is so effective it was even used at one time as an anesthetic agent.

Ingredients and Typical Effects

Little horse-specific research is available, so we listed the common human complaints/conditions.

Ingredient	Nervous System Effects	Typically Used For
Chamomile	Binds to the same brain receptors as benzodiazepines, like Valium.	Mild nervousness, anxiety.
Hops	Same as chamomile.	Mild nervousness, anxiety.
Ignatia amara (St. Ignatius's bean)	Contains the potent poison strychnine, a muscular and nervous-system stimulant.	Used in homeopathic concentrations for hysteria and grief.
Juahua	None known.	"Alternative"/balancing herb.
Kava kava	Influences excitability of brain neurons, affects brain chemicals. Should not be combined with valerian. Kava kava may negatively affect liver.	Insomnia, anxiety.
Lemon balm	Not known.	Mild anxiety.
Magnesium	Calming effects on a variety of brain-receptor types.	Anxiety, depression, irritability, jumpiness, migraines, PMS.
Myo-inositol	Important in receptor functions in nervous system cells.	Panic.
Passionflower	Mechanism not defined. Some evidence of binding to benzodiazepine receptors.	Anxiety, nervousness.
Skullcap	Probable benzodiazepine-like actions.	Mild nervousness and fearfulness.
Suan zao ren	Central nervous system depressant.	Irritability, anxiety, insomnia.
Taurine	Inhibitory amino acid in the brain.	Hyperactivity, autism, addictive behaviors.
Thiamine (B1)	Maintains integrity of the serotonin receptors.	Depression, anxiety, irritability, poor learning.
Tryptophan	Amino acid precurosor of serotonin.	Anxiety, aggression.
Valerian	Elevates levels of sedating brain neurotransmitters. Should not be combined with kava kava.	Insomnia, anxiety.
Vitamin B6	Required for conversion of tryptophan to the brain chemical serotonin.	Anxiety, easily stressed.
Wood betony	Unknown.	"Nervous headache."
Yuan zhi (polyganla)	Binds to dopamine receptors in the brain.	Poor memory and "focus."

Training and the horse's basic personality are the major determinants of how relaxed he will be.

Tryptophan is an amino acid that influences brain function. It was a popular "tranquilizing" and sleep-inducing supplement in people until problems arose with a painful muscle condition called eosinophilic myositis; it was pulled off the market, even though this problem was later proven to be due to a contaminant in the supplements, not the tryptophan itself.

Taurine, another amino acid sometimes incorporated into behavior supplements, helps maintain the normal structure of cell membranes and their receptors. However, effects of taurine on behavior are not clear. On the one hand, severe taurine deficiency in people caused profound depression. On the other, preliminary evidence suggests supplements may help with manic behavior in bipolar disorder, where people cycle between extreme activity (mania) and depression. A recent study in rats showed taurine reduced anxiety, but only at high doses.

Herbal-Based Ingredients

Not surprisingly, the pharmacology of most calming herbals has been found to resemble either the action of Valium-like sedatives or Prozac-like antidepressant and antianxiety drugs that influence serotonin levels in the brain. The two heaviest hitters in the herbal category are most definitely kava kava and valerian root.

A surprisingly high number of nervous horses respond quickly to simply filling a nutritional gap with basic essential nutrients.

The most potent kava kava products are methanol extracts of the leaves, with potency dropping as other plant parts are mixed in. Kava kava is also a frequently abused herb in Pacific island cultures and among the native populations of Australia. It's reported to have some narcotic-like effects, and use can be addictive. There is a tremendous difference in effect depending on the individual product, however.

Valerian root causes increased levels of a brain chemical that has sedating effects that interact with many other neurotransmitter systems.

Although neither kava kava nor valerian is reported to cloud thinking, the major use for both is in inducing sleep. High doses of either one can actually cause mania and excitement.

Field Trials

Each horse in the trial was tried on at least two products from different categories. No supplementation was used between products for three weeks or more, and the horse was observed to see if the behavior returned. It always did, usually in far less than three weeks.

- **Magnesium:** We had excellent results in all our problem categories with magnesium supplementation in the range of 3 to 10 grams per day. While results did vary depending on the problem, magnesium had a noticeable beneficial effect that was rated from good to excellent in respect to nervousness, anxiety, spooking, and overreaction to sound or touch, making it a top choice.

   Trailering issues are a major problem for many nervous horses, but should be dealt with by training, not supplements or drugs.

   Aggressive horses were less easily provoked, although they would still bite or kick when they were. Flank biting and phobias didn't respond. Magnesium carries no long-term side effects, and it doesn't drug the horse or change his chemistry in any way.

   Human supplements can be ground up, or you can buy magnesium oxide in bulk bags from a feed mill or other supplier. If the horse isn't receiving grain or doesn't accept powders well, we found Quiessence pellets effective and palatable, but pricey.

- **Thiamine (B1) And Vitamin B6:** Thiamine and vitamin B6 tended to be effective in the same horses that responded to magnesium, although magnesium gave better results. The combination of thiamine, B6, and magnesium was particularly effective in horses that showed diarrhea when stressed (a common symptom in horses that naturally tend to be high strung), and we liked the combinations in Seroquine, At-Ease, and Ex-Stress best. One of the poor-shipping horses did much better on this combination. He was obviously still nerv-

Performance horses need to have a level head to focus on the problems put in front of them.

ous about the whole idea, but loaded without help and scrambled less.

- **L-Tryptophan:** Tryptophan gave the best results in horses that became belligerent or pushy, which included all the racehorses that acted up in the saddling paddock. Even the gelding that liked to pick fights responded the best to tryptophan. A single dose of tryptophan prior to a race wasn't as predictable as feeding it for at least three days ahead of time.

  Our stall-confined horses also responded well to tryptophan, although we're not particularly comfortable with feeding tryptophan long term.

  We found a single dose of 4 grams three hours prior to competition also had aggression-modifying effects, but results were better with the multiple-day program. Best results were seen after three days' use, minimum daily dose of 4 grams of tryptophan, the last dose given about three hours before the competition (check rules).

- **Kava Kava and Valerian Root:** When we conducted our first trial, there were several products available that contained kava kava, some as the sole ingredient. It worked, and worked quickly, but those products have now disappeared. This may be because kava kava is now under close scrutiny here and in Europe as a result of possible liver problems associated with it. One horse we had on kava kava (a horse on stall rest for an injury) became very agitated after 2.5 weeks on the supplement, with no obvious reason found. He returned to normal over a few days when it was stopped.

  With the valerian-only trial, it took about a week to see a difference, while with valerian combination products, some calming was noted in a few days and became more noticeable after 10 days to three weeks.

  While the horses were calmer, or even "dopey" in their stalls, the effects didn't necessarily hold when the horse was stimulated. Horses that were hard to handle in the paddock, or spooky on rides, seemed to snap out of the effects of kava kava or valerian entirely under those conditions.

We especially liked Equilite's Equine Relax Blend, where the combination of valerian with milder but more rapid-acting herbs produced results quickly, with peak effect in about two weeks.

Bottom Line

We can't stress often enough that a horse that is too much for the rider to handle needs professional training or a new home. The horse that simply refuses to work with you may have issues, but the solution is retraining, not giving him an herbal calmative product. There's a big difference between a horse that adamantly refuses to cooperate and one that's easily startled by unexpected stimuli or gets highly excitable in understandable situations.

However, when you need help, first try adding magnesium oxide or thiamine alone to the horse's diet. If this doesn't work, we'd consider a commercial product that combines these ingredients. The nutritional approaches gave more consistent and reliable results with our test horses.

Of the products we tried, we found Seroquine, At-Ease, and Ex-Stress produced excellent, solid results in our field-trial horses. Seroquine gets the nod for potency and price.

Nervousness is a major impediment to forming a close bond with your horse.

More Is Not Better

Herbal supplements for "calming" should not be used indiscriminately. As with any medicinal substance, they can cause adverse reactions. For example, hops can interfere with cycling or pregnancy in high doses, and valerian root has antiprogesterone effects. In general, no herbals should be used in pregnant or lactating mares. No herb should be used with with any other tranquilizing or sedating drug. If the horse has been getting these and needs a tranquilizer or anesthesia, inform your veterinarian. Many of the most-active herbs can have exciting, rather than calming, effects if used in high doses. Liver damage is also possible with long-term and/or high-dose use.

If your nervous horse also gets aggressive, we suggest you try either tryptophan alone, as is found in B-Kalm paste (which may work at even a half dose), or in combination with magnesium and B vitamins, a combination we like in At-Ease.

Effects with the herbally based products were milder and less reliable in our test horses, but with valerian producing the most obvious effects when dosing was high enough. Equine Relax Blend, the valerian-based formula, worked the best.

Feeds and Nervousness

Some horsemen firmly believe grain makes a horse more hot-tempered, although it's never been scientifically proven. Conversely, substituting fat for grain calories usually calms a horse down. Before you start pumping your horse full of oil though, there are things to consider. If your sport requires speed or endurance, fat is not your answer. High-fat diets eventually lead to lowered levels of glycogen in the muscle that can adversely affect performance. In general terms, fat is a highly unnatural calorie source for a horse, as its normal diet would contain 3% fat at most. The source of calories can influence how calm or excitable your horse is, but you don't have to feed fat. Unless the horse is working very heavily, simply cutting grain and increasing hay will maintain the body weight very well. If hay is not enough, you can feed beet pulp or beet pulp and rice bran substi-

tuted for part or all of the grain ration rather than oils/fats. Approximate conversions are:

- 1 lb. oats = calories in 1.2 lbs. dry beet pulp or 1.08 lbs. rice bran
- 1 lb. sweet feed = calories in 1.25 lbs. dry beet pulp or 1.15 lbs. rice bran.

Additionally, if you find yourself feeding your horse more grain than you would like because of problems with keeping weight on him, your best answer might not be a calmative. We like Ration Plus (www.rationplus.com, 800-728-4667), which may help him utilize the hay portion of his diet better so that you don't have to feed so much grain. Another old favorite, Equi-Aide Products' Body Builder (800-413-3702), has repeatedly been effective in bulking up horses, and at the same time it often has a noticeable calming effect.

For Ladies Only

Our test horses included a 12-year-old mare who gave "alpha mare" a whole new meaning; a 2-year-old Thoroughbred race filly who was aggressive; a 3-year-old Standardbred race filly who got touchy mid cycle and nervous in the paddock; and a 13-year-old show mare who was basically push-button but unpredictable when she began cycling each year.

We first tried Hormonise on all four. The two aggressive mares responded extremely well. There was no change in the older show mare, but we believe that her minor ups and downs were really normal behavior. The 3-year-old lost her touchiness but remained anxious in the paddock. After letting all the mares and fillies go through one cycle with no supplements, we tried again.

Feisty Mare was fed to the aggressive two. It was moderately effective after 2.5 weeks for the 2-year-old but didn't make much difference with the older mare.

The Relax Her made a significant change in the show mare after a month, pleasing her owner. The 3-year-old filly was also fed Relax Her for a month and showed a bit more of a relaxed attitude in the paddock. She eventually was tried on a maintenance program of Hormonise with three grams of tryptophan starting three days before a race and did well with that.

Best Bets in Calmatives

Problem	Key Ingredients	Products
Nervous, shying horses	Magnesium and/or thiamine with or without vitamin B6	Quiessence, At-Ease, Megadose, Ex-Stress, Thiamine B1, Calm Ease
Nervous, aggressive horses	Tryptophan alone or with magnesium	Tryptophan Plus Gel, At-Ease Megadose, Easy Going
Very overactive stall-bound horses	Magnesium, B vitamins, valerian	Quiessence, Equine Relax Blend, or generic magnesium oxide
Slightly overactive stall-bound horses	Magnesium, B vitamins, herbal blends	Valerian-Free Relax Blend, Earth Lodge Calming Formula, Serenity, or generic magnesium oxide
Mares	Chasteberry, valerian	Hormonise, Relax Her

Equine Calming Products

Product	Active Ingredients	Comments
Ex-Stress Peak Performance Nutrients www.peakperformance nutrients.com 800-944-1984 $49/2 lbs.	Magnesium sulfate, thiamine hydrochloride, pyridoxine hydrochloride, riboflavin, niacin, folic acid	Consistent top performer over the years. No fillers means less to feed. Good middle of the road magnesium dose with high B levels so you can adjust down if too much effect without losing B potency.
Quiessence Fox Den Equine www.foxdenequine.com 540-337-5450 $27.50/5 lbs.	Good source of magnesium, trace amounts of B vitamins	Palatable magnesium supplement in a pellet form, perfect for magnesium responsive horses that are picky about powders.
Thiamine B-1 Equine America www.equineamerica.com 800-838-7524 $9.95/gallon	Thiamine hydrochloride liquid	Not concentrated enough for this purpose.
Thiamine Vitamin B1 Uckele Health and Nutrition www.uckele.com 800-248-0330 $14.95/2 lbs.	Thiamine mononitrate	Economical choice for the thiamine responsive horse.
Thiamine B-1 Solution Equine America www.equineamerica.com 800-838-7524 $13.95/qt	Thiamine hydrochloride liquid	Note: This is a different product from the one listed above with a similar name and is 5 times more concentrated. Effective at 2 oz./day for horses that are thiamine responsive.
Rlx-All Uckele Health & Nutrition www.uckele.com 800-248-0330 $21.95/2 lbs.	Thiamine mononitrate, L-taurine, valerian root extract	No additional benefit over effects of an equivalent dose of thiamine seen.
At Ease Megadose Select the Best www.selectthebest.com 800-648-0950 $10.40/60 cc paste $31.50/1.5 lbs powder	Magnesium oxide, L-tryptophan, thiamine mononitrate, pyridoxine hydrochloride	Excellent choice for the magnesium/B vitamin responsive horse. Depending on diet and individual animal, may need to add more magnesium to a single dose. Double dosing also gives full therapeutic dose of tryptophan, helpful in horses that are pushy/aggressive.
Calmex Paste Med-Vet Pharmaceuticals www.medvetpharm.com 800-366-8986 $4.95/tube	Thiamine hydrochloride, taurine, inositol	Effective dose of thiamine for those horses that respond to thiamine alone. No obvious difference in response compared to thiamine alone at an equivalent dose. Better effect when used for at least 3 days.
Calmex Powder Med-Vet Pharmaceuticals www.medvetpharm.com 800-366-8986 $22.50/2 lbs.	Thiamine, taurine, inositol, ignatia amara (homeopathic preparation)	Same as for Calmex paste.
Easy Going Pro-Formula Laboratories 800-525-3007 $6.88/tube	L-tryptophan 11.9%, valerian root, passionflower, kava kava, ginger root, hops, wood betony	Very good for horses that tend to be pushy/aggressive when nervous. Best results if used for 2 to 3 days prior to stressful event.

Equine Calming Products cont.

Product	Active Ingredients	Comments
So Kalm Paste Equine America www.equineamerica.com 800-838-7624 $5.00/tube	L-tryptophan 0.7%, thiamine hydrochloride	Helpful for horses sensitive to low dose thiamine. No tryptophan effect at suggested dose.
So Kalm Powder Equine America www.equineamerica.com 800-838-7624 $24/2 lbs.	L-tryptophan 0.7%, thiamine hydrochloride	Helpful for horses sensitive to low dose thiamine. Minimum of 2 oz. (double dose) for any tryptophan effect.
Tryptophan Plus Gel Horses Prefer/Vets Plus Inc www.vets-plus.com 800-468-3877 $5.95/tube	L-tryptophan and low doses of minerals and B vitamins	For pushy/aggressive horses. Best used for 2 to 3 days, as well as 2 to 3 hours, prior to stress. Double dosing most effective.
Calm Ease Equine Gold www.equinegold.com 800-870-5949 $69.95/2 lbs.	Suan Zao Ren, Yuan Zhi, Ju Hua, Sang Ye, Bai He, He Huan Pi, Mai Ye, Gou Teng, Bai Ji Li	More consistently effective as a calmative for use when the horse is out of the stall and working. May need to double dose for very anxious horses. Best results with regular use. Very pricey.
Calming Formula Earth Lodge Herbals www.earthlodgeherbals.com 860-237-8801 $70/lb.	Red clover, peppermint, German chamomile, yarrow, meadowsweet, goldenrod, nettle, thyme, burdock, celery seed, milk thistle seed	Calming effect is very mild, only detectable in stall-bound horses. Requires regular use. Aromatic, palatable, high quality herbs but very pricey.
Equine Relax Blend Equilite www.equilite.com 800-942-5483 $39.50/4 lbs.	Valerian, chamomile, hops, wood betony, passion flower	Excellent choice for a nervous, pacing, stall-bound horse. Some help with horses nervous under saddle, especially at the higher dose (2 oz/day).
Valerian Free Relax Blend Equilite www.equilite.com 800-942-5483 $39.50/4 lbs.	Chamomile, hops, wood betony, passion flower , blue vervain	Mildly to moderately effective with stall-bound horses. Not as effective as the valerian based formula under saddle, for shipping, etc.
Extra Calm Equine Science Products www.equinescience products.com (901) 380-1433 $33/3 lbs.	Alfalfa, valerian root, chamomile, queen of meadow, stevia, passion flower	Fairly effective with stall-bound horses. Mildly effective under saddle, but suggest higher dosing.
Hormonise Equi-Natural Products www.equinatural.com 972-752-5598 $43/liter	Vitex agnus castus (chasteberry) extract	Excellent choice for aggressive and irritable fillies and mares, especially when associated with strong or long estrus periods. Also calms geldings and stallions. Warning: Possible effects on stallion fertility.
Serenity Herbs for Horses www.herbsforhorses.com 888-423-7777 $52/2.2 lbs.	Lemon balm, chamomile, verbena, skullcap, passion flower	Mildly effective for stall-bound horses.

Equine Calming Products cont.

Product	Active Ingredients	Comments
Valerian Solution Equine America www.equineamerica.com 800-838-7624 $13.95/qt	Valerian extract	Mild effect noted in stall-bound horses only.
Tryptophan Plus Nutribites Horses Prefer/Vets Plus Inc. www.vets-plus.com 800-468-3877 $19.50/90 tablets	Very low doses of tryptophan, sodium chloride, potassium chloride, niacin, thiamine, riboflavin	Amounts of tryptophan and thiamine provided in the recommended feeding rate (1 tablet per 400 lbs body weight) way too low for any calming effect, but you may run across this product grouped with other calming/tryptophan supplements.
Quietex Powder Farnam www.farnamhorse.com 800-234-2269 $14.95/30 oz.	Valerian officinalis, Ignatia amara (homeopathic, 8X)	Mild effect with daily dosing in horses on stall rest. (Note: also available in paste form, $6.65/dose, which we found ineffective)
Calm & Cool Oralx www.oralxcorp.com 801-731-4050 $6.00/34 gram tube	Tryptophan, valerian, hops, wood betony, magnesium, taurine, thiamine, inositol	Mild effects at regular dose, obvious sedating effects at double dose.
Calm & Cool Pellets Oralx www.oralxcorp.com 801-731-4050 $23.50/6 lbs.	Same as paste	Same as paste.
B-Kalm Paste Horse Health www.farnamhorse.com 800-234-2269 $5.55/oz. tube	L-tryptophan	Good for horses that are both nervous and aggressive in stressful situations. Try half tube first. Obvious sedation in some horses at full dose. Best results with 2 to 3 days use.
Modipher EQ Vet Product Labs Vita-Flex www.vitaflex.com 800-848-2359 $27.95/7.5 mL	Nasal spray in dispenser bottle, contains "appeasing" pheromones	Mild to no obvious effects. Horses left undisturbed for at least 30 minutes usually appear very quiet, but are easily aroused again. Effect does not change with higher dosing than recommended.
Seroquine Uckele Health and Nutrition www.uckele.com 800-248-0330 $24.95/2 lbs.	Magnesium, taurine, thiamine, inositol	Highest magnesium and thiamine supplement. Excellent choice for horses that are jumpy, sensitive to sound and touch, overreactive.

Cushing's Disease

Cushing's syndrome is a collection of clinical signs and symptoms that are the result of hormonal imbalances. These are caused by either overactivity of the pituitary gland or a tumor in the gland itself.

The hallmark of Cushing's is an abnormally long, thick, curly, or coarse hair coat that does not shed in the spring. Poor immunity often develops, both to infections and internal parasites, related both to poor overall condition and the overproduction of cortisol, which suppresses the immune system. In advanced cases and/or with large tumors, blindness may occur due to pressure on the optic nerve. The horse may also tilt his head. Increased production of cortisol in response to elevated levels of ACTH from the pituitary also often results in insulin resistance and laminitis in these horses. Mares with Cushing's disease often develop enlarged mammary glands and may even produce milk. This suggests prolactin production is also increased.

Herbal Help

With these hormones in mind, we decided to try an herbal product, Hormonise, which is made from a plant called the Vitex agnus castus (chasteberry). It has been used in Europe to control a variety of human reproductive problems, including PMS, menopause, and polycystic ovaries. The common denominator in these syndromes is a high level of prolactin, a pituitary

A dense coat and visible ribs despite a large belly are some of the early signs of Cushing's disease.

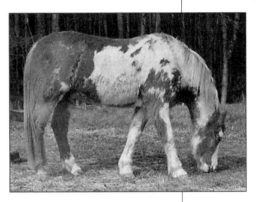

The classic scraggly coat is the least of the Cushing's horse's worries.

hormone that is known to be elevated in many cases of pituitary tumor in humans.

Our initial experience with Hormonise involved a 3-year-old that had a history of "mare" behavior problems. She was downright nasty. She was also cycling every 14 days. We didn't want to use Regumate or substances that had a calming or tranquilizing effect, so we tried Hormonise. Her response was excellent.

Since a high prolactin level is associated with both these mare-ish problems and pituitary tumors in some people, if even some of the horses with Cushing's disease had tumors of the type that secrete large amounts of prolactin, Hormonise might be helpful. We decided to find out.

A study in the 1993 *Hormonal Metabolism Journal* showed Vitex is capable of blocking the release of prolactin from pituitary cells. Despite this documented effect on pituitary prolactin levels, we couldn't find references to using Vitex in prolactin-secreting tumors, so we knew we were in largely uncharted territory. Vitex was also later shown to have a dopamine-like effect in the brain. It is now known that equine Cushing's disease begins with destruction of the dopamine producing neurons, which normally control hormonal output from the pituitary.

First Three Geldings

We initially gave Vitex to a horse and two ponies (all geldings) with classic Cushing's symptoms. We used the larger end of the recommended dosage scale and gave it daily, rather than in three-weeks-on/one-week-off cycles.

The response was rapid and dramatic. Within two to three weeks, shedding was occurring rapidly. One pony was white and would leave huge piles of hair around the field. The old hair had been coarse, dry, thick, and curly, but the new growth was normal and sleek, with a high shine.

All three geldings shed out completely for the first time in years, most with an early large loss of hair, followed by contin-

Hormonise

Herbal remedies are typically dried powders or extracts, which are prepared using high temperatures. Hormonise is a bit different.

The manufacturer believes their special processing results in a product with high biological activity but lower levels of the parent plant product. This may partially explain why we had no evidence of side effects, despite using dosages as much as four times higher than those commonly used in mares

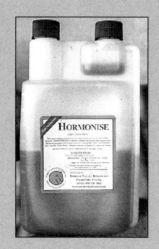

with cycling and behavior problems. The unique processing may also make it difficult to duplicate our results using powdered berries or standard extracts.

ued slower shedding or a few bursts of shedding until the abnormal hair was lost.

The other obvious change was increased energy levels. A chronically foundered pony was also getting around much better, even trotting, although no one would call him sound. It was difficult to tell if the increased activity level was related to his newfound energy or to improvement in the laminitis.

One pony failed to receive his Vitex for a three-week period, due to communication problems with the caretakers. Interestingly, his energy level dropped again and the abnormal coat began growing back rapidly. Resuming the Vitex led to another rapid shed and higher energy.

Welsh-Cross Gelding

Our next field test was a 17-year-old Welsh-cross pony gelding. At 12, he started problems with laminitis and weight gain. The initial laminitis was believed to be due to a vaccine reaction (a four-way vaccine was administered). The laminitis was handled by limiting his diet and grass time. In 1998, his caretakers noticed he did not shed out as well as in prior years and required body clipping.

By June 1999, his coat was obviously abnormal and he did little shedding. Abnormal fat deposits (looking like cellulite) were noticed across his rump. Energy levels sagged as well. He was described as being depressed and bad-tempered. Blood work in November 1999 confirmed Cushing's. His blood glucose was 278, insulin 192.5, both extremely abnormal (remember that different labs have different normal ranges for the tests they run).

He was started on cyproheptadine and responded with a small amount of shedding. He was on a maintenance dose at the time we began working with him in February 2000. He started on Hormonise and discontinued cyproheptadine in mid-February. Three weeks later, reports were that he was shedding like mad (mostly on the left for some reason), his feet were remaining cooler, and his energy levels had sky-rocketed.

Previously referred to as "Dan, Dan, the Old White Man," his movements had been described as elderly and slow. After three weeks on Vitex, he was squealing, kicking, rearing, and playing with the other horses—something he had not done for the previous three years. More objectively, after four weeks, his insulin had dropped to 119 and his glucose was down to 148. No further laboratory work was done. He continued to do well until supplements were stopped, at which point symptoms returned within three weeks.

Morgan Mare

For notes on this horse, see the "Tiffany" sidebar.

Tiffany: Before and After

Before Vitex: 3/22/00.

After Vitex: 5/31/00.

A 25-year-old Morgan mare had symptoms that developed gradually, since about age 17 or 18. Most prominent were the abnormal hair coat and abdominal distention, with some loss of muscle evident (see before photo). She had no clear pattern of increased water intake or increased urination. The first improvement was rapid shedding—a pattern that was to prove consistent with all horses. She also steadily lost the sagging and oversized abdomen. Her owner described her as looking "about seven months pregnant instead of 10½." She looked and acted five years younger (see after photo). Her energy level has remained high.

Morgan Gelding

A 23-year-old Morgan gelding (no lab work available) had been slowing down steadily for several years, attributed to old age. This year it was noted he had an abnormally thick and curly coat that did not shed out. He was started on Vitex and within 10 days began to shed heavily, growing in a normal, slick coat, which is also coming in this winter. Energy levels and general interest in life have improved significantly.

Tennessee Walker Gelding

A 20-year-old Tennessee Walker gelding had been diagnosed with Cushing's five or six years previously on the basis of abnormal hair coat, increased thirst, and increased urination. He was initially treated with cyproheptadine and had been switched to pergolide three years prior to starting the Hormonise.

Blood glucose before the Vitex, on pergolide, was running in the 300 to 366 range (normal is 60 to 125). Insulin just prior to Vitex was 30.47, with upper limit of normal being 30. These tests indicated the horse was entering the final stages of the disease—a true diabetes (insulin insufficiency) rather than just insulin insensitivity. He was on the supplement for one month, during which time there was no change in his condition.

The horse then came down with a serious lung infection and the owner preferred to switch him back to pergolide. We don't believe the switch to Vitex had anything to do with the lung infection, and the attending vet concurred. Infections and weakened immunity are common complications of long-term Cushing's disease.

This horse did have a somewhat lowered lymphocyte count in his blood at the start of the Hormonise, which is typical for immuno-compromised horses that have Cushing's syndrome. Nevertheless, under the circumstances, the owner's wishes and concerns were honored, and the horse was withdrawn from the field trial.

Thoroughbred Gelding

A 16-year-old Thoroughbred gelding had been showing early signs of Cushing's for three years. He had also been showing increased water consumption and urination over the past year. Blood chemistry and dexamethasone suppression tests in 1999 were normal.

In June 2000, blood chemistry showed his glucose was normal at 97 but insulin was 41.4—low for a Cushing's horse (indicating it was early in the disease), but about twice the upper limit of normal. He was started on Hormonise and shed out completely within three weeks. No other changes were noted. Repeat blood work after 2.5 months on Vitex showed glucose the same at 97, insulin 49.6. His winter coat also started growing in early and thickly. The rise in insulin at that time may have been caused by the seasonal ACTH elevations that occur in all horses beginning in late August.

13-Year-Old Mare

One of our most challenging horses was a 13-year-old mare who had symptoms suggestive of Cushing's dating back five years. When first purchased at 8, she had unusual mouth ulcers and a tendency to develop skin infections. She was extremely aggressive about her food. She had been noticed to leak fluid from her udder, which was very sensitive.

In 1999, she began to have excessive urination and thirst, urinating even when being worked. Over the winter of 1999 to 2000, her coat came in exceptionally long and thick and did not shed out completely. She stopped cycling. The owner insisted an insulin test be run, and it was markedly abnormal at 180. She was started on cyproheptadine and started to shed out within a week, but the increased thirst and urination continued unchanged. After three weeks on cyproheptadine the insulin was down to 131.

Shedding continued when the mare went on the Hormonise, and she was completely shed out in three to four weeks. She seemed to vacillate in how well controlled the thirst

Regular, gentle exercise will help the Cushing's horse maintain muscle and combat insulin resistance.

and urination were, having good days and bad. The same was true for energy levels. On days she did not drink excessively, urine color and amount were normal.

Within two months, she began cycling again and was showing strong estrus every 18 days, but was extremely "touchy" and irritable.

We eventually learned this mare was consuming huge amounts of salt, in excess of six ounces in an eight-hour period when it was measured. Limiting the mare's salt to what she needed resolved the increased thirst and urination to a large extent.

After six weeks on the Hormonise, her insulin level had dropped markedly, to 57. Urination and energy levels continued to gradually improve for this mare. However, her estrus behavior was also intensifying, and by the end of summer she was beginning to grow a thicker coat.

As of mid-October, her coat was thick and curly (she is half mustang) but not long. A repeat insulin test showed it was up to 96, which again was probably a result of the seasonal ACTH rises, which are often quite dramatic in a Cushing's horse.

Palomino Gelding

A 20-year-old palomino gelding was diagnosed with Cushing's five years before he entered our trial, with a history of laminitis dating back eight years. Diagnosis was confirmed via elevated ACTH level of 59.2 (normal is 3 to 39). He had the typical long, curly coat that did not shed out, increased thirst, voracious appetite, obesity with a cresty neck, poor heat tolerance, and a long-standing laminitis. He was never completely sound.

He had been on cyproheptadine for three years with little change.

Glucose prior to starting the Vitex and while on cyproheptadine was normal at 84. After about three weeks on Vitex, he started to shed out in large amounts and the new hair was softer. He was also laying down less than before the Hormonise and taking a much shorter time to come in at feeding, with some evidence of brighter attitude and more interest in his surroundings. He did well through the summer.

However, in late August, he began to grow in a winter coat that was again long and curly. He also had an exacerbation of his laminitis at this time, although it was noted that ground conditions were much harder than normal.

Bottom Line

All 10 horses in this field trial showed improved, rapid shedding of abnormal coat as a response to Vitex. Improved energy levels, lifting of "depression," and improvement in laminitic pain were noted in all horses that had these symptoms.

A drop in blood insulin levels was documented in two horses, one of which had a marked improvement over that seen with cyproheptadine treatment. Improvements were maintained over the summer. By late August, all horses were beginning to grow longer winter coats.

In two of these, which were also the most advanced cases based on history and blood work, the coat resembled a Cushing's coat, while in the others it was a normal winter coat. It appears that horses with advanced Cushing's changes, especially when they involve glucose metabolism, tended to have a less dramatic response to the Vitex. Also, it was unable to completely protect them from the seasonal ACTH rises and the elevated cortisol and worsening insulin resistance that causes.

Since our early trial, there have been two other field studies. One performed by the University of Pennsylvania reported no benefits with Vitex, but many of the horses in that trial were very advanced Cushing's cases requiring extremely high doses of the drug pergolide for control. A much larger two-year study was performed under the auspices of the Laminitis Trust, in the UK. The results of that study were very similar to those of our original small trial. Symptomatic improvements were obvious and dramatic in most cases. However, changes in blood work, including insulin and ACTH levels, did not necessarily occur. The researchers are currently in the process of taking another look at the laboratory results to see what role seasonal ACTH rises might have been playing.

Although Hormonise is available without a prescription, we don't recommend you use this supplement without involving your veterinarian. It can be a reasonable thing to try, especially in early Cushing's cases, but the drug pergolide is still the gold standard for treatment. For advanced cases and those with laminitis, pergolide offers more reliable control.

Hormonise is manufactured in the United Kingdom by Animal Health Company and distributed in the United States by Equi-Natural (www.equi-natural.com). It is not inexpensive. Effective dosage was found to be 10 cc/200 pounds of body weight. Cost is $43.95 per liter, which is about $2.20 per day for a 1,000-pound horse to treat Cushing's. The product used in the Laminitis Trust trial is a similar liquid extract called Evi-tex, available here from Emerald Valley Equine for $44.95 per quart, which equals 0.95 liters.

Nutrition and Management of the Horse with Cushing's

The hormonal changes with this disease typically result in insulin resistance, a condition where insulin is not as effective as normal in getting glucose into the cells where it can be used as energy. In severe cases, these horses are actually diabetic, with high blood sugars. When treatment controls the hormonal outputs, this will improve. However, pergolide alone is often not enough to completely control the pituitary hormones, and these horses do best on a low carbohydrate diet designed for insulin resistance. See chapter 16 for details.

Adaptogens for Cushing's Horses

Adaptogens are herbs that improve the ability to deal with stress. When cortisol output is low, they increase it slightly, and when it's high they lower it. How this happens used to be a mystery, but researchers have found that adaptogens are able to bind to the same receptors on the adrenal gland as ACTH. The adrenal gland is stimulated to produce cortisol when these receptors are activated. Because the effect is weaker than with ACTH, the stimulation is less than ACTH itself.

Adaptogens in Cushing's horses help block negative side effects of pergolide treatment and improve energy levels. Ones we have used include:

- APF, Advanced Protection Formula from Auburn Laboratories (www.auburnlabs.com), about $52 for 100 ml liquid. Use 5 to 6 ml/day.
- Jiaogulan (Gynostemma pentaphyllum), in bulk from HerbalCom (www.herbalcom.com), about $14/lb., lasts several months. Feed 1 to 2 tsp twice a day.

Many Cushing's horses are seniors and will benefit from measures such as support of the hindgut with pre- or probiotics, moistened meals, and hay pellets or cubes rather than loose hay. (Also see chapter 12.) Provision of a high quality protein often helps these horses maintain their weight better. If the overall diet is less than 10% protein, consider feeding 50 to 60 grams per day (about 2 ounces) of a high protein supplement like Uckele's Amino-Fac-41 (www.uckele.com, 800-248-0330, $34.95/40 lbs.). If total protein in the diet seems adequate but muscle loss is still a problem, specific amino acids may be more effective rather than increasing protein across the board.

Uckele's Tri-Amino with lysine, methionine, and threonine is a good choice and economical, $14.95 for 2 lbs. (53 daily doses). Helpful management adjustments include:

- Avoid stress.
- Limit vaccinations to those only absolutely needed and prevent the horse from coming in contact with horses other than his regular herd mates.
- Protect from extremes of weather, both cold and heat.
- Inspect the mouth regularly for infections or unexplained sores and maintain regular floating.
- Keep the feet trimmed at regular intervals. 🐎

Digestive-Tract Aids

The horse has a unique and complicated digestive tract. The upper portion, the stomach and small intestine, functions just like ours, but the lower portion, the cecum and colon, is much larger and ferments fibrous material and any other foods not digested in the small intestine, much like a cow's forestomach does. This rather complicated arrangement means that horses can derive more energy from fermenting fiber sources than dogs, but much less than cows. Horses require more preformed protein than cows in their diets (rather than protein obtained from digesting dead microorganisms from the forestomachs), but digest it less efficiently than species, like dogs, with a proportionately longer small intestine. These unique digestive and nutritional requirements leave the horse more sensitive to dietary changes. This coupled with some unique aspects of the digestive tract anatomy can combine to make colic a very real threat.

Risk Factors for Colic

Researchers at the University of Liverpool in the United Kingdom set out to answer the question of whether the time of year or season has an effect on the number of colic cases.

Using sophisticated statistical methods, they examined the university's colic case files dating back to 1991. As you might expect, strangulation of the bowel by the stalk of a lipoma—fatty tumors that hang on a long stalk and may become wrapped around the bowel like a bolero—showed no seasonal pattern. However, a clear fall/winter peak was found for impactions, spring for equine grass sickness (a problem in the United Kingdom likely associated with exposure to the bacterium that causes botulism), and peaks in both the spring and fall for all other types of colic.

Management factors were not specifically analyzed in this study, but the authors discussed how their findings might tie in with those of other studies that did look at management. These aspects included more time spent in a stall, reduction in level of exercise and/or turnout, and diet changes that were either higher or lower in roughage.

As a corollary to this, we would point out that reduction in grass consumption and substitution of hay for grass greatly reduces the amount of water the horse is taking in while eating. Grass is more than 80% water, while hay is about 10%. The authors also discussed a possible link between bad weather and colic, but stated it would be difficult to separate out whether it was the weather per se or the fact that horses are more likely to be stabled during bad weather.

This study drives home some basic and well-known truths regarding feeding and management specifically to avoid colic:

1. Make all changes in diet gradually, including both concentrates and hay, to give the intestinal tract a chance to adapt. Make substitutions over a period of a minimum of four days, preferably 14 days.

2. An unlimited supply of clean, fresh water should be available at all times and especially when horses are consuming hay.

3. Exercise is extremely important to normal functioning of the intestinal tract. A switch from turnout to stall confinement and from grass to dry hay puts the horse at particularly high risk for colic.

Regular exercise and plenty of down time, when the horse can be a horse, is an important part of digestive-tract health.

When real life intervenes (hay shortages, drought, horse moved to a new location with little or no pasture, turnout or riding must be cut back), there are some measures you can take to try and minimize risk:

- Add salt directly to the feed to encourage good drinking. Use a minimum of 1 oz. (2 tablespoons) of table salt in the winter, 2+ ozs. in the summer, divided between feedings.

- Hang an extra water bucket.

- Consider pre- or probiotic use (we recommend using Ration Plus) if an abrupt change in hay or grain cannot be avoided.

- If time for riding or turnout is at a premium, at least longe the horse for 20 to 30 minutes a day—or pay someone else to do it.

Less devastating than colic, but very common, are problems related to digestive inefficiency such as bloating, gas, and poor utilization of feeds, as well as gastric ulcers and chronic diarrhea. We'll walk you through some effective strategies for dealing with those problems.

Feeding Facts

Horsemen frequently wonder if multiple small meals truly are better than fewer larger ones. They wonder if hay and grain should be fed at the same time or if the type of grain they're feeding makes a significant difference.

These common feeding questions are usually answered more on the basis of personal opinion than scientific facts. A French study appearing in the *Journal of Animal Science* sheds some light, at least from the standpoint of the digestibility of starch in the small intestine.

Undigested starch that reaches the large bowel can cause problems. The cecum and colon can adjust to some extent to starch loads, but beyond a certain point problems become more likely. At the most minor end of the spectrum, there can be some bloating and loss of the organisms needed to efficiently digest hay. The worst consequence is grain overload resulting in colic, toxemia, and laminitis.

The researchers looked at the effects of multiple small meals, feeding meals with either high fiber or high starch, and the type of starch (potato, beans, corn, barley, oats, or wheat).

They found that the major determinant of how much starch would spill over into the large bowel was the type. Starch from oats was the most digestible, followed by wheat, corn, barley, bean, and potato. The size of the high-starch meal was also important. Feeding a high-fiber source at the same time as the starch tends to speed the meal along, but the meal size and type of starch were the most important determinants of how well it would be digested. Smaller, lower-starch meals seem to be better digested.

Impaction is a frequent cause of colic and is particularly likely to occur in the winter. Drinkable water is the most important element of good winter care. Note we said "drinkable." The complications of insufficient water intake—dehydration, shock, colic—can occur within just a day or two. Impaction colic is the most common symptom; although it may be blamed on the dry winter diet, less exercise, and even parasite problems, usually the reason is inadequate drinking levels.

Granted, a horse will drink less water in the winter than the summer because he sweats less—just as we do—but he still needs to consume a minimum of three to four times as much water as hay to keep his body functioning properly. If he's on hay and grain, he needs three times as much water as solid food. A good rule of thumb to remember is that a horse eating 20 to 25 lbs. of hay a day needs to drink at least eight gallons of water.

A major factor in winter impactions is insufficient drinking. Make sure water is a comfortable temperature for drinking, and add salt to meals to encourage water intake.

The basic ways to increase water consumption are:

- Add 2 tablespoons a day of table salt to your horse's feed (salt triggers the drinking instinct).

- Incorporate wet feeds and mashes as a source of supplemental water (it's not enough, but it helps).

- Like you, your horse prefers warmer water in colder weather. You can serve warmed water twice a day, with feedings, but you must do it consistently.

If the barn doesn't have a nearby hot-water supply, consider a bucket heater such as Farm Innovators' Bucket Heater (www.farminnovators.com, 800-277-8401). This large coil will warm five gallons of water to 100°F in about 20 minutes. It's thermostatically controlled and can be left in the bucket for constant heating, but we don't recommend this, as it's too tempting a toy for a bored horse. Cost is about $30.

For stalls and run-in sheds, consider investing in heated water buckets or tank deicers such as the product line of Allied Precision Industries (www .alliedprecision.com, 800-627-6179). These products have built-in thermostats to turn the heater/ deicer on and off as necessary, and the heater and thermostat are built into the bucket itself, so nothing floats around for the horse to play with. A standard stall-size bucket runs $30 to $35.

Winter is a high-risk time of year for impaction.

Forget the Natural Dewormers

A lot of the propaganda floating around about natural dewormers sounds pretty convincing, especially when it's presented with cautions about how harmful the chemicals in conventional paste dewormers can be. Parasites are a leading cause of digestive inefficiency, bloating, poor growth, and weight gain and are not to be taken lightly. If you are going to institute an alternative approach to dealing with parasites, you need to know if it's actually effective.

However, the fact of the matter is there are no studies that proved to us that commonly recommended natural dewormers effectively eliminate intestinal parasites. As for how harmful a drug dewormer could be, well, any drug, herb, or even mineral, for that matter, is potentially harmful and has its own safety profile and risk-versus-benefit ratio. Frankly, modern paste dewormers have a more favorable safety profile than common widely used drugs like penicillin or phenylbutazone.

Many herbals, as well as a variety of toxic metals (mercury, arsenic), have been used as dewormers both in humans and animals. However, most have the potential to be toxic as well, often with a narrow margin of safety, or even a direct contraindication in horses. For example, black walnut is a commonly recommended natural dewormer for people, but it will cause severe laminitis in a horse.

Oats are the most easily digestible of grains, and a good choice for horses that may have feed sensitivities.

Food Allergies

The role of food allergies in equine allergic symptoms is poorly understood. Although allergy testing often shows reactions to hays and grains, there are no good studies regarding the responses horses might have to foods.

In people, food allergies can cause immediate, life-threatening anaphylactic reactions, including throat swelling, or less severe chronic symptoms, which including respiratory problems, watery eyes, skin eruptions and/or itching, or digestive upset, nausea, and diarrhea. In horses, bloating, excessive gas, and production of more fluid along with formed manure may also be symptoms. In addition to genuine food intolerances, these symptoms could also be reactions to low-level mold contamination of the feed.

It's known from research with other species that a history of any type of allergy, including inhalant allergies (e.g., to pollens or molds) increases the risk of having food allergies as well.

An elimination diet is the best way to attempt to determine if any of your horse's foods are actually causing digestive upset symptoms. Try feeding nothing but very clean, fresh-smelling hay for a few days. If symptoms return with reintroduction of your grain mix, try the horse on grade I, triple cleaned, extra heavyweight oats. These premium oats are easy to digest.

Popular Natural Deworming Ingredients

Diatomaceous earth: The most popular ingredient in natural dewormers being marketed for horses is DE, or diatomaceous earth. DE is mined from ocean or lake beds and is rich in the skeletal remains of small organisms called diatoms. It is com-

USDA GRADES: CORN

Grade	Minimum weight in lbs./ bushel	Maximum % Heat-Damaged Kernels	Maximum % Total Damaged Kernels	Maximum % Broken Corn, Foreign Material
US No 1	56	0.1	3	2
US No 2	54	0.2	5	3
US No 3	52	0.5	7	4
US No 4	49	1	10	5
US No 5	46	3	15	7

USDA GRADES: OATS

Grade	Minimum weight in lbs./ bushel	Percentage intact oats	Maximum % of heat-damaged	Maximum % foreign material	Maximum % of wild oats
US No 1	36	97	0.1	2	2
US No 2	33	94	0.3	3	3
US No 3	30	90	1	4	5
US No 4	27	80	3	5	10
Heavy	38	n/a	n/a	n/a	n/a
Extra heavy	40	n/a	n/a	n/a	n/a

Substituting high-quality plain oats for multi-ingredient commercial grains often helps the horse with feed sensitivities.

posed of over 80% silicon dioxide and another 8% or so of aluminum oxide and iron oxide. The remainder is a mixture of calcium, magnesium, and other mineral oxides.

Finely pulverized DE powder is effective topically against ectoparasites (e.g. lice, ticks). It also works well in the environment to control a variety of insects. Microscopically, the powders have an irregular, sharp, spiny surface that damages the cuticles of insects, causing them to dehydrate rapidly and die.

DE is effective against all life stages of insects. The easiest to target are ground crawlers or larval stages, but it can also be mixed with attractants to lure in flying insects. However, once DE is wet, whether from water, saliva, or stomach fluids, it loses its microscopic "cutting" edges and is no longer effective against insects. It's also not a risk to the horse's intestinal tract, even for horses with ulcers.

DE is approved by the FDA and USDA as an additive to grains in storage facilities and as an aid in preventing insect infestations. It can be added at a rate of up to 2% in grains intended for feed (40 pounds/ton = 0.32 oz./lb.).

We're betting your interest is piqued. Ours was, too. But using DE as a topical insecticide is a big leap from using DE to kill parasitic worms inside the horse's digestive tract. In fact,

Regular deworming is easy, affordable, and your best investment in preventing colic and making sure your horse gets the most from his diet.

we found no solid evidence to prove that feeding DE will kill parasites in a horse's digestive tract.

Actually, when you think of it, why isn't there any substantial evidence available? A manufacturer should be able to confirm antiparasite action simply by taking two groups of horses with similar parasite burdens, feeding DE to one group and no treatment to the other, while all other management conditions remain the same. But no such studies exist to our knowledge. In addition, wetting DE destroys its ability to kill insects by contact, and your horse's intestines contain many gallons of fluid.

About the only way we think DE could help control intestinal parasites is if it has a feed-through effect. If manure containing parasite eggs is spread sufficiently thin to allow it to dry, the dried DE powder would again be active against any hatched larval forms. However, the powder has to be dry to work and that level of drying is itself lethal to parasite larvae.

If you want to try DE as part of a comprehensive parasite-control program, apply it liberally to the ground under and for a few inches around those areas where accumulated manure has been removed.

Garlic: Although garlic is a favorite natural dewormer ingredient, we could find no justification for its inclusion. Concentrated garlic liquids are sometimes used by gardeners to discourage vegetable worms from attacking root and bulb crops. But it doesn't kill them; it helps repel them. And some vegetable worms actually attack garlic bulbs.

The repelling effect also requires strong garlic solutions in far greater concentrations than would ever be achieved in your horse's intestine by feeding small amounts. Feeding large amounts or concentrated garlic liquids isn't a good idea either, because of the potential to cause Heinz body anemia in your horse.

Wormwood (Artemisia): Chemicals derived from sweet wormwood are currently being widely employed as a treatment for malaria, a protozoal blood disease. Wormwood has a long history of traditional use for treating parasitism, but, again, little to nothing that proves it is effective. We found nothing with a specific reference to dose or efficacy in horses.

We did find out that different species of wormwood may vary considerably in their activity. One, Artemisia absinthe, can be highly toxic to the nervous system. Essential oils from this variety have been shown to be highly effective when applied directly to insects such as mites, but the chemical responsible for this activity, thujone, causes toxicity.

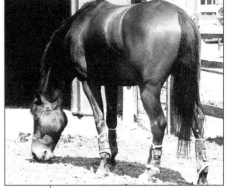

Again, despite so many claims that Artemisia will remove worms, there are no strong research studies to support this claim.

Clove: Cloves and clove oil are commonly recommended ingredients in alternative dewormers; the specific claim is effectiveness against parasite eggs. However, justification for this claim is lacking. Cloves and other aromatic spices do contain high concentrations of a chemical called eugenol, which is an effective insecticide when sprayed directly onto bugs and vegetable worms in high concentration. However, as with garlic, whether this translates into an effect when small amounts are eaten and greatly diluted in the intestinal contents remains to be seen.

Diet and management have huge roles to play in minimizing your horse's risk of colic.

Pumpkin seeds: Pumpkin seeds were a common parasite remedy in the late 1800s and early 1900s. They contain a substance called curcurbitin, which does demonstrate antiparasite activity in the lab. However, the traditional human dose is 200 to 400 grams, followed by a castor oil purgative "chaser." For the much larger equine digestive tract, a pound of seeds would be a very conservative estimate.

Bottom Line

We'd like to believe alternative deworming remedies could have some truth to them, but we could find nothing solid to substantiate effectiveness or required dosages. Plus, the potential for toxicity is a real concern.

On the other hand, modern paste dewormer drugs have a proven high efficacy, and most are safe at 20 to 100 times the required dose. The days of scary, toxic chemical dewormers, like the organophosphates, are long gone. We see no reason to settle for less than high efficacy in dewormers, especially just to hang a "natural" label on the product.

While you may get away with them in a mature, healthy horse, we do not recommend experimenting with an alternative dewormer in young or aged horses, as these animals are far too susceptible to serious parasite-related problems.

Prebiotics and Probiotics

Why are so many manufacturers jumping on the probiotic bandwagon? That's easy: It's an inexpensive ingredient that many horsemen seem to want, largely either due to talk around the barn or because they've taken probiotics themselves and believe probiotics positively affect the gut.

However, while probiotics do appear to help a number of horses, there isn't enough research for us to make a blanket recommendation. And, since most products contain ingredient levels that are woefully low, you may be wasting your money unless you feed three, four, or more times the label-recommended dose. So why are probiotics so popular?

What's a Probiotic?

The talk around most barns is that probiotics help horses get through necessary stresses like deworming and shipping with fewer physical problems, such as diarrhea. Many horsemen also say probiotics help the horse better utilize—or digest—his feed, meaning the horse gets more out of what he consumes. Claims even include that a probiotic ingredient can help clear up diarrhea, minimize colic, and prevent laminitis. Probiotics can make a difference in the right situation, but they don't deserve the "miracle-bug" title.

A probiotic is a live microbe that benefits the host—the animal ingesting it—by improving the animal's intestinal environment. A good probiotic should:

- Survive stomach acid and digestive enzymes in the small intestine

Probiotic products can help with a variety of digestive upsets, but few provide an adequate dose. Equine Generator does.

- Be able to adhere to the bowel wall

- Successfully establish itself and multiply in the host intestine

- Inhibit the growth of disease-causing (pathogenic) bacteria

- Improve fermentation in the gut

Studies on the effect of live bacterial probiotics in horses are sorely lacking. However, studies with other newborn and weanling livestock show probiotics decrease the amount of harmful bacteria shed into the environment by the animal. This means the probiotics likely caused there to be fewer harmful bacteria. Theoretically, this also makes the animal better able to fend off disease. Treated animals also showed better weight gain in the studies.

While the changes in the animals were clear, it wasn't proven whether the better weight gain in the probiotic-treated animals was related to their better utilization of the feed or because the animals didn't get sick as much. Research with humans and dogs shows that probiotics help with inflammatory conditions of the intestines. Overall, though, we agree that probiotics sound good, at least for most species.

Frankly, you won't hurt your horse by administering probiotics, but if you're looking for ways to trim your feed budget, you can eliminate probiotics. Most adult horses at a healthy weight don't need them.

We would consider using probiotics regularly for:

- Horses having trouble holding their weight

- Older horses that need some help with digestion and absorption

- Horses with a history of intestinal difficulties, including diarrhea, colic, gas, and bloating

- Foals and young horses up to age 1, as during this growth time their diets are constantly changing and they're still establishing populations of organisms in their guts

Probiotic-Type Products

Product	Price	Active Ingredients	Comments
Absorb-All Uckele Health & Nutrition www.uckele.com 800-248-0330	$32.95/4 lbs.	L. acidophilus 45 billion CFU/lb., L. lactis 45 billion CFU/lb., S. cerevisiae 340 billion CFU/lb, A. oryzae and B. subtillis unspecified amounts, digestive enzymes.	Species are appropriate. Label-recommended doses are a little low for estimated effective equine dosages.
Bio-Fax 10X Uckele Health & Nutrition www.uckele.com 800-248-0330	$10.95/2 lbs.	L. acidophilus 50 billion CFU/lb, L. lactis 50 billion CFU/lb., S. cerevisiae yeast 140 billion CFU/lb., enzymes (amylase, protease, cellulose).	Species are appropriate. Label-recommended doses are a little lower than estimated effective equine dosages.
DFM-EQ paste Horses Prefer www.horsesprefer.com 800-468-3877	$5.40/32 cc tube	10 billion CFU/10 cc of mixture of E. faecium, L. acidophilus, L. plantarum, L. casei.	Very good array of organisms at a recommended dose that actually exceeds the current estimated minimum.
DFM-EQ powder Horses Prefer www.horsesprefer.com 800-468-3877	$17.64/5 lbs.	12.5 billion CFU/oz. of mixture of E. faecium, L. acidophilus, L. plantarum, L. casei.	Half the lower end of recommended dose exceeds the estimated minimum effective dose.
Digest-Pro Select the Best www.selectthebest.com 800-648-0950	$28.95/5 lbs.	180 million CFU/lb. of mixture of L. acidophilus, B. thermephilum, S. faecium. Unspecified amount dried A. oryzae fermentation products.	Appropriate organisms, but label doses significantly lower than estimated effective equine dose.
Ener G Plus Rio Vista www.riovistaproducts.com 800-248-6428	$9.95/tube	Total lactic acid producing bacteria 3 billion CFU per 60-gram tube (derived from dried Enterococcus faecium fermentation product, dried lactobacillus acidophilus fermentation product) sodium 1.75% min – 2.25% max, potassium 2% min., magnesium 1.75% min., vitamin E 500 IU/lb.	Appropriate organisms. Label-recommended dose considerably lower than estimated effective equine dose.
Equi-Bac oral gel Kaeco Group www.kaeco.com 800-228-1211	$9.95/80 cc	Per 15 cc dose: 10 billion CFU of a mixture of Lactobacillus species, Enterococcus faecium, S. cerevisiae yeast, plus high-dose vitamin A, D, E, and B vitamins.	Species chosen appropriate. Label-recommended dose a little lower than estimated effective equine dosages.
EZ Travel RioVista www.riovistaproducts.com 800-248-6428	$9.95/tube	Total lactic acid producing bacteria 3 billion CFU per 30 gram tube (derived from dried Enterococus faecium fermentation products, dried Lactobacillus fermentation product), sodium 4.5% min. 5.5% max., magnesium 0.2% min., potassium 1.25% min., vit. E 500 IU/lb.	Appropriate organisms. Recommended dose much lower than estimated effective equine dose.
Fastrack Conklin www.conklin.com 800-888-8838	$23.50/5 lbs.	Lactic acid producing bacteria 2.5 billion CFU/oz. S. cerevisiae yeast culture, no amount specified, protease, amylase, fructo-oligosaccharide.	Appropriate organisms. Level of S. cerevisiae viable yeast not specified. Recommended dose too low compared to estimated effective equine dose.
Fastrack Equine Gel Conklin www.conklin.com 800-888-8838	$129.50 per 6 tube case, one tube holds 20 cc	Per cc: 1.25 billion CFU L. lactis and E. faecium 50 million CFU S. cerevisiae, fructo-oligosaccharide, vitamin A, vitamin E.	Appropriate species. Dose lower than estimated equine effective dose.
Foal Bac Royal Mile 952-469-3492	$10.15/4 lbs.	S. cerevisiae yeast 1.5 billion CFU/gm, mixture of Lactobacillus, Enterococcus, Bifidobacterium, Bacillus and Aspergillus organisms 100 million CFU/gm.	Appropriate species. Recommended dose lower than estimated effective equine dose.
Foal Response Vita-Flex www.vita-flex.com 800-848-2359	$12.95/30 cc	Lactobacillus and other lactic acid species 1 billion CFU/30 cc, bovine colostrums, vitamins A, C, D, E, B12, menandione, selenium.	Appropriate species. Dose significantly lower than estimated effective equine dose. Yeast amounts not guaranteed or specified but manufacturer reports 1 oz. Diamond V XP concentrates per regular serving (2 oz.).
Invigor Adeptus www.adeptusnutrition.com 866-233-7887	$39.99/10 lbs.	Proprietary blend of yeasts, including Diamond V an Alltech yeast in undisclosed amounts. Mannan oligosaccharides (MOS) 1 gram per ounce. Vitamin C.	Prebiotic product (yeast cultures). Appropriate species. The inclusion of MOS in this product makes it an attractive choice for operations with infectious bacterial diarrhea problems in foals, although label recommendations are likely low.

Product	Price	Active Ingredients	Comments
Micro Balance Vita-Flex www.vita-flex.com 800-848-2359	$14.35/80 cc	A. oryzae 141 thousand CFU/10 cc, Bacillus subtilis 372,000 CFU/10 cc, mixed lactic acid bacteria 112,000 CUF/10 cc, S. cerevisiae 3.56 million CFU/10 cc.	Appropriate species but high dose of live Aspergillus oryzae organisms could contribute to acidity in the colon. Dose much lower than estimated effective equine dose.
NutriBites Digestion Plus www.horsesprefer.com 800-468-3877	$19.99/90 tablets	Per tablet: L. acidophilus 600 million CFU; E. faecium 600 million CFU; L. plantarum 280 million CFU; L. casei 20 million CFU, with vitamin E 60 IU, vitamin D 2,000 IU, vitamin A 7,500 IU.	Appropriate selection of organisms, but recommended dosage below estimated effective minimum doses.
Power-Gest Paste Richdel Select the Best www.selectthebest.com 800-648-0950	$12.95/60 cc	72 billion CFU/tube of L. acidophilus, B. thermephilum, B. longum, E. faecium. Inulin fructooligosaccharide 150 mg/cc.	Good species, but low levels of organisms.
Pro-Bi ABC Plus www.a-b-c-plus.com 800-373-5971	$31.31/16 oz.	L. acidophilus fermentation products, aloe vera, chlorophyll liquid, peppermint, ginger, dandelion, and violet leaves.	Prebiotic fermentation products and herbs with a traditional use for digestive problems. No formal studies to establish dose and no guaranteed analysis.
Probios Equine One paste Chr. Hansen Biosystems www.chr-hansen.com 800-558-0802	$4.29/30 g tube	Not less than 10 million CFU/g. E. faecium, L. acidophilus, L. casei, L. plantarum.	Good array of appropriate organisms but dose low by estimates. However, a small University of Florida study documented lower incidence of foal heat diarrhea and less severe diarrhea.
Pro-Lactic DFM Horse Tech www.horsetech.com 800-831-3309	$15.95/2 lbs.	2 billion CFU/oz. of mixture containing B. coagulans, B. lichentiformis, B. subtilis, L. acidophilus, L. casei, L. plantarum, E. faecium.	Excellent array of appropriate species but recommended dose lower than estimated effective equine dose.
Ration Plus Cytozyme www.cytozyme.com 801-533-9208	$26/480 ml.	L. acidophilus liquid fermentation products.	Prebiotic liquid fermentation product. No live organisms. Documented equine effectiveness at label recommendations.
TPC Kaeco Group www.kaeco.com 800-228-1211	$16.42/2 lbs.	S. cerevisiae 1.36 billion CFU/lb., mixed Bacillus species 3.63 billion CFU/lb., mixed Lactobacillus and S. faecium 50 billion CFU/lb., vitamin E 3,000 IU/lb., B12 120 mg/lb., zinc 6,000 ppm, manganese 10,000 ppm, copper 5,000 ppm, cobalt 5 ppm, selenium 35.2 ppm.	Vitamin E and trace-mineral supplement with added probiotic organisms. Appropriate choice of organisms. Recommended dose provides much lower than estimated effective equine dose.
Yeast 100X Uckele Health & Nutrition www.uckele.com 800-248-0330	$24.95/5 lbs.	Live Saccharomyces cerevisiae yeast 10 to 15 billion CFU/gram.	Top dressed on grain. Very concentrated source of S. cerevisiae yeast.
Yea Sacc 1026 Farnam www.farnamhorse.com 800-234-2269	$25.70/3 lbs.	2 billion CFU S. cerevisia per daily serving (0.8 oz.).	Good choice for horses getting a lot of grain in their diets, but the documented effective dose is 5 times higher.
Equine Generator Bio-Vet www.bio-vet.com 800-246-8371	$31.25/7.5 lbs.	Over 12 billion CFU/oz. Blend of S. cerevisiae yeast, Lactobacillus species, Enterococcus species, and lactic acid utilizers.	Good broad spectrum choice for horse on any type of diet. Excellent potency.

What's the Difference: A Probiotic or a Prebiotic?

Probiotics contain live organisms—bacteria or yeast. The product labels should list the species, e.g. Lactobacillus lacti, and specify the potency in CFU, which stands for colony forming units. One CFU = 1 live bacterium capable of multiplying. **Prebiotics**, which are commonly lumped together with probiotics, are substances that either feed the types of beneficial organisms you're trying to encourage or provide growth factors that stimulate them.

Storing Live Organisms

The live organisms in your probiotic will not remain viable if the product is not properly stored. Products that contain live bacterial or yeast organisms need to be protected from extremes of heat. Refrigeration is not likely necessary if you use up the product in two to three weeks, but it is the ideal way to retain the highest numbers of live organisms possible.

The high moisture content and active enzyme activity in fresh grass make it highly digestible.

- Horses with hay bellies

- Horses on high doses of antibiotics

- Horses battling chronic low-grade colic.

Dose Is Important

Live probiotic organisms must overcome stomach acid, digestive "juices," and competition from the organisms already in the digestive tract in order to take a good hold.

Dr. Scott Weese at the University of Guelph points out that we don't even know for certain if the species of bacteria currently used are of benefit to horses. However, assuming they are, he estimates than an effective dose for an adult horse would lie somewhere between 10 and 100 billion organisms/ day. With Saccharomyces cerevisiae yeast, the dose necessary to show an acid-lowering effect in the horse's cecum has been established by studies to be 45 billion organisms/day.

If you're already feeding a probiotic and wonder if its recommended dosage is effective, use these figures to compare the active ingredient levels. Remember: one CFU (colony-forming unit) = 1 live bacterium capable of multiplying (or one organism).

Reasonable estimates for effective doses are:

- Foals/weanlings: Use probiotic bacterial species and S. cerevisiae yeast, alone or in combination, for bacterial diarrhea. Effective dose is estimated to be a minimum of 10 billion CFU/day in young foals; up to 45 billion CFUs cerevisiae per day for yearlings; from 10 to 100 billion CFU/day of bacterial organisms for yearlings. We suggest using it for the first two weeks of life. It's also reasonable to continue the probiotics for the foal's first year, while the intestinal tract is changing to adult feed and fermentation patterns.

- Horses on antibiotics: Probiotics given at 10 to 100 billion CFU/day for bacteria, 45 billion CFU/day for S. cerevisiae yeast may help restore bacterial populations after antibiotics have been stopped, but aren't necessary unless the horse developed diarrhea or other digestive upset while on the antibiotics. Probiotics can also be used at the same time as antibiotics to hopefully help prevent any problems, but the estimated required dose is high, 25 to 50 billion CFUs, three to four times a day.

Giving too low a dose is likely a waste. The organisms contained in the supplement are just as likely to be killed by the antibiotics as the ones the drug was meant to target. However, if the horse develops abdominal pain or diarrhea as a result of the antibiotic, using probiotics for a while after the antibiotics stop is reasonable. Research in humans taking oral antibiotics shows that probiotics at the same time can help avoid complications; however, the dosages necessary to do this properly are extremely high.

- Thin/debilitated/older horses having difficulty holding weight: Poor fermentation of fiber reduces the fermentation byproducts the horse can use as a calorie source and may be contributing to poor weight gain in these situations. Ration Plus has documented effectiveness in this regard. If using live organisms, it is estimated you will need to feed 10 to 100 billion CFU/day of bacterial species or 45 billion CFU/day yeast.

- Chronic colic: Recurrent episodes of colic, especially gas colic, may also be related to poor fiber digestion, but you need to be sure the horse is thoroughly checked out for other problems as well. Use the same doses as above for thin horses.

- Hay belly: A prominent abdomen disproportionate in size to the rest of the body can signal poor fiber digestion. If intensive deworming doesn't correct the problem, try probiotics as above for thin horses or chronic colic.

Healthy adult horses probably don't need a probiotic.

Ingredients

Pro- and prebiotics are relatively inexpensive ingredients. Many manufacturers include them in low amounts so they can add words like "digestive enhancer" to the product's list of claims. Don't be taken in.

If you're thinking the presence of probiotics on a label influences your choice of products, first check carefully to make sure the label specifies the species included and guarantees potency in terms of CFU, or colony-forming units.

Organisms identified as a probiotic for other animals and people won't necessarily benefit horses, especially at the same amounts. However, both bacteria-based probiotics and yeast-based probiotics have potential benefits for horses.

Bacteria

Fermentation products qualify as prebiotics, as they likely contain factors that promote bacterial growth. Aspergillus is a prebiotic, as is the Ration Plus formula. An intake of soluble fiber like psyllium, pectins, or complex carbohydrates that can't be digested in the small intestine are known to increase the numbers of beneficial bacteria in the large intestines of people, dogs, and other experimental species. However, a horse's diet is already rich in these nutrients from common feed ingredients.

Ration Plus is a liquid concentrate of fermentation products and contains no live organisms. Fermentation products refer to the material siphoned off vats containing actively multiplying bacteria. Studies of fecal bacteria before and after treatment in healthy adult horses show little change in bacterial counts but some increase in the diversity of species (see www.rationplus.com).

The most impressive research with Ration Plus was a study done on captured mustangs being held for adoption. Over a 51-day period, horses were divided into two groups. One was given Ration Plus, the other was not. The horses were otherwise fed, handled, and generally managed in an identical fashion. The horses, which were thin to begin with, showed weight gains of 86.3 pounds with the Ration Plus. Without it, they gained only 41.4 pounds, a difference of 108%.

Dried fermentation products containing variable counts of live bacteria are commonly used as sources of probiotic organisms in many different products, but we found no studies to show the dried fermentation products without live organisms have beneficial effects.

Yeasts

Saccharomyces yeast species fed to other species offer the same beneficial effects in terms of inhibiting growth of pathogenic organisms as probiotic bacteria.

The interest in them for adult animals is on their potential to improve utilization of feeds. A study in horses noted the most obvious effect when feeding Saccharomyces yeast was a reduction in acidity and lactate in horses being fed grain, more than likely because the yeast were themselves utilizing some of the lactate being produced.

Although yeast probiotic products are widely claimed to improve fiber digestion, this hasn't been scientifically proven to be significant in horses, except for those consuming large amounts of grain.

Aspergillus oryza is another yeast often listed as a probiotic. This organism produces lactic acid, so it has the opposite effect of Saccharomyces. However, dried Aspergillus cultures are used as food by many beneficial bacterial organisms and may be included in products in small amounts for that purpose.

Bottom Line

Probiotics may help adult horses having trouble utilizing their fiber sources, those with diseases that disrupt bowel activity, or when oral antibiotics are administered to the horse.

Probiotics can also help protect young foals from bacterial diarrhea, and in other species they appear to help prevent antibiotic-associated diarrhea when given at the proper time and at appropriately high dosages. However, except for Ration Plus, most of the products we evaluated in this trial have dosage recommendations that are likely too low to do the intended job.

For an overall choice of a prebiotic for your horse, we think your best choice is Ration Plus. This bacteria-based probiotic impresses us with its documented effectiveness and has been used in our test barns for years. We've found it especially helpful in reducing hay bellies, for low-grade colic, and to combat diarrhea.

If liquid isn't a feasible option or you simply prefer a powdered live probiotic, our choices for potency and price are Horses Prefer DFM-EQ powder or Equine Generator.

For yeast-based products, we like the products containing Saccharomyces cerevisiae best. Farnam's Yea Sacc 1026 contains the correct yeast, but recommended doses may be too low to get the job done.

For a product that combines yeast and probiotic bacteria, we suggest Foal Bac. A 3.5 oz. dose per day provides minimum estimated effective doses of bacteria and three times the minimum documented effective dose of S. cerevisiae.

For rapid establishment of beneficial strains in new foals, we like both Equi-Bac at a 15 cc dose and DFM-EQ paste at 10 cc/day.

Gastric Ulcers

You've read the ads, seen the endoscope studies results, and heard the talk: Gastric ulcers are incredibly common in domesticated horses. The incidence is higher in heavily stressed horses, like racehorses and endurance horses, but ulcers are being found in quiet horses that seem to have a plain, ordinary, easy life, too.

If your horse doesn't quite seem like himself at times, not colicky, but definitely somehow uncomfortable, he may be battling an ulcer. Or maybe he doesn't eat with the enthusiasm he used to have, or just lacks the "spirit" he used to have. You've ruled out other possibilities and are left to face the fact that you may well be seeing the symptoms of a chronic gastrointestinal (GI)-related problem, such as an ulcer.

Risk factors for developing ulcers include:

- Stall confinement

- Sporadic feeding rather than constant access to grass

- Exercise faster than a walk. This causes enough elevation in abdominal pressure to cause some acid to move into the unprotected areas of the stomach. The faster the horse moves, the more pressure and back wash of acid.

This is particularly a factor in racehorses that are frequently raced or trained on an empty stomach, without feed materials present to help absorb and buffer acid.

- Feeding processed feeds rather than whole grains
- Prolonged fasting (e.g., long trips, or a long period of time between the last feed of the day and the morning feed)
- Any problem elsewhere in the gastrointestinal tract
- Use of non-steroidal anti-inflammatory drugs and corticosteroids

The only way to definitively diagnose gastric ulcers is by examining the stomach directly with an endoscope at a veterinary clinic or doing a sucrose-absorption test. However, most horses are "diagnosed" by symptoms only.

Signs most suggestive of gastric ulcer include:

- Grinding of the teeth
- Belching noises
- Slow eating, often walking away without finishing meals all at once
- Picky appetite that includes the horse refusing foods or supplements that were consumed readily before

These symptoms aren't diagnostic of ulcers, but they do suggest discomfort associated with the upper GI tract/stomach. Less-specific signs frequently attributed to ulcers are:

- Sour, sulky attitude
- Poor coat
- Weight loss
- Poor performance
- Irritability
- Sensitivity to touch around the horse's lower belly/sternum area

Since the signs and symptoms are nonspecific—and overlap quite a bit with other causes of low-grade intestinal-tract discomfort and with pain from any cause—ulcers may be blamed when another problem is actually the cause. It's important to involve your veterinarian in the diagnosis and treatment.

While horses can develop some degree of gastric ulceration easily and under a wide variety of conditions, ulcers can and do heal spontaneously. On a scale of 1 to 3, with 1 being only obvious reddening of the stomach lining and 3 being a deep ulcer, a horse with a grade 3 ulcer is more likely to actually have symptoms as a result and definitely requires treatment, while a grade 1 stomach irritation could be symptom-free and resolve on its own.

Exercise as a Risk Factor

Studies performed at the University of Florida have shown that horses moving at a rate faster than a walk experience increased abdominal pressure that essentially back flushes highly acidic stomach contents from the lower, acid-producing (glandular) portion of the stomach back to the nonglandular portion. The Florida researchers found that when a horse is standing or walking, the pH of the stomach just inside the junction with the esophagus is in the range of 5 to 6, but as soon as the pace is picked up, the acid backflow can drop it to as low as 1.

The more time the horse spends moving around faster than a walk, the greater the exposure of these portions of the stomach to highly acidic conditions. It's a small wonder that a preliminary study looking for gastric ulceration in endurance horses found lesions in 67%. Most lesions were located in the nonglandular portion, the same location as in other performance horses, but 27% also had ulceration in the glandular portion, a condition that is usually only seen in horses following a critical illness of some type.

Given the prolonged, strenuous exercise in this sport, it was surprising that more horses did not show ulcers, but common practices on rides may be why. Many endurance riders feed alfalfa, which has an excellent buffering effect in the stomach. Beet pulp is another favorite and remains in the stomach longer than other types of feed. Allowing the horse to stop for water at every opportunity will also at least temporarily dilute the acidity.

Our Trial

Our field-trial horses included both horses with a documented history of gastric ulcerations and horses with symptoms suggestive of ulcers. As we stated, symptoms alone aren't enough to make an ulcer diagnosis. In addition, other digestive upsets, particularly from high grain feeding or poor digestive efficiency, may cause similar symptoms. However, since poor digestive efficiency or overfeeding will likely result in a drop in pH in the large intestine and some irritation of the mucosa there, it's possible that many of these products could be of benefit under those conditions as well. (The response to these products was judged solely on the basis of symptomatic control and doesn't necessarily correlate with actual healing.)

We found the antacid products were the most consistently effective in providing symptomatic relief for the greatest number of horses. Best results are obtained when using liquids administered by oral syringe for the first one to two weeks, a minimum of two times a day, before each feeding, preferably three to four times a day, as well as immediately before work. The appetites of the horses improved within one to four days and most rapidly with intensive treatment.

Studies on the use of antacids in horses usually call for much higher doses than we found effective for control of symptoms. However, those studies are focusing on the dose required to decrease acidity in a horse that has been fasted, while our horses were allowed constant access to hay and offered concentrates on their regular schedules. Since the presence of food in the stomach also has a buffering effect, this may explain the lower effective doses.

It's important in choosing a product for long-term use that it doesn't upset your horse's nutritional balances or intake. For example, magnesium is a common ingredient in many of these formulations. While low dietary magnesium can be a cause of excitability and nervousness in horses, overdoing magnesium can cause the same symptom, as it inhibits the absorption of calcium. Too little calcium can also cause nervousness,

Antacid-Type Ulcer Products

Product	Price	Comments
Allay, Adeptus www.adeptusnutrition.com 866-233-7887	$49.99/4 lbs.	Fine granules. Blend of antacid magnesium and calcium carbonates, licorice extract, yeast cultures. Well-accepted. Slower to work than the liquid antacids, but improvements start to become evident at about the one- to two-week mark. One horse developed bloating on this product (possibly a yeast sensitivity). Calming effect occurred within days in two horses, possibly from the mineral content.
Gold Buffer, Equine Gold www.equinegold.com 800-870-5949	$36.96/gal.	Calcium and magnesium buffers in a soothing, thick base of glycine, kaolin, methylcellulose, and pectin. Very well-accepted when dosed or put on feed. Effective at between 2 to 4 oz./dose, depending on severity of symptoms. Calming effect may be noted during periods of intensive treatment.
Pro-CMC, Absorbine www.absorbine.com 800-628-9653	$34/half gal.	Calcium and magnesium buffers in a pink liquid base thickened with natural and artificial thickeners. Pleasant aroma, fairly well-accepted. Most effective at higher than recommended doses (4 to 6 oz./dose). Calming effect may be noted during periods of intensive treatment.
U-Gard 2X, Corta-Flx www.corta-flx.com 800-838-7524	$26.99/2 lbs.	Fine powder with same formula as the U-Gard solution. Highly palatable. Horses with mild symptoms may show improvement as rapidly as within three days, especially if an extra dose suspended in water is given at night and before exercise. Best results if started with intensive dosing using the liquid product.
U-Gard Solution, Corta-Flx www.corta-flx.com 800-838-7524	$26.95/gal.	White calcium- and magnesium-based liquid antacid with kaolin, pectin, and other natural ingredients. Fairly well-accepted when dosed or put on feed. Effective at between 2 to 4 oz./dose, depending on severity of symptoms. Calming effect may be noted during periods of intensive treatment.
Ulsus, Peak Performance Nutrients www.peakperformancenutrients.com 800-944-1984	$49.99/3 lbs.	High potency, primarily calcium carbonate-based antacid, combined with marshmallow, licorice, and antioxidant support, including MSM. Fine powder, palatable. Results similar to U-Gard powder.

bone weakening, achy and weak muscles, and abnormal heart rhythms. The proper Ca:Mg ratio is 2.5:1.

As with any illness or disorder, always consult with your veterinarian first before instituting any treatment program.

Bottom Line

Our favorite liquid antacid was U-Gard Solution. Other liquids performed similarly at equivalent or higher dosages, but U-Gard then beat them on price.

Similar rapid results were obtained with Stomach Soother (use cautiously if the horse is showing severe symptoms and largely off feed), G.U.T. paste, and Rapid Response. These are much more expensive than the liquid antacids, and they avoid the possible calming effect seen with the high-dose calcium or calcium/magnesium products. The G.U.T. paste is less costly than Rapid Response, but Rapid Response doubles as an effective joint supplement.

If liquids or pastes aren't good choices, and for follow-up after a course of liquids or paste once the horse is eating well, powders are convenient. Again, the U-Gard 2X gets the nod for effectiveness and being most economical.

When prolonged symptom control is needed, effects of the antacids on the calcium/phosphorus/magnesium balance of the diet should be considered. To avoid the possible need to correct for mineral imbalances, consider using G.U.T. powder or one of the herbal formulations.

Chronic Diarrhea

Chronic diarrhea is a complicated problem. Except for the relatively rare cases of lymphosarcoma or a genetic immune deficiency, most cases result from either parasitism (especially immature tissue forms of parasites), viral, bacterial, protozoal, or rickettsial infections, or an allergy to a specific dietary component.

The inflammation and gut damage the initial problem causes lead directly to diarrhea and set the stage for altered

Non-Antacid-Type Ulcer Products

Product	Price	Comments
Digestion and Anti-Colic Formula, Earth Lodge Herbals www.earthlodgeherbals.com 860-237-8801	$30/lb.	Blend of dried Western herbs traditionally used for soothing and supporting the intestinal tract. Fresh, fragrant, high palatability. Interesting result with this in one belching horse that was immediately attracted to the product, would pick it out of his feed, and had relief of belching and improved disposition for 30 to 90 minutes after consumption. Otherwise, like the other dried whole herbs, it was slow to show effect, two to three weeks. Likely would be best to try as a maintenance supplement after initial symptom control with a more rapidly acting product like the antacids.
G.U.T. (Gastric Ulcer Transnutrients), Uckele www.uckele.com 800-248-0330	Paste $9.45/2 doses, powder 2 lbs./$37.95	Viscous base with blend of antacid, chlorophyllin, deglycerized licorice, gamma oryzanol, and probiotics. Bright green color. Highly palatable. Horses with mild-to-moderate symptoms showed greatly improved appetite and ability to finish meals within one to three days if started with paste treatments (given before meals), five to seven days when added to feed. We would suggest syringing this in to start. Horses with moderate symptoms may require double dosing first few days with a full syringe of paste or one ounce of powder mixed to a total volume of 60 to 80 cc. Hint: The paste syringe can be reused as a dosing syringe for powder mixed with water and a little corn oil.
Gastri X, Hilton Herbs www.chamisaridge.com 800-825-9120	$96.95/1.5 kg	Dried herbal blend containing traditional Western choices for soothing intestinal linings and calming cramping. High quality. Highly palatable. Doesn't work rapidly enough to be suitable for initial control of symptoms but a nice choice for maintenance of an ulcer-prone horse after the first 30 days of treatment. One trial horse that had moderate symptoms and did not respond satisfactorily to the dry herbs did show a rapid and obvious improvement when treated with a tea made from two of the ingredients, slippery elm and chamomile. A liquid formulation of this product might be a nice addition to their product line.
Gastro Aid, Cavalor www.farmvet.com 888-837-3626	$66.50/2.2 lbs.	Powder. Blend of traditionally used herbs, including licorice, bioflavonoid, and cabbage extract. Horses with relatively mild symptoms responded to this product alone after seven to 14 days when added to each meal. For more severe symptoms (e.g. very poor appetite, tooth grinding), begin with antacids until appetite is improved. Fair palatability.
GastroSaver, Figuerola Laboratories www.Figuerola-Laboratories.com 800-219-1147	$149.99/3 lbs.	Powdered extract of aloe, licorice and other herbs, zinc, MSM, lactic acid probiotics, multiple enzymes. One horse with confirmed gastric ulceration wouldn't eat it, and when given the product as paste became agitated after dosing (pawing, head tossing), was not continued on the product. Two others with mild symptoms showed either no improvement or a gradual reduction in symptoms over time. Not palatable but amount suggested is small.
Herbal Ulcer Blend, Equine Science www.herbs4horses.com 800-479-3537	$28.50/3 lbs.	Pelleted herbal blend including three of the most commonly used stomach soothing Western herbs (licorice, marshmallow, meadowsweet). Small pellets mix into meals well and are readily consumed. No improvements seen when fed as instructed, up to four weeks of use. Might be more appropriate as a preventative or maintenance supplement. Note: Contains Kava.
Natural Plan Stomach Soother, Healthmate Products www.stomachsoother.com 847-579-1051	$12 to $14/qt.	100% papaya puree. Dose 2 oz. twice a day. Palatable. Papaya has been documented to have a protective effect on gastric ulcers and may reduce acid secretion. Effective in horses with mild-to-moderate gastric ulcer/digestive upset symptoms consisting of poor appetite for grain, mild depression or irritability, and sporadic belching or tooth grinding. Rapid relief within three to five days. One horse with more severe signs (almost totally off grain, appetite very poor, gaunt) appeared in some discomfort after the initial dose and was then treated with antacids instead. Do not use in breeding stock. Refrigerate after opening. Note: Manufacturer also reports isolated cases of mild abdominal discomfort after a few days' use. The cause is unclear, but it may relate to some direct stimulant effect of the fruit on smooth muscles of the intestinal wall. We did not see this problem in our trial.
Rapid Response, Amerdon International www.amerdon.com 800-331-1036	$36.95/qt.	Aloe vera gel with proanthocyanidins (plant antioxidant), glucosamine, chondroitin. Extremely effective for rapid relief of ulcer symptoms, with appetite returning as quickly as in horses treated with antacids. Use 2 to 4 oz./treatment, same treatment schedule as with antacids. Once horse is back on feed, can be added to meals rather than dosed. Maintain with 2 to 4 oz./meal. Palatable. Expensive but does double duty as a joint supplement.

Product	Price	Comments
Succeed Digestive Tract Conditioner www.succeeddcp.com 866-270-7939	$125/30 tubes	Well-accepted and tolerated paste with faint oat aroma. Minimal to no change in symptoms with one tube/day dosing up to the 30-day mark. Same horses did respond rapidly to the liquid antacids. We didn't continue longer than 30 days. Company reports they have changed their instructions since our trial to two tubes/day during early periods of supplementation. An unpublished field trial conducted by the company documented improvement in average ulcer score in racehorses after 90 days of supplementation.
TractGard, Foxden Equine www.foxdenequine.com 540-337-5450	$27.50/5 lbs.	Combination of antacid ingredients, soluble fiber source, and mineral salts. We didn't see any effects of increased drinking or better hydration of manure as claimed, but at high doses (2 to 3 oz. several times a day) the product did appear to have an antacid effect, with improved appetite and longer eating times noted after two days of use. Palatable.
Ulcer-Plex, Multivet USA www.multivetusa.com 800-356-8776	$69/gal.	Liquid blend of both Western and Ayurvedic herbs to provide soothing effects, improve antioxidant status in the stomach lining, promote healing. Also contains antacid minerals. Palatable to most of our horses. Some immediate improvement in appetite noted when dosed shortly before offering feed, but this effect lasted only for that meal. Better results initially with repeated daily doses, before each meal. Gradual return to full appetite over two to three weeks in mildly affected horses.
Ulcrin, Med-Vet Pharmaceuticals www.unitedvetequine.com 800-328-6652	$41.50/2 lbs.	Powder. Same as G.U.T.
Ulseraze, Natural Animal Feeds www.naf-uk.com (no phone)	$98.99/1.8 kg	Powder. Blend of Western herbs, with whey and lactoferrin for healing support, designed to stimulate mucin production and provide antioxidant support. Fair palatability; be sure to mix the powder into feed well. Improvements are slow to occur (two to three weeks), but it's a good choice as a maintenance product for ulcer-prone horses after initial symptom control.

Ulcer-Treatment Guidelines

Symptoms	Classification	Action
Markedly depressed appetite, dull attitude, mild colic, sensitive to touch in the lower, cranial (toward the head) portions of the abdomen, possible weight loss.	Severe	Initial treatment with acid-suppressing medications is usually indicated in these horses. If the management and work level that precipitated the problem aren't changed, long-term treatment with either low-dose medications or intensive antacids may be needed to prevent recurrence. Efficacy of herbal approaches hasn't been formally studied.
Fails to finish grain on a regular basis but eats hay well, slow grain eating with multiple interruptions, may observe some tooth grinding or belching, little to no weight loss, possible attitude or performance changes.	Moderate	Intensive antacid therapy may control these symptoms without the need for expensive prescription medications, but if symptoms persist longer than 30 days, or fail to improve, a complete work-up, including scoping to confirm ulcers and determine severity, is indicated.
Goes off feed for one or more days following shipping, competition, or heavy work.	Moderate, intermittent.	Management changes to avoid having the horse go without access to hay for longer than three to four hours, combined with antacid use shortly before work, may avoid this pattern. Otherwise, use of half dose of Merial's Gastrogard, active ingredient omeprazole, or their new product, Ulcergard, is the only treatment FDA-approved for preventing gastric ulceration in horses. Treatment should start two to three days prior to the known stressful event, and be continued that day.
Picky about grain but cleans up, no weight loss, may be irritable or reluctant to perform.	Mild	Although mild gastric irritation could certainly cause these symptoms, this is the group where diagnosis is the least certain and upsets elsewhere in the intestinal tract may be causing the symptoms. If the horse responds well to intensive antacid treatment, index of suspicion is higher but this doesn't rule out hyperacidity, or some other irritation/inflammation, lower in the intestinal tract as a cause. This group is probably the best candidate for symptomatic relief from the multi-ingredient herbal products that target the entire digestive tract, but a work-up to determine the cause is indicated.

immune function and increased sensitivity to a variety of allergens or irritants that a healthy, intact intestinal tract would handle without problems. Populations of gut organisms can also be negatively affected.

By the time a vet sees a horse with chronic diarrhea, the original cause may have been resolved, and eliminating a parasite burden or infection may not immediately solve the problem. A return to normal may take time and involve one or more of these steps:

- Larvicidal deworming to eliminate possible high tissue levels of immature parasites

- Supporting the establishment of normal intestinal "bugs" through use of Ration Plus, high-dose live organisms, and exposure to the manure of normal horses

- Aggressive efforts to identify infectious organisms of all types

- Trials of oral antimicrobial drugs, even if an organism cannot be identified

- Use of oral equine serum or colostrum products

- Implementing a simple diet, such as only grass hay 🐎

Case History: Diet Saves Sasha from Inflammatory Bowel Disease

Although fortunately not too common, inflammatory bowel disease can be devastating, even fatal.

Sasha, an impressive dark bay warmblood, was foaled in the Ukraine and trained for dressage. As a six-year-old, he was shipped to a German dealer, who sold him to an American the following year. He was gelded that June and arrived in the United States on July 5. In early August, Sasha was dewormed and given a full round of vaccinations. About a week later, he colicked. That episode was followed by more deworming, which was followed by more colic and an increasingly obvious persistent weight loss.

While Sasha became enveloped in a steady downward spiral of colic, bloating, dramatic weight loss, and, eventually, inflammatory bowel disease (IBD), his owner aggressively pursued every avenue to find a cure.

Traditional Workups

A switch from grain to extruded feed and more-fibrous hay helped to slow the weight loss, but the colics continued. Initial blood work provided no clues, but a dextrose-absorption test revealed that the small intestine wasn't absorbing even this simple sugar. This led to a serum protein electrophoresis test, which separates out the proteins in the blood and can provide clues as to whether there's an inflammatory process, allergy, or malignancy.

The results looked like lymphosarcoma, but it could also have been due to IBD. Fortunately, a normal liver biopsy and liver/spleen ultrasound decreased the likelihood of lymphosarcoma.

The only procedure left was a biopsy of the abnormal sections of the intestine, which Sasha's owner was reluctant to do. Instead, she opted to try corticosteroids, which would relieve the IBD.

Sasha started on prednisone, a steroid, in the fall, then switched to injectable dexamethasone, a potent steroid with anti-inflammatory properties, on December 1. The dexamethasone did stop the severe colic, except for one episode in January after the horse was again dewormed.

In the meantime, the horse had literally become a steroid junkie and couldn't be tapered to a low dose. He required steroid injections every four days or he would colic badly. Even with the steroids, Sasha had frequent uncomfortable bloating episodes when manure production would drop. Even eating grass or just hay and weather changes would push him into colic.

All attempts to taper his steroids resulted in colic, sometimes severe enough to require Banamine and/or an extra steroid treatment. Exploratory surgery to remove abnormal sections of the intestines was suggested; however, the prognosis was poor. Things were looking grim. Determined, Sasha's owner got in touch with a progressive, never-say-die veterinarian who agreed to take the case.

Back to the Basics

It was clear that Sasha's IBD was at least partially due to stress—intensive training in Europe, gelding, and then the journey to the States—and that the vaccinations and dewormings may have pushed him over the edge. He was placed on a restricted diet in an attempt to get his inflammation under control while supporting a normal immune response.

A hair sample was sent to Uckele Health (www.uckele.com, 800-248-0330) for mineral analysis and a mineral supplement to correct any dietary imbalances or deficiencies. The vet put Sasha on Digest-All for assisting the small-intestine digestive processes, Equi-Pro to help rebuild muscle, and N-acetyl-cysteine to support the synthesis of the antioxidant glutathione, which is good for protecting the gut.

All grain-based feed was stopped, and Sasha was switched to beet pulp, which doesn't require a functioning small intestine for absorption and is well-tolerated. Sasha was allowed grass hay only and no fresh grass. The goal was to make his diet constant, avoid potential allergens and irritants in commercial grain mixes, and use feed that relied minimally on small-intestinal function. Since the small intestine is required for protein absorption, Sasha's dietary protein level was boosted with an easily digested and absorbed protein source, concentrated whey protein extract.

Intestinal function was further supported by Ration Plus (www.rationplus.com, 800-728-4667). He was also started on a few tablespoons of flaxseed oil for essential fatty acids and on APF (www.auburnlabs.com, 877-661-3505), a blend of Chinese adaptogenic herbs that strengthen immunity and modify inflammatory and allergic reactions. That left one more product to find: a source of bovine colostrum, which was known to treat IBD in experimental animals.

Vita-Flex was contacted about their Glutasyn (www.vita-flex.com, 800-848-2359), which would be an immune-system support and complement the N-acetyl-cysteine. However, at the time, Vita-Flex was developing a new bovine colostrum–based product called Rejuvenex, which produced positive responses in dogs. Sasha became the first Rejuvenex equine test case.

With the horse's diet in place, the focus shifted to getting him off steroids. On March 28, Sasha got his first dose of colostrum and was in the process of switching to the beet pulp and other supplements, which he was

handling well. He got a dexamethasone injection on March 31 because of bloating and diarrhea, which was considered likely due to the colostrum.

Determined to continue to use colostrum, the vet added Lactaid, the human product that contains an enzyme to break down milk sugar, to the Rejuvenex. That did it. Sasha looked so good that his owner skipped his next dexamethasone shot—without problems.

Off steroids, Sasha became more energetic, anxious for his food, and eager to go outside, which he did. Although he still had bloating, it was traced to new spring grass, so Sasha was fitted with a grazing muzzle. By mid-April, he had gained 50 pounds. His coat looked better, and he had gone five days without bloating.

He had one more episode of bloating severe enough to warrant dexamethasone, just in case, during a persistent period. The cause appeared to be a combination of too much grass, which necessitated taping the muzzle shut; too rapid an increase in supplements, and too little colostrum. By mid-May his energy levels were rapidly rising, he was shedding out well, and he was even being ridden.

Sasha was switched to a different source of colostrum (Fortius) and did well on this, too. He still had some shaky periods that were traced to either a hay change or too little colostrum, so he was switched to hay cubes to minimize hay changes. Progress was uphill. He was gaining weight, and the bloating episodes were increasingly rare. In November he went on plain oats.

Sasha is now back in work. He's eating hay cubes, oats, and beet pulp, plus a customized mineral supplement. His diet will have to be watched closely, and he will remain colic-prone, but it's a small price to pay. If Sasha's owner hadn't been determined to continue trying, he might not be here today.

Common Causes of Chronic Diarrhea

Cause	Tests	Treatment/Comments
Chronic parasitism, especially larval cyathostomiasis.	Fecal exam, but encysted larvae can't be detected. Blood count or fluid collected from the abdomen may show elevated eosinophils.	Treat with larvicidal deworming. Five-day double-dose fenbendazole is the most effective. This is probably the most common cause of chronic diarrhea.
Cryptosporidium or Giardia infection, possibly Globidium leukarti.	Fecal examination for pathogenic protozoa.	Treat with metronidazole (brand name Flagyl) or iodochlorhydroxyquin. Unusual cause but sporadic cases occur. Herd/group outbreaks possible. Well worth checking for since it's very treatable.
Lawsonia infection.	Fecal for Lawsonia PCR. Antibody titers.	Treat with oral erythromycin and Rifampin in foals. Also responds to oral doxycycline, which may be safer in older animals. See additional comments in text.
Salmonella infection, other bacterial infection	Repeated fecal cultures. Examination of fecal smears for white blood cells.	Treat by supporting growth of normal intestinal microorganisms through the use of probiotic-type supplements. This used to be considered the most common cause of chronic diarrhea in horses, but 10% or so of perfectly normal horses may culture Salmonella-positive. It's more likely to be the primary problem in a young animal. In adults, strongly suspect a component of immunodeficiency. Rhodococcus equi has also been found as a rare cause of chronic diarrhea in older animals. Several other strains of bacteria, such as Clostridia, are know to be associated with chronic diarrhea in people or other animals but are rarely tested for in the horse.
Fungal (e.g. Candida).	Fecal smears and cultures.	Treat with mare's milk/colostrum and encourage bacterial populations. Increased numbers of fungal organisms may be found in any chronic diarrhea, but are rarely the actual cause except in very young animals. Heavy fungal overgrowths, to the point they're the dominant organism in the manure, may be found in very young foals that received insufficient colostrum, have been heavily treated with antibiotics, or are orphaned and being raised on milk replacers.
Inflammatory bowel disease/ granulomatous enteritis.	Rectal exam. Biopsy. Serum protein electrophoresis. Absorption studies.	The usual therapy is corticosteroids but is often not successful. We have seen good results with a combination of oral colostrum and specialized diet. Can progress to severe diarrhea, weight loss, low serum protein. Horse may also have skin lesions. It's not clear if these inflammatory bowel disease cases are actually a separate disease, or the end result of particularly severe and long standing diarrhea of other causes (e.g. chronic infections).
Intestinal lymphosarcoma, a form of cancer.	Rectal exam. Biopsy. Serum protein electrophoresis. Absorption studies. Peritoneal tap cytology may be helpful.	No treatment. Progresses to severe diarrhea, weight loss, low serum protein. Horse may also have skin lesions.
Immunodeficiency disorders with chronic gut inflammation/ infection.	Serum protein electrophoresis. Fecal cultures. Specialized immune function tests.	You'll need a thorough evaluation for a correctible cause in order to determine treatment, e.g. insufficient colostrum, vitamin and mineral deficiencies, toxin exposures, chronic infections with organisms that cause immunosuppression. Rare as a primary disease, where defective immunity leads to chronic intestinal infections (e.g. Salmonella). May appear in a foal, or in young adulthood.

Electrolytes

Every cell in your horse's body acts like a tiny battery, highly dependent on correct concentrations of electrically charged particles (ions) both inside and outside the cells. These charged ions are electrolytes.

Electrolytes are nothing more than minerals dissolved in the horse's bloodstream. The horse must take in electrolytes and minerals year round to replace those lost in urine, saliva, bile, tears, mucus, and intestinal tract secretions. Electrolytes are also lost in sweat, but sweat losses reflect only part of the horse's total daily needs.

The major electrolytes in blood are sodium and chloride, which together make salt. Inside cells, potassium substitutes for sodium. Other important electrolytes (minerals in free or dissolved form) include calcium, magnesium, and phosphorus and the trace minerals zinc, iron, copper, and manganese. Bicarbonate ion is also an electrolyte. Your horse manufacturers this in a reaction that combines water and carbon dioxide to form hydrogen ions and bicarbonate ions.

Whether it's summer or winter, your horse's major source of electrolytes and minerals is his diet. For example, the daily potassium requirement for a 1,000-lb. horse doing intense work is about 40 grams per day, but most hays contain a minimum of 1% potassium, meaning just 10 lbs. of hay a day will meet or exceed the potassium needs of a horse at work (1 lb. of hay provides 4.5 grams of potassium). Of all the important electrolytes and minerals, the only ones that aren't present in adequate amounts in the diet are sodium and chloride—that's plain old salt.

Salt Is the Major Concern

At baseline, the horse needs to take in approximately 1 oz. of salt a day to stay optimally hydrated. Sodium is the major mineral controlling how much water is in the horse's body. Because it is in such short supply in their diets, horses have evolved to have a strong hunger for salt, and their bodies will also save sodium at the expense of losing other minerals if necessary.

When sodium is in short supply, horses adjust by secreting less sodium in the urine (substituting potassium instead), producing more concentrated urine, and "robbing" the tissues surrounding the cells of water to preserve the volume of their circulating blood. This loss of water in the tissues is what makes a dehydrated horse's skin remain tented up away from his body if you pinch it.

Horses that have not had access to salt can maintain their circulating blood volume well, but they're always somewhat dehydrated. If they never get stressed or exercised they'll probably be okay, but they quickly get into trouble with overheating, heat stress, and serious electrolyte abnormalities if temperatures climb or they're worked.

The major error that people make when using electrolyte supplements is to ignore the horse's basic salt requirement, believing the electrolyte supplement is all their horse needs. This simply is not the case. Most supplements contain far too little sodium to even begin meet baseline requirements.

Another common mistake is to add them to the horse's drinking water without also providing plain water. Some horses don't like the taste of electrolyte products or have mouth sores, ulcers, or abrasions that are irritated by the electrolyte-spiked water. Horses with stomach ulcers may avoid electrolytes too. The horse will also stop drinking supplemented water once his sodium hunger has been filled. The result of any of these things can be that the horse does not drink enough plain water.

With hard work or hot weather your horse's salt needs increase.

Easy Electrolytes

The first step in making sure your horse has adequate intake of electrolytes is to feed him a mineral-adequate diet with at least 10 lbs. of hay per day.

The next step is to provide free-choice salt or add salt directly to feeds. If you provide salt free-choice, monitor how much the horse actually eats. Loose salt, either in granular or fine (e.g., table salt) form, will usually be consumed more readily than salt in licks or bricks.

Make sure that the horse consumes at least 1 oz. of salt per day in cool weather, when inactive. That's a pound of salt every 16 days. With hard work and warm or hot weather, the horse's basic salt needs may increase to 3 to 4 oz. per day for an average-size horse.

Salt (sodium chloride) is the major electrolyte supplement your horse needs.

Supplements

There's a place for electrolyte supplements, but it comes after you are sure the horse's baseline requirements for minerals in the diet and plain salt have been met. It cannot be stressed often enough that failure to provide the horse with a balanced diet and to meet his minimum salt requirement of at least 1 oz. per day, whether working or not, will get you into trouble with electrolyte imbalances that electrolyte supplements can't fix.

Prolonged exercise (e.g., endurance rides) or shorter periods of intense exercise (racing, eventing) can result in large losses of sodium, potassium, and chloride via the horse's sweat. Since it's really not possible to "preload" the horse with extra electrolytes before the exercise starts, he'll have to make up those losses after exercise (and during, for horses that work all day). This can be done if your base diet is adequate, including adding more salt to make up for sweat losses, but it can take a day or two for heavy water and electrolyte losses to re-equilibrate.

While sweat is a major source of electrolyte loss, your horse loses electrolytes into urine and intestinal secretions all year long.

To prevent losses from accumulating in horses being regularly worked, and to avoid performance effects from losses during exercise that the horse can not replenish from available dietary stores in the gut, electrolyte supplements are useful. To replace losses accurately, the supplement should have the major electrolytes sodium, potassium, and chloride present in proportions that mimic those of sweat.

Sweat contains approximately 80% as much potassium as sodium and twice as much chloride as sodium. The quantity of electrolytes the horse needs depends on how much sweat he loses. Sweat losses during exercise vary, from about 2 quarts to over 10 quarts per hour. In terms of sodium lost, this amounts to anywhere from 5 to 25 grams an hour, which is a tremendous amount.

Electrolyte Precautions

Endurance horses lose tremendous amounts of electrolytes in sweat during a race. It's not surprising that supplementation of horses with concentrated electrolyte pastes at frequent intervals is a common practice among endurance riders.

Researchers at Oklahoma State undertook a study to determine the effects of this on the horse's stomach, particularly on gastric ulcer scores. There were 14 horses divided into two groups. One group received a placebo of 2 oz. of water every hour for eight hours. The other received 2 oz. of concentrated electrolyte paste on the same schedule.

The concentration of individual electrolytes per ounce was: 5,528 mg (5.528 grams) sodium, 11,886 mg (11.886 grams) chloride, 3,657 mg (3.657 grams) potassium, 754 mg calcium, and 153 mg magnesium. Horses had their stomachs scoped before and after the eight-hour period.

There was a significant increase in both the number and severity of gastric ulcers in the horses receiving the concentrated electrolytes, with the authors concluding that frequent dosing of electrolytes could be harmful to the stomach. It should be mentioned, too, that exercise itself is a risk factor for gastric ulcers, so this schedule of dosing in a horse that is also exercising could pose an even greater risk.

Maintenance and Light-Work Electrolyte Products

Product	Analysis	Comments
White salt brick—about $2 at your local feed store Loose tablet salt—about 49¢/lb. at your local grocery store	Sodium chloride 100%	The only electrolyte supplement you need for healthy horses at maintenance and at low-to-moderate work levels. Minimum consumption is 1 oz./day, up to 3 to 4 oz./day in hot weather. A four-pound brick should be gone in two months in winter, in about three weeks in hot weather.
Harvest Salt Buckeye Nutrition www.buckeyenutrition.com, 800-898-9467 $12.95/50 lbs.	Sodium chloride 93 to 96%, manganese 4,000 ppm, copper 2,500 ppm, zinc 5,000 ppm, cobalt 150 ppm, iodine 40 ppm	Very high salt content and each ounce provides about 25% of the daily requirement of trace minerals. The high manganese in this product is not suitable for many diets. Loose form, well consumed.
Su-Per Stress Less Gateway Products, Inc. www.buygpdirect.com, 888-472-2825 $8.20/4 lbs.	Per oz.: Potassium 1.94 grams, salt 1.5 to 1.6 g, calcium, magnesium, and other trace minerals in tiny amounts	Although product recommendation is for daily feeding to combat stress, amounts of major electrolytes are low and better proportions are needed. Major ingredient is sugar (dextrose).

Supplements to Replace Electrolyte Losses

Product	Analysis	Comments
Perfect Balance Electrolite Peak Performance Nutrients www.peakperformancenutrients.com, 800-944-1984 $19.99/2.5 lbs.	Per oz.: Sodium 6.2 g, potassium 5.5 g, chloride 14.2 g, calcium 485 mg, magnesium 337 mg, trace amounts of copper, zinc, and manganese	Perfectly balanced to match sweat losses. Very concentrated formula with no sugars or other fillers.
Perform N' Win Buckeye Nutrition www.buckeyenutrition.com, 800-898-9467 $19/4 lbs.	Per oz.: Sodium 1.12 g, potassium 0.91 g, chloride 2.8 g, calcium and magnesium as in sweat, 3% sugars	Ideally balanced for sweat losses, this product is backed by extensive research. Drawback is the low concentration of electrolytes/dose, meaning you have to use a lot more.
Ultra-Lyte Univet Pharmaceuticals www.univetpharm.com, 800-268-5069 $23.10/5.2 lbs.	Per 1.4 oz. dose: Sodium 2.83 g, potassium 3 g, calcium 2.3 g, magnesium 0.5 g, chloride 7.09 g, dextrose 14 g	Extra sugar in this product dilutes its potency. Sodium low compared to potassium. Calcium much higher than in sweat.
Jug EquiAide Products www.equiade.com, 800-413-3207 $5/8.3 oz. packet	Per 8.3 oz.: Sodium 3.7% (8.7 g), potassium 1.3%, calcium 0.3%, magnesium 0.2%, chloride 7.21%	Designed to be added to water. High dextrose. Good balances but could stand a little more potassium. One packet replaces sweat losses of up to about two hours work under moderate weather conditions.
Select Stress-Pak Richdel, Inc www.selectthebest.com, 775-246-3022 $10.45/2 lbs.	Per oz.: Sodium 14% (3.9 g), potassium 12%, chloride 23%, calcium 2 to 3%, phosphorus 2%, magnesium 2%, trace amounts iron, manganese, and zinc	Well-balanced (a little generous with the potassium). Calcium and magnesium higher than sweat losses.
Platform Complete Electrolytes Farnam www.farnamhorse.com, 800-234-2269 $19.50/2.8 lbs.	Per oz.: 0.85 g protein, 2.7 g sodium, 1.7 g potassium, 269 mg calcium, 500 mg magnesium, trace amounts of manganese, zinc, copper, cobalt	Falls short on potassium. Detailed list of amino acids but all in small amounts. Electrolytes in low concentration.
HydroAid Nutriscience, 215-542-8890 $35/3 lbs.	Per oz.: 80% carbohydrate, sodium 3.2 g, chloride 3.2 g, potassium 1.6 g, calcium 500 mg, magnesium 200 mg	This product is mostly carbohydrate. Fairly low levels of electrolytes. Chloride and potassium too low compared to sodium.
Endura-Max Kentucky Equine Research www.ker.com, 859-873-1988 $27.50/5 lbs.	Per oz.: Sodium 5.53 g, potassium 3.7 g, chloride 11.9 g, magnesium 153 mg, calcium 754 mg	This is a pretty well-balanced product. We'd like to see just a little more potassium. More concentrated than most.
Exer-Lyte Mobile Milling Services www.mobilemilling.com, 800-217-4076 $10.25/5 lbs.	Per oz.: Sodium 26.4 to 28.4% (minimum 7.5 g), chloride 50.5%, potassium 11%, magnesium 0.4%	No frills, highly concentrated electrolyte supplement at a great price. Potassium a bit low though. We would add 1.25 teaspoon of potassium chloride to get potassium up.
Su-Per Lyte Gateway Products Inc www.buygpdirect.com, 888-472-2825 $7.92/5 lbs.	Per oz.: Sodium chloride 52 to 56% (5.9 g sodium minimum), potassium 11.5%, small amounts of manganese, iron, zinc, copper, cobalt	At the listed range, it's a bit low for sodium at the lower percentage and a bit high at the higher percentage, but all in all this is a very well balanced and economical supplement.

Supplements to Replace Electrolyte Losses

Product	Analysis	Comments
Stress-Dex Squire Laboratories www.neogen.com, 800-477-8201 $13.95/4 lbs.	Per oz.: Sodium 2.4% (0.68 g), chloride 3.6%, potassium 3%, calcium 1%, dextrose, flavorings, trace minerals	A favorite with owners because their horses readily eat it. They should—it's mostly sugar! Extremely low levels of electrolytes, not correctly balanced.
Ride-Rite Electrolytes Advanced Biological Concepts www.a-b-c-plus.com, 800-373-5971 $20/3 lbs.	Per oz.: Sodium 10% (2.84 g), potassium 11%, chloride 26%, calcium 1.5%, magnesium 1%, phosphorus 0.5%, B6, vitamin C	Heavy on filler, this is a relatively dilute electrolyte supplement, too low in sodium, too high in calcium and magnesium.
Summer Games Electrolyte Kentucky Equine Research www.ker.com, 859-873-1988 $13.99/5 lbs.	Per oz.: Sodium 3.34 g, potassium 1.75 g, chloride 5 g, calcium 85 mg, magnesium 80 mg, trace amounts phosphorus, copper, iron, manganese, and zinc	Fairly good balance but needs more potassium. Relatively weak concentrations compared to other products.
Acu Lytes Vita-Flex www.vitaflex.com, 800-848-2359 $14.95/3 lbs.	Per 1.5 oz.: Sodium 4.25 g, potassium 1.3 g, calcium 807 mg, magnesium 345 mg, phosphorus 102 mg, low dose probiotics	More filler than electrolytes, potassium too low.
Apple-A-Day Finish Line www.finishlinehorse.com, 800-762-4242 $11.99/5 lbs.	Per oz.: Sodium 13.5% (3.8 g), chloride 15%, potassium 12%, calcium 5.9%, magnesium 0.5%, small amounts of trace minerals	Low concentration of electrolytes. Chloride too low.
Quench Horse Tech www.horsetech.com, 800-831-3309 $37.95/4 lbs.	Per 0.7 oz.: Sodium 4.4 g (= 6.28/oz.), chloride 10 g, potassium 3.96 g, calcium 344 mg, magnesium 238 mg, trace zinc, manganese, and cobalt	Just a bit more potassium than probably needed but overall a perfectly balanced electrolyte, very concentrated.

Troubleshooting: Low Blood Potassium May Be a Red Herring

Low blood potassium levels is a frequent electrolyte problem found in hard-working horses. The usual response, understandably, is to supplement with potassium, but that often doesn't work. Why? The reason is that many horses with chronically low-end potassium values are actually sodium, or salt, depleted. When making urine, the kidney secretes variable amounts of either sodium (Na+) or potassium (K+). Since the horse's body is set up to conserve sodium in preference to potassium, if the body's sodium levels are low, large amounts of potassium will be excreted in the urine.

Just five pounds of hay supplies all the potassium a horse needs for mainte-nance. Even potassium lost in sweat can be easily replaced with some extra hay or use of sweat balanced electrolyte replacer. If low potassium continues to be a problem, odds are that your horse is not taking in his maintenance amount of plain salt. Try adding a minimum of 1 oz. of salt to his meals for a few days. If you use table salt, 2 tablespoons = 1 oz. by weight.

Finally, when checking your horse's electrolyte status, wait at least an hour after doing any work. Electrolyte shifts occur during exercise but will reverse themselves without treatment once the horse stops working.

However, you should be able to minimize any potential harm from electrolyte supplementation by one or more of the following modifications of dosing:

- Administer electrolytes in drinking water.
- Administer concentrated electrolytes immediately after the horse has a chance to drink, preferably a few gallons.
- Wait until after the horse has eaten to give electrolytes. When you must syringe in the electrolytes, using a liquid antacid or corn oil as the carrier for electrolyte powders may help.

Finally, don't count on signs of colic to alert you that your horse may have gastric ulcers. Nervousness, poor performance, poor eating and drinking during the ride, even poor recovery rates, may be nonspecific signs caused by ulcers.

Note: A 2004 University of California study scoped endurance horses at the end of either a 50 or 80 km race and found that 67% had gastric ulcers.

Horses in moderate work in cooler weather probably do not require electrolyte supplementation.

Bottom Line

Unfortunately, most electrolyte supplements don't come close to making up for the losses the horse experiences in a one-hour period. Our pick for optimal concentration of electrolytes per ounce, price, and correct balances is Peak Performance's Natural Balance Electrolite (www.peakperformancenutrients.com). Second pick, also very well balanced, is Horse Tech's Quench, but New Balance is a better buy. Buckeye's Perform N' Win has ideal ratios but is much less concentrated. We find that some of the best choices, in terms of both concentration of electrolytes and their ratios, are Kentucky Equine Research's Summer Games, KER's Endura-Max (www.ker.com, 859-873-1988), Mobile Milling's Exer-Lyte (www.mobilemilling.com, 800-217-4076), Gateway Products Su-Per Lytes (www.buygpdirect.com, 888-472-2825) and

Any level of formal exercise in the heat increases your horse's electrolyte requirements tremendously.

Deciphering Electrolyte Labels at a Glance

- To make sure you are buying primarily an electrolyte supplement, not a lot of fillers, look for the amount of chloride to be 45 to 50%. This correlates to 12.78 to 14.2 grams of chloride per ounce. If quantities are significantly below this, it's heavily diluted. Look for sodium around 6 grams and potassium 4.8 grams. If the label lists a percentage as salt, look for 75 to 83% salt.

- If the label lists ingredients as their salts, e.g., potassium chloride or sodium chloride, look for one that has 2.5 to 3 times more sodium chloride than potassium chloride.

- Look for sodium to be somewhat more than half the level of chloride.

- If sodium and potassium are listed separately, potassium should be 80% of the sodium level, e.g., if 5 grams of sodium, you want 4 grams of potassium.

- Don't be swayed by flavorings. Horses have a natural taste for salt. All the flavored products still basically taste like salt (unless heavily diluted with sugar or other fillers) regardless of what they smell like.

- When comparing products that list their ingredients differently—by percentages versus grams and mg—some easy mental math to remember is that a level of 10% in a 1-ounce serving = 2.8 grams; 10% in a 2-ounce serving = 5.6 grams, etc.

Richdel's Select Stress-Pak (www.selectthebest.com, 800-648-0950).

Mobile Milling's Exer-Lyte and Gateway's Su-Per Lytes get the nod for a huge price differential. 🐎

Planning for Exercise in the Heat

Heat stress and exhaustion can be life-threatening complications of exercise in hot weather. Even relatively small amounts of dehydration and electrolyte imbalance have a negative effect on muscle function and can cause problems like "thumps" (an abnormality in nerve conduction that makes the diaphragm contract strongly with each heart beat), poor intestinal motility, or even heart arrhythmias.

While you can't start your horse's work day with extra electrolytes in the body tissues (the kidney rapidly clears any excesses), you can make sure he at least starts the day with his tank full and a reserve ready for absorption in his intestine by following these steps:

- Feed a minimum of 10 lbs. per day of hay, or allow constant grass access.

- Give a minimum of 3 oz. per day of plain salt, half divided between feeds, half syringed in after meals. Do this routinely, or at least starting 3 days before a day of planned heavy exercise in the heat.

- Avoid excessive calcium feeding. This can reduce the horse's ability to mobilize calcium from storage depots in bone if he needs it during exercise.

- If the horse is only sweating lightly, replace these losses with 3 to 5 grams of sodium and appropriate levels of chloride and potassium for every hour worked.

- For heavier sweating, double the above amounts.

- Get up early enough that your horse has a chance to eat a normal breakfast, including hay or grass, and to drink before exercise starts.

- If the horse will be working hard all day, give the first dose of electrolytes before exercise starts. This helps to match absorption to losses so that deficits do not occur.

Note: For optimal absorption, during exercise provide no more than about 1.5 grams of sodium and appropriate amounts of potassium and chloride per gallon of water consumed. A horse with a normal body level of sodium will drink freely. If you follow the steps above, your horse should easily drink enough water to allow for the hourly supplement amounts suggested, but it's still advisable to monitor water consumption between dosings to make sure that he does.

Checking for Dehydration

There are two simple tests you can do to check how well hydrated your horse is. One is called the pinch test. Pick up a fold of skin on your horse's neck and tent it (lift it) away from the body. If the horse is well hydrated, it will immediately snap back into place. If the skin is slow to return to its normal position, the horse is somewhat dehydrated. The longer it takes, the worse the dehydration. (In older horses, loss of normal skin elasticity can make this test unreliable when done on the neck. In an older horse, tent the skin at the point of the shoulder instead.)

The other test is to lift the horse's upper lip and press your thumb on the gums over the teeth with enough pressure to make the area blanch to white. This compresses the blood vessels. In a horse with normal hydration, the color will return in less than 2 seconds. Any longer than this means the horse is dehydrated. With severe dehydration, the gums will also feel dry and tacky rather than moist and slippery.

Additional Help for the Hard-to-Hydrate Horse

Horses that seem to easily slip into slight dehydration despite what should be adequate salt and water intake may have excessive sweat losses or losses along their intestinal tract. You'll need to stay on top of electrolyte supplementation, too, but these horses are often helped quite a bit by Uckele's Liqui-Fuel, a 25% betaine (trimethyl glycine) and 4.5% glutamic acid liquid supplement (www.uckele.com, 800-248-0330). Betaine (TMG) is very osmotically active and seems to help these horses retain better tissue levels of water, which in turn will pique their salt appetite. The glutamic acid supports health of the intestinal lining cells and also contains low levels of electrolytes.

Electrolyte-Related Performance Problems

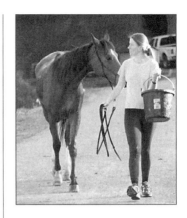

Bringing your horse's regular water bucket, or even water from home, encourages good drinking.

Muscular: Both dehydration and electrolyte abnormalities interfere with the ability of a muscle to contract normally. Overheating secondary to tissue dehydration also interferes with function and may damage the muscle cells. Consequences range from poor performance and fatigue to overt muscle damage and tying-up.

Heat Stroke/Exhaustion: Dehydration severely impairs the horse's ability to cool down his body. If forced to continue working, body temperatures may climb to 106 or above. This is a genuine medical emergency that may take your horse's life if not promptly treated.

Thumps: Electrolyte abnormalities (usually low levels of calcium, magnesium, and/or potassium) cause nerve irritability that may present as "thumps," a strong contraction of the muscular diaphragm that occurs with each beat of the heart.

Intestinal: Although the exact mechanisms are not clearly defined, dehydration and electrolyte abnormalities may put the horse at higher risk for developing an exercise-related decrease in intestinal motility. This is a fairly common reason for endurance horses to be pulled from competition at vet checks.

Feeding Pregnant, Lactating, and Growing Horses

As you might easily imagine, your pregnant mare's feeding needs differ from those of your other horses. You can get the job done with commercial feeds, but you'll need to read the feed tags to make sure nutrient levels are adequate.

The major difference between feeds suggested for use in broodmares and those for other classes of horses is a higher protein level. For broodmares, 14 to 16% is the usual, while 10 to 12% protein is the norm for other feeds. Pregnant and lactating mares do need a lot more protein, but even this level might not get the job done well enough.

Protein Levels

The difference between a 10% and 16% feed in terms of protein is only 27.2 grams/lb., while an 1,100-lb. mare in heavy lactation needs about 770 grams more protein in her daily diet. Look at what happens with a 1,100-lb. mare on a hay, then hay and grain pregnancy diet, when switched to a broodmare feed after she foals.

Pregnancy: 22 lbs./day of 8% protein hay = 800 grams of protein/day (adequate through the ninth month of pregnancy); 22 lbs./day of 8% protein hay + 3.3 lbs./day of 10% protein feed = 891 grams of protein/day (adequate up to foaling).

Lactating: 25 lbs./day of 8% protein hay + 6 lbs. 16% protein feed labeled for broodmares = 1,345 grams of protein/day

- Even 16% protein in feeds may leave the mare short of protein during lactation. Adding 1 lb./day of 50:50 alfalfa pellets and soybean meal to her diet will bridge the gap. Other options are ½ lb./day of soybean meal or sunflower meal.
- Feeds labeled for performance horses may do just as good a job as those for broodmares. Check your labels.
- For lactating broodmares being fed at the lower end of feeding recommendations (about 6 lbs./day of grain), choose a feed with 16% protein, 0.75% lysine, minimums of 0.75% calcium, 0.5% phosphorus, 50 ppm copper, 150 ppm zinc, 120 ppm manganese.
- Additional vitamin E, selenium, and iodine (iodized table salt a good source) will often be needed.
- Don't combine high-potency supplements with fortified grains if you are feeding at least the minimum recommended amount (usually 6 lbs./day).

(almost 200 grams short!). Since many of the grass hays fall below 8% protein, this deficit could be even worse.

Fortunately, nature provides a natural protein boost in the form of young pastures, where 20% protein is common. However, for the mare with little or no pasture access, you'll need to feed more protein.

Since the grains have a calorie value at least twice as high as most hays, it won't do any good to feed more grain because you would have to cut back the hay to avoid overfeeding; 2 lbs. of an 8% protein hay has the same protein content as 1 lb. of a 16% protein grain. In other words, if you increase a 16% grain by 1 lb. and cut back 2 lbs. on the 8% hay to keep calories the same, you're still feeding the same amount of protein.

Access to high-quality pasture with a mixture of grasses is a rich source of protein, vitamins, and minerals for pregnant, lactating, and growing horses.

Possible Solutions:

- Provide 2 lbs. per day of a 30% protein supplement. This will cover the protein needs, but since these products are highly mineral-supplemented, you'll end up overdoing it on the mineral front.

- You could solve the problem by adding 1 lb. per day of soybean (calcium:phosphorus = 1:2.46) or sunflower (Ca:P = 1:2.24) seed meal, or Uckele's Amino Fac 41 (Ca:P = 1:2.25), but this could upset your mineral balances.

- Another option would be a 50:50 mix of alfalfa pellets and soybean meal. This will provide 31.5 to 35% protein on the average and about 50% more calories than average grass hays, so you can feed more and provide more energy in the form of digestible fiber than with high-starch grains. 2 lbs. per day of the 50:50 soybean meal and alfalfa pellets has a balanced calcium:phophorus ratio, makes up the protein deficit without overdoing other minerals, and costs considerably less.

Next to consider is lysine intake. Lysine is the most important essential amino acid for normal growth and development, and the only one for which precise requirements are known. A mare in the last trimester of pregnancy that was on an adequately balanced maintenance diet before pregnancy with at least 0.3% lysine has a relatively small requirement for additional lysine. This can be easily met by feeding her 1 to 1.5 lb./day minimum of any commercial feed with a guaranteed lysine content of at least 0.6%. Even "regular" feeds like Triple Crown 10 or Nutrena Compete contain sufficient lysine, so there's no point in switching to a mare feed.

The lactating mare has a more sizeable deficit, even when increasing her feed by 70% and starting from a good base maintenance diet as just described. If you feed this mare 6 lbs. per day of a 0.6% lysine mare feed, she'll still be a little short. You'll need a feed with 0.7 to 0.75% lysine to provide enough. The

The mare's nutritional needs are even higher when she is lactating than when she is pregnant.

50:50 soybean meal and alfalfa mixture is also rich in lysine, about 1.8%.

What About Minerals?

Minerals are where we really count on mare feeds to get the job done. Any feed, whether labeled specifically for mares or not, will meet the trace mineral requirements if it contains at least 50 ppm of copper, 150 ppm zinc, and 120 ppm manganese, when fed at 6 lbs. per day along with 25 lbs. of hay that has been appropriately balanced. It's much more difficult to say with certainty if they are adequate for calcium and phosphorus.

With calcium, for example, grass hays may be as low as 0.3% calcium, or as high as 0.6%. Phosphorus also has a wide range. Six pounds of a 0.6% calcium feed provides 16 grams of calcium compared to a requirement during peak lactation of 59.1 grams, which could leave the mare a bit short of calcium during lactation. The mare in late pregnancy could also need more calcium than that provided by a small amount of a 0.6% calcium feed. We'd recommend making sure the calcium level in a feed being used for pregnant or lactating mares is at least 0.75% calcium, 0.5% phosphorus.

At 0.6 ppm selenium, 6 lbs. will provide 1.6 mg of selenium. This too may be a little light, so consider adding an additional 1 mg per day, or have the mare's selenium blood level checked and supplement accordingly. Many of these feeds also contain vitamin E, but it may not be stable for long in a feed. Supplementing pregnant and lactating mares with a separate vitamin E supplement is advisable.

Bottom Line

If your hay has 8% or less protein, is at the low end for calcium (i.e., around 0.3%), and you're going to be feeding the usually recommended low-end 6 lbs. per day of feed (about 2 lbs. per day in late pregnancy), you'll need a feed that contains:

- 16% protein
- 0.75% lysine
- 0.75% calcium
- 0.5% phosphorus
- 50 ppm copper
- 150 ppm zinc
- 120 ppm manganese

Nutrena Youth, Nutrena Develop, Buckeye GrassPlus Developer, and TDI 16 meet those high-end requirements, and we especially like that the TDI 16 specifies manganese content. When fed at the 6 lb. per day level, even these feeds could stand a bit of a protein and lysine boost from 2 lbs. of a 50:50 mixture of soybean meal and alfalfa.

For hay with 8% protein or higher, with calcium at least at 0.5%, you can get good results with either a 14% or 16% protein feed with a calcium minimum of 0.6%. Note that many of the feeds listed here are normally thought of as performance horse feeds, but will work well as a pregnant mare feed. If you go with a 14% protein feed and provide 8% protein hay, you'll need another 54 grams of protein on top of the 200 already mentioned when feeding 6 lb. per day of this combination.

Comparison of Feeds

	Purina Omolene 200	Purina Strategy	Purina Omolene 100	Nutrena Youth (Life Design)	Nutrena Develop (Farr)
Protein %	14	14	10	16	16
Lysine %	NG	NG	NG	0.85	0.85
Threonine %	NG	NG	NG	0.5	0.4
Methionine %	NG	NG	NG	NG	NG
Fat %	6	6	4.5	6	5
Calcium %	0.6	0.6	0.6	0.85	0.8
Phosphorus %	0.5	0.6	0.45	0.7	0.75
Iron ppm	NG	NG	NG	NG	NG
Copper ppm	55	55	35	60	60
Zinc ppm	220	220	140	180	240
Manganese ppm	NG	NG	NG	NG	NG
Selenium ppm	0.6	0.6	0.6	0.5	0.6
Iodine ppm	NG	NG	NG	NG	NG
Vitamin A IU/lb.	3,000	3,000	3,000	5,000	4,000

	Nutrena Compete (Life Design)	Nutrena Performance (Farr)	TDI 12	TDI 16	Tiz Whiz 16	Farnam Platform Mare and Foal
Protein %	14	14	12	16	16	16
Lysine %	0.75	0.75	0.5	0.8	0.78	0.7
Threonine %	0.3	0.35	NG	NG	NG	NG
Methionine %	NG	NG	NG	NG	NG	NG
Fat %	7	7	5	5	2.5	8
Calcium %	0.7	0.7	0.6	0.8	0.8	0.8
Phosphorus %	0.6	0.6	0.5	0.7	0.85	0.55
Iron ppm	NG	NG	200	350	NG	NG
Copper ppm	50	60	50	50	60	80
Zinc ppm	150	240	160	160	90	115
Manganese ppm	NG	NG	125	125	40	NG
Selenium ppm	0.6	0.6	0.6	0.6	0.3	0.6
Iodine ppm	NG	NG	0.25	0.25	NG	NG
Vitamin A IU/lb.	4,000	4,000	6,600	6,600	2,510	4,000

Warning: The recommendations used in this section are suitable for a 1,100-lb. mare whose base diet (both hay and grain) before pregnancy was known to be balanced and to meet the minimum National Reseach Council (NRC) requirements for protein, vitamins, and minerals. If the base diet was not balanced or adequate, that will change her requirements.

In the last trimester of the pregnancy, the mare's needs for increased minerals begin to outstrip the required calorie increase.

Specialty Products

Obviously you want your broodmare in peak health for conception, pregnancy, and lactation, but do you really need supplements that claim to target broodmares? If you're not feeding a diet that meets the specifications above, yes, your mare needs more.

There are special needs in late pregnancy and lactation, but the word "broodmare" in the advertising or on the label won't guarantee any particular product will meet those needs. Although there has been a great deal of interest over the years in looking into various nutrients to see what their effect on fertility might be, the bottom line is that fertility will not be improved by supplementation unless the mare was deficient to begin with.

The mare should be on a carefully balanced diet that provides needed amounts of all major and trace minerals (see sidebar, opposite), as well as adequate vitamin A (rarely a problem) and vitamin E (often deficient).

Thin mares have more difficulty conceiving, but overweight mares have more trouble with pregnancy, so aim for a middle of the road body condition score of 5 to 6—e.g., her ribs are covered, but the mare is not fat.

Approximately 80% of the growth of the foal is completed between the eighth and eleventh months of gestation. This is when the mare's nutrient requirements really begin to increase, and they are at their highest during the first three months of lactation.

The phrase "eating for two" applies even more to the mare that is producing milk than to a pregnant one. Take a little time to look at how much nutritional needs change. Protein requirements, for example, are almost double maintenance amounts in a lactating mare. The heavily lactating mare needs 1,000 grams—that's 2.2 lbs.—more protein than at maintenance levels.

Calcium requirements will more than double, from 20 grams per day to 59.1 grams. Since there's not much chance that any mare is going to be able to eat twice as much as she does at maintenance, her increased needs require some serious attention to nutrition.

Calculating Needs

If you're planning to meet your mare's needs with a supplement rather than grains, the amount you need to supplement your mare is simple: It's the difference between what her diet's providing now and what her pregnancy and lactation needs are.

Calculate Supplement Needs

If you start with a balanced diet meeting needs when not pregnant, and increase the amounts you are feeding by 20% in late pregnancy and 78% in lactation, you will meet her calorie needs. However, an 1,100-lb. mare will still come up short on minerals by these amounts:

Nutrient	Pregnancy	Lactation
Protein	78 grams	298 grams
Lysine	2.4 grams	10.5 grams
Calcium	13 grams	21.6 grams
Phosphorus	11.1 grams	22 grams
Copper	130 to 180 mg	Same
Zinc	490 to 540 mg	Same
Manganese	490 to 540 mg	Same
Selenium	2.4 to 4.4 mg	0.5 to 2.5 mg
Iodine	2.6 to 7.6 mg	3.3 to 8.3 mg
Vitamin A	0 to 15,000 IU	Same
Vitamin E	400 to 800 IU	0 to 300 IU

But remember, calorie increases don't necessarily match mineral and vitamin needs.

To figure out how much your mare needs, you first have to know what she's getting at baseline. If you don't, it's pure guesswork, and the price you may pay is the health and soundness of the foal. For this example, we'll use a 500-kg (1,100-lb.) nonpregnant mare whose maintenance diet meets NRC-suggested minimums. These are the amounts listed under "maintenance" in the table on page 126.

The reason some of these nutrients don't take a bigger jump with lactation is because the mare must eat considerably more of the base diet to hold her weight when lactating. In reality, most mares really don't or won't eat 70% more food when they are lactating, so this has to be taken into consideration. For example, if the mare ate 5 lbs. of grain and 15 lbs. of hay before pregnancy, she would have to eat 8.5 lbs. of grain and 25.5 lbs. of hay when lactating. If she won't clean up that much, you'll have to increase her supplements accordingly. If she'll only clean up half that much, you'll need to make up 50%

of that difference with supplements. Mares that are easy keepers and can't be fed as much will also come up short.

Mare Supplements

Let's take a look at some supplements and see how they compare to the numbers we came up with in the section above on calculating your mare's supplement needs.

Using commercial supplemented feeds can go a long way to meeting your pregnant and lactating mare's needs, but it's not ideal for every situation. Insulin-resistant and/or overweight mares don't do well with grain feeding. You may also be looking for a supplement that will allow you to feed your mare the same diet you did when she wasn't pregnant (just more, to meet calorie needs), or the same way you feed your nonpregnant and nonworking horses, without having to switch your feed brand.

Those of you who use a custom mixed and naturally balanced, but not supplemented, feeding program will also need more for your pregnant and lactating mares. Discuss adding a balanced protein/mineral supplement with your vet.

Bottom Line

We looked at widely available supplements targeting broodmares. Futurity Blend 30, Triple Crown 30, and Gro N' Win were the only ones we felt addressed the increased protein, amino acid, and mineral needs of pregnant and lactating mares. Of these, assuming you start from a base of balanced nutrients that at least meets minimum needs for maintenance, Buckeye's Gro N' Win gets the nod as best all-in-one product.

Growing Horses

There has been a lot of interest in recent years in rethinking the way we feed young horses. Recommendations in the last version of the NRC feeding recommendations were geared toward early weaning, when the young horse's digestive tract is not yet able to handle high-fiber hay or grass-based diets. As a result,

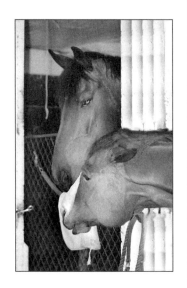

The nutritional needs of nonworking horses are vastly different than those of a young horse.

heavy grain feeding was recommended. It is now recognized that this can lead to significant peaks and valleys in hormone levels that may be a contributing factor to developmental bone disease.

The first step to raising healthy young horses is therefore not to be in any hurry to wean. Left to their own devices, young horses will gradually decrease their nursing and increase solid food intake until they are weaned completely by the age of 7 to 9 months. Delaying weaning until the foal is at least 6 months old allows more time for the gut to adapt to an adult diet, provides a longer period of access to nature's perfect food (the dam's milk), and also decreases the stress of weaning.

A 6- to 7-month-old foal has nutritional requirements that are very similar to those of a mare in early lactation with respect to the requirements for minerals as a function of calories (to identify the correct level of calcium per calorie, see the table in chapter 6, page 46). Therefore, one option is to feed them a scaled-down version of the diet above for lactating mares. Choose a feed that meets the protein and mineral requirements listed, and feed it at a rate of 1 lb. of grain for every 4 lb. of hay. Remember, though, that, as with the mares, this assumes that you know the hay has a reasonable mineral balance, or are supplementing to correct levels if it doesn't.

If you want to avoid feeding straight grains, any of the many "Lite" feeds on the market could be substituted, as long as their protein and mineral levels are appropriate. Most are going to fall short on protein for this age group, so count on feeding 1 oz. of our 50:50 alfalfa and soybean meal mixture for every 2% drop in protein below 16%. Otherwise, the "Lite" feeds are often a good choice because most are relatively mineral-dense and will meet or exceed the minimum mineral requirements.

Feeding the Young Horse

There is no time in a horse's life when diet is more important than when he is growing. Even a heavily pregnant mare carrying a rapidly growing foal can draw from her own body supplies.

Nutritional Requirements for Broodmares

Nutrient	Maintenance	Pregnant, last 3 months	Lactation
Calories/day (Mcal)	16.4	18.2 to 19.7	28.3 (11.9 above maintenance)
Protein/day (grams)	656	801 to 866	1,427 (771 above maintenance)
Lysine (grams)	23	28 to 30	50 (27 above maintenance)
Calcium (grams)	20	35 to 37	56 (36 above maintenance)
Phosphorus (grams)	14	26 to 28	36 (22 above maintenance)
Copper (mg)	100	250 to 300	250 to 300 (150 to 100 above maintenance)
Zinc (mg)	300 to 400	750 to 1,200	750 to 1,200 (450 to 900 above maintenance)
Manganese (mg)	300 to 400	750 to 1,200	750 to 1200 (450 to 900 above maintenance)
Selenium (mg)	2	4 to 6	4 to 6 (2 to 4 above maintenance)
Iodine (mg)	1 to 6 mg	keep under 35	keep under 35—conservative suggestion of 4 mg above maintenance
Vitamin A (IU)	15,000	30,000	30,000 (15,000 above maintenance)
Vitamin E (IU)	1,000 to 1,200	1,600 to 2,000	1,600 to 2,000 (600 to 1,000 above maintenance

The foal, however, is born with low-to-no tissue stores of key vitamins and minerals. The foal's body is starting from scratch, being built as it goes along. If something is in short supply, there's a problem. The young horse can't manufacture the amino acids and minerals he needs out of thin air. Since most of their growth takes place in the first year of life, "getting it right" is never more critical.

In nature, foals grow and mature normally on nothing but their dam's milk and grass. However, the trend over the last 20 to 30 years with domestic horses has been to rely heavily on grain and to wean early, sometimes as early as 3 months of age. Because the hind gut is not well developed at this age, recommendations were for feeding as much as 3 times more grain than hay for the first year of life. Current feeding recommendations also focus on rapid growth, tending to produce large, and fat, yearlings that appeal to halter judges and sales-ring

Don't Feed Your Weanling Like a Steer

The emphasize on oversized and fat babies is hard to overcome, but rapid growth and excess weight have clearly been identified as risk factors for developmental bone, joint, and tendon disorders.

buyers. As an outgrowth of this heavy grain feeding, manufacturers developed feeds that would deliver very high concentrations of minerals, supposedly to take the guesswork out of feeding the young horse.

There are several problems with this approach. First is that the young horse's mineral intake is tied to calories. If your young horse happens to be a perfect fit for the NRC growth rates and requirements, fine. Otherwise, you will end up either feeding more calories than the weanling needs to meet mineral needs, or cutting feed to avoid the youngster becoming fat but also cutting critical minerals in the process. Studies have also found that some young horses experience abnormally high blood sugar elevations after grain feeding and this puts them at risk of developing OCD, possibly as a result of wide hormonal fluctuations caused by the blood sugar swings (IGF-1—insulin-like growth factor). The third issue is whether or not these feeds actually get the job done.

The table on page 128 lists the nutritional requirements of a 6-month-old weanling weighing 475 to 500 pounds that will mature to a weight of 1,100 pounds, and nutrient intakes (from label information and feeding recommendations) when using some commercial feeds specifically labeled for use in weanlings.

This little guy's dam is producing more than 30 lbs. of milk a day to feed him.

Young Horse Feeds

	Requirement	Purina Junior Complete feed fed at full recommended amount	Nutrena Life Design Junior** Amounts from 4.4 lbs. feed	Triple Crown Growth*** Amounts from 6.6 lbs. feed	Farnam Platform Mare and Foal**** Amounts from 3.3 lbs feed
Mcal	15 to 17.2	15 to 17.2	unknown	unknown	unknown
Crude Protein (g)	750 to 860	754 to 855	300	420	240
Lysine (g)	32 to 36	unknown	15	24	10.5
Calcium (g)	29 to 36	36.4 to 41.3	17	30	12
Phosphorus (g)	16 to 20	28.6 to 32.4	14	18	8.25
Magnesium (g)	4 to 4.3	unknown	unknown	9	unknown
Potassium (g)	12.7 to 13.3	unknown	unknown	33	unknown
Vit A (IU)	10,000	15,600 to 17,700	19,800	39,600	13,200
Copper* (mg)	150	260 to 295	100	150	120
Zinc* (mg)	450	910 to 1,032	300	510	172.5
Manganese* (mg)	375 to 450	unknown	unknown	345	unknown

*Minimum estimate based on research showing possible key role of copper and zinc intake in joint cartilage development; manganese adjusted accordingly. **Fed with 1 to 1.75 lb. of hay per 100 lbs. bodyweight. Figures given are for middle of the recommended grain feeding range. ***Fed with hay. Figures given are for middle of recommended grain feeding range. ****Fed with hay, figures given are for the middle of the recommended grain feeding range.

Triple Crown Growth when fed in the middle of the recommended feeding range meets or exceeds all requirements except crude protein and lysine, and is possibly a little light on the manganese for keeping all trace minerals in balance. It also has the most extensive list of guaranteed levels so that you can actually be sure all the bases are being covered. To make up the protein deficit, all you would have to feed would be a little over 7 pounds per day of a 10% protein hay. The only problem with this strategy is that the hay intake is always going to be 50% or more of the young horse's diet. Unless you know your hay has a reasonably good mineral balance, you could be introducing mineral imbalances into the diet.

As you can see from the chart, Purina Junior, which is fed as a complete feed, also meets or exceeds the requirements for the nutrients they actually guarantee on the label. However, even with this abbreviated list, the levels of four key nutrients (manganese, potassium, magnesium, and lysine) are unknown for that feed. There's generous leeway with the copper, zinc, and vitamin A, but to get enough protein (the most expensive ingredient to add to a feed) you have to feed the full recommended amount. If your weanling is getting too fat on this level of feeding, any drop will provide inadequate protein. A drop of more than 25% will result in inadequate calcium intake, too.

The other two feeds are also fed with hay, but rely on it to provide key nutrients in needed amounts much than the TC Growth formula does. For example, if feeding Platform Mare and Foal in the middle of their recommended feeding rate, even a slow-growing 500-lb. weanling would still need:

- 436 grams of crude protein
- 18.6 grams of lysine
- 26.6 grams of calcium
- 13.25 grams of phosphorus
- 287.5 mg of zinc
- 0 mg of copper

To get that much protein, you would have to feed 7 lbs. of straight 14% alfalfa, which would give you more than twice as much calcium as needed and throw the calcium:phosphorus ratio out of balance. Life Design Junior, at the middle feeding range, leaves the youngster 376 grams short on protein, which would call for 8.25 lbs. of a 10% protein grass hay, which would probably also meet lysine needs (no guarantees, though). Whether or not it would correct the mineral shortfalls in a balanced manner depends entirely on the type of hay and its mineral profile.

Only the Purina Junior, which is fed as a complete diet, adequate covers the nutritional needs for the nutrients they actually list on the label. However, you have to feed their recommended amounts; the diet is about 30% forage, 70% high NSC concentrates; and there is no information or guarantee for several key nutrients. TC Growth, 6.6 lbs., with 7 lbs. of a 10% protein hay, is a little better but for this approach to work you need a hay analysis and it could still be too much concentrated sugar and starch for some.

What's the Alternative?

The alternative is getting back to raising, managing, and feeding the young horse like a horse.

- Wean as late as possible. Mare's milk is the perfect food for the developing horse, and the perfect supplement even late into the first year of life. Unless you have a rambunctious colt that is trying his dam's patience to the point of risking serious injury, you can allow the weaning process to occur naturally.

- Maintain the mare and foal on as large a quality pasture as possible, minimizing reliance on grains.

- Don't tie mineral intake to grain calories. Work with an independent equine nutritionist for determining your young horse's protein, mineral, vitamin and calorie needs and how best to meet these without having the horse become overweight or forcing rapid growth.

- Adjust calorie intake so that the ribs are always very easily felt. Ribs may even be visible when the horse is on a very rapid growth spurt but, as with a lanky teenager, this is normal.

- When supplemental calories are needed, include generous amounts of easily fermented fibrous foods to encourage development of the hindgut.

Putting It in Practice

We know of several youngsters that have been raised completely grainfree, while maintaining normal growth curves and even showing successfully in hand. Others have been raised with grain intakes considerably below what they are supposed to require for normal growth. In addition to the health benefits from not overfeeding grain, the approach below has the advantage of allowing you to feed all ages and classes of horses the same base diet, adjusting easily to individual calorie, protein, and mineral needs.

Step I. Start with a balanced base diet. Hay or pasture is the cornerstone. If relying on pasture, and/or hay from the same · fields all the time, speak with your agricultural extension agent ·

about the proper way to sample your fields for analysis. If you maintain the fields in the same way from year to year (seeding, liming, fertilizing, etc.) you will only have to sample every 3 to 5 years unless severe weather causes an obvious change in the types of grasses and plants that predominate. If you rely on hay and must buy it, you'll need to sample more

Pregnant and growing horses relying heavily on pasture should be supplemented based on a pasture analysis.

often but even those who don't have storage for large amounts at one time can make this do-able (see the chapter on insulin resistance for tips). Once you know what is and is not in your grass and hay, work with a nutritionist to come up with a supplement plan to balance this important part of the diet. If you set the supplement goals for adult maintenance, you can boost this with mineral or mineral/protein supplements to suit other classes of horses as need be (pregnant, lactating, growing). See Step III.

Step II. Concentrates. When more calories are needed than hay and/or grass alone can provide, use a concentrate that does not upset the balance you just achieved. Obviously a balanced grain mix will do this but so will these higher fiber alternatives with acceptable calcium:phosphorus ratios:

- beet pulp with 2 to 4 oz. of rice bran (no calcium added) or 4 to 6 oz. of wheat bran per lb. of beet pulp

- 50:50 beet pulp and whole, grade I oats

- 1 part alfalfa cubes or pellets, 2 parts oats

- 2 parts alfalfa, 1 part wheat bran

Step III: Boosting minerals. Once you have the base diet balanced in minerals, it becomes very easy to meet the higher needs of the growing horse by using a balanced commercial supplement. To maintain moderate growth, a 6-month-old weanling requires about 10% fewer calories than a mature horse his eventual adult size at maintenance, but 70% higher mineral intakes for bone and soft tissue development. Exactly how much more you need to feed will depend entirely on how your base diet worked out. With most hays, by the time trace minerals are balanced you will likely be feeding close to the weanling's requirement anyway and both commercially supplemented grains and the alternatives we've listed provide generous amounts of calcium, phosphorus, and magnesium. In most cases, the additional requirement of the weanling will end up being no more than 7 to 10 grams of calcium (maximum) above what the balanced base diet is already giving him, plus the proportional amount of other minerals a correctly balanced supplement will provide. If you like the convenience of a pellet, something like Triple Crown's 12% supplement will do fed at as little as 8 oz. day, or as little as 2 to 3 oz. day of a more concentrated mix like one of Uckele's economical Equi-Base supplements.

Step IV: Protein. Our sample 6-month-old weanling needs 750 grams of crude protein a day, and a diet that provides about 0.6% lysine if he's consuming 12 lbs. of hay/pasture, and concentrate per day. When pasture quality is high, this isn't a problem. If feeding 10% protein hay and one of the alternative feeds above, in equal amounts, the diet will provide from 11 to 13% protein depending on which feed you choose. In the worst-case scenario, he will need about 200 grams of additional protein, down to as low as 50 grams. There are many options for doing this, from high-protein and relatively low-mineral combination supplements like Buckeye's Gro N'Win, to both high-protein and high-mineral such as Triple Crown 30% supplement. If your mineral bases are covered, your nutrition consultant can give you advice about a protein supplement or make adjustments to your concentrate formula to boost the protein a bit more.

The hardest part about changing how you feed is changing how you think. That becomes a whole lot easier when you realize that your current feeding might not actually be doing all that you think it is, and the consequences this can have for a developing horse. We think the low-grain, low-fat, moderate calorie approach to feeding young horses, considering protein and vitamin/mineral needs separately from calories, is the safest and healthiest way to go. With a little professional help, you can be on your way in no time. Even if you choose to continue to go with high-grain feedings, remember you can't necessarily rely on the product you choose to cover all the bases, and a critical analysis of your entire diet, not just the grain, is necessary.

Signs of Possible Nutritional Deficiencies

Most of these symptoms can have multiple causes (e.g., parasitism), so always consult your vet to work through the problem.

- Slow shedding of the foal coat
- Dull coat
- Lethargy
- Poor immune function (runny eyes, runny nose, skin problems)
- Physitis
- OCD
- Splints

Does Insulin Resistance Cause OCD?

Developmental bone and joint problems, especially OCD, haunt every owner of young horses. While a recent study (*Journal of Animal Science,* 2005) did document some decrease in insulin sensitivity in yearlings that had been fed a high simple-carbohydrate diet since weaning, they compensated for this by disposing of glucose through pathways that do not require insulin so their glucose handling was still normal. Earlier studies had shown higher blood glucose response to feeding was a risk factor for OCD. While this had initially been blamed on insulin resistance, the insulin response to the higher blood glucose was actually proportionately the same as the insulin response in young horses whose blood glucose did not rise as high, so not likely to be related to insulin resistance. In other words, the problem is the magnitude of the glucose rise, not insulin resistance. The cause of this has not been determined, but may be related to differences in how long the meals are held in the stomach, the proportion of the meal that is "dumped" at any time into the small intestine for absorption, or how long the meal remains in the small intestine, where the absorption of digested sugars and starches into glucose occurs. 🐎

Busting Feeding Myths

It's an Inadequate Diet That Causes DOD

Inadequate copper intake, and subsequently zinc, is linked with higher risk of DOD, or developmental orthopedic disease. Foals nursing on copper-supplemented dams are protected, but the advisability of higher than NRC-recommended copper intake for growing horses is still being investigated. Still, it appears that growing stock should receive more copper.

It's not clear whether the higher need is related to higher body demand or to high levels of competing minerals in the diet. For example, high intakes of zinc will interfere with copper metabolism enough to produce joint disease. Iron, molybdenum, and manganese in excess could also have this effect. On the other hand, if zinc and manganese are too low, you may also see joint problems.

It's all adequate totals and correct balances. A sound course at the moment seems to be to guarantee the pregnant or lactating mare and growing horse receive higher levels of copper, then adjust zinc and manganese levels to a 1:3:2.5 to 3 ratio for copper:zinc:manganese, but no higher. Therefore, a youngster that was predicted to need about 100 mg a day of copper should also get about 300 of zinc and 250 to 300 of manganese, remembering that more is not better.

Protein Doesn't Deserve Its Bad Rep

Protein is often blamed for causing developmental bone disease, but it doesn't. Feeds supplemented to 14 to 16% protein levels are also invariably high-calorie, and it's the rapid growth rate stimulated by the high calorie intake—not the protein—that may be a factor. Adequate protein is essential for pregnant, lactating, and growing horses. When dealing with DOD, restricting calories is often part of the treatment. To avoid cutting protein while trying to reduce calorie intake, supplement protein or choose a high-protein/mineral supplement. It's important to remember, though, that the mineral profile of your protein supplement also needs to be considered in terms of its impact on the mineral balance.

Pregnant Mares Gotta Eat

You may hear broodmares don't require anything extra except for more feed when the foal gets large. This is good advice in terms of calories, but it can leave you short on key minerals beginning in the second trimester.

In the first trimester, the embryo and uterus don't place a huge drain on nutrients, but in the second trimester, the foal is gaining about 0.2 lb./day and making greater demands, while the uterus is taking up more room.

In the third trimester, when weight gains are averaging over 0.5 lb./day and the uterus takes up more abdominal space, the foal's demands are high while the mare's ability to eat gets more limited. You can cut down on the abdominal space needed to accommodate more calories by feeding more grain later in pregnancy but depending on what you feed you may be losing out on minerals.

Mares in the last trimester, if not before, require more calcium, phosphorus, zinc, and copper than would be predicted just by weight of the mare and foal if mineral requirements otherwise were the same as any adult horse. Meeting these needs significantly reduces the risk of OCD and DOD, such as epiphysitis.

These mares have increased nutritional requirements. The calorie requirements of maintenance compared to the last month of pregnancy rise by only 20%, but calcium and phosphorus needs double and copper needs are tripled. Obviously just feeding more of the same diet as for maintenance won't work.

Hay-Only Diets

With all the problems surrounding degenerative orthopedic disease in young horses, many people wonder if they should skip grain entirely. We don't think so.

It's unlikely you can support adequate body weight in the lactating mare and the early weanling without grain, although pregnant mares and young horses over 7 months may do okay on high-quality hay and/or pasture. However, you're still going to need to supplement minerals that match your hay. Select the Best's Mare and Foal Supplement I and II (made to match either grass or alfalfa hay) would be a good place to start looking for a complementary supplement to an all-hay diet.

12

Feeding Senior Horses

It wasn't too long ago that a horse was considered over the hill at age 10. But now, better health care and preventative medicine have greatly extended a horse's useful life, and many horses work into their 20s, some even longer. Not surprisingly, manufacturers have stepped up to the plate with products that target this growing population of older horses.

Offerings include more than supplements and arthritis remedies. Now you'll find specialized feeds for older horses right next to the bags for pregnant mares, performance horses, and growing horses. The questions for you to decide are whether or not that feed is the best one for your senior and whether that feed is worth your cash.

Gravity may take its toll on your older horse's back, but there's no reason she can't stay in good flesh.

Digestive Changes

As a horse ages, the ideal types of food don't change drastically. The bigger changes are his ability to process those feeds—as in chew and digest them— and his ability to ward off parasites that compete for the food he takes in. Regular deworming and good dental care are absolute necessities for your older horse's overall health and ability to utilize his feeds.

However, even if you have his teeth in as good shape as possible, his saliva production may lessen as he ages and the output of his digestive enzymes may drop. These factors combine to decrease his ability to properly digest fat, protein, and starches, meaning he'll get less out of everything you feed him.

- Remember your horse needs long fiber, indigestible stuff that keeps intestines moving.

- Additional fiber sources include hay, chopped forage, soaked hay cubes or pellets, beet pulp.

- Supplement B vitamins, vitamin C, and minerals.

- Use a probiotic to help with efficient digestion.

- Feed a source of EFAs— essential fatty acids.

Fiber can be a problem, too. Even if he manages to chew the hay and get it into his stomach, his intestinal motility and the ability to absorb those nutrients drop off over the years. The aged horse also has a weakened population of intestinal microorganisms, the good bacteria responsible for fermenting food that his own digestive enzymes cannot break down. All this means is that he's using what he's eating less efficiently than he could.

Adding a probiotic, like Ration Plus (www.rationplus .com, or 800-728-4667), to the horse's diet can increase nutritional efficiency, helping him produce and maintain the balance of microorganisms he needs for fiber digestion. With Ration Plus, we've found the horse gets more out of the food he eats—just what some struggling older horses need.

Special Nutrients

Your horse's mineral, calorie, and protein needs remain basically the same as when he was younger, except for a little extra attention to a few particular nutrients.

- **Protein:** Quality, not quantity, is the key with protein. Aim for 10 to 12% crude protein overall, meaning the average protein in your hay and your concentrate combined. A level of 12 to 14% crude protein in the feed with supplemental lysine and methionine is suggested.

Seniors are at high risk for tooth problems.

This added protein is a good insurance against any changes in protein digestibility related to lower levels of digestive enzymes in the horse.

- **Essential Fatty Acids:** Aging in other species interferes with the animal's ability to utilize essential fatty acids (EFAs), which are important for skin and hoof health and for battling arthritis. These are called essential because they must be supplied directly through the horse's diet, since he can't manufacture them himself. And since the older horse is less able to utilize what he takes in, he has a higher need for supplemented EFAs in his diet.

- **Vitamin C:** Horses generally manufacture adequate, but not optimal, vitamin C on their own, especially if they have access to fresh grass. However, the older horse is less able to accomplish this in even adequate amounts and should get vitamin C supplemented at a rate of 7.5 grams per day. Vitamin C is important for immune function, and an older horse is already battling a weak immune system.

- **B Vitamins:** Supporting a healthy population of intestinal bacteria will also improve your horse's B-vitamin status. B vitamins are important for your horse's immune system, his ability to withstand stress, and to maintain optimal red blood cells and a calm nature (aided by thiamine or vitamin B1).

- **Phosphorus:** Research in the past has shown poor phosphorus digestion in older horses, possibly due to cumulative damage from a lifetime of battling internal parasites. This information prompted many nutritionists to recommend the older horse receive higher levels of phosphorus. However, recent studies by Dr. Sarah Ralston show this may no longer be true, presumably because modern dewormers minimize parasite damage to the gut over a horse's lifetime. You do need to pay attention to the calcium:phosphorus ratio (Ca:P), in

Senior Feeds Guaranteed Analysis and Our Comments

Feed	Guaranteed Analysis	Comments
Buckeye Maturity/ Senior, www.buck eyenutrition.com 800-898-9467	Crude protein min 12%, crude fat min 4.5%, crude fiber max 15%, calcium 0.5 to 1.0%, phosphorus min 0.4%, copper min 30 ppm, zinc min 90 ppm, selenium min 0.3 ppm, vit. A min 3,000 IU/lb. Ca:P 1.25:1.	Basically a texturized/sweet feed with added soluble fiber. Too calorie-dense/grain-heavy to be our first choice but good for seniors having trouble maintaining their weight. It has middle-of-the-road mineral levels.
Superior Seniors, Agway/Southern States, www. agwaystores.com 804-281-1000	Crude protein min 14%, lysine min 0.65%, threonine 0.45%, methionine 0.25%, crude fat 10%, crude fiber max 17%, calcium 0.8% to 1.2%, phosphorus min 0.6%, copper min 60 ppm, zinc min 150 ppm, selenium min 0.3 ppm, vitamin A 9000 IU/lb., vitamin D min 450 IU/lb, vitamin C min 75 mg/lb., biotin min 0.450 mg/lb.	Pellets or texturized.
Life Design Senior, Nutrena Feeds, www.nutrenaworld. com 800-367-4894	Crude protein min 14%, crude fat min 5%, crude fiber max 16%, calcium 0.84% to 1.26%, phosphorus min 0.7%, copper min 40 ppm, zinc min 140 ppm, selenium min 0.3 ppm, vit. C 75 mg/lb., vit. A 6,000 IU/lb., vit. D 450 IU/lb., vit. E 75 IU/lb., biotin 0.45 mg/lb. Ca:P 1.2:1.	A middle-of-the-road calorie product with high-quality protein sources. However, we'd like to see the "products" and "byproducts" specified. Good vitamin and mineral levels for use either as a complete feed or to replace part of the regular ration.
Manna Senior, Manna Pro, www. mannapro.com 800-690-9908	Protein min 12.5%, fat min 4%, fiber max 16%, calcium 0.7%-1.2%, phosphorus min 0.5%, copper, min 33 ppm, selenium, min 0.3 ppm, zinc min 88 ppm, vit. A 3,000 IU/lb. Ca:P 1.4:1.	Pellets. A more calorie-dense feed, blend of grain and forage ingredients. Good choice for the advanced senior with a lot of trouble holding his weight, but try to also feed soaked hay cubes or chopped forage for long fiber.
Provide Complete Senior, Land O'Lakes, www. westernfeed. landolakes.com 206-282-2451	Crude protein min 12%, crude fat min 3%, crude fiber max 17.5%, calcium 0.8% to 1.3%, phosphorus max 0.5%,copper min 23 ppm, zinc min 92 ppm, selenium 0.3 ppm, vit. A 5,600 IU/lb., vit. D 500 IU/lb., vit. E 40 IU/lb. Ca:P 1.6:1.	Pellets. Trace-mineral levels are a bit low, but okay for a complete feed. Too low, however, for horses still taking in 1% of their weight as hay. Uses animal fats, which we don't like for horses. Uses the terms "byproducts" and "products" rather than naming all actual ingredients.
Purina Senior, Purina Mills, www. purinamills.com 800-227-8941	Protein min 14%, fat min 4%, fiber max 16%, calcium 0.6% to 0.9%, phosphorus min 0.4%, copper min 55 ppm, zinc min 220 ppm, selenium min 0.3 ppm, vit. A 3,000 IU/lb. Ca:P 1.5:1.	Pellets/extruded. Calorie-dense. Low on major and high on trace minerals. Best for horses that still eat hay but need more feed. Uses the terms "byproducts" and "products" rather than naming all actual ingredients.
TDI Senior, TDI Horse Feeds, www.tdihorsefeeds .com 800-457-7577	Crude protein min 13%, crude fat min 4%, crude fiber max 14%, calcium min 0.7%, phosphorus min 0.5%, magnesium min 0.25%, potassium min 1.8%, sodium min 0.3%, lysine min 0.75%, iron 320 ppm, copper 25 ppm, zinc 80 ppm, manganese 50 ppm, selenium 0.5 ppm, cobalt 0.6 ppm, iodine 0.6 ppm, vit. A 6,600 IU/kg, vit. D 660 IU/kg, vit. E 220 IU/kg, vit. C 45 ppm, riboflavin 6.6 ppm, thiamine 11 ppm, biotin 2.2 ppm. Ca:P 1.4:1.	The in-depth analysis information and company philosophy on their Web page, "We believe that you as a customer for premium feeds have a right to know what is in them," get a standing ovation. Higher reliance on digestible fiber and oil than grain in this product, making it a good first step for the horse that is not holding condition well on traditional feeds. Mineral levels a bit on the low end, unless you're feeding it as a complete feed.
Senior Formula, Triple Crown Feeds www.triplecrown feed.com 800-451-9916	Protein min 14%, fat min 10%, fiber max 17%, lysine min 0.6%, methionine/cystine min 0.35%, calcium 0.8% to 1.4%, phosphorus min 0.6%, potassium min 1.3%, magnesium min 0.37%, iron min 175 ppm, zinc min 150 ppm, manganese min 100 ppm, selenium min 0.3 ppm, copper min 60 ppm, vit. A 9,000 IU/lb., vit. D 450 IU/lb., vit. E 100 IU/lb, biotin 200 mcg/lb. Ca:P 1.33:1.	We like the reliance on high digestible fiber levels rather than grain, making it a good first step in the transition from regular diets to senior feeds. Added essential amino acids a big plus. Minerals well balanced. However, vitamin A is higher than the current proposed NRC upper-safe limit. When using this as a complete feed with no hay, be sure not to feed any additional A.
Senior Horse Feed, Tizwhiz, www. tizwhizfeeds.com 800-860-6789	Crude protein min 14%, crude fat min 4%, lysine min 0.7%, crude fiber max 18%, calcium 1% to 1.5%, phosphorus min 0.5%, salt 0.4 to 0.7%, copper min 60 ppm, manganese min 40 ppm, zinc min 90 ppm, selenium min 0.3 ppm, vit. A 2,500 IU/lb., vit. D 1,000 IU/lb., vit. E 150 IU/lb, biotin 2.7 mcg/lb. Ca:P 2:1.	Pellets. The trace mineral-profile isn't properly balanced, so we wouldn't recommend it as a complete feed, although it's designed to be fed as a complete feed or fed with hay.
Seniorglo, Moorman's www. moormans.com, 800-680-8254	Crude protein min 14%, crude fat min 5%, crude fiber max 16%, calcium 0.7% to 1.2%, phosphorus min 0.65%, salt 0.85% to 1.35%, copper min 45 ppm, zinc min 220 ppm, selenium min 0.88 ppm, vit. A 7,500 IU/lb. Ca:P 1.07:1.	Pellets. Designed to boost calories and vitamin/mineral intake but not as a complete feed. Excellent trace minerals, but zinc a bit high in relation to the copper. Needs additional calcium to balance phosphorus, but okay for horses on hay/pasture and needing more calories.
Vintage Senior, Blue Seal www .blueseal.com 800-367-2730	Crude protein 14.5%, crude fat 4.5%, crude fiber 12%, lysine min 0.65%, methionine min 0.3%, calcium 0.65% to 1.15% max, phosphorus min 0.65%, copper min 45 ppm, selenium min 0.52 ppm, zinc min 155 ppm, vit. A 5,000 IU/lb., vit. E 80 IU/lb. Ca:P 1:1.	Extruded. Low on fiber, so most suitable for horses having trouble holding weight on a high-fiber diet. The extrusion makes the grains more likely to be digested well in the small intestine. Needs additional calcium for a better calcium:phosphorus ratio.

EFAs for the Older Horse

Many senior feeds run 5 to 10% fat to provide extra, easily absorbed calories. This is fine for calories, but these stabilized fats are lacking in essential fatty acids. As level of feed processing rises and level of whole, natural feed intake drops, fragile essential fatty acids (EFAs) become in short supply. Consider adding one to two tablespoons/day of a cold-pressed flaxseed oil or stabilized flaxseed to boost the omega-3 EFAs (HorseTech, www.horse tech.com, or 800-831-3309 or Enreco Horse-shine, 800-962-9536). You

Flaxseed is a good source of EFAs.

can also boost the levels of the beneficial omega-6 EFAs and oleic acid for blood-sugar stability by feeding one to two tablespoons/day of either Uckele's CocoSoya oil (www .uckele.com, 800-248-0330) or a 50:50 blend of olive oil and cold-processed soy oil.

your horse's feed. This ratio needs to be no lower than 1.2:1 to avoid problems with excess phosphorus intake and to maintain strong bones.

Be aware that some manufacturers increased phosphorus levels in their senior feeds because of the past study, sometimes without increasing the calcium amount to match, resulting in a bad ratio.

- **Copper:** Copper is a trace mineral, meaning it's required in small amounts compared to the major minerals of calcium and phosphorus. However, copper is essential for hair pigmentation; controlling inflammatory responses; resistance to intestinal parasites; bone, tendon, and joint strength; and resistance to infections. Your older horse needs at least 40 ppm copper in his grain or other concentrate.

- **Selenium:** Selenium is another trace mineral that is deficient in most horses' diets. It protects the horse's muscles and is essential for proper thyroid hormone conversions. It is also an immune-system stimulant and beneficial antioxidant. Your horse needs at least 0.3 ppm in his grain or other concentrate.

Feeding the Senior

Maintaining good dental care, providing regular deworming, and supporting fiber digestive processes with probiotics may be all your older horse needs in order to remain on the same diet he had when younger. If he's still chewing fine and holding his weight on that diet, don't change a thing.

The horse should get most, if not all, of his calories from pasture and hay for as long as he holds his weight. As with any horse, we recommend you also feed a mineral supplement with a formula that complements your hay.

When older horses begin to have trouble holding condition, the most common cause is poor chewing. If he's dropping weight on a hay-only diet, increase the calorie density of the diet by adding some grain. We'd start by adding a regular grain, like easy-to-digest oats, rather than first trying a pricier senior feed, to see if a few pounds a day can stop the weight loss.

If he's having trouble chewing, try a different form, such as pellets or an extruded feed, both of which can be soaked if necessary. This is where the senior feeds begin to come into play, as they are designed to be easier to chew. In addition, hay cubes, pellets, and chopped forage can be soaked to make them easier to chew.

When hay, chopped forage, pellets or cubes, and regular grains aren't getting the job done, add or replace part of the hay with beet pulp. Soaked beet pulp is easier to chew than regular hays and delivers more calories per pound than hay,

Palatability, digestibility, and ease of chewing are all important factors in successfully feeding seniors.

When the horse can no longer chew regular hay efficiently, there are options.

though less than grain. Adding some rice bran or wheat bran to keep the major minerals balanced also boosts the calories.

Sometimes a bagged, chopped hay will be easier for an older horse to chew.

If the horse still can't hold his weight and also shows signs like quidding (dropping partially chewed sections of hay), and you find entire grains—meaning more than just the hull—in the manure, chewing problems are the culprit.

At this point, it's unquestionably time to try either a concentrated but easy-to-digest supplemental feed, like Seniorglo, or move to a complete or senior feed, while still providing at least five pounds per day of hay, chopped forage, or soaked hay cubes to provide the important nondigestible fiber.

A complete feed is designed to provide fiber for your horse's digestive health when he can't eat hay. However, you can also feed hay with a complete feed, if your horse can chew it, so don't be afraid to feed both.

Regular complete feeds that aren't labeled specifically for senior horses—and therefore often carry a lower price tag—are incredibly similar in ingredients and nutrition to those feeds that are designated for senior horses. If the regular complete feed is a better buy, we'd try it before purchasing the senior.

When fed as directed, both types of feed meet your horse's mineral needs. If your horse still can't maintain his condition, you may find the higher-fat and/or more highly processed senior feed is necessary.

Bottom Line

Supplements combining high-quality, easily digested protein and minerals, such as those targeting growing horses, can be ideal for seniors too.

If your older horse is doing fine on his hay-only diet, there's no reason to change a thing. We'd just add a good mineral supplement and a source of essential fatty acids.

If your older horse is only able to eat about 1% of his body weight in hay each day—meaning a 1,000-pound horse eats 10 pounds of hay per day—you definitely need to add a concentrate. Go to your local feed store and tell them you need a feed that provides good supplemental trace-mineral levels, at least 12% protein, guaranteed essential amino acid levels, and a high

Long Fiber and Seniors

A selling point often used with senior feeds is that they are higher in fiber. While this is generally true, and high levels of easily digested fiber are a good, safe energy source for a senior, these feeds still lack what is called "long fiber" or "scratch factor," the indigestible portion of hays and grasses that helps regulate motility in the intestinal tract and provides bulk. Most pellets or extruded feeds are low in this important type of fiber.

Even if your horse has few or no teeth, you should try to get some long fiber into him every day. Hay cubes or chopped

Chopped fiber sources can be fed right out of a bucket.

forage products can be soaked until very soft and mixed into the softened complete feed or beet pulp for these horses. This helps prevent problems with choke, impaction, or wood chewing that may develop otherwise. A minimum of 5 lbs. of long fiber per day for a 1,000-pound horse is advisable.

reliance on soluble fiber rather than grains as a calorie source, for intestinal tract health. Our favorites in this category are Vintage Senior, Triple Crown Senior, and Superior Seniors (see chart, page 139).

If your horse can only consume 0.5% of his weight (5 lb. for a 1,000-lb. horse) in even soaked hay cubes or chopped forage, you definitely need a concentrate that also provides a solid level of fiber. We still like those three feeds above, but we'd also recommend you consider the calorie-dense TDI Senior, which is a good first step for horses moving from hay diets. 🐎

Skinny Older Horse

Keeping older horses at a good weight is complicated. Weight problems are often a combination of poor ability to chew, inadequate saliva production, decreased digestive efficiency, and decreased appetite. Before focusing on what seems to be a poor appetite, consider that she may not be capable of eating as fast as she used to. Regular dental care is essential, but it doesn't necessarily improve the efficiency of chewing. Several modifications you can make may help the horse.

- Don't expect an older horse to clean up meals as quickly as a younger one. Segregate the horse for feeding, and allow as much time as needed for her to eat.

- Continue to offer hay, but also provide at least 1.5% of the horse's ideal body weight from either a pelleted complete or senior feed, or from hay pellets plus a pelleted mineral/protein supplement.

- Efficient digestion and fermentation require plenty of fluid. Because seniors often don't move around as freely, their water intake may not be optimal. In fact, impactions are a common problem. If your older horse still isn't blooming despite a switch to a pelleted diet, consider feeding soaked pellets. The extra water intake can make a big difference.

- A pro- or prebiotic may also help improve fermentation efficiency.

If providing a high-quality diet that requires a minimum of chewing still doesn't help the horse consume at least 1.5% of body weight, you need to have your vet check for an underlying medical cause for the poor appetite.

Hoof Support

Faulty nutrition isn't the only factor in hoof-quality problems, but it's a big player. Slow hoof growth, chipping, cracking, white-line crumbling, and inability to hold shoes are common. While genetics and faulty care are usually involved, inadequate nutrition can make the difference between the hoof with a potential for problems and one that actually develops them.

Hooves are built by specialized skin cells, and the same nutrients critical for healthy skin are also needed to build strong hooves. Nutrients documented to influence skin and hoof growth and quality include:

The same nutrients that contribute to skin and coat health and shine are essential to good-quality hooves.

- **B vitamins.** The Bs, especially biotin, B6, and folic acid, are important to your horse's hoof quality. While the horse's intestinal tract can synthesize enough B vitamins to avoid full-blown deficiency states, the levels may be inadequate for optimal health and hoof production. While the horse has been estimated to have a biotin requirement of 5 to 6 mg/day, doses of 15 to 20 mg may be needed to influence hoof quality.

- **Trace minerals.** Zinc is especially important to normal functioning of the cells that produce the hoof wall, but copper is also critical.

- **Protein.** The hoof wall is composed primarily of protein, and inadequate protein intake does result in poor hoof quality. But it's more likely the culprit is a deficiency of specific amino acids needed in high concentrations than the

Poor-quality hooves almost always have a nutritional component.

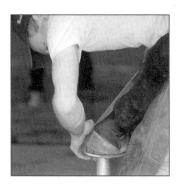

Horses with poor hoof wall quality that don't hold shoes well can cost a small fortune in farrier bills.

diet's overall protein level. These amino acids include cystine, cysteine, tyrosine, and threonine in the outer layers of the hoof wall and methionine for integrity of the white line.

- **Amino Acids.** Cystine, cysteine, and methionine are sulfur-containing amino acids. However, cystine and cysteine can be manufactured from methionine, so methionine is the one usually included. A comprehensive hoof supplement includes one or more other amino acids, plus methionine.

- **Fatty Acids.** A healthy hoof retains its natural moisture and pliability and resists absorbing water from the environment because of waxes and fats in the wall. Cholesterol compounds are the major source of fat—not a problem since the horse synthesizes cholesterol. However, the wall also contains essential omega-3 and omega-6 fatty acids that must be obtained from the diet.

Horses getting their nutrition from fresh grass take in anywhere from 6 to 20 times more omega-3 fatty acids than omega-6, while horses on hay or hay and grain diets consume exactly the opposite. Even the commonly used oils are all higher in omega-6. Many horses with dry, splitting feet that don't respond well to other supplements improve when fed whole flaxseed or flaxseed oil.

Bottom Line

Knowing what ingredients to look for is a start, but you've also got to know what levels are required to make a difference. Biotin levels in the supplements we surveyed ranged between just over 6 mg to 50 mg; zinc between 45 to 566 mg; and methionine between 75 mg to 7,500 mg.

Read labels carefully. Our chart is designed to help you choose the hoof product that will best fit into your horse's existing diet, while targeting likely deficiencies.

Horses on mineral-balanced diets with adequate-quality protein rarely have hoof problems. For those that do, our choice would be Bio-Flax 20, which covers possible deficiencies of omega-3 fatty acids, biotin, B6, and methionine.

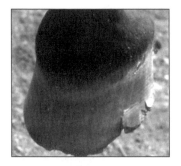

Problems with brittle and chipping hooves often need to be fixed from the inside out.

If the horse has access to pasture so that omega-3s aren't a concern, Uckele's Equi-Hoof Complex is a good choice, providing adequate methionine, biotin, and B6.

For horses receiving at least 5 lbs. a day of balanced or supplemented grain mixes but no supplementation to correct imbalances that may remain because of their hay, look for more trace-mineral insurance in ratios that won't interfere with the balanced grain. Your best choices here are Master Hoof Blend and Ascend Hoof Gel.

Horses receiving no or little supplemented grains, with unknown mineral intakes from hay, should try one of the more comprehensive hoof supplements such as Hooflex+, Farrier's Formula, Shoer's Friend, or Nu-Hoof Accelerator. Nu-Hoof Accelerator is a definite best buy because of the higher biotin levels at the lowest price.

If your horse also has skin or coat problems, a nutritional link to quality issues is even more likely. Some common dietary deficiencies that can affect both skin and the feet include:

- **Zinc.** A common deficiency in hays, often made worse by excesses of competing minerals such as iron and manganese.

- **Protein.** Including the essential amino acids lysine and methionine, which may be deficient even if the total crude protein in the diet is adequate.

- **Essential fatty acids.** Processed grains and dried hays lose much of their essential fatty acid content, especially the omega-3 fats.

- **Copper.** Another common deficiency, made worse by excess of other minerals. Copper is essential for the formation of the connective tissues.

- **Cobalt.** Cobalt containing vitamin B12 derivatives is essential for cell division and protein metabolism. B12 is synthesized from cobalt in the diet.

- **B vitamins.** Everyone connects biotin with hoof health, but the other Bs are also important for normal protein metabolism and skin and connective tissue health. 🐎

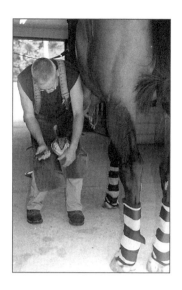

Regular, competent hoof care is just as important as nutrition in building and maintaining healthy hooves.

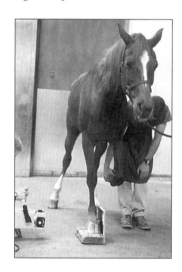

Foot problems account for the vast majority of equine lamenesses.

Weak hoof structure can lead to nagging foot pain.

Hoof Supplements

Product	Price	Formula (Per Serving)	Comments
BioFlax 20 Horse Tech www.horsetech.com 800-831-3309	$36.95/5 lbs.	20 mg biotin in a base of flax with added lysine, methionine	Excellent choice for a horse on a balanced hay-and-grain diet and no grass.
Biotin II 22X MVP www.medvetpharm.com 800-366-8986	$52.95/5 lbs.	22 mg biotin, good methionine (also lysine and cystine), low levels trace minerals (zinc 45 mg), pyridoxine	Best for a horse on a balanced diet but suspected to need biotin and/or methionine for hooves.
Super Bio-Zin Mobile Milling www.mobilemilling.com 800-217-4076	$42/7 lbs.	22.7 mg biotin, high levels methionine, lysine (also proline, tyrosine, glycine), high zinc at 566 mg with 53 mg copper, vitamins	High potency, palatable supplement best for horses on primarily low-zinc hays or pastures.
Focus HF Source www.4source.com 800-232-2365	$19.50/3.5 lbs.	6 mg biotin, 213 mg zinc, 42.6 mg copper, high level of methionine, broad spectrum of ultratrace minerals from kelp	High methionine but middle-of-the-road levels of zinc, biotin, and copper make this a good choice for horses eating low-to-moderate levels of supplemented grains and low-zinc hay.
Biotin ZM-80 Vita-Key www.vita-key.com 800-539-8482	$28.99/5 lbs.	High methionine, 200 mg zinc, 15 mg biotin, yeast base	High methionine and biotin. Middle-of-the-road zinc. Safe choice even for horses eating supplemented grain mixes but low-zinc hays.
Grand Hoof Grand Meadows www.grandmeadows.com 800-255-2962	$44.80/5 lbs.	20 mg biotin, high methionine, 250 mg zinc, 25 mg copper, 20 mg B6, plus lysine in a yeast base	High biotin and methionine, with moderate zinc and copper. Good complement for horses receiving supplemented grain but low-zinc hay. Moderate B6.
HB 15 Farnam www.farnamhorse.com 800-234-2269	$26/3 lbs.	High biotin, moderate B6, extremely low lysine and methionine	Only biotin and pyridoxine in significant amounts, so best used with balanced diets when biotin deficiency is suspected.
Horseshoer's Secret Farnam www.farnamhorse.com 800-234-2269	$21/11 lbs.	15 mg biotin, 300 mg zinc, 100 mg copper, very low lysine and methionine, plus stabilized flax (amount not specified) and a high-protein base	Good broad-spectrum supplement choice for horses receiving some supplemented grain and hay that has not been tested for nutritional levels.
Master Hoof Blend Vita Flex www.vitaflex.com 800-848-2359	$33.50/3.75 lbs.	20 mg biotin, 50 mg B6, good methionine (plus low cystine and lysine), low zinc (45 mg), plus 50 mg manganese, 15 mg copper	Good B6, biotin, and methionine levels. Trace minerals, including zinc, are low. Best for a horse on a balanced diet suspected to need biotin, vitamin B6, or methionine.
Vita Biotin Horse Health www.farnamhorse.com 800-234-2269	$9.95/2.5 lbs.	Biotin supplement, 6.25 mg/dose	Moderate level biotin supplement.
Biotin Plus Paragon Performance Products www.grailhorse.com 800-356-5222	$30.95/2.5 lbs.	50 mg biotin, 500 mg pantothenic acid, low methionine, in a base of linseed meal, stabilized rice bran, brewer's yeast, wheat germ, spice, yucca	High biotin, with levels of amino acids and other B vitamins getting a boost over labeled amounts from the high vitamin, protein, and fatty acid levels in the product's base.

Product	Price	Formula (Per Serving)	Comments
Biotin 100 Crumbles Equine America www.equineamerica.com 800-838-7524	$9.95/2.5 lbs.	Biotin supplement, 6.25 mg/dose	Moderate-level biotin supplement.
Bio-Hoof Vets Plus www.horsesprefer.com 800-468-3877	$32.75/5 lbs.	Biotin 20 mg, B6 30 mg, low zinc, methionine, and lysine, plus vitamins A, D, E	Good biotin, moderate B6. Low in other nutrients. Best used for horse whose primary problem is a biotin deficiency.
Next Level Equine Hoof Fluid Farnam www.farnamhorse.com 800-234-2269	$18.25/liter	Biotin 20 mg, good methionine and lysine, low zinc (53 mg), copper, low-dose MSM in corn-syrup base (liquid)	Levels of biotin and methionine good. Best tried for a horse already on a mineral-balanced diet.
Shoer's Friend Equine America www.equineamerica.com 800-838-7524	$32.50/11 lbs.	Biotin 6.25 mg, methionine 7,142 mg, vitamin C 1.3 g, vitamin B6 40 mg, zinc 266 mg, copper 95 mg, manganese 160 mg, other vitamins and amino acids	High methionine, moderate biotin. This is a broad spectrum supplement best used for horses on unsupplemented diets.
Farrier's Formula Life Data Labs www.lifedatalabs.com 256-370-7555	$37.25/11 lbs.	Methionine 5,355 mg, biotin 20 mg, zinc 226 mg, copper 92.6 mg, plus vitamin C (unspecified amount), cobalt, iodine, and naturally occurring levels of other amino acids	High levels of trace minerals, biotin, methionine. Broad-spectrum formula. Good choice for horses on unbalanced, unsupplemented diets.
Nu-Hoof Maximizer Select the Best www.selectthebest.com 800-648-0950	$37.78/2.5 lbs.	Methionine and lysine in good amounts, 30 mg biotin, good zinc (250 mg) and low copper, also iodine, riboflavin, folic acid	High biotin with mid-range amino acid and zinc levels. Best for horses on low levels of supplemented grain and low-zinc hay.
Hoof Biotin Uckele www.uckele.com 800-248-0330	$28.45/18 oz.	Biotin 32 mg, zinc 200 mg, methionine 500 mg	Low methionine but high biotin and zinc. Concentrated formula.
Equi-Hoof Complex Uckele www.uckele.com 800-248-0330	$37.95/3.3 lbs.	Biotin 20 mg, methionine 2,500 mg, B6 50 mg, zinc 50 mg, copper 20 mg, manganese 40 mg	High biotin, methionine, and B6. Low levels of trace minerals. Best for horses on balanced diets or generous levels of supplemented grains.
Horse Shoe Finish Line www.finishlinehorse.com 800-762-4242	$15.95/3 lbs.	20 mg biotin, 2,500 mg methionine, 2,800 mg gelatin, very low zinc (6.5 mg), also MSM and small amounts of other ingredients	Best used as a source of supplemental biotin and methionine for a horse on a balanced diet.
Hooflex+ W.F. Young www.absorbine.com 800-628-9653	$59.95/17 lbs.	2,750 mg lysine, 3,000 mg methionine, 15 mg biotin, with a comprehensive and balanced trace mineral package, including high zinc, 360 mg, low level vitamin A, E	Good levels of amino acids and biotin, with a mineral package that won't upset a balanced diet and light enough on the manganese to be helpful with many commonly encountered hay imbalances.
Ascend Hoof Gel Farnam www.farnamhorse.com 800-234-2269	$26.95/51 oz.	Methionine 3,000 mg, lysine 2,000 mg, 20 mg biotin, low levels copper and zinc (about 85 mg) in canola oil and corn syrup base (liquid)	Good levels of amino acids and biotin. Best for horses on a properly mineral balanced diet.
Su-Per Hoof Gateway www.gatewayproductsinc.com 719-537-6383	$18.39/4 lbs.	Biotin 15 mg, methionine 75 mg, lysine 125 mg, B6 20 mg	Moderate doses of biotin and pyridoxine, but methionine and lysine too low. This is essentially a biotin supplement.

Non-Nutritional Factors

Inadequate hoof care is a major factor in hoof quality that doesn't get enough emphasis. Hooves grow more rapidly in the spring and summer and require more frequent trimming than the every six-to-eight-week schedule many people use. As the hoof grows forward and under the bone column, more stress is placed on the quarters and heels, predisposing to cracks, while in the forefoot the white line tends to be stretched and widened and may lose its integrity and provide an entry point for organisms. The flaring of the hoof wall away from the sole predisposes to chipping.

Flares on feet that are not properly balanced are also weak points predisposed to chipping. Shoes help protect the ground surface from chipping, but they can increase the chances of heel and quarter cracks when the foot is overgrown, since they concentrate weightbearing along the hoof wall. Movement at nail holes eventually widens them, providing an easy entry point for organisms and resulting in loosening of the shoes.

Take care to avoid over-rasping the hoof wall to smooth ridges or rings for cosmetic reasons. This strips the wall of its natural outer waxy and fatty covering, leading to excessive drying. Hoof shines and polishes, and the harsh chemicals needed to remove them, do the same thing.

Save Your Money

A number of other ingredients may show up in hoof supplements, but are of questionable, if any, benefit to your horse's hooves. Avoid paying for them, if you can. These include:

- **Vitamin A:** Rarely deficient, but added to virtually every other supplement and to grain mixes.

- **Vitamin C:** Questionable benefit for most horses, since horses manufacture their own vitamin C.

- **Silica:** It's not clear if it's even an essential mineral, but it's abundant in mature grasses, straw, and grain coats.

- **Sulfur:** The horse requires sulfur-containing amino acids, but we've found no evidence to support a further benefit from inorganic sulfur or MSM.

- **Gelatin:** While long a folk remedy for human brittle nails, there's no data to support use of gelatin for hooves. It is about 90% protein, but the only hoof-important amino acid present in high amounts is glycine, which the horse can easily synthesize. The only sulfur-containing amino acid it contains is methionine, but it would take over 3 oz. of gelatin to get just 600 mg of methionine.

Immune-System Support

Poor immune-system function puts your horse at risk for serious infections, sometimes caused by unusual and difficult-to-treat organisms.

How Can You Tell?

Routine blood tests, such as a complete blood count (CBC) and blood chemistry, won't always accurately predict how well a horse will respond to an infectious challenge, but there may be some clues that can help you determine if your horse's immune system isn't right where it belongs.

From the CBC results, look for low total white blood cell (WBC) count, low lymphocyte count, and elevated ratio of neutrophils (aka segs) to lymphocytes. Anemia may also be present.

On the blood chemistry results, low levels of globulin may be founding evidence, or the enzyme GGTP may be high normal or elevated, with other liver enzymes and liver function tests, like bilirubin, at normal levels. GGTP can be elevated as an isolated finding when the immune system is trying to fight all its battles using primitive inflammatory responses.

If the horse is an adult, fecal exam may turn up evidence of parasites not normally found in healthy adults, such as roundworms and pinworms.

There are outward changes in the horse that can tip you off too, including:

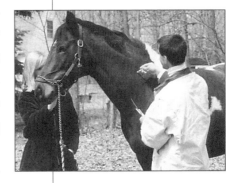

Without a vigorous immune system, your horse won't mount a good antibody response to vaccines either.

- Goopy eyes

- Increased nasal discharge

- Dry cough

- Pot belly

- Tail rubbing

- Skin infections, itching, lice

- Poor coat

Be especially suspicious of poor immune system functioning when the horse that develops these problems is the only one in the group to have them. It's easy to dismiss isolated problems as "just overly sensitive to flies," "has some allergies," "needs a deworming," etc. and not realize that they're actually symptoms pointing to poor immune system functioning.

When the horse is in poor physical condition, it's a safe bet his immunity is weak.

When immunity is weak, the horse's body is more likely to respond with exaggerated inflammatory and allergic-type reactions than with the organism-specific antibodies and killer T cells he needs to actually overcome challenges, including parasites. This in turn makes him more sensitive to environmental irritants, too.

What Can You Do?

A thorough veterinary exam is in order to determine if there is an underlying medical problem that is weakening the horse's immune response. If nothing is found, support consists of doing what you can to eliminate factors that stress his immune system and providing the nutrients the immune system needs to function well:

- If the horse is in work, back down on intensity and skip a few competitions.

- Stable the horse during periods of extreme weather, such as heat or cold and rain or snow.

- Make sure a horse on group turnout is not being bullied.

- Be sure the horse is not battling a parasite burden.

Beware Immune-Stimulant Herbs

A variety of herbs have been shown to be capable of stimulating one or more types of immune reaction. However, the arms of the immune system they stimulate aren't necessarily the ones that are underactive in horses with weakened immune systems. In fact, it often is exactly the opposite. Immune-system stimulant herbs given to otherwise healthy horses with normally functioning immune systems may help give a "wake-up call" or "red alert" that has their first-line defenses primed and ready for an infection, but this is rarely where the problem lies in horses with suppressed or weakened immune systems. Before considering these products, you need to consult with someone who is familiar with the specific immune system effects of the herbs.

Consult your vet or a nutritionist to make sure your diet is balanced and meets minimum trace mineral requirements, including selenium, and that both total protein and essential amino acid requirements are being met. Remember that both younger and older horses have increased protein needs.

Immune System Supplements

To build a horse with a strong immune system, you have to start with the basic diet. If his body doesn't have adequate levels of the tools it needs for a smoothly functioning immune system, no amount of "stimulation" is going to help. If working with a nutritionist, you will need a hay analysis and a rundown of your feeds and supplements. See the sidebar on page 156 for our best picks. The Triple Crown vitamin-and-mineral supplement line has consistently done the best job of balancing a variety of hay and grain combinations. Nothing can substitute for knowing exactly what is in your hay and balancing accordingly, but this product line has the best batting average. Use the TC10 if you know your diet is likely to have adequate protein. Otherwise, TC30 will also give you a good boost of protein and essential amino acids.

Horses exercising heavily and those stressed by illness, shipping, or injury, as well as older horses, may have increased

Horses exercising heavily may put additional stress on their immune system.

needs for antioxidant vitamins and minerals. Antioxidants help by protecting the immune system from the effects of "friendly fire" as it goes about its job of reacting to invading organisms or chemical substances. Vita-Key's Antioxidant Concentrate is our favorite in this category.

When protein quantity or quality is unknown or poor, whey protein can be a good choice. This is the highest quality, most bioavailable type of protein source. Ten to 20 grams per day will provide the horse with a good supply of essential amino acids.

Vitamin E needs to be supplemented in all equine diets, except for horses on fresh grass. This fragile vitamin is rapidly destroyed during the process of curing hay and provided in low amounts in other types of feed.

Many supplements are flaxseed-based.

Vitamin E is a critical antioxidant with immune-boosting effects. It is best absorbed when given with some fat at the same time. Uckele's Liquid E-50 is a convenient and well-priced vitamin E in oil supplement.

The immune system also relies heavily on essential fatty acids—simple fats that the horse's body is not able to manufacture and which he must get from the diet. These include the omega-3 and omega-6 fatty acids. The omega-6 fats are important to generating a robust immune response, while the omega-3s work to keep the response in check and also protect the immune system from damage. Grains, vegetable oils, brans, nuts, all seeds except flax, and (to a lesser extent) hays are all sources of omega-6 fatty acids, while only fresh grass contains appropriate levels of omega-3s. For this reason, most horses need supplemental omega-3s in the form of a ground, stabilized flaxseed product like Omega Field's Horseshine or the Horse Tech line.

A wide variety of herbs have been suggested for "supporting" immune function. Like injectable immune-stimulant drugs, they work because they activate the immune system. Most herbs are more stimulating to the primitive, inflammatory types of immune responses. Spirulina platensis, a blue-green algae, is different. It has been shown to specifically improve the production of IgG antibodies, while down-regulating allergies associated with IgA antibody responses. For recommended feeding levels, see the chart.

If your horse continues to experience problems such as frequent infections, you need to contact your veterinarian for a work up to determine possible underlying causes, and for further suggestions.

Trial 1

If your horse is otherwise healthy and you are interested in trying to keep his immune system "pumped up" so that he is better primed in the event of exposure to an infectious disease, an immune system supplement may help.

We undertook a 10-week feeding trial of immune supplement products, conducted at a busy racing and training stable with a large number of young horses in training. As always, this was a field trial with products used in real barns and under real conditions, not a scientific study. However, we were careful to avoid introducing factors that could directly affect the outcome.

Horses traveling to competitions are at high risk of exposure to infectious organisms.

All horses had been residents for at least four weeks, which allowed them to acclimate to their surroundings and diet. No vaccinations were given during or for four weeks preceding the trial. No trial horses were shipped off the premises during the study (although there was movement of other horses in the barns). Supplemented and unsupplemented horses were matched by age group (under 2 years, 2- to 3-year-olds, or 4- to 7-year-olds).

Diets used during the trial were started four weeks in advance of any supplements. Horses not in work were fed at 1.75 to 2% of body weight. Horses in training (moderate work

Recommended Immune-Boosting Products

Product	Comments
TC12 or 30 Triple Crown Feeds www.triplecrownfeed.com 800-451-9916 About $25/40 lbs.	A comprehensive vitamin, mineral, and protein supplement that consistently does the best job of balancing the widest variety of rations. Available in 12 or 30% protein.
Antioxidant Concentrate Vita-Key www.vita-key.com 800-539-8482 About $50/20 lbs.	A potent vitamin and trace mineral supplement for boosting levels of key nutrients the immune system needs to function properly and keep its cells in good repair. Best for horses that are on diets that are reasonably balanced but unsupplemented.
Whey protein concentrates or isolates (Human natural food stores) About $28.97/5 lbs.	Milk protein is well documented to help support the immune system, has a good array of essential amino acids including glutamine and lysine, and is highly digestible. Choose unflavored or vanilla varieties. Supplement from 30 to 100 grams/day, depending on protein needs.
Liquid E-50 Uckele Health and Nutrition www.uckele.com 800-248-0330 $18.95/pint	Vitamin E is easily destroyed by interaction with air, bacteria, and other ingredients in multi-ingredient mixes. For best effects, supplement E separately, 1,500 to 2,000 IU/day. This product is a concentrated source of E (2500 IU/tsp) in an oil base for best absorption. Many horses also readily consume human soft gelcaps containing vitamin E in oil.
Horseshine Omega Fields www.omegafields.com 877-663-4203 $34.95/20 lbs. **Nutra-Flax** Horse Tech www.horsetech.com 800.831.3309 $29.95/12 lbs.	Stabilized flax is a concentrated source of omega-3 essential fatty acids, needed to keep the anti-inflammatory arm of the immune system's checks and balances functioning optimally. For horses not on fresh grass, feed 4 to 6 oz./day. If the horse receives no grain, or only a highly processed feed, add 2 oz./day of rice bran as a source of omega-6 fatty acids, also very important to immune-system functioning.
Spirulina platensis Herbalcom www.herbalcom.com 888-649-3931 $13.65/lb. **Spirulina Wafers** Springtime www.springtimeinc.com 800-521-3212 $24/180 wafers **Spirulina** Horse Tech www.horsetech.com 800-831-3309 $24.95/2 lbs.	Spirulina has given us very good results in controlling sensitivities to allergens and irritants, while research in other species shows that at the same time it strengthens the immune system's ability to mount antibody responses. Also an excellent source of highly digestible protein and essential amino acids. Feed 20 grams (1 oz. by volume measure of powder or 10 wafers) twice a day to start. May be able to drop to once a day as horse improves.

level) were fed at 2.25% of body weight. Unsupplemented test horses received 14% protein (all vegetable sources) commercial sweet feed and mixed hay; some were on joint nutraceuticals and occasional electrolytes, but no other supplements were given.

All supplemented trial horses also received supplemental antioxidant vitamins and minerals (Vita-Key Antioxidant Concentrate, www.vitakey.com). This was done to ensure there were no deficiencies of key vitamins or trace minerals that could make the immune stimulating supplements less effective.

About 2.5 weeks into the supplementation period, the farm was hit by an outbreak of flu-like respiratory disease. Unfortunately, many of the products tested reported 30 days supplementation was required to reach full effect, making interpretation of results somewhat difficult. Despite this, there were measurable differences observed between the supplemented and unsupplemented horses.

Unsupplemented Horses

There were 35 unsupplemented horses. All 2- and 3-year-olds developed the respiratory disease, with fevers (up to 104°) and depressed appetite for three to five days. It took two to three weeks for symptoms to disappear, particularly coughing, despite treatment with antibiotics in several cases. Change in nasal discharge from clear to white or yellow pus was common in this group. Seven of the 35, all 2-year-olds, had coughs that persisted beyond the three-week mark.

Antioxidant Supplement Only

Three horses were supplemented with antioxidants only. All developed the disease, with high fevers for two to three days, but appetites returned after 24 to 36 hours. Nasal discharge remained clear in two of the three. A third required antibiotics after the discharge changed to yellowish. All three recovered completely in 10 days.

Antioxidant Supplement plus 50 grams/day of Whey Protein Stack (Champion Nutrition)

This group had their protein intake supplemented with highly bioavailable whey protein in addition to the vegetable protein sources. Raw whey protein has been shown to contain a variety of immune-stimulating proteins, including lactoferrin, lactalbumin, and others.

We had no way of knowing if this product (marketed as a muscle-building aid for humans) actually contained these proteins, or in what amount, but chose it because it was low-heat processed, maintaining the natural protein forms, and a high-quality protein source. Both horses in this group developed the respiratory disease with high fevers, but temperatures returned to normal by the 36-hour mark. No significant appetite loss was noted and nasal discharges remained clear. A cough lasted 8 days in one horse; 10 in the other.

High performance leads to competition between body systems for key nutrients, with the immune system often coming up short.

There is no true flu season for horses, but the combination of cold-weather stress and low intake of antioxidant foods can make winter a higher risk time of year.

Antioxidants and Actimune (ActiVet Bio Ltd)

Actimune (www.activet.com) contains IgY immuno-proteins harvested from the eggs of chickens immunized with some common equine pathogens that provide both local passive protection and also stimulate the immune system. Another key ingredient is a patented form of the bacteria Lactobacillus, which binds to harmful bacteria, neutralizes toxins, protects the gut wall, and stimulates the immune response. Also included are live yeast cultures, fermentation products from beneficial bacteria, vitamins, and minerals.

The two horses receiving Actimune were the only two that didn't become ill during this outbreak of disease. However, they were also the only two not being actively worked at the time of the outbreak. One was a yearling and the other a 3-year-old sidelined two weeks after the start of the study with a foot abscess. It is virtually impossible to say how much the stress of training influenced disease susceptibility in the other supplemented horses, compared with what was almost certainly a greater vulnerability in the yearling (the highest risk group for infectious disease) and the stress caused by the foot abscess. Four of the 35 unsupplemented horses were not being actively trained, but all developed the infection.

Trial II

The major ingredients in herbal immune-boosting products have been proven in scientific studies to have clear-cut activity on various parts of the immune response. There is no reason to think they would work differently in horses, although details of safety and dosage need to be worked out.

We field-tested a variety of rapidly acting herbal immune-stimulant products in a group of horses showing early symptoms of respiratory infection. A virus was making its way from barn to barn, causing dry coughs, low grade fevers in about 70% of affected horses, and frothy white nasal discharge. Six horses, between the ages of 2 and 5 years, were involved.

The Internal War: Barbarians and Sharp Shooters

The disease-fighting forces within the horse's body can be divided into two camps: the primitive immune system and the sophisticated immune system.

The primitive immune system's activities are about as subtle as a horde of invading barbarians. These cells include macrophages, neutrophils, and mast cells. This bloodthirsty group will savagely attack any substance—bacteria, virus, protein, etc.—that it does not recognize as belonging to the body. Invaders are attacked with destructive enzymes, exploded in reactions that involve oxygen, and engulfed by cellular death chambers where they are dissolved and spit out again. The primitive immune system is also responsible for disposing of organisms (or portions thereof) that have been tagged and bound with antibodies produced by the more sophisticated immune system.

The sophisticated immune system uses cells that are more like sharp shooters, the B and T lymphocytes. Antibodies are produced, targeting one or more components of the invader's outer wall or genetic material. This inactivates the targeted organism or foreign substance and at the same time creates a large complex of antibodies bound to the invader that is easier for the primitive immune system to recognize. This limb of the immune system also produces substances that can either enhance the overall response and stimulate the nonspecific immune cells or curb/suppress immune and inflammatory reactions.

We used products based on echinacea, a proven immunostimulant in horses. Higher recommended dosages were used. Both groups contained one 2-year-old. All four treated horses had a white, frothy nasal discharge, one had a temperature of 101.5°, and one had a spontaneous dry cough.

Both untreated horses had the same nasal discharge, but neither coughing or running fevers at the start of the test. Symptoms had been present for 24 to 36 hours. All horses were continued in light work.

The young foal's immunity gets a boost from preformed antibodies present in the mare's milk.

By 48 hours after starting treatment, all symptoms in the herbal supplement group had disappeared. Of the untreated horses, one still had the nasal discharge and seemed to tire more easily with exercise, and the other (the 2-year-old) had developed a fever (101.8°) and cough.

All treated horses continued in their training schedules without problems. The unsupplemented 2-year-olds had to be stall-rested, as exercise greatly aggravated the cough.

This was a fairly mild respiratory virus, and responses might not have been as good if the horses were being challenged by a virulent flu, but nonetheless we were impressed, especially since supplementation was not started until after early symptoms had begun to appear.

Bottom Line

The horses in our trial receiving only enhanced nutritional support (antioxidants alone or antioxidants plus high-quality protein) showed milder symptoms, fewer complications, and more rapid recovery. These results reinforce our continual recommendation that antioxidants and a high-quality diet are of particular importance to horses under stress.

Echinacea-based products also showed a clear benefit, although the virus challenging this group was not as severe.

Those receiving specific immune-stimulating products showed a tendency toward an even greater reduction in the severity of disease. Only Actimune provided full protection compared to the untreated horses when matched for age and level of stress. However, the stressors those horses were under were different from those receiving the other products, and the other products might have needed more time to reach their full effect.

It appears from our findings and available solid research that commercial immune-stimulating products do affect the immune system and may be worth the money for horses in stressful situations and heavy training or in areas with high incidence of infectious diseases.

Allergies—Too Much of a Good Thing

An allergy is an exaggerated and imbalanced immune system reaction to something in the environment that normally shouldn't cause any detectable response.

Genetics do play a role, but family history doesn't automatically mean the horse is doomed to allergies. Respiratory allergies, for example, may develop following immune system activation by a viral infection and persist long after the infection has been cleared. Nutritional factors may play a large role in determining how your horse can control allergic reactions.

Diagnostics

Allergy testing can help identify triggering substances so that you can try to avoid them and can also help identify specific allergens in order to begin desensitization injections.

Horses have access to two types of testing, intradermal injections and blood antibody tests (RAST testing). False negatives and false positives can occur with both.

False negatives are most likely when testing is done during a time when symptoms are quiet, but strong allergies are still likely to be detected at this time. Testing during an asymptomatic period can reduce the number of false positives obtained.

False positives are most likely when testing is done while the horse is actively having problems. Reactions are generally considered false positives if they aren't consistently present, or disappear as symptoms quiet down, and are believed to arise because of the overly sensitive nature of the immune system during allergy attacks. It's still helpful to identify the false positives, since avoiding those substances can help calm down the allergic responses in general.

When allergy testing does identify the major allergic triggers, a series of densensitizing injections can be helpful. However, the process of testing, formulating the injections, and administering the series is expensive and should only be done by an expert in this field.

Feed to Fight Allergies

We can make a difference for our horses by making sure they are provided with the correct nutrients, which allow the immune system to implement counterbalancing responses.

Like all body systems, the immune system has cells that both initiate inflammatory and allergic-type reactions and cells that keep those reactions in check. Unfortunately, many of the nutrients that are critical to maintenance of good anti-inflammatory responses are the ones most commonly deficient in equine diets. A normal and healthy immune system is also a balanced immune system. While it may seem counterintuitive to support the immune system if you are fighting allergies, general immune system nutritional support, as above, is beneficial. (Also see the chapter on Skin and Coat for more details.) What you do want to avoid for the most part is herbal immune stimulants, since these nonspecific immune system irritants often prime the pathways you are specifically trying to avoid.

We are impressed with the preliminary results of feeding spirulina for allergy symptom control. Horses with seasonal respiratory allergies may also benefit from additional intake of potent plant antioxidants from products like HemoCease (www.peakperformancenutrients.com, 800-944-1984) or PhytoQuench (www.uckele.com, 800-248-0330).

Alleviate Symptoms

Runny Eyes: Red, irritated, and tearing eyes are a common allergic problem in horses. Most cases are caused by insect irritation and sensitivity. Your best defense against this is simple but underused—a well-fitted fly mask. Even if there is an element of pollen sensitivity involved, simply eliminating the mechanical irritation from flies on top of that can drastically decrease the severity of the problem. Horses with pink skin around their eyes will also have an element of sun sensitivity, adding to the problem.

When tearing and irritation persist despite protection from light and insects, there's likely an element of pollen or airborne mold sensitivity. Soothe the eyes with either human eye drops or Farnam Clear Eyes (www.farnamhorse.com, 800-234-2269), or use a tuberculin (1 cc) syringe to drop sterile saline solution across the horse's eyes.

For an extra soothing effect, keep your drops or saline in the refrigerator. Store in a self-sealing plastic bag to avoid contamination of the container with refrigerator molds, which may be invisible to the eye.

COPD/Heaves/Asthma: Lung allergies are particularly difficult to control in horses because, in addition to specific allergen hypersensitivities, horses are also highly sensitive to dust, inhaled chemicals, and weather changes, such as cold or high humidity with high levels of suspended irritants. Careful attention to vitamin and mineral intake is helpful and should be maintained year round. Spirulina is certainly worth a trial. Avoid heavy exercise or other stresses at times of the year when the horse is most prone to attacks. Pelleted complete diets minimize dust exposure from feeds. Be vigilant about any types of mold, many of which you can't easily detect. Avoid dusty bedding, like straw. Shake out any hay and soak it to reduce or eliminate dust. A 30-minute soak is recommended.

Skin Problems: Most seasonal skin problems are related to insect hypersensitivities. Careful attention to diet and supplements can calm these reactions considerably. Permethrin-based chemical repellents are the most effective across the board, but reactions can develop to these, as well as to "natural-ingredient" fly sprays. Horses with sweet itch, a severe sensitivity to Culicoides bites, need special measures since the fly repellant chemicals don't faze these insects.

Use fly sheets and allow the horse free access to shelter to escape the pests. Large fans positioned to blow across, or out, doorways may discourage many flying insects.

Soothe the horse's eyes with eye drops.

Sweet Itch/Midline Dermatitis

Tiny biting insects, called Culicoides—aka biting midges, no-see-ums—cause a lot of misery for many horses and ponies. Icelandic ponies are particularly prone to the problem, but no breed is safe. Symptoms are raw, open, oozing, and extremely itchy areas along the under-surface of the belly, and/or excessive mane or tail itching, also sometimes with open, oozing areas. These tor-menters are particularly diffi-cult to control since they virtually ignore regular fly/mosquito sprays. However, they are stopped by mechani-cal barriers and find camphor and phenol particularly offen-sive. The recipe for a repellent and soothing formula we've found particularly effective is below. It's also effective for other tiny insect pests, like chiggers.

Sweet-Itch Remedy: Mix ¼ teaspoon of the human product Campho-Phenique (available in drug stores) and ¼ teaspoon of Calm Coat (www. calmcoat.com, 888-396-0004) into a 13 oz. jar of petroleum jelly (Vaseline or a generic). The petroleum jelly provides a barrier, while the Campho-Phenique is a bar-rier, repellent, anesthetic/dis-infectant. Calm Coat is thick, providing a barrier, soothing essential oils, and repellent action. Generously apply to the affected areas two to three times a day or any time the horse becomes itchy.

Food Allergies

The role of food allergies in equine allergic symptoms is poorly understood. Although allergy testing often shows reactions to hays and grains, there are no good studies regarding the responses horses might have to foods.

In people, food allergies can cause immediate, life-threatening anaphylactic reactions, including throat swelling, or less severe, chronic symptoms, which include respiratory problems, watery eyes, skin eruptions and/or itching, or digestive upset, nausea, or diarrhea.

It's also known from research with other species that a history of any type of allergy, including inhalant allergies (e.g., to pollens or molds) increases the risk for having food allergies as well.

When a horse with seasonal allergies turns up as positive for a grain or hay type that is fed year round, odds are this is either a false positive or a sensitivity that has arisen because the primary allergy has made him more reactive in general. Either way, the wisest course of action is to avoid any foods that test positive, at least when the horse is actively fighting allergy symptoms.

Obviously, if your horse's hay and/or grain haven't changed when summer arrives, these aren't likely to be a major factor, but sensitivity to something in the pasture could be.

If you're fairly certain your horse's skin reactions aren't insect-related, try turning him out with a muzzle that prohibits grazing for a few days to see if it makes a difference. This would indicate an allergy to a plant in the field. 🐴

15

Joint Support

Horse Journal published the results of its first joint nutraceutical trial in November 1997. There has been literally an explosion of joint supplement products over the ensuing 10 years, and each trial we have done includes more products, with more ingredients and in different combinations.

Competition among manufacturers for a niche in this product category is fierce. When we first started field trials, products were limited to the flagship combination product Cosequin, or individual ingredient products containing glucosamine, chondroitin, or Perna mussel. Before too long, Nutramax, the manufacturer of Cosequin, decided it was too costly and time-consuming to attempt to track down and prosecute all the other equine combination products that were surfacing. Since then, the number of products has sky rocketed, and hyaluronic acid has joined the ranks of active oral ingredients.

The first trial we did of oral hyaluronic acid featured the pioneering product Conquer gel. Responses were very impressive. (See sidebar on page 176 for those results.) Next, we decided to see what benefits might be obtained by adding hyaluronic acid (HA) to an existing joint supplement product. This trial was not designed to oust the basics of glucosamine, Perna and chondroitin sulfate. If your horse is doing well on his current supplement, there's no reason to change it. In fact, your best bet remains to try the simplest, most cost-effective product first. That may well be Corta-Flx, a plain glucosamine, one with supportive ingredients, like Grand Flex, or any combination of

How Do They Work?

Hyaluronic acid seems to offer its major effect as a barrier, preventing substances like fibronectin from gaining access to the cartilage cells and triggering breakdown (*Osteoarthritis Cartilage,* September 1997).

Reports also continue to mount that the combination of glucosamine with chondroitin is more effective than either one alone, at least under laboratory conditions.

Using the same experimental model of a fragment of fibronectin triggering cartilage breakdown, a study published in the March 2006 issue of *Osteoarthritis Cartilage* found that the combination, at levels that can be achieved in the blood after oral intake, was effective in blocking or reversing cartilage breakdown and also in stimulating healing, while the individual agents alone showed only a mild anti-inflammatory effect.

basic joint ingredients. If that's not enough, you're going to want to go further. That's where our information will help you.

This trial was interesting, to say the least. We used horses within a wide range of ages and activity levels, comparing responses to those observed with prior supplements, as well as multiple products used with one horse. Each product was used on three to 14 horses for a duration of one to six weeks. Problems included arthritis, acute and chronic synovitis, OCD, and other joint problems. For details of the results, see the table on page 178. (Note: Some of these products may no longer be available, or may have changed their ingredients since the time of this trial. We're including them in their form at that time for historical purposes.)

We then assessed the results by considering expected and unexpected improvements and the horses' overall environments and histories.

All the oral HA products consistently performed well. The gels and liquids gave faster results than the powders and, in some cases, the results were also stronger. The response to the gels was somewhat better than to the liquids. However, it's not

Not a Cure-All

Joint nutraceuticals are effective for a wide range of problems, including OCD, early to advanced degenerative arthritis, and certain back problems that may involve changes in the joints that allow movement of the spine. Since joint nutraceuticals only directly address problems related to joint cartilage, incomplete responses or failures may be related to the exact pathology involved.

For example, a horse experiencing pain related to osteophyte formation around a joint or joint fractures or dislocations will continue to have this problem. Muscular spasm or pain, ligamentous pain, or pain related to chips of bone or cartilage or cartilage flaps will also be unchanged. Accurate diagnosis of all components contributing to pain is essential to matching the treatment program to the horse.

clear if this was because there was less chance with the thicker gels of a portion of the supplement being spit out or leaking out than with the liquids.

This kind of light, effortless movement is only possible with pain-free joints.

Many horses also responded extremely well to combination products without HA. We saw solid improvements with Absorbine Flex+, In Motion, Lubron Plus, and Matrix 4 that were extremely close to those obtained with straight oral HA.

We also found that when we added HA to any of the glucosamine/chondroitin/Perna combinations, we got an even better response. In fact, the greatest improvement in lameness grades was clearly with Chondrogen EQ, a product that combines glucosamine, chondroitin, HA, and manganese, although we're not sure the manganese is a factor in its success.

To evaluate the effect of adding HA to your present supplement plan, try purchasing a small supply of an HA gel; use it at ¼ to ½ of the recommended dose for one to two weeks to see if you get further improvement. If so, consider adding HA.

Glucosamine Sulfate versus Chloride

The battle rages on concerning whether glucosamine hydrochloride (HCl) or glucosamine sulfate is preferred. The sulfur is important to the formation of strong cross-bridges in connective tissue, but there's no evidence that the horse requires sulfur in any form other than the sulfur containing amino acids in protein. No studies definitely prove glucosamine sulfate has a better clinical effect than glucosamine hydrochloride. We didn't see a difference either. You get more glucosamine per ounce with the chloride form, and some horses are more reluctant to eat the sulfate.

Choosing a Joint Supplement

With so many products on the market now, with a wide variety of ingredients, it's difficult to know which one to choose. What works well for one horse may not for another. Several factors should be taken into consideration when trying to decide if you should use a joint supplement at all and, if so, which is most likely to help.

- Stage of disease: A horse with advanced arthritis, including loss of cartilage and poor fluid production (seen on X-rays as a narrowed joint space and denser bone around the joint) and/or one with extensive buildup of bone around the joint, isn't going to respond as well or as quickly as one with early arthritic changes.

  However, joint nutraceuticals may be able to help halt progression of the disease and improve joint fluid production. A horse like this may also benefit from an anti-inflammatory or analgesic herbal product or a joint supplement that contains these ingredients.

- Cause of the problem: When joint problems are caused, or aggravated, by conformation defects, when poor hoof trimming causes uneven loading of the joints, or if there is soft-tissue damage to stabilizing ligaments or other

Devil's claw is an herbal anti-inflammatory.

Beyond the Basic Ingredients

In our October 2003 issue, we targeted a few "specialty" products for joints that went beyond the usual chondroitin, glucosamine, hyaluronic acid, or Perna. Cutting inflammation, blocking cartilage breakdown, and supporting healing are the cornerstones of a nutraceutical approach to arthritis treatment. The four products in this field trial address one or more of these concerns in a new way.

Results

We tried **EquuSea** supplementation first on horses with chronic arthritic conditions. Most were already on, or had been on glucosamine and/or chondroitin, but with residual pain and stiffness. In every case, there was decreased lameness, more spontaneous movement, and better mobility. The response was rated as equivalent to one to two grams of phenylbutazone in every case. Time to response was from two days to two weeks. Two of the horses had been tried on MSM and hadn't responded.

Next, we tackled acute inflammation. These cases ranged from synovitis to acute worsenings of chronic conditions. Again we saw an obvious response, with improvement noted in two to five days. Compared to bute, the response took longer and the pain control was not as good. However, the resolution of swelling and heat was equivalent to bute. Plus, EquuSea's high palatability was a pleasant surprise, given its sea-based ingredients, which horses often object to in feed tubs.

Recovery packs the strongest punch in terms of glucosamine, chondroitin, and MSM at recommended dosages of any joint supplement we have seen—double the loading dose of other products. It's therefore no surprise that it performed well with arthritic horses, even at half dose.

To find out if the addition of the plant polyphenols and the MSM were enhancing the response, we compared improvements to Recovery vs. improvements with glucosamine and MSM alone.

One mare with arthritic hocks and ankle and back pain showed equivalent pain response to glucosamine alone in her joints, and no added benefit with MSM. However, with Recovery, she had a noticeable decrease in joint effusion and the back pain also responded partially.

A three-year-old with arthritic changes in both knees and one fetlock improved more than one lameness grade with glucosamine alone and had no further improvement adding MSM. He was sound on Recovery, deteriorating again when taken off of it. He became sound when restarted on Recovery.

A nine-year-old mare with suspected autoimmune-related arthritis responded about the same to high-dose glucosamine and MSM as she did to being on Recovery.

An 18-year-old gelding with multiple arthritic joints had a significantly better response to Recovery than he did to just equivalent doses of glucosamine and MSM. Improvement held at the maintenance dose.

A 25-year-old mare with marked lameness and extensive ringbone showed better response to Recovery than to equivalent doses of glucosamine and MSM alone, decreased overall stiffness, and more time moving around, but still noticeably lame.

Rapid Response makes a wide range of claims. We found the time to a response in common arthritic joint conditions was longer than with many joint supplements, taking one to two weeks. We didn't find results notably different than that obtained with glucosamine and/or chondroitin supplements in terms of pain and movement in the involved joints.

However, one filly, retired from racing because of a severe ankle arthritis with beginning fusion, responded extremely well to Rapid

Response, better than to glucosamine or Adequan. We also noted that horses on Rapid Response all tended to move significantly more freely overall after two weeks or so on this supplement.

We also had excellent responses with back pain that hadn't been responsive to regular joint supplements. Several youngsters that had been on Adequan for months for stifle or ankle OCD turned the corner rapidly when put on Rapid Response. In fact, the cysts resolved, according to radiographs. How much of this was related to time and repeated Adequan treatments finally working couldn't be determined, but the impression was that Rapid Response had made a difference.

Some of the most dramatic responses came in horses with ringbone that had been lame for months to years and unresponsive to anything except pain medications. The X-ray changes were at least arrested and, in several cases, the excess bone decreased on radiographs.

An incidental observation in a mare being given Rapid Response for multiple joint problems and back pain was that a large callus of bone at the site of a kick sustained a year before began to shrink after about two weeks. After four weeks, it was gone.

A common thread was that this product appeared to be effective in degenerative conditions that involved the bone rather than just cartilage. A Thoroughbred with a severe sesamoid fracture sustained as a foal became pasture sound after a year on Rapid Response and will soon attempt training, although the fracture remains unchanged on X-ray.

A horse with a navicular cyst, wide fracture line, and extensive navicular demineralization, for whom euthanasia was recommended, was slow to respond but after seven months had complete filling-in of the cyst with bone and only a narrow fracture line remaining.

At this point, he had improved from grade 4 (worse) to grade 1 (mild) lameness at the walk and was trotting comfortably in a straight line. Whether either of these horses can return to formal use remains to be seen, but even this level of improvement would normally not be expected.

Another added benefit of Rapid Response is control of gastric-ulcer symptoms. One horse with diagnosed gastric ulcers and one suspected on the basis of clinical signs returned to normal eating within 18 to 24 hours of beginning Rapid Response.

The manufacturer recommends simultaneous topical and oral use. We found the product difficult to work with topically. Oversoftening of the skin, requiring leaving the leg open for a while, commonly occurs. Testers who couldn't wrap or gave up on wrapping seemed to have equivalent results by increasing the oral dose, essentially giving the same amount they'd have used on the leg orally. We can't rule out benefits from local application as well, though.

The response to **Joint Saver** was typical of a good glucosamine/chrondroitin product, with improvements in three to five days. However, we didn't find any notably better response to Joint Saver than these same horses had to plain glucosamine and chondroitin supplements.

Bottom Line

Recovery was our favorite overall with respect to arthritis since, even at maintenance doses, it packs the same punch in terms of glucosamine and MSM as loading doses of other joint products. Its price at this level of use is comparable. On the other hand, Rapid Response is expensive. That said, it's the best we found in conditions like ringbone that involve proliferation of bone. It's also the only joint product we've used that gave good results with back pain. It also proved helpful with two fractures and severe, refractory OCD.

EquuSea is a good alternative to NSAIDs for chronic inflammation. Use it alone or with glucosamine/chondroitin for more joint support.

For further details, see the table on page 178.

internal joint structures, joint supplements may provide a bit of relief, but it's not realistic to expect much effect from joint-specific nutraceuticals alone.

- Use of the horse: This can be a significant factor when it comes to both types of products and dosages. Lower-dose ranges for glucosamine and chondroitin may provide enough effect for horses not in work, but those being used regularly and heavily usually need more. Nonworking horses or those in light work are also more likely to respond well to simple glucosamine, while a multi-ingredient product may be the best choice for a working horse.

- Active inflammation: If the condition is acute, or the horse is prone to flare-ups with heat and swelling, a product with high-dose MSM, hyaluronic acid, or anti-inflammatory herbs (boswellia is excellent) will probably work best.

Hyaluronic Acid

One of the most recent additions to joint choices is hyaluronic acid, also known simply as HA. There is much to be learned about exactly what HA does in an arthritic joint and how it interacts with other joint nutraceuticals. In this field trial, we observed a clear benefit with liquid or gel forms of HA versus powders in controlling acutely inflamed joints. The liquids or gels are effective at ½ to ¼ the amount required for powdered HA. However, even relatively small amounts of HA used in combination with glucosamine/chondroitin can make a significant difference.

The question always comes up regarding whether any joint nutraceutical can even survive digestion and be absorbed into the body. While there are no studies available on the extent of absorption of hyaluronic acid, it's known that HA makes a good carrier for the delivery of medications through the skin.

Pay Attention to Labels

Not all joint supplements are created equal and there can be substantial differences in potency, even between products from the same manufacturer. Joint nutraceuticals can vary widely in the amount of active ingredient they provide per recommended dose. Sometimes, we believe, recommended doses may be listed at the lowest possible effective levels in an attempt to reduce the daily cost of the supplement. They also may not take into account your horse's weight, especially if you have a big warmblood or draft cross.

We recommend you read all product labels closely. If the amounts aren't provided per dose in milligrams, do the math to figure out what you really need to be feeding. The daily dosages we list in our chart on page 175 are per 500 to 550 lbs. of body weight and are those we found to be the most effective in our field trials. Adjust up or down according to your horse's or pony's weight. If your horse weighs 1,000 pounds (get out the weight-measuring tape), you'll need to double our recommendations.

Remember, too, that horses in regular work that involves heavy joint stress—such as upper-level dressage, eventing, endurance, combined driving, jumping, roping, reining, or cutting—may need to be maintained on the full/loading dose for best effect.

Older, retired horses that are in no work/complete turnout may respond to lower doses than younger, active ones. However, older horses that are worked may require the highest doses. What's considered light work for a young horse can actually be stressful for older horses, both in terms of fatigue and how much arthritic joints can take without worsening. This comment isn't to discourage working older horses, of course. Exercise is extremely beneficial to them. You just need to understand their limits and increased needs.

Most effective combination products are those that contain a full, recommended dosage of at least one ingredient, which is usually glucosamine.

Chondroitin Fights Inflammation

A published article (*J of Eq Vet Sci*, Vol 18, No 10, 1998) showed chondroitin sulfate in distilled water (identical to Arthroglycan) at a dose of 2,500 mg/day to be effective in protecting cartilage and controlling inflammation in an experimentally induced model of noninfectious arthritis. A unique property of chondroitin is its ability to reduce the activity of destructive enzymes within an inflamed joint. Although the arthritis created in this study was quite severe and not typical of naturally occurring disease, the findings suggest that chondroitin would be an effective addition to the treatment plan of acute arthritis problems where heat, increased production of joint fluid, and joint-fluid abnormalities, including significantly elevated protein levels and cell counts, are found.

Our Trial

For our 2005 trial we used horses of a variety of ages and uses. Acutely inflamed joints, either new conditions or flare-ups of old ones, were examined daily for five days to check for any effects.

Horses with chronic conditions were all affected enough that they were consistently lame. Lameness was graded according to the American Association of Equine Practitioners (AAEP) grading scale. Horses were graded by a veterinarian before starting the supplements, at two weeks, and at four weeks. Trainers and owners were instructed to keep a log of changes observed between examinations.

Note: Results may vary with different horses. As always, if your current product is working, there's no reason to switch.

Bottom Line

Although pain relief is slower to occur with glucosamine than the newer combination products, it remains an excellent economical option. Glucosamine doesn't have a significant effect on active inflammatory processes, so this must be dealt with

Horse Journal Dosage Recommendations

Amounts listed are per 500 to 550 pounds of bodyweight, meaning a 1,000- to 1,100-pound horse requires twice the amounts.

Ingredient	Loading Dose	Maintenance Dose	Combination Products*
Glucosamine	5,000 mg	2,500 mg	1,250 to 2,500 mg
Chondroitin sulfate	3,750 mg	1,875 mg	500 to 1,000 mg
Hyaluronic acid	50 mg	25 mg	10 to 25 mg

* Combination products are those that contain more than one of the listed joint-supplement ingredients.

separately in acutely inflamed joints. However, regular continued use can inhibit future inflammation.

Added ingredients like antioxidant vitamins and yucca typically take longer to reach full effect than plain glucosamine, so further improvement may be noted beyond the four-week mark in products that include these ingredients. However, we expect to see improvement within 14 days of starting a product. If you don't, consider changing products.

When trying your horse on joint supplements for the first time, go with a no-frills, basic glucosamine or glucosamine/chondroitin combination. Uckele's plain glucosamine products are the least expensive we saw, followed by Joint Renew, a pure glucosamine sulfate, from Peak Performance. Grand Flex, from Grand Meadows, remains a top economical choice, given the addition of important trace minerals and antioxidants.

For a combination glucosamine/chondroitin product, Foxden Flex gets the nod at $1.38 per day for a high-dose treatment. Corta-Flx, now with added HA, remains an excellent choice.

Another option is to move up to a combination product that offers more in terms of antioxidant protection, such as the high potency but well-priced Senior Flex, $1.78 per day at a high dose.

For the really tough problems, or to maintain status quo, in regularly working horses, you want a stronger performer. After narrowing down the best products, we looked at price, and Lube All Plus is most the economical.

Regular use of joint supplements can reduce lameness-related vet bills.

Conquer Is Impressive

It's available over the counter and administered the same way you do a paste dewormer.

A relative newcomer to the scene is Conquer from Kinetic Technologies (www.kinetictech. net, 877/786-9882, $14/three-dose tube). This product is an oral hyaluronic acid (HA) given at 100 mg/day. By comparison, intravenous Legend is a 40 mg dose, and the usual intra-articular dose of hyaluronate is 20 mg. Conquer is a lightly apple-flavored gel that administers in daily 10 cc doses, is well accepted, and is available over the counter.

A controlled study of Conquer looked at weanlings with spontaneously occurring moderate synovitis of the fetlocks. The weanlings were dosed with 100 mg/day (approximate average weight 400 lbs., so this is double the dose recommended for small horses) and kept on usual turnout and management, without other treatments or drugs. Response was excellent compared to untreated controls, with resolution of symptoms occurring as rapidly as one week.

Impressed with the idea of an oral HA, we tried Conquer on a 2-year-old in race training with evidence of synovitis in multiple joints, a 3-year-old with a check ligament inflammation, a 9-year-old racehorse with chronic arthritic problems, and a retired aged show horse with multiple arthritic joints.

The check ligament didn't respond, but we didn't expect it to, since even injectable HA is of no real benefit with tendon/ligament injuries.

The other three horses showed good-to-excellent response with clear benefit by the end of the first week and maximal benefit after two weeks of 100 mg/day.

They were then tried on reduced maintenance dosing of every other day. The 2-year-old, who had become completely sound after one week on Conquer, maintained the benefit on alternate-day dosing for the next three weeks. He'd been treated before the Conquer with three doses of Legend and had responded well but not completely. Two weeks after the third Legend dose, he was back to the same condition, at which time we tried Conquer.

The 9-year-old didn't hold her improvement on alternate-day dosing. In addition, when the speed of her workouts increased, she showed some heat and filling the day after. However, double-dose Conquer the day before and day of the speed work eliminated the heat-and-filling problem.

The retired horse maintained his improvement on the alternate-day therapy, but we weren't able to stretch it to once every three days.

After five weeks on Conquer—two weeks at full dose, three weeks at alternate-day dose—the 2-year-old's supplementation was stopped and he had no further problems. Both the 9-year-old and the aged horse did regress to their original condition within three weeks of stopping Conquer. The 2-year-old and the 9-year-old had been treated previously with Legend and were already on joint nutraceuticals.

We found the overall response to oral Conquer every bit as good as intravenous HA, and it was well-tolerated. In addition, we believe it has potential as a good follow-up to a joint injection.

When more direct pain relief from herbals is needed, our pick is Arthrigen, with a full spectrum of cartilage-specific nutraceuticals, as well as devil's claw and antioxidants. Finally, for complex problems involving soft tissue other than joint lining or cartilage, Artri Matrix and Rapid Response are worth a try.

Acutely inflamed joints are a special problem, and in this situation HA excels. Results with liquids and gels were clearly superior to the powders in quieting down hot, swollen joints. Lube All or its multi-ingredient companion product, Lube All Plus, are the most economical options, but all the HA gels performed well, as did the high-potency powder HA, Celadrin.

We subject our horses' joints to many unnatural stresses.

There are still some skeptics who don't believe joint nutraceuticals help, but these products are definitely more than just trendy. Their overwhelming acceptance and use by owners and trainers is a testimony to their effectiveness. Our own trials have shown overwhelming effectiveness as well. Among the benefits are:

- Decrease in stiffness
- Improved freedom of movement
- Improved lameness scores
- Reduced joint heat and swelling
- Reduction in the number of horses that actually require injectable joint products for control of symptoms, and greatly increased intervals between those injections when oral joint supplements are used

Maintaining normal joint flexibility is essential to the horse being able to perform safely and well.

Liquids versus Powders

Liquid is "in" for supplements. It offers more flexibility in feeding than powders. Horses on plain grain mixes (without molasses) can be more easily supplemented with a liquid, as it adheres better to the grain. Horses on hay only can be treated by oral syringe. You could even spray it on the hay, but unless the horse enjoys the taste and will actively seek out the treated hay, you are likely to end up with some waste and erratic dosing this way.

Joint Nutraceuticals Field Trials

Note: The "improvement grade" is based on the AAEP lameness scale.

Product	Price	Ingredients	Comments
Absorbine Flex+ Absorbine www.absorbine-animal.com 800-628-9653	$41.39/5 lbs. $1.17/day maintenance. $2.34/day loading.	Per 64-gram dose: Stabilized rice bran 57.432 grams, glucosamine sulfate 2,460 mg, N-acetyl glucosamine 780 mg, MSM 780 mg, yucca powder 3,300 mg.	Results were similar to straight HA, although we used a higher dose than the label recommended to maintain effect in three out of four horses. Average lameness grade improvement was 1.
Chondrogen EQ Kinetic Technologies www.kinetictech.net 877-786-9882	$59/50 doses. $1.18/day maintenance. $2.36/day loading.	Per dose: Glucosamine sulfate 5,000 mg, chondroitin sulfate 500 mg, hyaluronic acid 20 mg, manganese sulfate 20 mg.	The degree of improvement in our trial horses was strongest with this product, at 1.5+. Although two trial horses didn't respond at all, both also didn't respond to intravenous or intra-articular hyaluronic acid. They responded to intra-articular corticosteroids.
Hylarin B Uckele www.uckele.com, 800-248-0330 OR MVP, www.unitedvetequine.com 800-328-6652	Gel $11/30 cc. $23.95/80 cc. $3/dose. Powder $82.50/300 grams. $2.75/dose.	Gel per 10-ml dose: 125 mg sodium hyaluronate, 500 mg boswellia. Powder per 10-gram dose: 125 mg sodium hyaluronate, 500 mg boswellia.	Average time to response with the gel was six days, with the powder 10 days. Some deterioration in improvement noted in four horses when switched from gel to powder. Overall movement in laminitic horses improved. Good additive effect noted in horses on glucosamine/chondroitin combinations. Average lameness grade improvement was 1+.
Hyla Rx gel or liquid Select The Best www.selectthebest.com 800-648-0950	Gel $14.95/60 cc or $2.49/day Liquid $59.95/gal. or 94¢/day.	Gel: Sodium hyaluronate 100 mg/10 cc Liquid: Sodium hyaluronate 100 mg/2 oz.	Initial response time was about six days. Additive effect when combined with other joint supplements. Laminitic horses moved better overall, likely due to secondary joint-pain relief. Average lameness improvement was 1.
In Motion 4 Equine Therapy www.4equinetherapy.com 866-321-0665	$60/2 lbs. $1.88/day maintenance. $3.75/day loading.	Per oz.: MSM 10,000 mg, vitamin C 5,000 mg, glucos. HCL 2,500 mg, glucos. sulfate 2,500 mg, devil's claw 2,320 mg, chondr. sulfate 1,750 mg, manganese 480 mg, lysine 400 mg.	Excellent response in the active dressage/cross-country horse and held on maintenance dose. Obvious, but not complete, response in the racehorses, which also required continued loading dose. Good additive effect with HA. Average lameness improvement was 1.
Lube All and Lube All Plus Equi-Aide Products www.equiaide.com 800-413-3702	Lube All $48.95/16 oz. $3.05/day. Lube All-Plus. $66.95/16 oz. $4.18/day.	Lube All: 100 mg sodium hyaluronate/oz (liquid). Lube All Plus: 100 mg sodium hyaluronate/oz. (liquid), 4,000 mg MSM, 2,500 mg glucosamine sulfate, 400 mg chondroitin sulfate.	Response at 7-10 days. Additive response using Lube All with glucosamine/chondroitin powders. Superior response with Lube All Plus, including in horses switched from Lube All to Lube All Plus. Average improvement was 1+ with Lube All; a bit more with Lube All Plus.
Lubron and Lubron Plus Uckele Health and Nutrition www.uckele.com 800-248-0330	Lubron $34.95/240 grams. 58¢ to $1.16/day. Lubron Plus: $54.95/2 lbs. 92¢ to $1.84/day.	Lubron per 8 g dose: Glucos. HCL 3,000 mg, glucos. sulfate 3000 mg, chond. sulfate 2,000 mg. Lubron Plus per 30 g dose: glucos. HCL 3,500 mg, glucos. sulfate 3,500 mg, chond. sulf. 2,500 mg, boswellia 500 mg, yucca extract 3000 mg, grapeseed ex. 1,000 mg, pyridoxine 50 mg, panto-thenic acid 50 mg, ascorbic acid 1,000 mg.	One lameness grade improvement with both products. Average time to first improvement with Lubron was eight to 10 days. Average time with Lubron Plus was three to six days. Good additive effect with oral HA.
Matrix-4 MVP www.unitedvetequine.com 800-328-6652	$108/ 4 lbs. $1.68/day maintenance. $3.36/day loading.	Per ounce: Glucos. sulfate 5,000 mg, chond. sulfate 1,800 mg, MSM 11,652 mg, Ester-C 3,200 mg, yucca 1,325 mg, copper chelate 30 mg, zinc chelate 140 mg, manganese 100 mg, vitamin E 200 IU.	Response of at least one full lameness grade in all horses except one that also didn't respond to intra-articular hyaluronic acid. The average time to first obvious improvement was 10 days.
Maximum Strength Natural Flex Vets Plus www.horsesprefer.com 800-468-3877	$23.50/1 lb. $1.47/day maintenance. $2.94/day loading.	Per oz: Glucosamine HCL 1,820 mg, chondroitin sulfate 160 mg, Perna mussel 2,500 mg, manganese ascorbate 75 mg, biotin.	Improvement varied with horses, with one achieving 1.5 improvement on the lameness scale and the others 0.5. The average time to first response was three weeks. The label doses are on the low side in this supplement, so you may need more time to get a full effect.
Senior Flex MVP www.unitedvetequine.com, 800-328-6652	$69.75/5 lbs. $.83/day maintenance. $1.63/day loading.	Per ounce: Glucosamine sulfate 5,000 mg, chondroitin sulfate 500 mg, MSM 3,000 mg, Ester-C 1,200 mg, yucca 5,500 mg, vitamin A 15,000 IU, vitamin D 5,000 IU, vitamin E 1,000 IU.	Mild improvement initially, then leveled off after 2 to 3 weeks. Test horses were seniors, the least-active group. Their little formal exercise likely influenced the results when compared to the products used on active horses. Average improvment was 0.5.
Trilube, Uckele www.uckele.com 800-248-0330	$64.95/2 lbs. $1.22/dose.	Per 17-gram dose: MSM 10,000 mg, chondroitin sulfate 2,000 mg, glucosamine hydrochloride 5,000 mg.	Average improvement was almost 1. One horse showed no difference, one was better because of the MSM, and one didn't respond until HA was added.

The New-Generation Joint Choices

Product	Ingredients	Form/ Palatability	Comments
EquuSea, Coastside Bio Resources, www.seacucumber. com, 800-732-8072, $70/7 lbs., one-month supply	Per dose: Sea chondroitin (patented preparation sea cucumber extract) 15 grams, MSM 1 gram, kelp 2 grams (providing approximately 1.4 mg iodine).	Pellet/Excel-lent.	MSM dose is low, more in line with natural intakes of a horse on pasture than therapeutic levels. According to product patent information, the specially prepared sea cucumber extract in this product reportedly gave significant clinical/subjective improvement in people taking it for a variety of arthritic conditions in uncontrolled trials. Marked anti-inflammatory effect, equivalent or superior to corticosteroids, was documented in the laboratory using two standard models of chemically induced inflammation. Proliferative capacity of rheumatoid arthritis cells was greatly reduced.
JointSaver, Figuerola Laboratories, www. figuerola-labs.com, 800-219-1147, 3 lbs. $149.99, approximately 2-month supply at full dose	Per 2 scoops: Glucosamine hydrochloride and low molecular weight chondroitin sulfate (10 grams each), MSM 5 grams, SAM-e 200 mg, collagen complex including cartilage matrix glycoprotein, vitamins E/A/C, trace minerals.	Powder/Fair to poor.	Product is recommended to be given on an empty stomach, so consider dosing this as a paste made with water, juice, or apple-sauce. Contains recognized therapeutic doses of glucosamine and chondroitin, with chondroitin in the more highly bioavailable low-molecular-weight form, low-dose MSM, low-dose SAM-e for a horse, good vitamin and mineral levels. Dosage of the collagen complex/matrix glycoprotein is low compared to other products and on a metabolic body weight basis for the horse.
Rapid Response, Amerdon, www.amerdon.com, 800-331-1036 $149.95, approximately a 2- to 4-week supply	Aloe and other plant sources of mono- and polysaccha-rides, proanthocyanidins, glucosamine, papaine, complex carbohydrates from inulin, vitamins A/D/E/B, naturally occurring mineral levels.	Thick, almost "chunky" liquid-gel/ Excellent.	The details of this formula are proprietary and can't be released, but ingredients are nontoxic and nothing is present in amounts that would interfere with dietary balance. For details of potential actions of the ingredients, see sidebar on page 11. For details of recom-mended wrapping methods for local applications, any questions during use, and assistance with individualization of dosage, contact the manufacturer.
Recovery, Biomedica Labs, www. biomedicalabs.com, 866-334-2463 $79.95/kg, 25-day sup-ply at full dose for a 1,000-lb. horse	Per scoop (dose of one scoop/600 lbs): 750 mg of plant polyphenols in-cluding epigallocatechin gallate, proanthocyanidin, epicatechin, resveratrol. Glucosamine HCl 10 grams, DMG 1,000 mg, MSM 10 grams, vitamins C/E, magne-sium, and zinc.	Fine powder/ Good to fair.	Very high levels of glucosamine at the full therapeutic dose (e.g. 20 grams/1,200-lb. horse). Therapeutic level of MSM. Excellent plant polyphenol levels. Note: Product cakes easily because it does not contain any anticaking agents and is hydroscopic. High level of MSM may have limited palatability to some extent, but all test horses did consume it in their feed after some initial hesitation.

Liquids also are absorbed more quickly, but this is only if the liquid is taken on an empty stomach. Large volumes of fluid are able to pass quickly through the stomach, even if it contains grain or hay, but an ounce or two of fluid will not trigger this bypass, especially if it is absorbed onto the hay or grain before the horse eats it.

Finally, a 1998 Italian study demonstrated that chondroitin sulfate is absorbed more quickly and more efficiently when it is dissolved in a liquid instead of encapsulated. The amount actually absorbed, however, was still relatively low (18% for rats, 12% for humans).

A variety of joint nutraceuticals and herbal anti-inflammatories are available to help the horse with joint problems.

Disadvantages

Liquids aren't perfect. They are definitely messier than powders. Residues in the feed tub will support bacterial growth and fermentation more readily, especially in hot weather. If you use a liquid and your horse does not lick his tub clean, cleaning and rinsing between each feeding is a must.

Liquid formulas as a general rule are also less stable than powders and therefore have a shorter shelf life. Stability in liquid is known for some forms of minerals, but not for chondroitin or glucosamine. Other ingredients, like antioxidant vitamins (e.g. Ester-C), may also be less stable in liquid form, and minerals may interact more easily in liquid formulations.

The tricks with liquid supplements are to buy only what you can use in about 30 days, keep them out of the sun and temperature extremes, and never buy a supplement that looks like it has been sitting around for a long time. In fact, it doesn't hurt to ask when the shipment containing your supplement came in or look for a lot number and check with the manufacturer regarding how old the bottle is. (These guidelines are also important with powder supplements or any feed, for that matter.) 🐎

Joint Nutraceuticals

Product	Price	Cost per day/ high dose	Comments	Best For
Acti-Flex 4000 Cox Veterinary Laboratories www.acti-flex.com 803-581-4747	Liquid $26.50/qt. (32 days at low dose, 16 days at high dose) $58.50/5 lbs. powder (80 days at low dose, 40 days at high dose)	$1.46	Low (maintenance) to moderate (loading) levels of glucosamine, chondroitin, MSM, SOD, boswellia, vitamin C. Improvements of up to 1.5 lameness grades in chronic conditions within the first week. Liquid works faster. Horses in moderate to heavy work continued to require the higher dosage level to maintain their improvements. Some reduction in heat and swelling in acutely inflamed joints noted within 3 to 5 days with the liquid.	Chronic conditions that do not respond well to chondroitin/glucosamine alone, up to moderate levels of inflammation.
Adult Flex Vapco www.vapco.com 800-523-5614	Powder $62.99/4 lbs. (64 days low dose, 32 days high dose)	$1.97	Moderate levels of glucosamine and chondroitin, high MSM, vitamin C and bromelain with low levels of magnesium and trace minerals. At loading doses (2 oz.), improvements of 1 to 1.5 lameness grades at the 2-week mark in horses with chronic arthritis at no, low to moderate levels of work. Improvements held at lower doses in horses not in work, while those being used continued to require the higher doses for the same control. Improvement of up to 1 lameness grade in high-performance horses.	Horses in up to moderate work not responsive to chondroitin/glucosamine alone.
Advance HA Peak Performance Nutrients www.peakperformance nutrients.com 800-944-1984	Powder $72.99/lb. (60 days at low dose, 30 days at double dose)	$2.43	Moderate dose glucosamine, vitamin C and hyaluronic acid, with anti-inflammatory effects from boswellia, bioflavonoids, also glutamine and trace minerals. Improvement of 1.5 to 2 lameness grades by 1 to 2 weeks, including 2 horses that did not respond well to full dose glucosamine. The lower dose is effective in older horses and horses in low level work; higher dose may be needed for maximal benefit in high-performance horses. For more rapid control of pain and inflammation in acute problems, combine with additional HA.	Chronic conditions in all classes of horses that are not responsive to glucosamine/ chondroitin alone.
Arthrigen Uckele Health & Nutrition www.uckele.com 800-248-0330	Powder $89.95/2.5 lbs. (28 days)	$3.21	High-dose glucosamine, chondroitin, and MSM, moderate hyaluronic acid, antioxidant/anti-inflammatory herbs, plant extracts, and other nutrients Highly effective combination product including in a horse with longstanding coffin joint arthritis and one with extensive hock arthritic changes, improvement up to 2 lameness grades. Very good and rapid control of the soft tissue swelling and joint effusion in acute arthritis flare-ups as well. One horse who also had a chronic suspensory problem showed significant improvement in that also. Dose can be safely increased for severe inflammatory problems, may be lowered for maintenance of chronic problems.	Acute conditions and chronic conditions not responsive to chondroitin/glucosamine/ hyaluronic acid products.
Arthrisoothe-Gold NaturVet www.naturvet.com 888-628-8783	Liquid or powder $45.08 / liter for liquid, $42.35/2.25 lbs. powder	$2.35	Moderate (maintenance) to high-dose glucosamine plus MSM (higher in the powder), hyaluronic acid, Perna, boswellia, yucca, Ester-C, manganese. Improvements of 1.5 to 2 lameness grades by the 2-week mark in both active and inactive horses with chronic joint problems. Horses on the liquid showed improvement more quickly, obvious by the 7-day mark. Horses not in work maintained their improvement on 1 oz./day, but horses being worked needed to be maintained on the 2 oz./day dose. No obvious effect on resolution of swelling or heat with acute problems. Note: We saw no obvious difference between the 2 and 4 oz./day dose.	Chronic conditions in all classes of horses that are not responsive to glucosamine/ chondroitin alone.
Artri-Matrix Cavalor www.farmvet.com 888-837-3626	Powder $159.99/90 15 gram individual (pony size) doses, or as loose powder in 5 kg (11-lb.) bulk containers (22 days at loading; 30 days at performance dose; 45 days at low activity dose)	$5.30	Glucosamine, chondroitin, hyaluronic acid, collagen matrix proteins, whey protein isolate, minerals, essential fatty acids, anti-inflammatory herbs. Although slower to work than some other products, it was worth the wait. A 10-year-old carriage horse receiving it for an arthritic knee (old chip fracture) improved a full lameness degree in his knee and also showed obvious reduction in swelling and heat in an old suspensory injury and a stifle strain, despite being driven more during the test period than was usual. A 4-year-old trotter with severe carpitis (X-rays negative, joint swollen and inflamed) that had been on 2 months of stall rest with no improvement improved 1.5 lameness scores by the 4-week mark, and an old (several months) high suspensory lesion in a hind leg also improved. Bilateral gonitis (stifle inflammation) in a 2-year-old improved 1 lameness grade at the 4-week mark, after having been unchanged and unresponsive to other supplements for the 3 months prior to this.	Advanced or complex problems not responsive to glucosamine/chondroitin/hy- aluronic acid based products.
Blue Stallion Flx-Team J. M. Saddler, Inc www.jmsaddler.com 800-627-2807	Liquid $37.49/qt. (32 days at low dose, 16 days at high dose)	$2.34	Low (maintenance) to moderate (loading) glucosamine, vitamin C and chondrotin, plus MSM and hyaluronic acid. Improvements of up to 1.5 lameness grades in chronic conditions within the first week. Horses in moderate to heavy work continued to require the higher dosage level to maintain their improvements. Some reduction in heat and swelling in acutely inflamed joints noted within 3 to 5 days with the liquid.	Chronic conditions not responsive to glucosamine/ chondroitin based products.
Celadrin/HA Foxden Equine, Inc www.foxdenequine.com 540-337-5450	Powder $85/250 grams (50 servings at lowest dose, 25 at high dose)	$3.40	Highest concentration of hyaluronic acid/serving of all products, also contains a patented anti-inflammatory acetylated fatty acid at high dosage. Good control of heat, swelling and pain of acutely inflamed joints within 3 to 5 days at the lower dose, dramatic improvement in 24 to 48 hours at the high dose. Improvements of 1.5 to 2 lameness grades at 2 weeks in a chronic fetlock arthritis. Because the acetylated fatty acid has been shown to take longer to reach full effect in other species, further improvements may be noted with longer use. Because of the high concentration of hyaluronic acid in this product (400 mg/5 gram dose), it is an economical choice as a "booster" for glucosamine/chondroitin based products.	Acutely inflamed joints, alone or in economical low dose addition to basic glu- cosamine/chondroitin prod- ucts for chronic problems.

Product	Price	Cost per day/ high dose	Comments	Best for
Chondrogen EQ Kinetic Technologies www.kinetictech.net 877-786-9882	Powder $59/25 oz. (50 days at low dose, 25 days at high dose)	$2.36	Moderate glucosamine combined with low-dose chondroitin, HA and manganese. A previous *Horse Journal* choice. Improvement of 1 to 2 lameness grades by 1 to 2 weeks, including in an older horse that failed to respond to full dose glucosamine. The 0.5-oz. dose is effective in older horses and horses in low-level work; 0.75 to 1 oz. may be needed for maximal benefit in high-performance horses. For more rapid control of pain and inflammation in acute problems, combine with additional HA.	Chronic problems not responding well to glucosamine/chondroitin based supplements.
Conquer Kinetic Technologies www.kinetictech.net 877-786-9882	Gel or powder $11/3 dose syringe, $16/6 dose syringe (best price), $120/50 dose tub of powder	$4.80 powder $2.66 gel	High-dose hyaluronic acid. This is the original oral HA product for horses. At regular doses, good control of heat and swelling in acute problems within 3 days (more rapid at higher doses). Improvement of as much as 2 lameness grades by 1 to 2 weeks in both acute and chronic problems. The gel works more quickly and is more effective overall. Dose of powder needs to be doubled, or more, to achieve the best effect in acute inflammation. One quarter to half doses of the powder can be added to other joint nutraceuticals to boost their effectiveness.	Acutely inflamed joints; chronic problems not responding to glucosamine/ chondroitin based supplements, either alone or added in lower doses to other products.
Corta-Flx Corta-Flx Inc. www.corta-flx.com 888-294-1100	Liquid $32/qt. (32 days at low dose, 16 days at high dose), also available in 16 oz. $3.25	$2	Proprietary isolates of key molecules in chondroitin and glucosamine, with added hyaluronic acid. This old *Horse Journal* favorite, also documented to be effective by gait analysis studies at Michigan State, continues to offer rapid improvements of as much as 1.5 lameness grades within the first week of use. In fact, in terms of pain the addition of hyaluronic acid to the formula didn't make much difference but this formula did offer more rapid resolution of the heat and swelling of acutely inflamed joints.	Chronic problems in all classes of use.
Direct Complete Equine Direct, LLC www.equinedirect.net 866-955-1314	Coarse Powder $104.50/10 lbs. (80 days)	$1.31	Moderate dose glucosamine, chondroitin and MSM, high vitamin C and biotin, flax, "multi" vitamin and mineral. Improvements of up to 1 lameness grade after 4 weeks in horses doing no to low levels of work. No significant effect in horses at higher work loads. May be a good choice for these horses in terms of price if the mineral profile matches your needs.	Low-level chronic problems in horses doing little work.
Direct Complete HA Equine Direct, LLC www.equinedirect.net 866-955-1314	Coarse Powder $129.50/10 lbs. (80 days)	$1.62	Same as Direct Complete but with hyaluronic acid added. The addition of hyaluronic acid led to as much a 1.5 lameness grade improvement at the 4-week mark, with obvious reduction in joint swelling in one horse. One high performance horse also responded with an improvement of 1 lameness grade. No obvious effect on acutely inflamed joints.	Moderate chronic lameness in all classes of use.
Direst Flex Equine Direct, LLC www.equinedirect.net 866-955-1314	Coarse Powder $131/10 lbs. (160 days at low dose, 80 days at high dose)	$1.64	High-dose glucosamine with moderate MSM in a complete "multi" vitamin/ mineral base. No obvious effect on acute inflammation but improvement of up to 1.5 lameness grades in chronic conditions, both older horses and active younger horses but the active horses required a 2 oz./day dose.	Moderate chronic lameness in all classes of use.
Emerald Valley Ultimate Equiglobal USA Ltd www.emeraldvalleyequine. com 888-638-8262	Liquid $67.95/liter (20 doses at lowest dose, 5 doses at highest dose)	$13.59	Low dose MSM, glucosamine, vitamin C even at full loading dose (40 cc/200 lb.), devil's claw base. At the higher dosage range, modest improvements of up to 1 lameness grade in both acute and chronic conditions seen in horses in low work, or not being worked. Some reduction of heat and swelling (when present) was seen within 24 hours, likely as a result of the devil's claw. Poor response in chronic conditions in horses in heavy work, although again some improvement in heat and swelling within 24 hours on the highest dosages. Note: Treatments were discontinued at the 2-week mark when horses failed to show significant improvement, but the manufacturer notes response may take 3 to 4 weeks.	Not recommended. Other products produce speedier results for less money.
Farrier's Magic Winning Formula Berlin Industries www.farriersmagic.com 800-544-3635	Liquid $49.95 /16 oz. (30 days at lowest dose)	$6.24	Low-dose chondroitin, glucosamine, collagen and hyaluronic acid. Despite the relatively low doses of active ingredients in this product, we found surprisingly good and rapid results, especially in older horses with chronic problems where changes of up to 1 lameness grade were seen with the 0.5 oz. dose, 1 to 2 lameness grades at the 1 oz. dose. 1.5 to 2 oz./day required for good control of acute or chronic conditions in high performance horses. Improvements evident within 3 to 5 days.	Chronic joint lameness in horses doing low-level work.
Flex+ Absorbine/W.F. Young, Inc. www.absorbine.com 800-628-9653	Powder $58.40/4.3 lbs. (30 days maintenance, 15 days loading)	$3.89	Low-dose glucosamine and MSM combined with yucca and N-acetyl glucosamine (a naturally occurring metabolite of glucosamine) in rice bran. Although a bit slower to show results (maximum results at the 4-week mark, with initial improvement seen at 2 weeks), this product produced from 1 to 2 grade lameness scale improvements in chronic arthritic problems. High-performance horses required the higher dose to maintain these improvements. Proven in a research study to provide an anti-inflammatory effect equivalent to phenylbutazone after 50 days of continuous use. Although too slow to work for best results in acute problems, this is an excellent choice for the chronically arthritic horse.	Chronic conditions in all classes of use, especially horses prone to joint flare-ups.
Flo-Flex HA Med Vet Pharmaceuticals, Ltd www.medvetpharm.com 800-366-8986	Liquid $74/64 oz. (64 days at maintenance, 32 days at high/loading dose)	$2.31	Good levels of glucosamine and hyaluronic acid, with moderate levels of MSM, vitamin C, bromelain, yucca, grape seed and a trace-mineral package. Rapid improvements noted as soon as 3 to 5 days in chronic problems on loading doses of 1.5 to 2 oz./day. Improvements of as much as 2 lameness grades noted by 2 weeks, maintained at 1 oz./day in horses not in work; maintenance requirement for 1.5 oz./day in working horses. Quieting of actively inflamed joints noticeable within 3 days.	Both chronic and acute joint problems in all classes of use.

Product	Price	Cost per day/ high dose	Comments	Best for
Fluid Action Finish Line www.finishlinehorse.com 800-762-4242	Powder or liquid $32/1.875 lb. powder (32 days at low dose, 16 days high) or 32 oz. liquid (32 days low dose, 16 days high)	$2	High-dose (at 2 oz. serving) glucosamine and vitamin C, with small amounts of B vitamins, MSM and yucca. This supplement delivers the kind of results we've come to expect with high-dose glucosamine. Improved freedom movement and decrease of at least 1 lameness grade by 1 to 2 weeks in horses with chronic arthritis that does not involve excessive proliferation of bone. When used for acute problems, additional control of inflammation and pain may be indicated short term, as determined by your vet.	Chronic arthritis problems that do not have much bone proliferation.
Fluid Action HA Finish Line www.finishlinehorse.com 800-762-4242	Liquid or powder $36/1.875 lb. powder or 32 oz liquid (32 days at low dose, 16 days high) or 32 oz liquid (32 days low dose, 16 days high)	$2.25	High-dose (at 2 oz. serving) glucosamine and vitamin C, low-dose hyaluronic acid, with small amounts of B vitamins, MSM and yucca. The addition of hyaluronic acid makes this product as effective overall as the original Fluid Action, but at the lower 1 oz. dose in older horses and horses not in heavy work. High-performance horses did best with 1.5 to 2 oz./day. More rapid onset of action (3 to 5 days), even with acute problems, but doesn't have as much anti-inflammatory action as full-dose HA or high-dose MSM. The small price differential compared to the original product is well worth it.	Chronic arthritis problems.
Foxden Flex Foxden Equine, Inc www.foxdenequine.com 540-337-5450	Powder $50/600 grams (54 days at low dose, 36 days at high performance dose)	$1.39	Contains moderate levels of glucosamine and chondroitin, low-dose magnesium and trace mineral chelates, low-dose alpha-lipoic acid. At the recommended dose of 1 g/100 lbs. of body weight, improvements of up to 1.5 lameness grades at 2 weeks in chronic conditions in horses doing no to low levels of work. Horses in heavy work responded best to 1.5 g/100 lbs., also with improvements of up to 1.5 lameness grades at 2 weeks. No appreciable rapid anti-inflammatory effect in acute problems was noted, but improvement in lameness by the 7-day mark.	Chronic arthritis problems in all classes of use.
Glucosamine HCL or Glucosamine Sulfate Uckele Health & Nutrition www.uckele.com 800-248-0330	Powder $19.95/8 oz. (30 to 60 days)	67¢	Improvement of up to 1.5 lameness grades can be seen at 2 to 4 weeks, with best results obtained in joints that do not have extensive changes on radiographs.	Chronic arthritis problems that do not show extensive bone changes on X-ray.
Glucosamine XL Plus MSM Med Vet Pharmaceuticals, Ltd www.medvetpharm.com 800-366-8986	Pellet $37.95/5 lbs. (45 days at regular dose, 30 days at 1.5x regular dose)	$1.27	High-dose MSM, glucosamine and Ester-C with added vitamins, amino acids and trace mineral chelates. Improvements of 1 to 1.5 lameness grades at regular dose with up to low levels of exercise, up to 1.5 lameness grades by 2 weeks with 1.5 to 2 times regular dose with moderate to high exercise levels, in both chronic and acute joint problems. Good control of swelling/heat in acute problems in 5 days.	Arthritis problems prone to inflammatory flare-ups.
Grand Flex Grand Meadows www.grandmeadows.com 800-255-2962	Powder $35.00/1.875 lbs. (30 days at low dose, 15 days at high dose)	$1.24	Moderate to high (at loading dose) glucosamine, high-dose vitamin C, methionine, trace minerals with additional antioxidant ingredients. Always a top *Horse Journal* choice in the glucosamine category, often providing more rapid results than plain glucosamine. Grand Meadows also has a water-soluble version available that includes MSM, if you're looking for a liquid.	This product is a good place to start for any horse, especially if there is any question about adequate intakes of trace minerals.
Glucoflex Pellets Equine America www.equineamerica.com 800-838-7524	Pellet or powder $39.95/4 lbs. (64 days low dose, 32 days high dose)	$2.33	Moderate level of glucosamine with low-dose MSM. Improvements of up to 1 lameness grade with pellets, 1.5 with powder, after 2 weeks in both inactive and active horses with chronic joint problems. Horses with moderate to high work loads continued to require the high dose to hold their improvements. No obvious effect on heat or swelling in acute problems.	Chronic arthritis problems that do not show extensive bone changes on X-ray.
Hy-Flex Med Vet Pharmaceuticals, Ltd www.medvetpharm.com 800-366-8986	Meal $107/5 lbs. (80 days at low dose, 40 days at high dose)	$2.67	Moderate to high levels of glucosamine, yucca, plus moderate MSM, hyaluronic acid and Ester-C. Rapid improvements seen in chronic conditions, up to 1.5 lameness grades, including 2 horses that did not respond well to chondroitin and glucosamine alone. High-performance horses may require the higher dose to maintain those improvements. Significant improvement in heat and swelling with acutely inflamed joints seen by 3 to 5 days.	Chronic arthritis problems that do not respond well to glucosamine/chrondroitin products alone.
Hyalun Hyalogic, LLC www.hyalun.com 866-318-8484	Liquid $35/30 cc	$1.17	Low-dose hyaluronic acid. One older horse showed improved freedom of movement and 1 lameness grade improvement (hock arthritis) after 2 weeks of use at recommended dose. A 2-year-old in training with fetlock inflammation showed no improvement, and no significant improvement in an 8-year-old racehorse with knee arthritis. Higher doses were not tried.	Horses in low-level work with mild arthritis problems.
HylaRx Complete Select the Best www.selectthebest.com 800-648-0950	Powder $44.95/2.5 lbs. (30 days low dose, 15 days high dose)	$2.99	High potency hyaluronic acid and glucosamine, with moderate doses of MSM and chondroitin. Anti-inflammatory/analgesic effects not as rapid as with HA in gel form, but acute problems like osselets or carpitis quiet down rapidly over 4 to 5 days. Improvements of 1 to 2 lameness grades by 1 to 2 weeks.	Good choice for seniors who do not respond well to glucosamine/chondroitin alone, and for active horses with both acute and chronic problems.
Hylarin B Uckele Health & Nutrition www.uckele.com 800-248-0330 and Med Vet Pharmaceuticals, Ltd www.medvetpharm.com 800-366-8986	Paste or powder $10.95/3 dose tube; $23.95/8 dose tube; $78.50/30 dose jar of powder	$3.65 gel $5.23 powder	High concentration of hyaluronic acid/dose, plus a generous serving of the effective anti-inflammatory boswellia. Extremely rapid control of swelling and heat associated with acute inflammation. For example, a 2-year-old colt with stifle strain that was poorly responsive even to NSAIDs showed 80% reduction in heat and swelling within 24 hours with double dosing, resolution within 48 hours with only slight residual lameness. The gel works more quickly and was more effective overall. Dose of powder may need to be doubled, or more, to achieve the best effect in acute inflammation. One quarter to half doses of the powder can be added to other joint nutraceuticals to boost their effectiveness.	Rapid control of acute inflammatory conditions, as an add on to chondroitin/ glucosamine products when horses do not respond well to those alone.

Product	Price	Cost per day/ high dose	Comments	Best For
Hylasport OTC HorseTech www.horsetech.com 800-831-3309	Meal $71.95/4 lbs. (32 days at high dose, 64 days at low dose)	$2.25	High-dose glucosamine, vitamin C with moderate levels of MSM, hyaluronic acid and chondroitin, manganese, flax base. Improvements of up to 1.5 lameness grades in chronic conditions by the 2-week mark, in both inactive and active horses. Horses in moderate to high levels of work continue to need the 2 oz./day dose. Noticeable improvements by 1 week. No appreciable effect on the heat and swelling of acutely inflamed joints by the 5-day mark, but joint effusions in chronic conditions were improving by 2 weeks of use.	Chronic arthritic conditions in all classes of use.
Joint & Bone Uckele Health & Nutrition www.uckele.com 800-248-0330	Powder $21.95/227 grams (30 days at low dose, 15 days at high)	$1.46	High dose of natural source chondroitin (trachea), supplemental calcium/ phosphorous. Little effect on acute joint problems or acute flare-ups of old ones, but improved freedom of movement overall and up to 1 lameness grade improvement at the 4-week mark. Interestingly, one 2-year-old put on the product for a hock strain also had physitis at the knees that had been a problem for several months. This showed significant improvement at the 2-week mark and was resolved at the 4-week mark.	Showed some promise with developmental bone problem but needs more testing.
Joint Flex + Equine Products Inc www.equineproductsinc.com 800-821-5363	Powder $134.95/35 oz. (105 days at low dose, 52 days at high dose)	$2.59	Moderate levels of glucosamine and chondroitin, low MSM and vitamin C. At the suggested feeding rate of 1 teaspoon twice a day, moderate improvements of 0.5 to 1 lameness grade with chronic arthritis pain in horses doing no or low level work; 3 to 4 teaspoons per day needed for moderate improvement in high performance horses. Minimal to no obvious analgesic/anti-inflammatory effect in acute joint problems.	Chronic arthritis problems in all classes of use.
Joint Guard Equine Gold www.equinegold.com 800-870-5949	Powder $38.95/lb. (39 days at lowest dose, 26 days at higher dose)	$1.50	Moderate level chondroitin, glucosamine, MSM and vitamin C. Average of 1 lameness grade improvement at 2 scoops/day in horses with chronic problems doing little work. Horses in moderate to heavy work required 3 scoops/day for similar levels of improvement. Little anti-inflammatory/analgesic effect noted at up to triple doses in acute problems. Manufacturer currently recommends 4 scoops/day for 3 days after heavy exertion. This change was made after our trial was completed. We did not evaluate the 4 scoop/day dosage.	Chronic arthritic conditions in all classes of use.
Joint Powder Combo Equine Racing Systems www.equineracing.com 360-837-3700	Powder $71/3 lbs. (42 days at low dose, 26 days at high dose)	$2.74	Low levels of chondroitin, glucosamine and hyaluronic acid, with antioxidant action from betaine, ascorbic acid and Ester-C, bioflavonoid, trace minerals, plus vitamin B6. Although a little slow to take effect, improvements of up to 1 lameness grade were seen at the 2-week mark, with continued improvement up to 1.5 lameness grades at 4 weeks. High-performance horses responded best to double dosing, with improvements up to 1.5 lameness grades at 2 and 4 weeks at this level of feeding.	Chronic arthritic problems in all classes of use.
Joint Renew Peak Performance Nutrients www.peakperformance nutrients.com 800-944-1984	Powder $225/5 lbs. (454 days at low dose, 227 days at high dose)	99¢	Pure glucosamine sulfate. Improvement of up to 1.5 lameness grades can be seen at 2 to 4 weeks, with best results obtained in joints that do not have extensive changes on radiographs. Glucosamine does not have any significant effect on active inflammatory processes, so this must be dealt with separately in acutely inflamed joints. However, regular continued use of glucosamine can inhibit future inflammation.	Chronic arthritis conditions that do not involve extensive bone changes on X-ray.
Joint Renew II Peak Performance Nutrients www. peakperformancenutrients.com 800-944-1984	$70/600 grams (30 days)	$2.33	High-dose glucosamine and Ester-C with added low-dose devil's claw, bioflavonoids, manganese and zinc. Improvements of up to 1.5 lameness grades at the 2-week mark in both active and inactive horses with chronic joint problems. Inactive horses may hold their improvement at half the regular dose. No significant changes in heat or swelling in acutely inflamed joints, but steady reduction in joint effusions in chronic joints.	Chronic arthritic problems in all classes of use.
Legacy Select the Best www.selectthebest.com 800-648-0950	Pellets $27.30/5 lbs. (40 days at low dose, 20 days at high)	$1.37	High-dose yucca and vitamin E, with moderate MSM, chondroitin, glucosamine and vitamin C. Designed specifically for seniors, the levels of chondroitin and glucosamine in this product are not sufficient for a horse in active work. At 2 oz./day, more freedom of movement noted by the 2- to 4-week mark, but problem joints still obvious. At 4 oz./day, average of 1 lameness grade improvement in problem joints.	Seniors with early arthritic problems. Good choice as a preventative or for the stiff, achy older horse.
Lube All Equiade www.equiade.com 800-413-3702	Liquid $44.95/500 cc (33 to 50 days)	$1.36	Hyaluronic acid. At 10 to 15 cc/day, quiets inflammation and pain of acute problems or flare-ups of chronic problems within 3 to 5 days. Improvement of 1 to 1.5 lameness grades in acute conditions. Very useful as an add-on for horses that do not respond as well as hoped to glucosamine/chondroitin based supplements.	Acute joint problems and active flare-ups of old problems.
Lube All Plus Equiade www.equiade.com 800-413-3702	Liquid $64.95/500 cc (33 to 50 days)	$1.97	High-dose hyaluronic acid with moderate levels of glucosamine, MSM and chondroitin. This combination product performed extremely well with two very difficult cases that were poorly responsive to other supplements—an older mare with extensive knee arthritis related to a previous fracture, and a 4-year-old with a previous hip injury that had been severely lame for months and improved 2 full lameness grades.	Acute and chronic problems in horses at any level of work.
Lubrin Uckele www.uckele.com 800-248-0330	Powder $33.20/240 grams (30 days at low dose, 15 days at high dose)	$2.21	Low (2 scoops/day) to high (4 scoops/day) glucosamine and chondroitin supplement. Ineffective at less than 2 scoops/day. At 2 scoops/day, gradual improvement of 1 lameness score in inactive horses by the 2 weeks mark. At 4 scoops/day, freedom of movement significantly improved overall, with improvement of up to 1.5 lameness grades in both inactive and active horses. Fair control of the pain of acute problems by the 5-day mark at the higher dosing.	Chronic arthritic problems.

Product	Price	Cost per day/ high dose	Comments	Best for
Lubrun Plus Uckele www.uckele.com 800-248-0330	Powder $52.20/2 lbs. (43 days at low dose, 21 days at high dose)	$2.49	Slightly more potent version of Lubrun, with additional anti-inflammatory effects from boswellia, yucca, grape seed, vitamin C and B vitamins. Ineffective at less than 0.75 oz./day. In terms of lameness grading, 1.5 oz/day equivalent to 4 scoops of original Lubrun. Horses in regular work usually require the 1.5 oz/day dose to maintain their improvements. Good control of acute problems by the 5-day mark, and gradual reductions in joint effusions (filling) seen over the course of the 4 weeks in horses with chronic problems.	Both acute and chronic problems in horses in all levels of work.
Matrix 4 Med Vet Pharmaceuticals, Ltd www.medvetpharm.com 800-366-8986	Powder $111.25/4 lbs. (64 days at low dose, 32 days at high dose)	$3.48	Moderate (maintenance) to high (loading) levels of yucca, glucosamine and chondroitin with high levels MSM, Ester-C, modest levels of vitamin E and a balanced trace-mineral package. Very comprehensive package with control of swelling and heat within 3 to 5 days with acute problems or flare-ups, improvement of up to 1.5 lameness grades at 2 weeks at 2 oz./day, further improvement to 2 lameness grades at 4 weeks. Horses in heavy work required continued 2 oz./day dosing to hold their improvements.	Both acute and chronic problems in horses in all levels of work.
Mida-Blue Mida Enterprises, Ltd www.midaplex.com 877-422-0222	Large pill/wafer $39.95/30 (30 days)	$3.32	100 mg hyaluronic acid/treat. Although the horses all thought these were great treats, no response was seen at up to 3/day. Higher dosages, or combination with other Mida products, was not evaluated.	Not recommended. Other products produced preferable results.
Mida-Gold Mida Enterprises, Ltd www.midaplex.com 877-422-0222	Large pill/wafer $39.95/120 (30 days)	$3.32	Low levels of glucosamine, chondroitin and MSM plus anti-inflammatory boswellia, vurcumin and guggulipid. Highly palatable. No improvement in acutely inflamed joints after 5 days, but a horse with a persistent (2+ months) joint effusion and mild lameness after OCD surgery showed 50% improvement after 2 weeks.	Long-term control of low-level inflammation.
Mida-Plex Mida Enterprises, Ltd www.midaplex.com 877-422-0222	Large pill/wafer $39.95/120 (30 days)	$3.32	Low-dose glucosamine, chondroitin, very low MSM and vitamin C. No effect at this level of feeding in a high-performance (race) horse, but 2 older horses improved 1 lameness grade by the 4-week mark, and were moving more freely overall at 2 weeks.	Chronic low level arthritis in horses at no to moderate work.
Multiflex Nupro www.multivetusa.com 800-356-8776	Powder $55/3.75 lbs. (60 days at low dose, 30 days at high dose)	$1.83	High levels of glucosamine, chondroitin, Perna and MSM, as well as moderate vitamin C and trace minerals. Improvements of at least 1 lameness grade at 1 oz./day in horses with chronic arthritic pain not in active use. Best results at 2 oz./day for high-performance horses. At 1.5 to 2 oz./day, control of pain and inflammation within 3 to 4 days in acute arthritis flare-ups.	Chronic arthritic problems, including those prone to mild flare-ups.
Rapid Response F Amerdon Inc www.amerdon.com 800-331-1036	Liquid $79/quart	$9.88	Contains glucosamine, chondroitin, oligomeric proanthocyanidins in a base of aloe vera gel. Feed 2 to 6 oz., once or twice a day. Because of the high price of this product, we reserved it for some particular difficult cases. At 2 oz. twice a day it resolved an acute flare-up of osselets (synovitis and capsulitis of the fetlock) in a racing colt who had been battling the condition for 2 months. Sound after 2 weeks. A retired horse with severe hock arthritis with a history of only partial response to several different joint nutraceuticals became pasture sound at walk and trot after 4 weeks and was still moving well 3 weeks after stopping. A 2-year-old Standardbred filly with a history of a kick to the shoulder as a foal (but no fractures found) was showing abnormal movement of the previously injured leg that severely impaired her ability to pace. She overcame this at low speeds but showed lameness and abnormal gait again when speed work was introduced. Minimal to no improvement with NSAIDs or other joint supplements. Within 2 weeks of starting RR, her lameness resolved and she is continuing to train well.	Both acute and chronic lameness problems, including those involving problems with tissues other than the synovial lining or cartilage. If you have a difficult or complicated lameness, don't give up on supplements helping until you try this one.
RE-NU Membrell www.membrell.com 800-749-1291	Powder $61.25 (32 days)	$1.91	Eggshell membrane as a natural source of chondroitin, glucosamine, hyaluronic acid and collagen. We tried this with 2 older horses with moderate arthritis involving multiple joints, and generalized stiffness. In one, there was no change. The other horse showed more willingness to move in general, but lameness grade was unchanged at 2 weeks.	Very mild arthritic changes in older horses.
Senior Flex Med Vet Pharmaceuticals, Ltd www.medvetpharm.com 800-366-8986	Meal $71.75/5 lbs. (80 days at maintenance, 40 at loading/high dose)	$1.79	Moderate (maintenance) to high dose (loading) yucca, glucosamine, vitamin E and Ester-c, with low to moderate chondroitin and MSM, vitamins A/D. Potent formula with both cartilage support and antioxidant defenses. Improvements of 1.5 lameness grades in 2 senior horses, 2 lameness grades in a third. Improvements were well maintained on the maintenance dose.	Seniors with up to moderate levels of arthritis pain.
Senior Flx Equine America www.equineamerica.com 800-838-7524	Powder $34.79/4 lbs. (32 days)	$1.09	Moderate-dose chondroitin sulfate, digestive aids, supplemental lysine and methionine. No obvious effect on acutely inflamed joints at suggested dosing. In chronic conditions in older horses, improved freedom of movement overall is noted, with gradual reductions in amount of joint swelling by the 4 week mark, improvement of 0.5 to 1.0 lameness grade in problem joints.	Low level arthritis problems in older horses.
S.T.P. (Stop the Pain) Equimed USA 800-765-6040	Liquid $36/900 cc (30 days at low dose, 15 days at high dose)	$2.40	High hyaluronic acid, moderate glucosamine, chondroitin and Perna, with low dose moswellia, MSM, superoxide dismutase and yucca. Assists in control of heat and swelling with chronic conditions, improvements noted by 4 to 5 days. Improvements of up to 1.5 lameness grades in chronic conditions after 2 weeks. Horses in work need to stay on the higher dose to maintain their improvements. Reduction in joint effusions in chronic conditions noted.	Control of chronic conditions in horses at all levels of work, including those prone to mild joint flares.

Product	Price	Cost per day/ high dose	Comments	Best for
Su-per Sound Gateway Products www.buygpdirect.com 888-472-2825	Powder $34.07/2.5 lbs. (40 days low dose, 20 days high dose)	$1.70	Moderate to high glucosamine, low-dose MSM, full spectrum of collagen based amino acids, low dose bromelain and Yucca, B vitamins and trace minerals. No appreciable effect on heat and swelling with acutely inflamed joints. Improvements of 1 to 1.5 lameness grades at 2 weeks if kept on the loading dose. Higher doses required to hold the improvement in active horses. Inactive horses may maintain improvement on lower doses.	Control of up to moderate chronic arthritis problems in horses at all levels of work.
Su-per Glucosamine C.S. Gateway Products www.buygpdirect.com 888-472-2825	Powder $34.35/2.5 lbs. (40 days low dose, 20 days high dose)	$1.73	Moderate to high dose glucosamine and mixed chondroitins from collagen. No appreciable effect on heat and swelling with acutely inflamed joints. Improvements of 1 to 1.5 lameness grades at 2 weeks if kept on the loading dose. Higher doses required to hold the improvement in active horses. Inactive horses may maintain improvement on lower doses.	Control of up to moderate chronic arthritis problems in horses at all levels of work.
Su-per Powerflex H.A. Gateway Products www.buygpdirect.com 888-472-2825	Powder $74.95/2.5 lbs. (20 days)	$3.75	High-potency mix of MSM, glucosamine, chondroitins from collagen, hyaluronic acid, E/Se with additional antioxidant herbs and nutrients. Highly effective product providing rapid control of acutely inflamed joints and obvious pain and joint effusion relief even in severe chronic conditions and those likely to involve soft tissue problems as well (e.g. stifles). Improvement of up to 2 lameness grades.	Control of both acutely inflamed and chronic arthritic problems in horses at all levels of work.
Super-Flx Equine America www.equineamerica.com 800-838-7524	Powder $21/2 lbs. (32 days at low dose, 16 days at high dose)	$1.31	Low-dose chondroitin and glucosamine, with unspecified amounts of glutamine, vitamin C and trace minerals. At the lower feeding dose, at 4 weeks modest improvements in freedom of movement and up to 1 lameness grade seen in chronic conditions in horses doing no or very low level work. For more active horses, double dosing needed to achieve the same level of improvement. No apparent effect on acutely inflamed joints.	Low-level chronic arthritic problems.
Super-Flx Glucosamine Solution Equine America www.equineamerica.com 800-838-7524	Liquid $21.75/32 oz. (32 days at low dose, 16 days at high dose)	$1.36	Glucosamine sulfate, at low dose, high levels at high dose. Moderate levels of improvement of up to 1.5 lameness grades can be seen at 2 to 4 weeks, with best results obtained in joints that do not have extensive changes on radiographs. One 5-year-old racehorse took his lifetime best winning time on this product, and was able to skip hock injections he had been receiving monthly. Glucosamine does not have any significant effect on active inflammatory processes, so this must be dealt with separately in acutely inflamed joints. However, regular continued use of glucosamine can inhibit future inflammation.	Chronic arthritis conditions that do not involve extensive bone changes on X-ray.
Special Joint Blend Equine Science www.herbs4horses.com 800-479-3537	Pellet $55/3 lbs. (48 days at low dose, 24 days at high dose)	$2.29	Yucca, devil's claw, chondroitin sulfate, alfalfa, glucosamine, MSM. No effect on acutely inflamed joints was noted, but gradual decrease in joint swelling with chronic conditions by the 4 week mark. Improvement of up to 1 lameness grade by 4 weeks in chronic conditions, with double dosing required to achieve this in horses in active work.	Horses already on a glucosamine/chondroitin supplement that need an anti-inflammatory effect, or could try by itself for mild chronic problems.
Tri-Lube Uckele Health & Nutrition www.uckele.com 800-248-0330	$64.95/2 lbs. (50 days at low dose, 25 days at high dose)	$2.60	Moderate (low dose) to high (high dose) glucosamine, chondroitin and MSM. One older, retired horse on lower dose showed rapid improvement of 1 lameness grade at the 2 week mark, continued improvement in overall freedom of movement at 4 weeks. One acute flare-up of knee arthritis in an older horse came under control rapidly (3 to 4 days) with double dosing, and maintained inflammatory control with an improvement of 1 lameness grade on the lower dose. One actively racing horse with chronic fetlock problems had some improvement at the low dose but significantly better results at the high dose, with resolution of joint swelling and improvement of 1.5 lameness grades after 2 weeks.	Arthritic problems with poor response to glucosamine/ chondroitin only, including for control of those prone to joint flare-ups.
Tri-Lube Xxtra Uckele Health & Nutrition www.uckele.com 800-248-0330	Powder $74.95/2 lbs. (50 days at low dose, 25 days at high dose)	$2.99	Moderate levels of glucosamine, chondroitin and hyaluronic acid in the 20 gram dose, high-dose MSM. Same excellent anti-inflammatory effect in acute conditions, with best results at 40 grams/day (double dose), as with the original Tri-Lube. In 2 out of 3 test horses, we didn't see any obvious clinical difference in response as a result of the added hyaluronic acid, but this may be because the generous levels of MSM in this product were already providing rapid control of swelling and pain. However, one older history with a history of poor synovial fluid production in a fetlock that had been treated repeatedly with corticosteroids in the past showed a dramatic improvement of 1 additional lameness grade when switched from original Tri-Lube to Tri-Lube Xtra.	Arthritic problems with poor response to glucosamine/ chondroitin only, including for control of those prone to joint flare-ups.
Trisport HorseTech www.horsetech.com 800-831-3309	Meal $49.95/4 lbs. (64 days at low dose, 32 days at high dose)	$1.56	Same ingredients as HylaSport, but without the addition of hyaluronic acid. Improvements of up to 1.5 lameness grades in chronic conditions by the 2-week mark, in both inactive and active horses. Horses in moderate to high levels of work continue to need the 2 oz./day dose. Noticeable improvements by 1 week. No appreciable effect on the heat and swelling of acutely inflamed joints by the 5-day mark.	Chronic arthritic conditions in horses at all levels of work.

Laminitis/Insulin Resistance

The first time we discussed insulin resistance was in 2000, when we did a field trial with magnesium supplementation of chronically laminitic and cresty horses and ponies. We wanted to see if there might be any truth to the folklore that magnesium can help with laminitis.

What we saw were amazing, observable changes in many of the supplemented animals in terms of foot comfort, obesity, and abnormal fat deposits. This led to the question of whether many cases of chronic laminitis might be linked to insulin resistance (IR). It is well documented that people with IR are frequently deficient in magnesium and that supplemental magnesium is beneficial for them. Three to 5 grams/day is a conservative trial dose, but for long-term administration you should find out how much is in your horse's diet and supplement to achieve a calcium:magnesium ratio between 2:1 and 1.2:1.

The link between IR and laminitis in ponies was first made back in the 1970s, by Dr. J. R. Coffman. Coffman documented significant differences in insulin sensitivity in ponies that had a history of laminitis versus those that did not. At the time, the connection was documented only in ponies, but Coffman suspected that Morgans might also be affected.

Vets largely believed then that IR in horses was only evident as a complication of Cushing's disease. In 2002, Dr. Philip Johnson coined the term "equine metabolic syndrome" to describe easy weight gain and high laminitis risk in horses without a pituitary tumor that were insulin-resistant. (Metabolic syndrome is the term used for humans with IR, a pre-diabetic state that is also associated with changes in circulating levels of cholesterol and triglycerides.) This idea met with considerable resistance among veterinarians, and the concept that IR could exist independent of Cushing's disease was slow to filter through to practitioners or be accepted by researchers. But 2006 was a pivotal year for research into IR, with some of the most vocal critics making a complete about-face and not only using the term metabolic syndrome, but demonstrating that IR was indeed a risk factor for laminitis.

Coffman had also reported on lipid and fat abnormalities in ponies with IR, and noted, as have many others, that IR is a component of the often fatal hyperlipidemia syndrome in ponies and miniature horses or donkeys. Changes in fat metabolism aren't as dramatic in full-size horses, but Dr. Nicholas Frank, at the University of Tennessee, reported in a recent study that full-sized obese, insulin resistant horses do indeed have abnormal levels of fats and cholesterol in their blood.

Obesity and IR

Your horse may not be thrilled, but muzzling is an excellent way to limit or prevent grazing without depriving your horse of the exercise and social contact he gets on turnout.

The role of obesity in insulin resistance has not been completely sorted out. The prototype insulin-resistant horse or pony is a very easy keeper, overweight, with abnormal fat deposits, like a prominent, fatty neck crest. It's also true that even a normally insulin-sensitive breed, like the Thoroughbred, will show a decline in insulin sensitivity along with obesity. It's not entirely clear whether it is the obesity per se that causes it or the high-grain and often high-fat diets they must consume to become overweight. In any case, a poll of 605 owners of insulin resistant horses and ponies, members of the 4,460 member Yahoo Equine Cushing's and Insulin Resistance Group (pets.groups. yahoo.com/group/EquineCushings), showed that the most consistent symptom, in 29% of the cases, was known or suspected laminitis or foot pain. This was followed by abnormal fat deposits in 23%, while only 18% responded that the horse was actually overweight at the time of diagnosis. The bottom line is that while most insulin-resistant horses will gain weight easily, preventing excessive weight gain is not enough to prevent insulin resistance or laminitis. Furthermore, not every overweight horse is insulin resistant, at least not to the degree that can be easily detected on screening tests.

Exercise, on the other hand, is a potent tool for helping horses with insulin resistance. Regular exercise, even a single bout of exercise, significantly improves insulin resistance and glucose handling. There have been many cases of Arabians who were lean, kept on pasture, and fed grain when they were in endurance training, but begin to gain weight rapidly, and even develop laminitis, when exercise was stopped for even a few weeks.

Diagnosis

Researchers use a variety of complicated tests involving oral or intravenous glucose administration, intravenous insulin, and multiple blood samples to investigate and confirm insulin resistance. However, at the simplest level, all that is necessary is to document higher-than-normal levels of insulin in a horse that has not been recently fed a high simple-carbohydrate meal. Complete fasting should not be done, since insulin resistance is a dynamic condition, an abnormal response to feeding.

On the day of testing, the horse should be fed nothing but low-NSC (nonstructural carbohydrate) hay or well-soaked hay, if the NSC is not known. Blood should be drawn for glucose testing at the same time. Although glucose is rarely elevated above normal in IR horses, the ratio of insulin and glucose to each other is abnormal. In other words, an IR horse produces more units of insulin per unit of blood sugar than a normal horse.

Researchers have developed some logarithmic equations to describe insulin resistance in horses, but an easier approach widely used in human IR, and found to be just as sensitive as the more complicated equations in people, is the G:I ratio; that is, glucose divided by insulin. The details for these numbers have yet to be worked out in horses, so we can only give you guide-

Outward appearances may be suspicious, but not all overweight horses are insulin resistant. Confirm the diagnosis with blood work.

Believe it or not, even the amount of high-sugar grass a horse can get by reaching under the fence line can be enough to trigger laminitis.

lines. There also may be breed differences, comparable to racial differences among people. That said, when glucose is within normal ranges, G:I ratios below 4.5:1 likely represent uncontrolled insulin resistance; 4.5:1 to 9:1 compensated insulin resistance, while 10:1 or greater is normal insulin sensitivity.

Treatment

The best news about insulin resistance is that once you know what you're dealing with you can control it. If the horse is over 13 years old, he should also be screened for Cushing's, since diet alone may not be able to take care of the problem without treatment of the underlying high-cortisol output. If you're fortunate enough to avoid laminitis, daily exercise is the place to start. An absolute minimum of 30 minutes per day, mostly trot-

Ponies and miniature breeds are particularly prone to insulin resistance.

ting and cantering (if the horse is fit enough to tolerate this) should be done. If you can't ride, longe the horse or find someone to do it for you.

Consistent exercise may be enough to avoid other changes, but it's wise to eliminate or greatly reduce any concentrated carbohydrate sources until the horse is a normal weight, has lost any abnormal fat deposits, and is fit. The lower the NSC of the diet, the more liberally you will be able to feed your horse. With exercise, free-choice, low-NSC hay with appropriate supplementation usually works out well.

If exercise is absolutely out, strict diet control is essential. The cornerstone of treatment is a low-NSC diet, meaning 10% or lower for most horses. Careful attention to mineral intakes is also important, since insulin resistance in all other species is associated with oxidative stress and some key mineral deficiencies, as well as overabsorption of iron, which worsens IR and inflammatory tendencies. The recommendations below were developed by the author and published in the February 2004 issue of *Compendium on Continuing Education for the Practicing Veterinarian*. They will also appear in the new textbook *Equine Podiatry*.

Recommendations

- Base diet: Grass or alfalfa/grass mix hay (Note: Some laminitic horses are sensitive to alfalfa), with NSC of 10% or lower.

- Molasses-free beet pulp as a carrier for supplements. (Note: Some brands do not list molasses on the bag, but contain molasses anyway. Beet pulp should always be thoroughly rinsed before soaking, until the rinse water runs clear. This removes both surface molasses and any contaminating soil, which is high in iron.)

- 2 to 6 oz. per day of ground stabilized flaxseed for essential fatty acids. Its ratio of omega-3 to omega-6 is most similar to grass and is high in anti-inflammatory omega-3 fatty acids.

- 2000 IU of vitamin E.

- Intake of all minerals at a minimum of 150% of current NRC (National Research Council) requirements, using the following ratios:

    Calcium:Phosphorus:Magnesium 2:1:1.
    Iron:Copper 4:1 (maximum 10:1 if the horse is not iron overloaded).
    Copper:Zinc:Magnesium 1:3:2.5.

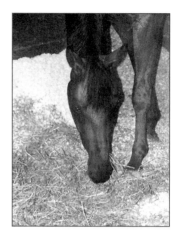

Hay with low levels of simple sugars and starch is the cornerstone of the diet.

Start by feeding low-NSC hay at 2% of the horse's ideal body weight, or 1.5% of the horse's current body weight, whichever is higher. Check weight with a tape weekly and adjust hay as needed. Horses that are highly immobile because of pain may need to be fed slightly less. Be careful, though; starvation diets may cause rapid weight loss, but will not get rid of abnormal fat collections and may make the horse more insulin-resistant.

There are currently only a few commercially available feeds that we're sure are both low enough in NSC and correctly mineral balanced. These are:

- Ontario Dehy Balanced Timothy cubes* (www.ontario dehy.com, 877-289-3349): 10% or less NSC, minerals added as dictated by analysis of the hay in the pellets. Contains both hay and beet pulp. Can be used as a

The Air Fern

If you determine your horse's situation and find he is overweight but his calorie intake isn't higher than the average estimates, you have what has been coined an "air fern" or "easy keeper." There are some horses that are just efficient in converting their feed, but if you are more than 10% or so below average requirements and your horse is still fat, you should consider having him tested for insulin resistance. Talk with your vet about testing.

Insulin resistance (IR) is most common in ponies, minis, donkeys, Morgans, Arabians, and horses of Spanish/South American descent. The ability to pack on fat easily was a survival advantage for their ancestors, but backfires in the face of domestication and a constant, often generous calorie supply. We've covered the feeding of these horses in detail elsewhere in this chapter (see also back issues at www.horse-journal.com), but the key points are:

- Absolutely no grains, seeds, brans, etc. except for a few ounces per day of flaxseed for the essential fatty acid content.

- Graze with extreme caution, if at all. The sugar/starch level in pasture grasses fluctuates widely, even over the course of a day, and is often too much for these horses to handle.

- Type of calories is extremely important. Beet pulp and grass hays need to form the core of the diet. Rinse beet pulp before soaking to make sure all molasses is off it. Hay should be tested for mineral levels, starch, and sugar content. Some IR horses will tolerate hays with a combined sugar

and starch content in the low teens, others need it below 10%. Soaking before feeding may help lower sugar.

Exercise combined with an appropriate, mineral-balanced diet is the only treatment available, but it will work.

Weight Gain on Pasture

Horses gain weight on pasture for the same reason they do on other diets—too many calories and not enough exercise to burn them off. Grass is the horse's perfect food, packed full of vitamins and enzymes, plus high water content that keeps conditions in the colon favorable for fiber digestion.

The calorie level in grass is always relatively low because of the high water content, but horses can consume huge amounts of it in a day, obviously enough to hold or gain weight if they have an unlimited supply. Immature, growing grasses have the lowest level of unfermentable fiber and the highest of simple sugars, starches, other plant sugars, and soft, fermentable fiber. Protein content can also be high, over 20%.

The higher digestibility and calorie yield of young grasses is what puts that spring bloom, and often blimp, too, on a horse. Stabling or dry lotting the horse for part of the day may not work. He'll only gorge himself when he does get out on the grass. If you're going to use restriction, the horse will probably have to spend a lot more time off grass than on it. A better solution is often a grazing muzzle like the Best Friend Grazing Muzzle (www.best friendequine.com).

grain replacer or as a complete feed. All you need to add is ground stabilized flax and vitamin E. Feed with 1 to 2 oz. per day of iodized table salt. Widely available in the United States. Hays for every batch are analyzed.

- Sterett Brothers Low Carb Complete Feed* (www.sterett broshayandfeed.com, 425-822-9011): Pelleted hay with less than 10% NSC. Sold with separate balancing minerals in a flax base. Grain replacer or complete feed. Each batch of pellets is analyzed. Add only vitamin E and iodized salt. Availability limited to the West Coast.

- Triple Crown Safe Starch* (www.triplecrownfeed.com, 800-267-7198): Chopped low-NSC hay with pelletized vitamins and minerals. Grain replacer or complete feed. Some additional ground stabilized flax and salt round out the diet. Check availability in your area.

- Spillers Happy Hoof (www.spillers-feeds.com): A blend of chopped hays and other low NSC ingredients that now contains no molasses and has safe NSC levels. Magnesium, zinc, and vitamin E are lower than we would like to see, though, and iron and manganese are not specified or guaranteed. Also need to add flax and salt. Limited to the South.

- Poulin Carb Safe (www.poulingrain.com, 800-638-3112): This is another low-NSC option, based on hays, beet pulp, and flax. Again, mineral guarantees are incomplete, but vitamin E and disclosed minerals are good. It's available mainly in the New England region.

Otherwise, there are a host of feeds being advertised as "safe" or "low" carbohydrate that contain combined sugar and starch levels ranging from the teens to 20 or 30+%. This level is lower than a straight grain mix, but usually not low enough for an insulin resistant horse.

There are also many manufacturers using the term NSC to include only starch, instead of both sugar and starch. Be

Products that guarantee low NSC and have good nutritional balance.

Magnesium deficiency plays a critical role in insulin resistance in other species, and the early Horse Journal trials with supplementing this nutrient found good results in horses as well.

wary of any feed claiming to be safe that contains molasses, significant amounts of rice bran, grains or grain products (except distiller's or brewer's grains), or flours.

Restrictions

No grain, carrots, apples, or horse treats. A few sunflower seeds or alfalfa pellets can be substituted.

Hay or a hay-based complete feed comprises the vast bulk of the diet. To know the hay is safe and how much of each mineral the horse requires, hay analysis is necessary. To make analysis realistic, you need to buy your hay in bulk. If this isn't the case, you have a few options:

1. Talk to your hay dealer to see if it would be possible to have a several-month supply of hay earmarked for you only, so that testing is a reasonable option.

2. Locate a nearby farmer who will rent you loft space (usually quite reasonable) so that you can purchase a large load and store it.

3. Convert some unused space to hay storage (weather-tight outbuildings, empty stalls, etc.).

4. Convert the horse to a 100% diet of a known, safe feed.

If worse comes to worst, soak all your horse's hay and research the average mineral profiles for the hay type and the region where it was grown. The state university's agriculture department is the place to start.

Bottom Line

Getting started on the diet changes is the hardest part of managing a horse that is diagnosed as insulin resistant. Like any other management change, once you get rolling it will become routine.

The important thing to remember is that halfway measures will get halfway results. This is a full lifestyle change for these horses. Most people only become committed to properly caring for IR horses after they have run into problems with laminitis, but if they were aware of how to deal with it and instituted a correct diet and exercise program, the suffering could have been avoided.

The extra effort to really do it right is well worth it. We've seen horses that have been struggling with weight problems and repeated episodes of laminitis for many years that have been able to trim down and be put back into active use with the correct diet, management, and hoof care.

Another study published in the May-June 2006 issue of *Alternative Therapies in Health and Medicine* compared the response of insulin-resistant people to diet therapy alone or diet plus Jiaogulan supplementation. Both groups improved, but the people on diet plus Jiaogulan showed greater improvement. Many insulin resistant horses are given Jiaogulan to help them with laminitis and encourage good hoof growth, although there are no studies on treating IR in horses with Jiaogulan.

Insulin resistance, obesity, and Cushing's disease all put your horse at risk for laminitis. The metabolic changes associated with these conditions require strict limitation of sugars and starches in these horses. Obesity can also affect fertility and greatly increases joint stress.

While horse owners try all kinds of things to keep these horses healthy—from drugs to shoes to "miracle" supplements— nothing is going to be a real fix if you don't get back to the basics: diet.

Beet Pulp

A few years ago, beet pulp was considered a bad choice for horses with metabolic disorders because of its high NFC (non-fiber carbohydrates) content. However, we now know that most of that NFC is actually pectin, a soluble fiber that's removed by the same analysis techniques that pull out sugar and starch. In fact, beet pulp without molasses is the best thing to feed these horses. Plain beet pulp has the lowest glycemic index of common equine feeds, lower even than most grass hays.

The glycemic index of a feed describes how high a spike in glucose/sugar is produced after the horse eats it. And you don't want a sugar spike in these horses any more than you do in a human diabetic. As much as 30 to 40% of the horse's diet by weight can come from beet pulp. At higher amounts, hay intakes may drop off because beet pulp is filling.

Because beet pulp has a calorie level higher than grass hay, if the horse is overweight, substitute beet pulp for hay at a rate of 1 pound of beet pulp (weight before soaking) for each 2 pounds of hay removed. For normal-weight horses, feed 1 to 1.5 pounds of beet pulp for each 2 pounds of hay, adjusting as needed to maintain the correct weight. For horses that are underweight, substitute on a pound-for-pound basis to encourage weight gain.

Stabilized flaxseed meal and rice bran are good choices as grain substitutes in terms of their effect on blood sugar and insulin, but they're both high in fat, which may be a worry. Feed these products only at levels necessary to provide essential fatty acids (1 to 2 oz. each). If your horse's weight is appropriate, you can feed up to 6 oz. a day to help with mineral balances. We recommend a rate of 2 oz. per 1 pound of beet pulp fed.

Hay Choices

Be careful with alfalfa hay, which can cause laminitis flare-ups in some horses. The mechanism for this isn't clear—and technically it shouldn't—but the fact of the matter remains that some horses are sensitive to it. If your horse tolerates alfalfa well without foot pain, you can include it, up to 20% of the hay ration.

Grass hay has always been the staple of the diet for overweight and laminitic horses. However, research by agricultural consultant Katy Watts presented at the 2003 Laminitis Conference showed that not all grass hays are equal when it comes to their safety for these horses. A safe level of sugar and starch in the hay appears to be 10% or lower. Most strains of Bermuda grass have the lowest levels, making it your first choice if you can get it. Timothy is second.

Orchard grass, oat hay, and other grain hays are the worst choices. Their sugar content can be close to 20% or higher.

Drug Therapy for Insulin Resistance

Several drugs are available to people to assist in control of insulin resistance. One of these is metformin.

A study at the Maxwell Gluck Equine Research Center at the University of Kentucky, reported in the *Journal of Reproduction, Fertility and Development*, looked at the effects of treating obese insulin resistant mares with metformin—an oral medication used to control high blood sugar in diabetic humans.

It's has been known for quite a while that overweight mares tend to continue to cycle over the winter, when leaner mares don't, and that these overweight mares are insulin resistant compared to more slender mares. Mares were given 3, 6, or 9 grams of metformin per day. The study found improved insulin sensitivity after one month in the mares given 3 grams per day, but no effect at one month with 6 or 9 grams per day. When tested two or more months after starting the 3 grams per day dose, there was no longer any improvement evident. It was determined that the drug metformin had no real, long-lasting effect for these horses.

Other factors that influence the sugar content of a hay include growing stresses and rapid curing conditions.

But don't underfeed either. The best results are obtained when the horse is fed hay at a rate of a minimum 1.5% of his ideal body weight. For example, if the horse currently weighs 1,200 pounds but should only weigh 1,000, feed him a minimum of 15 lbs. of hay a day. Cutting back to near starvation rations can actually worsen insulin resistance and is rarely effective in producing weight loss. This also cuts back too far on the protein and minerals the horse needs. 🐎

Muscle Support

From sales yearlings to seniors, halter horses to endurance horses, building and maintaining good muscle is a concern. While a number of nutritional supplements on the market claim they can help you do that, be sure you have the basics covered before you spend a penny.

The horse can't build and maintain good muscle without the raw material to make, fuel, and repair them. Those key ingredients are:

- **Water and salt:** Like all soft tissues in the body, muscle cells are mostly water, and they're bathed in body fluids, again mostly water, that carry nutrients, hormones, and other signals to the muscle cells. Dehydrated horses look, and are, smaller.

  Rule #1: Provide fresh water, at a comfortable drinking temperature, at all times and a minimum of 1 oz. of salt per day in the winter. Increase to 2 to 4 oz. per day in hot weather.

- **Calories/Fuel:** Muscles obtain most of the fuel they need to function and build from energy in the form of carbohydrate (glycogen) and fat they store right inside the cells. These energy stores also contribute to the muscle's size.

  Muscles are the body's major consumers of glucose. Glucose is taken up from the blood and either burned for energy or stored as glycogen.

  Glucose metabolites are also key components in the burning of fats. Muscles store more glycogen than fat, because they can't obtain enough from the blood to keep functioning during exercise. If a muscle runs short of glucose metabolites during work, it will begin to break down the protein in muscle cells to convert it to glucose and glucose metabolites.

After exercising, the horse's muscle is primed to readily take up glucose to replace glycogen stores that were used. Correct feeding of meals and supplements allows this natural ramping up of the muscle's "hunger" for glucose to rapidly resupply depleted muscles.

Rule #2: Provide sufficient calories and carbohydrate to maintain energy stores and prevent protein breakdown with work.

- **Protein:** Everyone knows muscles are high-protein. To build and maintain muscle, the horse needs adequate total protein in the diet and sufficient amounts of key amino acids (the building blocks of protein molecules). Amino acids of particular importance to muscle are the BCAAs, or branched chain amino acids, of leucine, isoleucine, valine, lysine, and, in the case of horses in extremely hard work, possibly arginine.

Rule #3: Provide adequate protein from varied sources for a good mix of amino acids, and consider a BCAA or HMB (a derivative of the BCAA leucine) supplement if problems with muscle mass remain evident.

- **Antioxidants:** Working muscles generate large amounts of potentially damaging oxygen byproducts (oxygen-free radicals) when burning their fuels. Maintaining adequate levels of key antioxidants to neutralize these free radicals is essential to protecting the muscle cells from damage. Vitamin E and selenium are two of the most important.

Rule #4: Provide 2,000 IU/day of vitamin E to horses in light work, 5,000+ IU/day for horses in moderate to heavy work, and a minimum of 2 mg/day of selenium. Blood selenium levels should be checked to determine

A well conditioned, properly fed performance horse is lean but with well developed muscles.

the individual horse's requirements, because there is considerable individual variation.

- **Vitamins and Minerals:** This is too big a topic to cover in detail in this section (see chapter 1 for more information), but adequate levels and balances of vitamins and minerals are critical to nerve function, protein metabolism, energy generation, and muscular relaxation and contraction.

Rule #5: Adequate and balanced vitamins and minerals are essential for muscular development, repair, and function.

- **Exercise:** You can pump the horse full of all the calories and protein you like without improving muscle mass if the horse is not being exercised. "Use it or lose it" definitely applies to muscle tissue. Even the muscle wasting in older horses (unless related to disease) can be largely prevented and even reversed with regular exercise.

Rule #6: Regular exercise with proper nutritional support builds muscles.

- **Fat versus Muscle:** Your horse has a layer of fat under his skin, which can vary tremendously in thickness. If you aren't familiar with truly fit horses and how well-developed muscles look and feel, you can be easily fooled into thinking that a fat horse has good muscle bulk. The body-condition scoring systems, like the 9-point Heineke condition scale used in this country, or the 5-point system of Drs. Carroll and Huntington use in Australia, are geared to the amount of fat the horse has, not muscle. Many areas that people commonly think indicate good muscling, like the back and neck line from withers to poll, are actually prone to depositing fat. It's entirely possible for a horse to put on weight, even be fat, and have poor muscle development underneath it. Conversely, a horse with little fat covering over his ribs may have excellent muscular development.

Our Trial

For our trial of muscle-building products, we used a variety of horses, from yearlings to performance horses to seniors. We evaluated the products for a range of concerns: sales prep, poor muscular development in both young and old horses, and horses training and racing experiencing trouble holding and building muscle or with low-grade muscular problems.

Regular exercise combined with proper nutrition produce the lean, athletic muscular body type seen in this horse.

To evaluate the effects, we chose to measure fore-arm circumference, as fat in this area is usually minimal. Muscular development along the muscular arch of the neck and muscle belly definition along the chest and shoulder were assessed. Horses were also body-condition scored according to the 9-point Heineke scale to assess any changes that might actually be due to increased body fat. Special attention was paid to the amount and texture of fat along the chest wall and over the ribs, since there are no large muscles under the skin in that area.

- **Vitamins and Minerals.** To see the difference vitamins and minerals could make, we took at a look at three products: PalaMountains Equine, Oxy-Equine, and Sport Horse. Both switching to a vitamin and mineral supplemented feed and use of Oxy-Equine resulted in improvements in both body-condition score and muscling, with no added advantage to adding the Oxy-Equine to a diet already containing a supplemented feed. Sport Horse significantly improved body condition and muscling in two yearlings that were already receiving good quality hay and a vitamin-and-mineral supplemented grain. Try this first if there's any suspicion your vitamin and mineral bases may not be adequately covered.

- **Gamma Oryzanol-based.** Gamma oryzanol is a plant steroid with a structure similar to animal steroid hormones, including sex hormones. Its anabolic (muscle building) effects have not been well researched in formal studies, but gamma oryzanol derived from rice bran oil is one of the most common ingredients in equine muscle supplements. Some improvements in muscling were seen with several products, but the standout in this category was Body Builder, with consistent improvements noted even in horses on well supplemented diets with adequate protein, calories, and lysine levels. No improvements in performance were noted.

- **Creatine.** Creatine is the darling of human body builders but doesn't produce the same dramatic results in horses. We tried one creatine product and found no obvious changes in muscling. We'd skip the creatine.

- **Protein and Carbohydrate.** Fat Cat was most effective in preventing muscle loss and maintaining body-condition score when fed immediately after work. A specific muscle-enhancing effect was not noted, though. Try this as a supplementary calorie source for a horse in work having trouble holding both weight and muscle bulk. The other product in this category, Cell Mass, is higher in protein and targets muscle-cell volume. Effects were seen when used in a diet where protein intake was likely borderline.

- **BCAAs and HMB.** Our best results in terms of muscle bulk and exercise performance were seen with this category. We tried the products with horses receiving what should have been adequate diets in all respects but that still had trouble holding and building muscle mass, with evidence of some soreness. Best results were obtained with Su-Per HMB and BCAA Complex, when given close to exercise.

Bottom Line

The findings in our product trial highlighted once again the importance of the base diet. Before trying a muscle-building product, get assistance in evaluating your basic feeding plan. Correcting any weaknesses there will also benefit the horse overall and may eliminate the need for a muscle supplement. The "Troubleshooting Action Plan" table will help you sort through this.

Troubleshooting Action Plan

Horse Class	Problem	Suggestions and Product Picks
All ages and uses	Poor body-condition score, poor muscling	1) Deworm. 2) Evaluate diet for adequate levels of calories, protein, and lysine. 3) Consider switching to a vitamin/mineral supplemented feed, or adding a high-potency vitamin-and-mineral supplement, such as Sport Horse or Oxy-Equine.
All ages and uses	Diet analyzed and adequate, no performance issues, overall body weight OK but muscles not well defined	Body Builder
Performance	Adequate calories, vitamins, and minerals but possibly borderline protein, body-condition score OK to borderline, losing muscle definition or not building muscle with exercise	Fat Cat Cell Mass
Performance	Adequate calories, protein, lysine, vitamins, and minerals but losing muscle mass, low-grade muscle problems	Su-Per HMB BCAA Complex

Note: Any horse showing dramatic weight and/or muscle loss should be evaluated by a vet.

We recommend you troubleshoot and choose the product that most closely matches your horse's nutritional situation. If everything is ideal, we'd go with Body Builder for all ages of horses.

Serious Support for High-Level Performance

From Gatorade to those sophisticated-sounding concoctions sold in health-food stores, sports drinks for human athletes are everywhere. These drinks maintain the body's hydration level and provide essential nutrients, like electrolytes and energy sources, which then boost endurance and strength during physical exertion—just what we want to do for our horses.

And they're fluid for good reason: Delivering nutrients with water is the most efficient route of replacement. The carbohydrates and glucose in solid food, like candy, aren't as effective. Nutrients in water pass right through the stomach and into the small intestine for immediate absorption, even if the stomach already contains food. No waiting period.

Of course, you're thinking you already give your horse a "sports drink" when you provide electrolytes in a separate bucket of water. But what if there were a way to get more out of that bucket than just electrolyte replacement? What if you

Use a Sports Drink To:

- Give your horse a boost on long show days.

- Quickly replenish tired muscles.

- Get him beyond a "wall"

- in strength or endurance training limits.

- Help him hold his build.

- Change his attitude from tired to eager.

could actually boost performance, like some human sports drinks do?

Best Ingredients

Of course, the most important ingredient in any sports drink is water. Not only is it a vehicle for other ingredients, but even a tiny amount of dehydration can also affect performance. And, of course, electrolytes are an absolute must.

In addition, we want carbohydrates such as dextrose, glucose, or longer-chain sugars in the drink to provide energy. Fat is not the ideal energy source it is sometimes held up to be, although horses working at low intensities do use a lot of mobilized body fat. However, fat taken in during work won't do you any immediate good.

For the muscles, we need amino acids, in particular branched chain amino acids (BCAAs), which the muscles use up at a significant rate during exercise.

Various vitamins, trace minerals, and metabolically important substances like lipoic acid, Co-Q 10, and carnitine are also sometimes added to sports drinks, again in small amounts—often amounts too small to make a difference.

Last, but not least, is creatine. As in all mammals, the creatine phosphate system is an integral part of energy metabolism in a horse's muscle, especially in the fast-twitch (speed) muscle fibers.

Creatine and BCAAs

When it comes to creatine, more is definitely not better.

We tried dosages varying from 20 to 120 grams/day of pure creatine. After two to three days of dosages over 60 grams/day, many horses developed increased tension and tone on palpation of the muscles. At 80 to 120 grams/day, two horses developed stiffness and one appeared to tie up after exercise, although muscle enzymes remained normal, indicating there was no actual damage. Human creatine users report cramping as a side effect.

Our problems occurred after high loading dosages and resolved within a week after stopping the creatine. In a human study, changes induced by long-term ingestion took up to 30 days to resolve—something to keep in mind if you're considering creatine use.

Creatine and BCAA Products
BCAA Complex—Peak Performance Nutrients (800-944-1984). $79.99/2 lbs. $1.78 per 20-gram dose.

Creatine—Uckele (800-248-0330). Pure creatine monohydrate. 454 g./lb. $21/lb. 93¢ (20 grams) to $1.86 (40 grams) per dose.

Equi-Pro—Uckele (800-248-0330). Contains creatine 5,000 mg., L-leucine 1,000 mg., L-valine 1,000 mg., HMB 1,000 mg., glutamine 3,000 mg., L-isoleucine 1,200 mg., chromium 2 mg., glycine 1000 mg., base of maltose, sucrose, and dextrose (about 60 g.), bicarbonates, phosphates, lipoic acid, electrolytes. $12.95/100 gm packet.

Creatine and Muscle Levels

Creatine supplementation increases muscle levels and improves athletic performance (primarily short-term bursts of speed) in many species, but studies in horses fed creatine showed no change in blood or muscle levels.

When we tried creatine in a previous field trial (March 1999), our results also were less than convincing, although it's bugged us ever since. Work in progress in the United Kingdom using a creatine assay specially selected for equine blood casts doubt on the common assumption that horses can't absorb creatine. Therefore, creatine should work, but why didn't it in our trials?

Several factors play into effective creatine supplementation, including dosage, whether the athlete is training actively, insulin level in the blood at the time the creatine is absorbed, and level of training. Our prime suspect in our first trials was poor absorption from the intestines.

Creatine is fragile and readily broken down into creatinine, a waste product. We suspect feeding creatine with a meal might not be the best method. However, delivering it in water would give it a non-stop route to the small intestine. Guaranteeing that blood insulin was up at the same time, by including simple carbohydrates, should help absorption.

That's when the light went on for us: What about an equine sports drink that would deliver carbohydrates, creatine, and BCAAs to the horse, in various combinations?

You Can Lead a Horse to Water

We designed four basic sports-drink mixtures:

1. A 7% solution of maltodextrins, a dissolved glycogen-loader with carbohydrates (plain carbs),

2. A 7% solution with BCAAs only,

3. A 7% solution with creatine only, or

4. A 7% solution with creatine and BCAAs.

That was easy and fun. But convincing the horses a sports drink is a good idea is another matter. When we offered these solutions in a small bucket or bowl, most horses gave us a blank stare or sniffed at it and snorted the stuff all over the place. A few even nudged it away. Back to the drawing board.

After much experimentation, we hit upon using a few tablespoons of frozen grape-juice concentrate or a cup of carrot juice as flavoring agents. Three of the seven horses accepted this mixture—one mare liked her grape juice drink so much she licked the bowl.

Since we wanted to observe effects of administration both before and after exercise, the three horses who accepted the mix became the pre-exercise group. The other four received their supplements as a paste immediately after they consumed at least two liters of water when being cooled out after exercise, or mixed in the first two liters of water they were offered after work.

Note: While carbohydrates and BCAAs are stable in water, creatine is not. Be sure to mix up the solution or paste immediately before giving it to the horse.

Field Trials

In addition to looking for different effects from the mixtures, we wanted to see if sports drinks pre-exercise would influence attitude and performance and if there was any obvious value to using them after exercise.

The seven Standardbred racehorses in our trial were all at a tough stage in training—making the transition into serious speed (anaerobic) work at, or close to, race speeds. This is a difficult time metabolically for many horses, and it's not unusual to find that, while they may have progressed effortlessly prior to this time, they "hang up" at a speed and have trouble making further progress. All seven horses were "hitting the wall."

To qualify for the trial, the horses must have had three consecutive speed training sessions or races where they were unable to meet their next milestone in terms of improving in speed. All were screened for lameness and respiratory problems.

Plain Carbs: Before we looked at combinations, we needed to know what effect the plain carbohydrate drink would have. We knew that glycogen-loading protocols and a high-carbohydrate feeding 1.5 to two hours prior to racing or training can have a dramatic effect. We had never checked for effects of a single carbohydrate boost without prior loading, though. The results were positive.

All the horses receiving a pretraining or racing carbohydrate drink (50 to 70 grams per liter, two liters), given 30 to 60 minutes before work, showed obviously alert attitudes and an eagerness to perform. After receiving these pre-exercise supplements daily for 7 to 10 days, their ability to maintain speed and finish more strongly was also evident, with times for a mile dropping an average of one second over the best time for the previous three training sessions.

Branched chain amino acids specifically prevent muscle tissue from breakdown.

Horses in high-performance sports can often use some muscle support.

Sharp turns and speed work can strain muscles as well as joints.

Carbs plus BCAAs: We next tried combining the carbohydrate with 20 grams BCAAs. Two horses performed exactly as they had with the carbohydrate only. One was worse.

Creatine and Carbs: We next added 40 grams of creatine monohydrate to the carbohydrate mixture. After a week of this carb-and-creatine drink before exercise, two of the three horses were more aggressive about wanting to race and pulling more than usual during training. They were described as finishing with more ease. Times improved almost another full second over the initial improvement with carbohydrates alone. The third horse showed no change in attitude or strength when finishing, but also improved his time almost another full second.

Note: This equaled almost two seconds over their best efforts for the three training sessions prior to starting with sports drinks.

The trainers stated the creatine mix made a noticeable difference in eagerness and how well the horses performed. However, it was difficult to differentiate whether the additional improvement in time was related to the horses' training and/or to additional carbohydrate being supplied versus the creatine.

In an attempt to get a better handle on creatine versus carb effects, we selected two other racehorses considered to be racing at their potential. For their next two races, they received either a five-day creatine-loading protocol alone (80 grams per day for five days, split 50:50, with half given 30 minutes prior to the morning feeding and the other half immediately after finishing the day's exercise; on race day, half was given as usual in the morning, half three to four hours before racing), or the same creatine program plus 70 grams of a glycogen-loading product at the same time intervals.

In both horses, creatine alone produced no changes in attitude or performance, while the creatine with glycogen-loader resulted in a dramatic improvement. One of the horses improved his race time by four seconds on the creatine-and-glycogen combo, and bested his time for the last quarter of the race by two seconds, despite less-than-stellar track conditions.

The Right Mix for the Problem

Problem	Suggestion
Racing/speed training: Horse having trouble meeting milestones for speed or improving speed.	7% maltodextrin solution with 20 to 40 grams creatine pre-exercise (within 30 to 60 minutes). Or post-exercise (immediate) 2 liters of the solution or double-dose Equi-Pro.
Dull attitude, lack of interest.	7% maltodextrin solution with or without creatine pre-exercise—2 liters (70 grams of glycogen-loader product/liter), or double-dose Equi-Pro.
Horse lacks strength and/or tires easily but "hot" attitude not desired.	Try 7% maltodextrin solution with 20 grams BCAAs pre-exercise (try at home first!). If still too eager, try same post-exercise only for a week or longer, or 7- to 10-day course of Equi-Pro post-exercise.
Horse having trouble maintaining weight and/or muscle mass, muscle soreness.	Both carbs alone and carbs plus BCAAs helped these horses. When BCAAs were used, improved muscle definition was also obtained. Equi-Pro, with good carb levels and lower doses of BCAAs and creatine but a synergistic effect from the combination (and a small amount of HMB), was an effective way to combat muscle problems while avoiding any possible negative effects from higher doses.

The other's time improved 1.5 seconds, all of it in the last quarter of the race. The horses were then only lightly exercised for two weeks, with one training session at 85% of race speed after the first week.

For the third race, both received glycogen-loading only, no creatine. The horse that had improved four seconds showed only a three-second improvement this time, while the one that had improved 1.5 seconds improved by a full two seconds. However, the drivers of both horses, who were not aware of the trial, commented the horses were unusually eager and strong for the races when they had received creatine.

Post-Exercise

An energy boost before performance is one thing, but equally important was quickly replenishing hard-working muscles. Human athletes know carbohydrate sources taken after hard work enhance the rebuilding of glycogen stores. They also favor the conversion of growth hormone into its active anabolic form, IGF-1 (insulin-like growth factor) and help from the carbs toward preventing muscle soreness.

The most recent research into post-exercise supplementation also discloses an important role for BCAAs in the preservation and building of muscle mass, as well as prevention of muscle damage, as evidenced by increased blood levels of muscle enzymes after exercise and soreness. We've seen this muscle-preserving and soreness-preventing effect with tying-up products. It's also been found in people that the effects of carbohydrate and BCAAs enhance carbohydrate effects.

Most recommendations regarding creatine supplements in humans call for taking them several times a day. However, a study in the *Journal of Applied Physiology* shows that muscles exercised first take up more creatine than those that aren't, and ingestion of creatine at the same time as carbohydrates improves the levels of both in the muscle compared to taking either one alone. Sounds good, but we wanted to see how it translated in a real-life barn.

The horses in our post-exercise-supplement group ranged in age from 3 to 8. All had a history of at least one past episode of prolonged muscle soreness or tying-up and were prone to stiffness, elevated muscle tone, and soreness on muscle palpation for a few days following speed training. However, muscle enzymes at the time of supplementation, while in active training, were confirmed to be normal.

One horse received post-exercise carbohydrates only, one a combination of carbs and creatine, one carbs and BCAAs, one carbs, BCAAs, and creatine. A 2-year-old filly was put on Equi-Pro. She had no history of exercise-related, training, or muscle pain or stiffness problems but was having trouble maintaining her muscle mass and weight, so her trainer took things slowly with her for fear of overfacing her. Supplementation was given after work, during cooling out.

All the horses showed brightened attitudes without muscle soreness or stiffness and were eager to perform. They had no difficulty meeting their next training milestone for speed and had no evidence of a dull attitude or loss of appetite after heavy work, which had been common before the supplementation.

The trainers concluded unanimously that the supplementation had benefited them. The horses on carbs and BCAAs (with or without creatine) also showed a visible improvement in muscle definition. The filly on Equi-Pro was easily able to maintain her weight and muscle mass with no other change in her diet.

Pulling the Results Together

For horses willing to drink them, pre-exercise sports drinks with about 7% carbohydrate as maltodextrins (70 grams per liter) provide an energy boost that translates into an eager and willing attitude. With regular use, after seven to 10 days, the horses improved in their ability to maintain speed, similar to the effects seen with a glycogen-loading protocol. This also occurred when the sports drinks were supplied immediately after exercise.

BCAAs appear to have a negative effect on speed, at least when given pre-exercise, and to dampen the "up" attitude from the carbohydrate. Plus, studies show that BCAAs markedly depress anaerobic-energy generation, which is an integral part of speed work. Of course, if you just need to put more bottom, or strength, in your horse, this could work to your advantage.

Long-term (seven to 10 days plus) use of carbohydrates with BCAAs alone, or with BCAAs plus creatine, given in close association to work, improved muscle definition. In our trials using anabolic alternatives to steroids, we got the same results, but it took higher dosages and a longer time period with BCAAs alone.

The jury's still out on creatine, although when given with carbohydrates and water on an empty stomach, we feel it shows more promise than before. Our trainers consistently reported horses were more eager to perform and felt stronger than with carbohydrates alone. Unfortunately, however, this didn't translate into any clear advantage in speed over carbohydrates alone.

Bottom Line

Regular use of "sports drinks" can benefit horses in heavy training or on intensive competition schedules. Use the drink before exercise or competition to give the horse an energy boost and brighter attitude. Horses that have trouble meeting their goals for speed or distance or that tire in the middle of a long show day can benefit from drinking cooling-out water blended with a sports-drink mixture of either carbohydrate alone or carbohydrate with BCAAs or creatine to help them replete their muscular energy stores more efficiently. The same approach worked well for horses with lackluster performance, muscle pain, and trouble holding muscular bulk.

We found no ineffective products in our trial. The "combo" products, Equi-Pro and Turbo III, were convenient but more expensive than mixing individual products. All our glycogen loaders got the job done, with a nod for price going to Uckele's Carb-O-Load. For the most economical sports-drink mixture, we'd combine Carb-O-Load with Uckele's pure creatine and/or the Peak Performance BCAA Complex.

Special Needs of High-Performance Quarter Horses

Post-exertion muscle soreness and strain can happen to any horse, but the high demands placed on the muscles of a Quarter Horse can easily lead to some soreness. Add to that the fact that they're also prone to some breed-related muscle problems, and you know you need to pay attention to their muscles.

Slow, careful conditioning is the best preventative. Training improves both strength and flexibility of muscle groups and the tendons attached to them. Practicing movements in a controlled training setting will fine tune the reflexes the horse needs for quick changes of direction or fast starts. Training also improves levels of the stored carbohydrate glycogen within the muscle, the only fuel that can support speed.

There are a variety of muscle massage tools on the market that horseowners can use on their horses.

Feeding

There's some evidence to support fat supplementation (up to 8%) of the grain portion of the diet in the hard-working Quarter Horse, despite our overall concerns about feeding fat to horses. Studies have found both improved sprint times and higher lactate production during sprints (an indicator of glycogen use) when grain was supplemented with fat.

The likely explanation for this is that the muscle learns to make better use of fat for maintenance energy requirements and during low level, slow work, allowing for better preservation of glycogen stores, which are then available for the high speed work. It's important to note, though, that this only works when fat is supplemented in addition to grain, not as a substitute for it as is done to treat equine polysaccharide storage myopathy (EPSSM). The horse still needs grain to build glycogen stores.

To benefit the most from training and recover glycogen stores quickly after exercise, the muscle needs glucose. Studies in multiple breeds have shown that horses are slow to replenish their glycogen stores, taking up to three days to do so after a major effort. However, some recent studies have found that both intravenous and oral supplementation of simple carbohydrate can hasten this process. This trick has been practiced by human athletes for many years.

Details of how much, and when, for maximal benefit have yet to be worked out and confirmed by studies, but muscle in other species is most "hungry" for glucose in the first hour or two after exercise stops, with increased uptake by muscles continuing over the next 24 hours, but dropping rapidly during that time. Providing the horse with 2 to 4 oz. of a glycogen-loading product as a paste shortly after heavy training or competition, and again in a grain meal about two hours after the exertion, should give him a good head start on repair and replenishment of hard-working muscle.

Antioxidants are also important to hard-working muscles. They won't boost performance per se, or prevent injuries, but they're extremely important in mopping up the free radicals produced during exercise and preventing injury to cell structures.

Vitamin E and selenium should always be supplemented, according to the type of diet and selenium levels in your area.

Tying-Up

Isolated episodes of tying-up can also happen to any horse and don't necessarily indicate an underlying muscle disease. Severe overexertion may cause it, and electrolyte abnormalities may contribute to muscle cramping and pain. The precise cause of isolated episodes of tying-up often goes undiagnosed.

Horses that are in the early stages of being introduced to serious speed work and very fit horses that miss exercise sessions are at highest risk. Cutting or even eliminating grain on days these horses are not formally worked can help decrease the risk, probably by avoiding excessive glycogen build up. Keeping horses outside, rather than stall confined, is also helpful.

Muscle is protein, and building and maintaining muscle requires protein. Most performance-horse diets contain more than enough protein to get the job done, but if the horse is failing to build or maintain muscle as expected, supplementation with HMB (hydroxymethyl/butyrate) or a branched chain amino acid product may help.

HYPP

Repeated episodes of severe cramping tying-up symptoms are another story. HYPP and EPSSM are the most likely causes in a Quarter Horse. HYPP, hyperkalemic periodic paralysis, isn't actual tying-up, but it looks like it.

As most Quarter Horse owners know, HYPP is a genetically determined disease, tracing back to descendants of the great halter horse, Impressive. It's really a disorder of electrolyte balance within the muscle, disturbing and reversing the normal condition of low sodium and high potassium inside the cell. In the early stages of an HYPP attack, muscles tremble and may spasm, leading to confusion with tying-up, but there are important differences.

Recommended management strategies include:
- Avoid stress, changes in management, changes in diet.

Don't Blame Lactic Acid for Muscle Pain

Most people firmly believe that lactate, or lactic acid, is the cause of muscle fatigue, "burning," and tying-up. They'll purchase supplements, believing the products can reduce lactic acid, and they'll make dietary changes for the same reasons. But lactic acid's relationship to muscle fatigue is terribly misunderstood. Lactic acid isn't the enemy.

Muscles and Energy

Muscles produce lactic acid continuously. It's generated during the breakdown of glucose as an energy source. If the horse is moving slowly, most of the lactate is further broken down to pyruvate and goes into aerobic energy pathways. However, as the horse moves faster and needs to produce energy quickly to keep up with demands, the aerobic pathways are too slow and more energy is generated anaerobically, producing lactate.

Lactate isn't a waste product or a toxin. It's beneficial. Lactate is used by the liver and by muscle cells that aren't being worked as hard. Lactate is also a buffer, a way that muscle cells can carry harmful acidity out of the cells. This is because the lactate molecule binds the acidifying hydrogen ions and carries them into the circulatory system.

People who have been used to thinking of lactate as harmful have trouble accepting this concept, but many studies have failed to find any relationship between lactate levels after exercise and poor performance. In fact, it's often found that the superior-performing horses are those with the highest lactate levels after exercise.

A similar association between high lactate production and superior performance has been found in human athletes.

Bottom Line

What this all boils down to is that blood lactate after exercise is nothing more than an indicator of how hard or fast the horse worked. It's not connected to tying-up or muscle damage. Instead of being harmful, lactate is actually a source of energy and reduces the acidity inside hard-working cells by carrying the hydrogen ions out of the cell. High blood lactate levels are associated with superior performance, not fatigue. Next time you see advertising for a supplement or grain that claims to make your horse work harder or longer by lowering lactate, pass it up.

- Keep the horse on a regular exercise program.
- 24/7 turnout may be beneficial.
- Avoid high dietary levels of potassium.
- Treat with acetazolamide, a diuretic that encourages potassium excretion, for horses that are not well-controlled with management and diet.

Although some types of hay have been recommended as lower-potassium alternatives, the fact is that all hays are many times higher in potassium than the horse actually requires. Grass is, too, especially young growths of grass, but the high water content of grasses means the potassium is significantly diluted. Beet pulp without molasses is the lowest potassium feed, and grains are much lower than hays and will deliver a load of glucose at the same time, to help drive potassium into the cells where it belongs. Substituting wet beet pulp for part of the hay, offering frequent small grain feedings, and soaking hay before feeding, which will lower potassium content, are feeding strategies that help avoid swings in blood potassium.

In fact, the ability of insulin and glucose to drive potassium back inside the muscle cells where it belongs is the basis for the owner's first-aid emergency treatment of administering corn syrup, or encouraging the horse to eat grain (preferably corn). HYPP attacks are also a veterinary emergency, since the weakness can involve the breathing muscles, and severe attacks can kill a horse. Your vet will use intravenous glucose, possibly intravenous calcium and insulin, and acetazolamide.

EPSSM

Repeated episodes of true tying-up in a Quarter Horse, like in their heavily muscled cousins, the drafts, are most likely to be caused by EPSSM. Muscle biopsies of horses with EPSSM show high levels of glycogen, as well as a substance that is not normal glycogen.

The exact nature of the defect in metabolism in these cells that makes them prone to damage with exercise isn't clear, but it appears they rely too heavily on carbohydrate and not enough on fat. Limiting carbohydrate intake and feeding increased fat appears to "train" muscles to make better use of fat as an energy source, which relieves many of the symptoms.

Definitive diagnosis can only be made by muscle biopsy, although many opt for a trial of low-carbohydrate, high-fat diet instead. The current basic diet recommendation for an EPSSM horse consists of hay, with alfalfa pellets substituted for the grain ration, and up to two cups of vegetable oil. One cup of oil is the calorie equivalent of about 2.5 to 3 pounds of grain. Improvements in the form of more relaxed muscle tone and less frequent and severe symptoms of tying-up may appear rapidly or may take time.

Any oil will do, but Uckele's Coco-Soya (www.uckele.com, 800-248-0330) can be a good choice. This blend of coconut and soy oils is cold pressed and unprocessed, retaining high levels of natural antioxidants. It's highly palatable. The coconut oil is high in medium-chain-length triglycerides, which are able to enter the muscle cell without requiring a carrier protein like the longer-chain triglycerides found in other vegetable oils do.

Treatment of an EPSSM-related tying-up episode is the same as for any other type of tying-up. Movement can worsen muscle damage and should be avoided. Muscle relaxants, tranquilizers, and intravenous calcium and magnesium may be used to help the stiff, painful muscles relax. Intravenous fluids help prevent muscle pigments from clogging the kidneys.

Gleam & Gain is a high-fat supplement.

Muscle Tears

Another problem that frequently occurs in Quarter Horses is muscle tears, due to the combination of heavy muscling and the type of work many Quarter Horses do. These typically involve long, large muscle groups of the upper hind leg, when viewed from behind.

Soreness and stiffness present at the time of the initial injury may resolve, only to be followed by the development of a shortened gait on the involved side and a characteristic slapping down of the foot, called goosestepping. This occurs when the injured area of muscle heals by formation of a thick, tight scar that lacks the ability to stretch that normal muscle has.

The condition is called fibrotic myopathy. In some cases, calcification or calcium deposits may also form, called calcific myopathy. Surgical removal of the scarred and/or calcified portion of muscle is the usual treatment. Shock-wave therapy also has been tried. 🐎

Products to Promote Muscle Growth

BCS= Body-Condition Score

Product	Price	Dosages	Comments
BCAA Complex Peak Perfomance Nutrients www.peak performancenutrients.com 800-944-1984	Powder $75.99/900 grams (45 days) $1.78 per day	Per 10 g: 4,500 mg leucine, 3,800 mg valine, 1,600 mg isoleucine (these 3 are branched chain amino acids), 350 mg glutamine, plus low levels magnesium, zinc, chromium, and B6	Modest but visible improvements in neck and shoulder muscling, up to 0.75 cm increases in forearm circumference, no change in BCS after supplementation for 2 weeks in the feed of two 2-year-old fillies in heavy training. Best results seen in a 3-year-old filly having problems with muscular cramping, mildly elevated muscle enzymes, and poor muscling. That filly received 10 grams immediately before and after exercise, as a paste with 2 oz. of maltodextrin powder. After 2 weeks, her forearm circumference improved 1 cm, muscle stiffness was relieved, muscle enzymes normalized, and her trainer reported she was working much more easily.
Blitz Peak Perfomance Nutrients www.peak performancenutrients.com 800-944-1984	Gel $12/80 cc dose $12 per day	Electrolyte/mineral (profile similar to sweat, plus good levels of magnesium), high-dose B vitamins, and moderately high BCAAs and other amino acids	Designed as a preperformance booster. Can be used as a daily supplement but $12/day is pricey for most for regular use. The vitamin-B profile is conducive to efficient energy generation without making the horse "hot." We tried it on a 2-year-old filly who was on the nervous side, prone to low-grade muscular cramping/pain, had a poor appetite and was beginning to lose some muscle definition over her shoulders, chest, and rump. Product was administered 1/2 tube half hour before and after exercise. She was calmer, ate better, showed no more evidence of muscle pain after 4 days, and also filled out but with no change in forearm circumference, so this may have been as much a result of improved appetite as an actual muscle building.
Body Builder Equi-Aide www.equiaide.com 800-413-3702	Liquid $84.95/32 oz. (64 days) $1.33 per day	Per 0.5 oz., 1,000 mg gamma oryzanol in a corn oil and rice bran oil base	One weanling on sales prep, one 2-year-old gelding in heavy training, and one 5-year-old racing gelding, all on high-quality diets with generous protein and adequate calories, all with poorly defined muscling, were supplemented for 30 days. Obvious improvements in muscling were seen, with a 0.5 grade increase in BCS. The weanling showed a 0.5 cm increase in forearm circumference, 2-year-old increased by 1.5 cm, 5-year-old by 1 cm. No improvements in training or race performance were noted.
Body Pro II Med-Vet Pharmaceuticals www.medvetpharm.com 800-366-8986	Liquid $69/32 oz. (64 days maintenance, 32 days loading) $1.12 per day maintenance	0.5 oz. gamma oryzanol 1,250, 264 mg creatine in soy and coconut oil	We fed this to one weanling on sales prep, a 2-year-old gelding in training who was poorly muscled, and a 20-year-old retired gelding with poor teeth that had been losing muscle mass. All were on high-quality diets (the older gelding on soaked pellets), with generous intakes of protein, adequate calories, above NRC recommended levels of lysine. The weanling showed no changes compared to other weanlings in the same group. The 2-year-old appeared somewhat better muscled overall, with a 0.75 cm increase in forearm circumference, but also increased rib fat, and he was reported to be eating better. There was no change in the older gelding.
Cell Mass Uckele www.uckele.com 800-248-0330	Powder $33.20/2 lbs. (32 1 oz. doses) $1.04 per day	Per 1 oz.: 16 grams hydrolyzed gelatin, rice bran extracts, Sasparilla root (may be mildly androgenic in geldings), with supplemental L-glycine, L-glutamine, ornithine alphaketoglutarate (growth hormone stimulant), moderate dose creatine	We tried this supplement with three 2-year-old geldings in training on different diets. All were receiving adequate calories and NRC-recommended minimum levels of lysine, but different protein intakes, either 10%, 12%, or 14% protein feeds (8 lbs./day), and free-choice grass hay (good quality but untested protein content, lysine guesstimated at 0.2%). Three more 2-year-olds were not supplemented and fed the same diets. The horses on the 10% protein feed did not build muscle well, with or without the supplement. With the 12% protein feed, addition of the supplement led to a 0.5 cm increase in forearm circumference and better muscular definition overall with no differences in BCS. With the 14% protein feed, no differences were found between the test horses, and both showed good muscular development.
Creatine XL Med-Vet Pharmaceuticals www.medvetpharm.com 800-366-8986	Powder $21.50/lb., (100 low-dose servings; 25 high-dose servings) 22¢ per day low	Per dose: 4,540 mg creatinine (3 to 4 times this for loading)	No change in subjective muscling, forearm circumference, or BCS after 30 days at low-dose feeding, added to meals. One 3-year-old filly was given the 4X dose for 5 days, drenched immediately after work. She showed a 0.75 cm change in forearm circumference on day 5, along with stiffness in movement. An 8-year-old gelding treated the same way showed no changes, but trainer reported faster sprint speeds, less effort, in a training session.

Product	Price	Dosages	Comments
Fat Cat Vapco www.vapco.com 800-523-5614	Powder $23.99/5 lbs. (27 days at high dose) 89¢ per day high dose	3 oz./day for high performance. A 24% protein, low fat, dextrose based supplement with low levels of added biotin, salt, major minerals, lysine, methionine, probiotics/digestive enzymes	We fed this to two 2-year-old fillies in training who were having difficulty maintaining both a good BCS and building muscle despite increases in feeding and a high-quality diet. One was fed the product in her regular feeds, the other was given it mixed with water, as a gruel (highly palatable) immediately after exercise. The one receiving it in her feed stopped losing weight, but the one getting it immediately after work actually showed an improvement in BCS, looked more filled out overall, but no change in forearm circumference.
Foxden Muscle Mix Foxden Equine www.foxdenequine.com 540-337-5450	Powder $35/300 grams (30 days) $1.17 per day	Per 10 g: 2 g threonine, 2 g tyrosine, 1 g lysine, 1 g glutamine, 300 mg methionine, 200 mg ALA, 1.5 g CLA	This product was given to two 2-year-olds known to have adequate lysine and crude protein in their diet, and response compared to two unsupplemented 2-year-olds on the same diet. After a month on 10 g/day, there was no change in BCS or forearm circumference.
M.A.S.S. Kinetic Technologies LLC www.kinetictech.net 877-786-9882	Liquid $35.20/32 oz. (32 days) $1.11 per day	1,500 mg/oz gamma oryzanol with low-dose lysine and threonine	Recommended amount was fed to one 3-year-old filly, one 3-year-old gelding, and one 18-year-old gelding. The filly showed no changes. The 3-year-old gelding showed 0.75 cm increase in forearm circumference, no change in BCS, slight change in general muscling through the neck and shoulders. The 18-year-old gelding showed a 1.0 cm increase in forearm circumference, slight increase in BCS as judged by sponginess of rib fat, improved muscular contours through the neck and shoulders.
More Muscle Corta-Flx Inc www.corta-flx.com 888-294-1100	Liquid $25/qt. (64 days) 39¢ per day	1/2 oz. 1,000 mg gamma oryzanol in a base of rice bran oil, thickeners	Three 3-year-olds in training, one filly and two geldings, on vitamin/mineral supplemented diets and adequate intakes of calories, protein, and lysine, were supplemented for one month and compared to four unsupplemented 3-year-olds on identical diets. No changes in BCS. One colt in the supplemented group showed a 0.5 cm improvement in forearm circumference but no obvious change in neck or shoulder muscle definition.
Muscle Build Cavalor www.farmvet.com 888-837-3626	Powder $190.99/90 packets (11 to 30 days) $6.37 per day at 3 packets	2 to 8 packets per day. A high-carbohydrate, 29.2% protein supplement, Gluta Syn, low levels of lysine, methionine, threonin, cystine, vitamins, herbs	Three low-BCS poorly muscled 2-year-old geldings in training were intensively dewormed then put on: A) high-quality hay/grain and vitamin-supplemented mineral-balanced diet, adequate protein; B) Same with three packets per day Muscle Build; C) Same with 10 packets per day Muscle Build. All three showed similar improvements in BCS and forearm circumference. The one on 10 packets had better muscle definition, better excercise tolerance, and was felt by the trainer to be subjectively stronger.
Muscle Builder Equimed USA 800-765-6040	Liquid $64/qt. (64 doses) $1 per day	0.5 oz 1,250 gamma oryzanol, 300 mg DHEA, 300 mg pregnenolone in rice bran and corn oils	Due to hormone precursors in the product, it wasn't used on breeding-age fillies/mares. Two 2-year-old geldings who were having trouble maintaining muscle mass in training, despite adequate intakes, showed improvement in forearm circumference, no change in BCS, better muscling through the neck and shoulders. One 19-year-old barren broodmare showed a 1 cm increase in forearm musculature, improvement through her neck and shoulders, 0.5 grade increase in BCS.
Oxy-Equine Bonina www.bonina.com 509-297-4480	Pellet $160/25 lbs. (100 days) $1.60 per day	4 oz./day, vitamins and minerals with octacosanol. 35% protein, base of soybean and linseed meal, with brewer's yeast, yeast, brewer's grains, wheat germ, and vitamin E oil	This product was fed to two similarly sized late yearlings in poor body condition, both receiving adequate calories, protein, and lysine, one with a vitamin and mineral supplemented feed, one not. Both were intensively dewormed prior to starting the feeding trial. Both improved significantly over the trial, better muscle tone and development overall, improved 1 BCS, 0.75 and 0.75 cm increases in forearm circumference.
Sport Horse Uckele www.uckele.com 800-248-0330	$47.45/15 lbs. (40 days) $1.19 per day	6 oz./day, high-potency vitamin-and-mineral supplement, with good grapeseed extract, high dose probiotic, levels of lysine, methionine, threonine, and low-dose creatine	Two weanlings in poor body condition had been intensively dewormed and put on a diet of high-quality hay and vitamin/mineral supplemented grain but continued to show poor muscular development, pot-bellied appearance, low energy. After two months there was an improvement in overall BCS of 1 grade but they had not gained in height. After 30 days on Sport Horse, the pot-bellied appearance was gone; chest, shoulder, and neck muscle definition clearly improved, 0.75 and 1.0 cm increases in forearm circumference.
Su-Per HMB Gateway Products, Inc www.buygpdirect.com 888-472-2825	Powder $66.88/2.5 lbs. (20 servings) $3.35 per day	2 oz./day, 10,000 mg HMB	One 2-year-old filly in training and two 5-year-old racing geldings, all having trouble holding muscle mass despite adequate intake, were fed 2 oz./day in a small feed either 30 minutes before or after working. Within 2 weeks, improvement in forearm circumference of 0.75 cm for the filly and 1.5 cm for the geldings was noted, with improved muscling through the neck and shoulders. Top lines improved without any change in fat at the tail base or over the ribs. One gelding had his first win in 20 starts after 2 weeks.

Obesity

OK, your horse is fat. You know it—maybe your trainer told you, and heaven knows your veterinarian would point it out. The overall health of overweight horses, just like overweight people, is jeopardized. Horses can become more susceptible to injury, laminitis, breathing difficulties, and hormonal problems. You've got to take action.

We've become so accustomed to seeing shiny, sleek-coated horses with lots of extra flesh that we easily forget they're actually fat. Some people use the phrase "well conditioned," a term that should be reserved for fit athletes. Round ponies are called "cute," rather than "chubby." Carrying extra weight around is no more healthy or desirable for horses than it is for us. But even if you recognize your horse needs to lose weight, you may be unsure how to go about it without starving or depriving your horse. Stop worrying. Trimming down your horse doesn't have to be stressful for either one of you.

The first step in setting up a weight-loss diet is to determine what your horse's ideal body weight is. Use this information to determine how much hay the horse should be fed. For safe but steady weight loss, if the animal is being worked daily, feed a minimum of 1.5% of his current body weight and 2% of his ideal body weight in hay. For a horse getting no formal exercise and confined to a stall or small paddock, feed between 1% of the current body weight and 1.5% of the ideal body weight. For example, assume our fat pony's current body weight is 700 pounds and his ideal body weight is 500 pounds. He's getting no formal exercise. We'd fed him between 7 and 7.5 pounds of hay per day (1% of current weight to 1.5% of the ideal weight of 500 pounds).

No Crash Dieting

If your horse or pony is already on a grain-free, reduced-hay diet that would make any other horse look like a rack of bones, but weight loss is slow, you may decide to cut feed even further. Don't do it.

Ponies, minis, donkeys, and even full-sized horses whose weight problem is metabolic react to severe calorie restriction by becoming increasingly resistant to the effects of insulin and mobilizing large amounts of fat in an effort to "feed" their cells that way. The fat mobilization can be so severe that the blood looks milky and organ damage can occur.

If you're in this situation, go back to square one; determine your target weight, feed accordingly, and make sure you allow no grain, grass, or high-sugar hays. If you choose the diet correctly, your horse or pony can eat a normal amount and still lose weight.

Knowing how much you are actually feeding your horse, in pounds, is the first step in determining if you may be overfeeding.

Hay's Number 1

The type of hay you choose is important. Hays vary tremendously in their calorie and sugar content. The bright green, tender, dairy cow–quality cuttings of alfalfa lead the pack in calories. The stemmier alfalfas usually available to horse owners often contain the same or fewer calories than young cuttings of some grass hays.

In general, however, we recommend you avoid high quality alfalfa, brome, peanut hay, any crop-type hay (e.g., peavine, soybean), the grain hays (wheat, oat, milo, triticale), and young, tender cuttings of any type. The best hays for weight loss are prairie hays, native meadow hays, and mature cuttings of Bermuda grass, timothy, or orchardgrass.

Excess weight comes from feeding more calories than the horse needs, but weight loss doesn't require starvation diets.

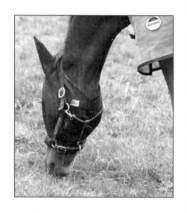

Nothing packs on pounds faster than good pasture.

Calculating his grain and fat intake is simple: None. We're all conditioned to think that the horse's nutrition comes from his grain and that you must "feed" the horse, meaning a concentrate or grain of some type. It's just not so. Grains and fat are extremely calorie-dense and have no place in the diet of a horse that needs to lose weight. The culture shock this creates puts a major roadblock to weight loss in the path of many horses. Even more importantly, if your horse or pony's weight issue is related to a metabolic problem, to get that under control, it's essential to avoid feeding grain or fats.

If you just can't bear the idea of not "feeding" your friend—or he throws a fit because the other horses get goodies in their tubs and he doesn't—substitute something more appropriate. Beet pulp packs about the same calories per pound as oats, but because it can soak up water to a volume four times its dry measure, you can give a good-sized, filling beet-pulp meal at a fraction of the calories.

For a full-sized horse, one pound of beet pulp per day (dry weight) divided into two feedings and "seasoned" with 4 to 6 oz. of ground stabilized flax makes a tasty, good-sized meal that's mineral-balanced for the major minerals, supplies all the fat the horse needs for health, and meets his requirement for omega-6 and omega-3 fatty acids. All you need to add is the hay and a mineral supplement suitable for the hay you've chosen.

Straw

Straw may look low-calorie and unappealing, but the fact is straw can provide as many calories as average grass hays and is often high in sugar. It's readily consumed, especially by horses on diets. We recommend you bed the horse on shavings or another type of alternative bedding.

Grazing

Nothing packs the pounds on a horse more reliably than good pasture. Nature intended grass to be the horse's perfect food,

- Get your horse's current weight, using a weight tape or scale, if possible.
- Determine your horse's ideal body weight.
- Calculate your horse's current daily calorie intake.
- Find your horse's daily calorie requirements for his ideal body weight.
- If calorie intake is excessive, change feeding to reduce it by 25% of the current intake or to the average requirements for his ideal body weight, whichever is larger.

- Exercise!
- If your horse still does not lose weight, consider testing for insulin resistance, since this will mean strict attention to the sugar and starch content of the diet.
- Maintain adequate and balanced intake of all minerals, vitamin E, and any other nutrients suggested by your vet.
- Did we mention exercise?

but it didn't plan on horses having an unlimited supply without covering many miles a day to get it.

One of the most difficult things to accept is that grass intake will have to be limited if not prevented. You can still allow the horse or pony the benefits of moving around on turnout by using a grazing muzzle that sharply limits grass intake. For extremely overweight animals or those with metabolic problems, grass intake should be prevented entirely. Our favorite muzzle is the Best Friend Muzzle from www.bestfriendequine.com.

Lo-Cal Treats

Your horse should have an advantage over a person trying to lose weight since he really can't cheat. Unfortunately, keeping to the prescribed diet seems to be harder on owners than it is on the horses. Be careful not to project your own feelings about dieting onto the horse, or make assumptions that your horse is craving certain things or feeling deprived. The fact is that most horses adapt extremely well to a weight-loss diet.

Automatic feeders that dole out small amounts of hay pellets at more frequent intervals can help alleviate boredom and long intervals between feeding when stalled horses need calorie restriction.

Average Calorie Needs for Horse at 1,100 lbs. Mature Weight

Category	Calories	Hay Equivalents
Maintenance	16.4 Mcal	19 lbs.
Breeding stallion	20.5 Mcal	25 lbs.
Mare, late pregnancy	19.7 Mcal	23 lbs.
Mare, lactating, first 3 months	28.3 Mcal	33 lbs.
Mare, lactating, after 3 months	24.3 Mcal	28.5 lbs.
Light work	20.5 Mcal	25 lbs.
Medium work	24.6 Mcal	29 lbs.
Heavy work	32.8 Mcal	38.5 lbs.

Replacing grain with a pound or so of a protein and mineral supplement reduces calories without sacrificing nutrition.

If you want to share some treats, forget the grain-and molasses-based treats or, worse yet, donuts or any human food you used to use for treats. Sugar-free candies, like an occasional peppermint, are okay, but it's better yet to substitute along the same healthful lines as recommended for human diets. A carrot, a handful of grapes, a prune, or a few alfalfa pellets are much better choices. Fresh carrot and fruit bits are better than dehydrated or dried because the natural water content dilutes the calories. Think portion size, too. Don't give your horse that whole apple; split it with him. Thanks to growing awareness about the health risks of excess calories, especially sugars and starches, there are even guaranteed, tested, low-sugar and -starch treats available now: Skode's Horse Treats (www.skodes horsetreats.com).

Problem Solving

Temporary Weight Problems

Let's say that Mary's horse, Sonic, was being trail ridden for an hour four days a week and longed 20 to 30 minutes another two days. Trail rides were mostly trotting. Sonic's work level is

Calories in Hays versus Grains

A lot of people are under the impression that hays are nothing more than fiber, something you give the horse to chew on to keep him occupied. Nothing could be further from the truth. Hay is not only your horse's major source of minerals, it contributes substantially to protein intake—and definitely calories too.

The calories in hay are expressed as DE (digestible energy) and given as Mcal/lb. (megacalories/lb.). Hays actually vary widely in their calorie content, from 0.7 Mcal/lb. or less for poor-quality hays, to over 1.0 Mcal/lb. Most decent-quality hays are between 0.8 and 0.9, so we will use a figure of 0.85 Mcal/lb. to illustrate calorie intakes. 20 lbs. of average hay provides the horse with 17 Mcal of energy.

To reduce a horse's calorie intake and still feed grain, you have to make significant cuts in his hay. There's a big difference between hays and grains. Plain grains have twice as much digestible energy

(DE) as hay. Commercial feeds, because of the added fat and molasses, are often three times as calorie-dense as hay. If you substitute 5 pounds of commercial grain mix, usually the minimum recommended on the bag, for 5 pounds of hay, the horse will get a hefty increase in calories:

- 20 lbs. of hay x 0.85 Mcal/lb. = 17 Mcal/day

versus:

- 15 lbs. of hay x 0.85 Mcal/lb. = 12.75 Mcal/day

PLUS

- 5 lbs. of grain x 2.55 Mcal/lb. = 12.75 Mcal/day

TOTAL 25.5 Mcal/day

To keep the calorie intake of a horse fed 5 lbs. of commercial grain a day the same as a horse fed hay only at 2% of his body weight, you would only be able to give him 5 lbs. of hay a day! That's way too little hay for his digestive health.

moderate. Mary hurts her ankle, can't ride, and in four to six weeks, Sonic's weight jumps quite a bit.

When she was working him, Sonic was getting 2.5 lbs. of a commercial grain morning and night, and about 15 lbs. of hay. Sonic's working weight, before the gain, was between

Why Exercise?

Exercise changes how the horse's body uses its calories. Most calories are used by your horse's muscles. Muscles in motion burn more than resting muscles, but it goes beyond that. Exercise also improves the ability of the muscle cell to burn fuels and directs calories away from fat and into the muscle, both as fuel and to be stored. The body contour changes that accompany exercise aren't just because there is less fat, but reflect larger, healthier, better functionng muscles.

Whenever possible, an important strategy is to add exercise or increase the amount the horse is already doing. Turnout does not count as exercise. Aim to get the horse moving for a minimum of 30 minutes a day, no breaks, no stops to enjoy the scenery or chat, definitely no munching along the way.

If the horse is unfit and heavy, walking may be all that he can handle at the start. Shoot for a pulse of between 80 and 100 beats per minute during the exercise. Make sure the horse's feet are correctly trimmed and balanced (he's putting a lot of weight on those feet!), and keep a close eye on the legs for any filling or heat as you go along. You can hand walk, longe, pony from another horse, or ride. Just get him moving!

Substituting a small amount of hay pellets for your grain greatly reduces calories but still allows you to feed a "meal."

1,050 and 1,100 lbs. A quick calorie check shows that was just about right for a horse his size in moderate work, but too much for normal maintenance in an inactive horse. In fact, he was getting enough calories to support a weight of over 1,600 lbs. at maintenance.

There are two simple solutions here. If Mary doesn't want to change his feeding routine, she can substitute 4 to 5 lbs. of a complete feed for her grain mix and add a suitable mineral supplement to make up the difference in mineral levels between the complete feed and the fortified grain. Or, she might stop the grain and actually feed him more hay than she's doing now, which is a big help with boredom, and give him all the minerals he needs from a mineral supplement, mixed into a small amount of soaked beet pulp (soaked has only ¼ the calories of dry beet pulp) and a few ounces of flax for essential fatty acids.

Note that neither one of these approaches involves feeding Sonic less food—just a change in the types of food.

If we take the same scenario as above, but find that Mary is now ready to start riding again, Sonic will lose the extra weight once he gets back up to his former level of exercise, so there's really no pressing reason to do anything about it, although if he finds it more difficult to work with the extra weight (more huffing and puffing, legs filling), it's smarter to cut back a bit on the grain until he's back to full work.

Serious Weight Problem Requiring Major Long-term Revision

Peppermint Twist is an "only horse," a 14.3-hand Morgan mare with a body condition score of 8+; she weighs in at 1,200 pounds when she should weigh about 800. She's out on grass in a high-quality pasture (clover and mixed grasses, not overgrazed) for 12 hours a day, fed 15 pounds a day of early cutting hay from the same pasture and 3 lbs. per day (weight before soaking) of a 50:50 mixture of wheat bran and beet pulp. She gets no formal exercise at all since her owner went to college. This was the same diet Peppermint had when she was eventing.

Because of the early cutting of her hay, it probably has a higher than average DE. Assuming a DE of 1 Mcal/lb. from the hay, for a total of 15 Mcal for the day, and another 3.6 DE from

Mildly overweight horses are common in the show ring, but this practice only adds to the burden on the horse's lungs, heart and joints.

Calorie/Energy Content of Common Feed Ingredients

Feed	Calories/lb.
Fats and oils	3.61 Mcal
Commercial grain mixes	2.5+ Mcal (varies widely depending on exact ingredients and amount of added fat)
Horse cookies/treats	2+ Mcal
Seeds and nuts	1.5+ Mcal
Corn	1.54 Mcal
Wheat bran	1.33 Mcal
Oats	1.3 Mcal
Rice bran	1.19 Mcal minimum (many have added fat)
Beet pulp	1.06 Mcal (this is the official estimate, recent work suggesting calorie yield may be closer to oats)
Alfalfa hay	0.85 to 1.1 Mcal ("average" quality)
Grass hay	0.8 to 0.9 Mcal ("average" quality, varies widely)
Straw	0.6 to 0.7 Mcal
Fresh carrots and apples	0.2 to 0.25/lb. (high water content)
Molasses	1.2 Mcal

the beet pulp and bran, Peppermint Twist was getting 18.6 Mcal for these sources alone. Her maintenance need is about 12.8. But, even at that, for her to be as heavy as she is, she must be taking in quite a lot of grass when on the pasture. This is what many people forget to factor into their calculations.

A completely sealed grazing muzzle is the first step for her weight-loss plan, since it's impossible to know, or control, how much she is eating on the energy-dense pasture. If the owner drops the amount of hay, beet pulp, and bran down to a total of 12.8 Mcal, that alone will equal a 25% drop. If this is combined with not allowing grass, it would be a drastic calorie cut, which we want to avoid.

Instead, the plan devised for Peppermint was to:

• Divide turnout into one 4-hour turnout during the day and an 8-hour turnout at night, always with a sealed grazing muzzle.

Few horses genuinely work for a living the way they did in the past.

- Keep her on a dry lot the rest of the time and feed a 25% reduction in calories, which would be 13.6 Mcal. She can get that from 12 lbs. of hay and a pound of beet pulp, with 6 oz. of flax used as a carrier for her minerals.

- Once she reduces to around 900 lbs., shave her calories down to the 12.8 Mcal she should need to maintain a normal weight of 800 lbs. by giving 12 lbs. per day of her hay, with a total of 0.5 lbs. of beet pulp and 3.5 oz. of flax a day, divided into two feedings. 🐎

Performance

Many "performance" supplements have hit the market. What exactly is a performance supplement? In the broadest sense, it should be something that will help your horse perform better. Turns out, though, that manufacturers have some widely differing ideas about what ingredients are necessary to accomplish that.

Common sense alone will tell you that if something is beneficial for the performance of a racehorse, it might not be what you're looking for to support an endurance horse.

Because this category of products contains such a wide variety, we have to recommend that you look at them product by product. The products we included are by no means the only ones advertised as performance supplements, but they are examples of common categories, including:

- **General vitamin and mineral products labeled as "performance":** Dietary deficiencies can certainly have a negative impact on how the horse handles the physical stress of performance, but should be approached by correctly balancing the diet appropriate to his level of work. There's no evidence that megadosing vitamins or minerals will make the horse perform better.

- **Antioxidants:** Exercise does increase antioxidant requirements. You'll want to make sure the horse is getting at least 2,000 IU per day of vitamin E, 2 to 4 mg of selenium, and perhaps a little vitamin C, 1 to 3 grams a day. Horses under particularly heavy stresses may also benefit from some of the plant-based antioxidants.

- **Muscle builders/protectors:** We covered muscle-building problems in depth in chapter 17. Some of the best products in that category, including glycogen-loaders and branched chain amino acid (BCAA) products, are included again here. Working muscles do require high levels of branched chain amino acids, which are broken down as energy sources during work and must be replaced to both prevent muscle loss and build more muscle tissue. Decreasing levels of BCAAs in the blood during prolonged or endurance exercise may also lead to higher concentrations of tryptophan in the brain, causing fatigue.

- **Energy boosters:** Energy basically means calories. When it comes to hard-working muscles, this means fats, carbohydrates (the premier fuel), and branched chain amino acids. Fat can only be efficiently utilized for slow work, since it is metabolized too slowly to meet the energy demands of moderately high and high speed. Hard-working horses having trouble maintaining their weight on adequate grain and hay rations may benefit from the inclusion of small amounts of fat in their diet, to spare other energy sources when they're not working hard, but feeding too much, or substituting too much fat for carbohydrates, may negatively impact performance. Burning fat also requires intermediates that are derived from carbohydrate metabolism. Fat has its place, but carbohydrate is the king of exercise fuels.

- **Adaptogens:** Ginsengs and some other herbs are adaptogens that have been proven to moderate the cortisol response to exercise or stressful situations, so the horse reacts more like a trained animal, with responses that are less exaggerated. Moderation probably occurs because such herbs are structurally similar to the mammalian hormones. Horses that are sour or have poor energy levels and appetites often show a favorable response to adaptogens, which includes Ginseng.

Few things can compare with the beauty of an equine athlete in peak health and condition.

Avoid These!

Even a quick look at human exercise/performance supplements will show you there is a huge array. Some work, some don't. Some also are of use in horses, some aren't. Worse yet, the castoffs on the human end, products well known not to be helpful, may end up in equine supplements. Some things to avoid include:

Chromium: Not likely to be deficient and won't help if it isn't. Chromium is important to proper utilization of glucose by muscles, but unlikely to be deficient unless horse is eating hays/grains grown in alkaline soils (Southwest). Horses on high-grain intakes or using glycogen loaders may need more chromium. Heavy exercise also increases chromium losses in other species, but it's not proven in horses.

Inosine: This is a waste product of ATP breakdown, and high levels are harmful to energy generation.

Lactate and Pyruvate: The muscle and liver can utilize these byproducts of carbohydrate metabolism, but there's no shortage of them during exercise and there are much more efficient ways to provide energy.

Creatine: Although creatine is well-documented as useful in human sports medicine to improve intense muscular efforts in humans, the value to horses remains questionable. Equine literature and our own field trials have found no or equivocal results. Very high doses have caused cramping in some horses. It's also expensive. We'll pass.

DMG (dimethylglycine): Although still widely touted as a way to lower lactic acid production, this supplement does not work in people, and there's nothing to support its use in horses either. The precursor of DMG, TMG/betaine, does appear to be of benefit to untrained horses starting exercise, or those entering more strenuous stages of exercise training. A 1999 study published in the *Journal of Animal Science* found horses supplemented with 80 mg/kg of body weight of betaine (40,000 mg for a 500 kg/1,100 lb. horse) showed lower levels of lactate production and lower release of fatty acids, indicating more efficient aerobic ultilization of glucose. Betaine also improves muscle bulk while decreasing fat in other species. However, no performance benefit has been found in horses that are already fit.

Bottom Line

Equine-exercise research is finally starting to catch up with human investigations. Studies have now shown that either intravenous or oral glucose supplementation improves glycogen levels in muscles compared to conventional feeding regimens. So if you're looking for a true performance enhancer, we'd probably start with muscle builders, including glycogen loaders like maltodextrin, and BCAAs.

Because it's important to choose the product based on your horse's particular needs, it's difficult for us to make a No. 1 pick here. That said, we think the standouts in our chart include: APF, Power Pak, Blitz, BCAA Complex, Carbo Load, Carbo Charge, Glycogen Loader, and Advanced Glycogen Loader. 🐎

Properly fueling a racehorse can give the competitive advantage.

Muscles properly fueled with glycogen perform faster and longer.

Performance-Enhancing Supplements

Product	Ingredients	Comments
Performance Horse Supplement Merrick's Inc. www.merricks.com 800-637-7425 Price not available/25 lbs.	16% protein, 60% fat (from animal fat preserved with BHA) 12,500 IU vitamin A/lb., 50 IU vitamin E/lb. Suggested feeding: 1 to 1.5 lbs./day.	This is basically a fat supplement that would be equally at home with fat-based weight-gain products. We also don't like the idea of feeding horses animal fat.
Maximum Performance Horse Maximum Performance, Inc. www.maxperfeq.com 502-817-1947 $65/20 lbs. (60 days)	Digestive enzymes, 22% calcium, 8% phosphorus, 2.26% salt, 3,000 ppm zinc, 200 ppm copper, 2,600 ppm manganese, 70 ppm iodine, 20 ppm selenium, 200,000 IU/lb. vitamin A, 30,000 IU/lb. vitamin D, 176 IU/lb. vitamin E. Suggested feeding: 5 oz./day.	This is basically a mineral and vitamin A/D/E supplement that is heavy on the calcium, low in copper, good levels of selenium and iodine, heavy on the A, and light on E. We found no specific performance-enhancing ingredients in this supplement.
Opt-E-Horse Complete Weaver Leather www.weaverleather.com 800-932-8371 $25/3 lbs. (48 days)	Per 0.5 oz: Zinc 85 mg, copper 71 mg, manganese 99.5 mg, iodine 2 mg, selenium 0.5 mg, vitamin A 15,000 IU, vitamin E 125 IU, D 3,125 IU, low dose B vitamin complex, including biotin (0.55 mg). Recommended feeding: 0.5 oz.	This is a low-potency trace-mineral and vitamin supplement, heavy on the copper. Might be useful for plugging some trace-mineral gaps in areas that have low-copper hays, but vitamin E, selenium, and B vitamins are very low, and we found no performance-enhancing or energy ingredients.
Cool Calories 100 Performance Horse Nutrition www.performancehorse nutrition.com 208-549-2323 $21.00/8 lbs. (16 to 64 days)	Beaded vegetable-oil supplement, preserved with vitamin E. Recommendation: 2 to 4 oz./day for horses in work, up to 8 oz./day if underweight.	Sane feeding level recommendations on this product. When used as directed, can be of assistance to hard-working horses having trouble holding their weight. Vegetable oil source, with all natural (vitamin E) preservative. Introduce gradually to avoid digestive upset and diarrhea.
Ultimate Equine Booster Bio-Logics Inc www.ublcorp.com 888-205-9957 $92.40/4.4 lbs. (17 to 35 days)	Whey protein isolate with unspecified amounts of creatine and chromium added. Recommendation: 2 to 4 oz./day in divided feedings.	Feeding whey protein isolate is beneficial for many hard-working horses, both for immune system support and for providing high-quality protein, but you can buy high-quality human whey protein isolate products for about half this price. We'll also pass on the creatine and chromium.
Recovery Eq Biomedica Laboratories www.recoveryeq.com 866-344-2463 $72.99/2.2 lbs. (20 to 40 days for a 1,200-lb. horse)	Per 600 lb. dose: 1,000 mg green tea and grape seed extract, 10,000 mg glucosamine, 10,000 mg MSM, 1,400 mg vitamin C, 1,000 mg DMG, 750 IU natural vitamin E, 525 mg magnesium. Loading dose: 26 grams/600 lbs, maintenance 13 grams/600 lbs, 26 gram scoop provided.	Although it won't necessarily make your horse run faster, cut quicker, or jump higher, this supplement is designed to help counteract degenerative processes and tissue damage related to oxygen free-radical generation during exercise. All ingredients are at high potency and appropriate doses for performance horses. Pricey, but in the sense of you get what you pay for.
HY-XL Race Fuel Uckele Health and Nutrition www.uckele.com 800-248-0330 $7.55/80 g tube/1 dose	Paste with sodium, potassium, calcium, magnesium, and B vitamins in good dosages, small amount DMB, amino acids, including BCAAs, carnitine and bicarbonate precursors in a base of maltodextrin, dextrose, fructose.	Effective electrolyte support based on sweat losses, B vitamins, amino acids and glycogen loader. Mini glycogen loader effective within an hour before high-speed work, as a substitute for a powder glycogen load away from home, as a premixed dose of glycogen loader and protein immediately after work, as a good energy boost between classes, or every 2 hours in an endurance race.
APF Auburn Laboratories www.auburnlabs.com 877-661-3505 $59.95/120 ml (20 to 30 days)	Liquid extract blend of the adaptogenic herbs Eleutherococcus senticosus (Siberian ginseng), Schizandra chinensis, Rhodiola orsea, Echinopanax elatus. For performance horses: 4 to 6 ml/day.	Ginseng/adaptogens included. The specific combination in APF has been shown to reduce time to fatigue in laboratory animals. These ingredients also have high antioxidant potential. APF improves energy levels, alertness, and attitude without causing nervousness.

Product	Ingredients	Comments
Power Pak Paste or Powder Peak Performance Nutrients www.peakperformance nutrients.com 800-944-1984 $19/80 cc (one pre-event dose) $35.99/3 powder (3 doses)	Paste formulation blend of American ginseng, cordyceps, and Eleutherococcus, plus undisclosed amounts of creatine monohydrate, calcium pyruvate, lipoic acid, inosine, and carnitine.	Another adaptogen-based product, designed to be used for three days pre-event (powder in feed) and/or a few hours before event (paste formulation). We've seen an energizing effect from this product, particularly the paste formulation, in prior trials.
Blitz Peak Performance Nutrients www. peakperformancenutrients.com 800-944-1984 $12.99/80 cc (2 doses)	Combines an electrolyte (including calcium and magnesium) and trace mineral package well balanced to sweat losses (high-speed race or about an hour of endurance work), high potency B vitamins, licorice extract for stomach protection, and a full spectrum amino acid package with the focus on branched chain amino acids and glutamine.	This is an intelligently formulated "work horse" of a supplement that addresses the stress and electrolyte losses of exercise, plus the amino acid needs of working muscle. Useful support for horses on intensive schedules, after high-speed workouts or races, at multiclass shows, between phases at an event. A bit pricey for use for an entire endurance race, but worth trying at least late in the race in horses experiencing problems with weak finishes with electrolyte supplements alone. Will not cause nervousness or excitability.
B.C.A.A. Complex Peak Performance Nutrients www.peakperformance nutrients.com 800-944-1984 $75.99/2 lbs powder (45 days) $14.99/80 cc paste (2 doses)	A balanced blend of branched chain amino acids, glutamine, and B6.	BCAA supplementation is worth trying for any exercising horse having trouble holding muscle mass. For horses that work at moderate to high speeds, we've had best results combining 10 to 20 grams of BCAAs with 3 to 6 oz. of a glycogen loader and administering after work. Can be used after race for endurance horses, or as a supplement during the race to help with fatigue.
Nutragard Vita-Flex (Division of Farnam) www.vita-flex.com 800-848-2359 $125/4 lbs. (21 to 43 days)	Per 1.5 oz dose: 1.6 g lysine, 494 mg iron, 1,350 mg vitamin C, 360 IU vitamin E, low to moderate zinc, copper, manganese, B vitamins, low dose probiotics, undisclosed amounts of citrus bioflavonoids and aloe.	Although claiming to be a potent antioxidant supplement, we don't see it from the guaranteed analysis list. For this kind of money, we want to know what we're paying for.
Liqui Fuel Uckele Health and Nutrition www.uckele.com 800-248-0330 $18.95/gallon (32 to 128 days)	Per oz.: 7,100 mg of betaine, 1,275 mg glutamic acid.	This is a product we've found useful for horses that have problems with dehydration despite adequate electrolyte supplementation. The betaine can also help with energy metabolism in horses just beginning training or entering heavy training.
AMP Fuel Uckele Health and Nutrition www.uckele.com 800-248-0330 $12.30/85 gram tube (½ to 1 dose)	High doses of BCAAs and whey protein isolate, bicarbonate precursors, adaptogenic, anti-inflammatory, circulation-supporting and stomach-protecting herbs, phosphate source and AMP (adenosine monosphosphate) for support of ATP regeneration, antioxidants, DMG and TMG, B vitamins. Recommendation: 1 to 2 tubes 4 to 6 hours before competition.	Designed as a pre-event support, this supplement concentrates on energy generation, support, and protection of hard-working muscle. Ingredients are present in amounts large enough to make a difference.
Carbo Load Uckele Health and Nutrition www.uckele.com 800-248-0330 $50.30/20 lbs. (40 to 80 servings)	100% maltodextrin.	Easily digested and absorbed glucose source for hard-working muscle. Replenishes glycogen stores. Feed 3 to 6 oz. maltodextrin immediately after hard works or competition, with an additional dose in a small grain feed 1 to 2 hours later. Horses on endurance rides may benefit from 2 to 4 oz doses every 1.5 to 2 hours.
Equi PRP Uckele Health and Nutrition www.uckele.com 800-248-0330 $12.30/packet (1 dose)	Per packet: 10 grams creatine, 6.4 g BCAA, 1 g HMB, 6 g glutamine, 2 g DMG, 10 g monosodium phosphate. Recommendation: 1 packet 1 to 3 hours prior to exercise and after exercise.	The value of the DMG and creatine is questionable, but the HMG and branched chain amino acids provide good muscle support.
CarboCharge Vita-Flex (Division of Farnam) www.vita-flex.com 800-848-2359 $15/3 lbs.	Long chain maltodextrins, thiamine, and chromium.	Glycogen-loader product with added thiamine and chromium for glucose handling (may or may not be needed). Easily digested and absorbed glucose source for hard-working muscle. Replenishes glycogen stores.
Glycogen Loader Equine Racing Systems www.equineracing.com 360-837-2102 $49.95/10 lbs.	Rapidly digested maltodextrin chains, with chromium.	This is the original glycogen-loader product designed by the late Tom Ivers. It's a pioneer product in this category, used successfully both in short-distance and endurance racing.
Advanced Glycogen Loader Equine Racing Systems www.equineracing.com 360-837-2102 $99/12 lbs.	Longer chain length maltodextrin than original Glycogen Loader, plus a wide array of nutrients to support energy generation and glucose utilization.	Designed more for use as a precompetition glycogen-loading product, this is administered several times daily for 3 to 4 days prior to speed competition.

How to Glycogen Load

Glycogen loading is borrowed from human sports medicine, where time and time again it has been proven to improve performance. In fact, glycogen loading is one of the few things that safely and legally improves athletic performance. For years horses were believed to be different from human athletes because they took so long, typically as long as three days, to replace the glycogen they had used during a hard exercise bout. Although reports from different researchers remain somewhat contradictory, more recent studies have shown that glycogen repletion can be accelerated if the horse is provided with a sufficient amount of extra glucose either intravenously or orally. This strongly suggests that the reason horses were taking so long to recover their glycogen levels was simply an inadequate supply of readily available carbohydrate in their diet.

There are no specific studies on performance effects of simple carbohydrate supplementation, but very clear evidence that low glycogen stores have a negative effect on performance. Our trials on glycogen loaders have shown clear benefits.

There are a variety of feeding recommendations for these products—close to the event, added to meals; once, or for several days straight. However, exercise greatly increases the muscle's "hunger" for glucose, an effect that peaks within 1 to 2 hours of exercise, then declines over the next 24 hours. A protocol that we have found to be very effective for horses in heavy training or competition is:

On hard work days:

- 3 oz. of powdered glycogen loader or 6 oz. of corn syrup (not high fructose) either added to the first gallon of cool out water or given by dose syringe within 30 minutes after stopping work.
- 2 oz. of powdered glycogen loader or 4 oz. of corn syrup (not high fructose) with 2 to 2.5 pounds of grain 2 hours after stopping work.
- Same amounts of loader or corn syrup as above, given by dose syringe (or let the horse eat it if he will) 3.5 hours after stopping work.
- Same amounts as above in the last grain feeding of the day.

If the horse is prone to muscle soreness, or you know he has worked particularly hard, especially if the effort was more intense than he's been sufficiently conditioned for, adding 20 grams of BCAA to the first dosing can help decrease the risk of muscle stiffness.

This post-exercise supplementation, after competitions and on hard training days, makes an obvious difference in the horse's energy level the next day and gives him a jumpstart on repleting glycogen stores so that he's ready to continue working without interruptions in scheduling.

Respiratory Aids

"Good wind" is one of the most valued attributes in a horse. Anything that interferes with the horse's ability to freely get air or oxygen has an immediate negative impact on athletic ability—not to mention comfort and general well being.

Stable Cough and Heaves/COPD

The term "stable cough" refers to a syndrome affecting horses that start coughing when they're confined to a barn. The problem isn't related to respiratory infections, although it does put the horse at a higher risk of developing one. Nasal discharges due to stable cough are more thin or frothy, as opposed to the thick, discolored discharges associated with an actual infection. The stable cough is dry and hacking. More significant than the cough is the reason for the cough, which is caused by airway spasm and inflammation called recurrent airway obstruction (RAO). Once irreversible injury to the lungs has occurred, the changes begin to resemble chronic obstructive pulmonary disease in people (COPD).

The most common trigger of RAO is the mold found in straw and hay. Even hay and straw that look clean and smell sweet may contain some level of mold. Environmental molds growing on untreated wood or concrete areas may also contribute. Although this sounds like an allergy, a Swiss study found no increase in IgE, the allergy immunoglobin, in lung tissue samples from horses with RAO. Other studies have found

You can purchase "cough drops" for horses in the form of a paste syringe.

increased levels of IgE specific for common molds. It appears that while allergies may certainly trigger it, nonspecific lung irritants like dust and ammonia from urine may also be to blame.

All the studies describe increased numbers of mast cells, which can release histamine and are involved in tissue remodeling and scarring, as well as infiltration with lymphocytes and neutrophils, suggesting that RAO is primarily an inflammatory problem.

Some people dismiss stable cough as a minor problem, as long as the horse isn't running a fever or acting sick. This is a mistake. Left uncorrected, RAO will progressively worsen and eventually cause permanent lung damage. RAO also has been found to predispose high-performance horses to lung bleeding, or exercise induced pulmonary hemorrhage (EIPH).

The terms "heaves" and "stable cough" may be used interchangeably, though heaves is typically reserved for the most severe cases. And often, heaves goes by a new name these days—chronic obstructive pulmonary disease, or COPD. New name; same old disease.

Heaves is one of the more descriptive names given to an equine disease. It reflects how the horse's sides and chest must work and heave to try to get enough air into and out of the body. Like "strangles," it immediately paints a vivid picture of the condition of the horse when in the throes of an attack. The lining of the nasal passages is often bright red. The horse is, literally, air hungry.

Also obvious in advanced cases is the "heave line," which is a muscular indentation running along the outline of the rib cage and curving up into the flank along the last rib. It is caused by the horse forcibly using his diaphragm and abdominal muscles to expel air. It is most obvious during an attack. but can be observed in advanced cases even when the horse is breathing fairly comfortably.

The list of symptoms is rounded out by coughing, which may also be present between attacks, and wheezing. In some cases, the wheezing is audible when standing near the horse; in others it can be heard with a stethoscope. As you may imagine, these horses have decreased exercise tolerance. They tire

Management Strategies for Heaves and Stable Cough

Steroids, bronchodilators, and antihistamines are the cornerstones of therapy for respiratory problems, but they're expensive prescription drugs and illegal in competition horses. They also may have side effects. You may get symptomatic relief with a simpler focus: mucus production.

A Michigan State University study confirmed that horses with heaves (chronic obstructive pulmonary disease) have increased mucus accumulations in their lungs. The mucus response was also found in normal horses when exposed to common environmental irritants, like dusty hay. Antibiotics won't help. You need to target the mucus:

- In a German study of patients with severe bronchial asthma, one of the aromatic compounds found in eucalyptus, a potent mucus-thinning agent, reduced steroid use by about one-third.
- An Italian study found that intravenous and nebulized NAC (N-acetyl cysteine) dramatically reduced the inflammatory activity of white blood cells without interfering with immune responses.
- A Polish study found that long-term oral NAC use resulted in significant reductions in active inflammation in the lungs with mucus thinning.

Many of the cough/breathing supplements we've found effective do thin the mucus, as do many highly aromatic substances. Mucolytics worth trying to help a horse with COPD, lung allergies, or stable cough include:

- **Vicks VapoRub:** Apply liberally to the nostrils several times a day.
- **Wind Aid:** A potent, aromatic cough remedy (Hawthorne, www.hawthorne products.com, 765-768-6585).
- **Air Power:** A potent, aromatic equine cough remedy (Finish Line, www.finish linehorse.com, 800-762-4242).
- **Equitussin:** A soothing, well-priced aromatic cough remedy (Select the Best, www.selectthebest.com, 800-648-0950).
- **Resprun:** Gentle enough for mild-to-moderate problems (Uckele, www.uckele.com, 800-248-0330).
- **Hilton Freeway:** Provides fast, effective relief. Gentle and well-accepted. Has some long-term therapeutic benefits (www.chamisaridge.com, 800-743-3188).
- **Jet Breath:** Blend of Chinese herbs with both mucolytic and bronchodilating properties. Potent (www.justwin.net, 800-227-2987).
- **Breathe Ease:** Blend of Chinese herbs with both mucolytic and bronchodilating properties. Potent (www. equinegold.com, 800-870-5949).
- **Cough Free:** Good herbal blend for stable cough and milder conditions. (Sure Nutrition, www.farnamhorse.com, 800-234-2269).
- **Generic N-acetyl cysteine (NAC):** 2.5 to 5 grams, once or twice a day. Available in capsule form from human health/supplement stores.

more easily, cough during and after exercise, and take much longer to cool out or stop blowing after exercise.

With advanced COPD, the symptoms are so dramatic and the horse in so much distress he will need emergency attention.

Changes earlier on are more subtle and insidious, waxing and waning until there are irreversible changes in the lungs.

What to Do

- **Fresh air:** Whenever possible, horses with stable cough/RAO and heaves should be kept outside. Removing exposure to the offending irritants is by far the most effective treatment. Healthy horses tolerate cold well and will remain comfortable as long as they have ready access to shelter.

  If they must be stabled, it's imperative not to close the barn up and to make sure there is a constant flow of air through the barn. Opening windows above head level of the horses and doors located at the ends of aisles will keep air moving without subjecting the horses to direct drafts. If the barn isn't well ventilated, consult a contractor for how best to correct this.

- **Bedding:** Straw might not be the best choice here, due to its natural dust and molds. Shavings are better, but the aromatic oils may bother some horses, and shavings are sometimes infested with mold as well. Kiln-dried, low-dust shavings cost more but can make a big difference. You might also consider a pelleted or cardboard-based bedding.

  It doesn't do any good to only replace bedding for the coughing horse. All stalls have to be treated the same way. When using pelleted products, be sure to follow directions for wetting them slightly to rehydrate; if you run across bags with large amounts of fine, dusty materials, return them for a refund. These products are too expensive to settle for less than precisely what you need.

- **Diet:** For mildly affected horses, or when the problem is excessive dust rather than molds, thoroughly wetting and dunking the hay before feeding it may do the trick. Actually soaking the hay for 15 to 30 minutes before feeding is even more effective. If that's not enough,

Management Strategies

- Consider allergy testing to help identify food sensitivities.
- Change hay types or find a hay of the same type without seed heads.
- If the hay change makes no difference, stop feeding concentrates entirely or put the horse on plain soaked beet pulp only.
- Avoid carrots, apples, or commercial treats of any kind during the diet trial. Cross-reactions can occur with pollen allergies.
- If changing hay and going to beet pulp with no treats doesn't help, stop there. Food allergy as a component to the symptoms is highly unlikely.

- If the beet pulp only diet does help, try adding in single ingredients one at a time to test the effect—plain oats, soybean meal, etc.—making only one new addition every two weeks.
- You can also try feeding the horse a commercial grain that is as different as possible in ingredients from the one you were originally using. If this also makes the horse worse, compare the two ingredients lists to see if you can narrow down the list of possible offenders, looking for the common ingredients.

cubed or pelleted hays are a better choice, since the grasses used in these are typically harvested at a higher level of moisture, then cut and heat dried before processing, reducing the chance of mold growth. Pelleted complete feeds also work well for many affected horses. Grains can harbor their own assortment of molds and are problematic for some horses. In that case, switching to a pelleted, beet pulp–based, and grain-free feed or soaked beet pulp alone will help.

- **Antioxidant Supplements:** Several studies have consistently shown reduced levels of antioxidant nutrients in the lungs of horses with RAO and COPD. A 2002 study from Belgium found that supplementing horses with vitamin C, vitamin E, and selenium was effective in improving the levels of these antioxidants, as well as glutathione (an important antioxidant protein), and also improved exercise tolerance and inflammation in the lung. In fact, one of the reasons these horses do so much better on pasture may be the presence of natural antioxidant vitamins and omega-3 fatty acids in live grasses.

- **Other Supplements:** Spirulina, at 20 grams twice a day, may be helpful as a natural antihistamine and for immune system moderation. We've also found that breathing is eased, exercise capacity increased, and recovery times improved with a blend of Chinese herbs. Human studies have found that airways are often hyper-responsive with magnesium deficiency and that treating with magnesium can help them open up again, but this treatment may only work when given intravenously or as an aerosol. Magnesium effects haven't been studied in horses.

- **Vicks:** Not too exciting, but plain old Vicks VapoRub or a generic equivalent applied liberally below the nostrils or used in a nebulizer or vaporizer effectively relieves airway spasm and irritation and thins mucus so that it is more easily eliminated from the respiratory tract. This simple, symptomatic treatment can make a world of difference, but you have to use it consistently.

- **Drugs:** A wide variety of bronchodilating, antihistamine, and corticosteroid drugs are available for use orally, by injection, or by inhalation. However, attempting to control RAO with only drugs is like trying to treat a chemical burn without removing the chemical from the skin.

For many horses, all that is required to fix the problem is to get them outside. Don't consider using drugs until all the other suggested approaches have been exhausted.

Herbs for Bronchospasm

Jiaogulan and Spirulina

Jiaogulan (Gynostemma pentaphyllum) is a vine indigenous to remote mountainous regions of south China. It's been

"Cough Drops" for Fast Relief

If you use menthol cough drops yourself, you understand the rationale behind the eucalyptus, peppermint, and menthol in cough products: fast, temporary relief. However, equine preparations with these ingredients are far stronger than the effect you get from sucking a cough drop. Many horses act obviously irritated after they're administered, shaking their heads and making chewing motions. Most will stop eating for a while, possibly due to an irritant effect on the stomach. Several test horses also coughed more severely immediately after the treatment than before, again likely due to irritation. These ingredients do traditionally help thin mucus and ease breathing, but we'd rather use Vicks on the nostrils for equal or better effect. Only Resprun appeared to be free of violent reactions from the horses.

Although much more expensive, our clear choice in quick relief both for effectiveness and absence of side effects is the Freeway. Coughs are calmed immediately, and the product is gentle and well-accepted. A close second, and also the best buy, is Richdel/Select the Best's Equitussin. This also appears to be more soothing than irritating, although we would prefer to avoid the harsh aromatic oils entirely if possible.

Product	Ingredients	Comments	Field-Test Ratings/Evaluations
Air Power Finish Line 800-762-4242 www.finishlinehorse.com $14.95/pint $4.25/single-dose syringe	Honey, apple-cider vinegar, aloe vera, ethyl alcohol, menthol, lemon juice, oil of eucalyptus.	0.5 oz (15 cc) before work and may repeat in evening.	"Mentholated" cough remedy.
Equitussin Richdel, Inc. www.selectthebest.com 800-648-0950 $10.95/qt./$28.95/gallon	Glyceryl guiacolate, ammonium chloride, potassium iodide, mentholated white-pine syrup, eucalyptus and peppermint oils in a molasses-syrup base.	2 to 4 oz. given two or three times daily or before work	"Mentholated" cough remedy.
Hilton Freeway Hilton Herbs www.chamisaridge.com 800-743-3188 $44.95/liter	Licorice, marshmallow, ginkgo, cleavers, coltsfoot, plantain, garlic extracts in a base of apple-cider vinegar and honey.	30 to 40 cc/adult horse twice a day, OK in feed.	Fast, effective relief while being gentle and well-accepted. Also has some long-term therapeutic benefits.
Resprun Uckele Health & Nutrition www.uckele.com 800-248-0330 $4.24 per single-dose tube	Syrupy paste containing camphor, menthol oils of eucalyptus, wintergreen, orange and clove, aloe, valerian, kelp, glycerin, vinegar, juniper berry, honey.	Full tube one to four hours before work or in a nebulizer, can use on the nostrils.	Least reactions for "mentholated" cough remedies in our trial, although it's pricey.
Wind Aid Hawthorne Products www.hawthorneproducts.com 765-768-6585 $15.53/qt. $2.50/tube	Sodium iodide, eucalyptus oil, peppermint oil, glycerin.	2 oz. once a day for 3 days prior to competition and 2 hours before; give 2 to 3 times a day for heavy lung congestion. 1 oz. tube is equivalent to 2 oz. of liquid.	"Mentholated" cough remedy.

consumed for centuries as a tea or vegetable and as a medicine for relieving fatigue and cold symptoms.

Scientific studies into the activities of this plant have revealed that it is an extremely potent inducer of nitric-oxide enzyme systems—eNOS (e for endothelial, NOS = nitric oxide synthetase)—inside blood vessels that are critical to keeping the vessels dilated and blood moving smoothly.

When tissue is injured in any way, the normally inactive eNOS enzyme system is activated. Nitric oxide is then produced at levels much higher than normal, which shuts down the eNOS system and is part of the cascade that triggers an inflammatory response. Jiaogulan has the unique ability to tone down the iNOS (inductible "turned on" during inflammation) inflammatory response while it supports the eNOS circulatory and healing one.

An article published in the August 2005 issue of the *Journal of Pharmacy and Pharmacology* showed that Jiaogulan reduced baseline resistance to air flow, inhibited histamine-induced bronchoconstriction by 68%, and inhibited inhaled allergen-induced bronchoconstriction by 80%.

We decided to try it in combination with spirulina (see below) for horses with symptoms of allergic or reactive lung disease that were free of symptoms on spirulina at rest, but still had prolonged respiratory recovery times after work and poor exercise tolerance. A dose of 2,000 mg of Jiaogulan was used in combination with 20 grams of spirulina, twice a day, with the Jiaogulan given 20 minutes before feeding. The response was excellent, with eight of eight test horses showing normal respiratory recovery rates and exercise tolerance on this combination.

Some other research into the effects of Jiaogulan that are of interest include one in the March 2006 issue of the *Journal of Biomedical Sciences* that found Jiaogulan inhibits release of the inflammatory cytokine (cellular messenger) called NF-Kappa-B. This is the same cytokine suppressed by aspirin and also the one that activates the eNOS enzyme system described above. This probably explains how Jiaogulan is able to activate vascular nitric oxide production but suppress inflammatory nitric

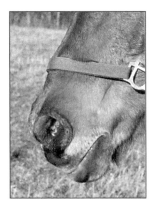

Several different nutrients and herbal supplements can help ease breathing in horses with respiratory problems.

oxide pathways at the same time. It also shows a direct anti-inflammatory activity for this herb.

Spirulina platensis is a microscopic blue-green algae that grows in the shape of a coil or spiral, which is how it got its name. Spirulina is one of the earth's oldest plants, estimated at 3.6 billion years old. It's been used as a dietary staple in Africa and parts of the Americas for hundreds of years and can be found on the shelves of most supplement and natural-food stores. Always on the lookout for ways to help our horses, we decided to find out if spirulina could benefit horses with allergic problems. So far, results have been excellent.

We obtained our spirulina as a bulk powder from www.herbalcom.com. At $13.65/lb., 60¢ is the 20-gram dose cost. We mixed it well into sweet feed. If you're feeding plain grain or pellets, moisten the feed so the powder adheres well. It arrives in a brown wrapper with the spirulina powder inside a blue plastic bag. The product looks somewhat like powdered spinach.

Case 1

A 5-year-old Standardbred gelding's seasonal problems were interfering with his performance. He had a history of seasonal headshaking and severe pulmonary allergies, with heavy mucus production in the summer. Cultures from the lung had been negative, and the horse showed no response to antibiotics. He did improve with bronchodilators and therapy to thin the mucus.

The year before, his headshaking lasted from early April to September. Supplementation began at 10 grams twice a day of spirulina powder added to his feed after headshaking had started again the next spring and he was showing a thin nasal discharge. Some improvement was noted, but it wasn't dramatic, so dosage was increased to 20 grams twice a day. At this level, headshaking and nasal discharge disappeared.

Spirulina was stopped three times between April and September. Each time, the symptoms returned within one to two days, disappearing again within a day of restarting the spirulina. His lungs have remained perfectly clear.

Cleaning Buckets

Molds and bacteria can grow in feeding equipment and cause problems, so special care is needed for the horse with breathing difficulty. A 5% acetic acid vinegar—the same as sold in grocery stores—kills 99% of bacteria, 80% of molds, and even some viruses.

Use full-strength vinegar to clean your equipment, rinsing out if needed, but otherwise just wipe out the excess and leave the residue in there. Most horses like the taste of some vinegar.

Safety of Wet Feed

Wetting hay and feed decreases fine particles, but it may also support mold and bacterial growth. Always wet feed immediately before feeding and feed only an amount that will be consumed within two to three hours in warm weather and six to eight hours in cold weather. Remove uneaten hay or feed after these times, wipe the feeder/trough clean, and dry with a towel.

Commercial Feeds

A variety of feeds are marketed as being more suitable for a horse with lung allergies or COPD. Specially processed bagged forages, like Lucerne Farms' line of forage feeds (www.lucernefarms.com, 800-723-4923), undergo dust extraction and high-heat processing/dehydration, so they contain less dust and mold than traditionally baled hays.

Conventionally processed bagged, chopped forages that are molasses-coated also have a lower "dust" factor but may still support mold growth.

Feeding a complete feed that relies heavily on beet pulp and dehydrated alfalfa meal as the fiber source, as most do, will help eliminate the problem of hay from your horse's diet. However, complete feeds don't offer any other particular advantage unless they also eliminate one or more other ingredients that could be causing your horse's problem.

Case 2

A 25-year-old Morgan gelding suffered from COPD, also known as heaves. He was not doing well with conventional therapy of steroids, antihistamines, and bronchodilators and had a poor tolerance for any level of exercise, evidenced by coughing. After being off medications for a week, he was started on spirulina at 20 grams twice a day. Within three days, his owner was riding him again, at trot and canter, with no heaving and no coughing. Prior to the spirulina he would be heaving and having uncontrollable coughing after just walking. He also began again to actively play in the field with his buddies.

Case 3

A 13-year-old imported warmblood mare with respiratory allergies and mild exercise intolerance had a tracheal wash that revealed large numbers of mast cells. She required constant antihistamines, but her exercise tolerance was still not good. Antihistamines were stopped and spirulina started at 20 grams twice a day. Symptoms of cough and nasal discharge were gone in 24 hours, with exercise tolerance greatly increased. She was tapered down to 10 grams daily.

Case 4

A 28-year-old pony had severe "asthma"/heaves. He was non-responsive to brochodilators, steroids, antihistamines, and inhaled medications. He was started on 10 grams of spirulina twice a day but showed no improvement.

Bottom Line

The responses impressed us, and all the horses eventually accepted the product in their feed. Four additional horses were given 60 grams of spirulina twice a day for two weeks with no side effects noted. Always talk to your veterinarian before starting a supplement when your horse has a medical problem.

Horses with chronic obstructive pulmonary disease—COPD, or "heaves"—require strict management to control the disease to a level in which the horse is still useful and comfortable.

A variety of inhaled potential allergens and irritants are found in dusty feeds and hays. These allergy triggers can include: proteins or complex carbohydrates in specific types and species of hay or grains, other feed ingredients, molds or fungi, bacterial products, pollens, insect droppings, and tiny insect body parts.

Anyone who has one of these horses knows to avoid these noticeably irritating feeds—even whole oats can be too dusty—but even low levels of allergens and irritants can irritate a horse with sensitive airways and lungs. Fine particles of hay, grain, and dirt can be physical irritants.

To understand how dusty your horse's diet really is, take a sample of the plain or pelleted feed or hay and put it in plastic sandwich bag. Shake or stir it around well. The small particulate matter will adhere to the sides of the bag. In most cases you'll be able to clearly see it. If you're not sure, swab the inside of the bag with a cotton ball to see how much debris you pick up. Your best bets for minimizing aerosolized allergens and irritants include:

- Use cubed or pelleted hay rather than baled. Even these can benefit from being lightly moistened.

- If feeding baled hay, dunk or soak each flake thoroughly, wetting it to the center and then shaking it apart.

- Sweet feed has the least potential for aerosolized particles, but don't feed the fine material at the bottom of the bag or bin.

- Pellets have less dust than plain grains, but both should be moistened slightly with water or lightly sprayed with oil before feeding.

- Plain grains can be further cleaned by shaking them in a colander with a fine mesh before feeding.

- Never feed broken grains or pellets at the bottom of a bag or bin, as there's a high risk these could be mold-contaminated.

Exercise-Induced Cough

An exercise-induced cough means the horse coughs when exercised, rarely coughing in the stable. His resting respiratory rate may or may not be elevated, and he may or may not have a nasal discharge when exercising.

All our field-test horses in this category that didn't have elevated respiratory rates at rest were endoscoped to make sure there was no anatomical problem to cause irritation and account for the cough.

Meticulous environmental control of dust and allergens, plus the regular use of mentholated rubs, like Vicks, at the nostrils, are simple but usually effective control measures for

Nutraceutical and Herbal Long-Term Cough Remedies

Product Information	Ingredients	Comments	Field-Test Ratings/Evaluation
Bioquench Uckele Health & Nutrition www.uckele.com 800-248-0330 $19.95/2 lbs.	Beta-carotene, bioflavonoids, folic acid, grape seed, riboflavin, thiamine, vitamin C, vitamin E.	Blend of antioxidant vitamins (A,E,C), B vitamins, bioflavonoid for suppression of allergy or inflammatory response due to infection.	Good control of allergic symptoms, such as cough or nasal discharge. Best when combined with Herbal-Mune.
Breathe Herbs for Horses www.herbsforhorses.com 888-423-7777 $33/2.2 lbs.	Hyssop, garlic, white horehound, red clover, euphatorium.	Blend of western herbs.	Good choice for stable cough and mild lung problems, including early heaves. High-quality, aromatic, and palatable whole herbs.
Breathe Ease Equine Gold www.equinegold.com 800-870-5949 $97.95/2 lbs.	Bei Sha Shen, Dan Shen, Gui Zhi, Huang Qi, Jie Geng, Kun Bu, Nan Sha Shen, Wu Wu Jiao Shen.	Immune-supporting, expectorant and stimulant herbs.	Effective in easing work of breathing, blocking exercise-induced respiratory distress and cough, similar to albuterol.
Cough Free Farnam Sure Nutrition www.farnam.com 800-234-2269 $24.99/lb.	Elecampane root, fenugreek seed, ferrous sulfate, sulfur, kelp, dicalcium phosphate, comfrey, charcoal, calcium carbonate.	Blend of expectorant/tussive minerals and traditional western herbs.	Good choice for stable cough and mild lung problems. Fine powder. Helps to moisten feed to cut dust and improve adherence.
Cough Less Equine America 800-838-7524 $24.50/2 lbs.	Fenugreek seed powder, kelp, garlic powder, echinacea, astragalus, elecampane root, sulfur, gentian, comfrey, aloe vera, acetic acid, glycerine, oil of eucalyptus.	Mixture of immune-stimulant herbs, herbals, and minerals to thin mucus.	Palatability poor due to strong eucalyptus odor. Manufacturer recommends molasses or other flavor-enhancers, but we didn't find these too helpful.
Equinacea Equilite, Inc www.equilite.com 800-942-5483 $55/2 lbs.	Echinacea, osha, eyebright, cat's claw.	Blend of immune-stimulant, immune-modulating, and mucus membrane-soothing herbs.	Some temporary symptomatic relief of mild stable cough. Effectiveness may have been hampered by poor acceptance. Product does have a result in 72 hours or money-back guarantee.
Grape Seed Extract Med-Vet Pharmaceuticals www.unitedvetequine.com 800-366-8986 $66/5 lbs.	Grape seed extract.	Antioxidant with 20 times the potency of vitamin C, 50 times vitamin E.	Good choice for immune-system effects when dealing with both allergic and infectious problems. Combine with an antioxidant for better control of symptoms.
Hackaway Hilton Herbs www.chamisaridge.com 800-743-3188 $53.95/3.3 lbs.	Garlic, plantain, euphrasia, elder flowers, thyme, cleavers, licorice.	Western herbal blends.	Helps in control of stable cough, cold symptoms.
Hemo Cease Peak Performance www.peakperformance nutrients.com 800-944-1984 $39.99/2 lbs.	Ester C, mixed citrus bioflavonoids, rutin, hesperidin, quercetin, mullien leaf powder, hawthorn berry, vitamin K.	Potent antioxidant ingredients with some herbal support.	Palatable, aromatic, and obviously high-quality herbs. Effective in eliminating or reducing stable cough, chronic nasal discharge, mild early heaves symptoms. Excellent symptomatic relief from mild cough and chronic nasal discharge. Helps control wheezing and bronchospasm.
Herbal-Plex Med-Vet Pharmaceuticals www.unitedvetequine.com 800-328-6652 $34.95/2 lbs.	Hesperidin, vitamin C, aromatic orange oil.	Antioxidants. Block activation of neutrophils in inflammatory reactions. Reduce bleeding and fluid leakage. Protect against chemical irritation.	Good control of cold and allergy symptoms, especially effective when combined with Herbal-Mune.
Hesperidin Biocomplex Uckele Health & Nutrition www.uckele.com 800-248-0330 $27.95/2 lbs.	Licorice, marshmallow, ginkgo, cleavers, coltsfoot, plantain, garlic extracts in a base of apple-cider vinegar and honey.	Blend of western herbs.	Rapid, excellent relief of dry coughs. Palatable. Long-term use provides good control of stable cough, helps clear mucus from lungs.
Hilton Freeway Hilton Herbs www.chamisaridge.com 800-743-3188 $44.95/liter	Huang Qi, Jie Geng, Ku Bu, Wu Jai Shen, Nan Sha Shen, Bei Sha Shen, Dan Shen, Gui Zhi.	Blend of immune-supporting expectorant and stimulant herbs.	Effective in easing work of breathing, blocking exercise-induced respiratory distress and cough, similar to albuterol.
Jet Breathe Just Win, Inc www.justwin.net 800-227-2987 $150/3 lbs.	Stinging nettle, peppermint, yarrow, comfrey leaves, german chamomile, mullein, red clover, milk thistle seed.	Blend of western herbs.	Reliable and rapid relief of nasal discharge, cough, mild heaves symptoms.

exercise-induced coughs that don't involve lung problems. However, an exercise-induced cough is a different story from the horse with stable cough.

We didn't have much luck controlling these problems with the "cough-drop" products alone, although after a week of Freeway the severity and frequency of coughs were less. Our quickest results by far were obtained with the Chinese herbs Jet Breath and Breathe Ease, with marked improvement obvious within a few days.

We also had excellent results with antioxidant/immune combos and the western herbal blends, although these sometimes took a little longer to work. There is considerable overlap of this particular symptom with other problems. Some horses cough only at the start of exercise, apparently as a way of clearing their airways. Others are irritated by exercise and cough more the longer they go or cough the most after you stop work.

We found that when exercise was a factor in the coughing, and no active infection was present, there was a good chance the horse also had lung disease to some extent.

Chronic Nasal Discharge

It's often difficult for people to decide what is and what is not normal in terms of a nasal discharge. If drainage is clear, it's usually a matter of degree. Most horses don't have much, if any, clear drainage when at rest. Immediately after exercise, some increase may be noted. Cold weather normally makes a horse's nose run more, just like it does ours. The combination of cold weather and exercise can even result in a thin but frothy whitish discharge (like watery, whipped egg whites).

A frothy white discharge at rest, though, is not normal—even though it may reflect irritation from dusts and ammonia in a closed-up winter barn more than it does an allergic or infectious problem.

Thick white, gray, or yellow discharge is always abnormal, especially if you see it when the horse is at rest. However, a horse that has been stall confined for a day or more will sometimes have a thicker-than-normal, off-color discharge after his first exercise. This occurs because secretions can build up in the airways when there is no exercise at all.

Most horses with abnormal nasal discharges also have, or eventually get, coughs. This seems to be one of the earliest and most nonspecific signs of upper-respiratory-tract irritation. Environmental control—better ventilation, avoiding dust, switching from straw to shavings, and wetting hay—can virtually eliminate the problem in many early cases. The next step would be antioxidant supplementation, or antioxidants with an herbal immune-stimulator if the horse also has a cough. The antioxidants alone provided significant symptomatic relief, often within three to five days at the most.

We found most horses with persistent problems responded well to Uckele's Bioquench. If problems persist on Bioquench, move through the sequence for stable cough, but also get the horse scoped to rule out follicular pharyngitis or a gutteral-pouch problem.

Although horses can have outdoor allergies too, most with lung problems do better on turnout.

Coughs Related to Conditions Involving Lungs

More serious and, unfortunately, more insidious are problems involving the lungs themselves. We tend to count on coughs and nasal discharge to warn us of lung problems, but these symptoms don't necessarily indicate lung involvement.

The first sign of lung involvement may be nothing more than a mildly elevated respiratory rate at rest or prolonged respiratory-rate recovery after work. Eventually, the horse's work capacity decreases, whether it's in the amount of time he works, the intensity of the work, or both. Because these changes are gradual, it's easy to overlook or dismiss them in the early stages. The horse with a lung problem is often labeled lazy, but it's not that he doesn't want to work harder—he actually can't.

Lung involvement should be suspected any time the respiratory rate at rest is elevated and/or when it takes the horse longer than normal to come back to a resting rate after work. It should also be considered when he breathes harder with and after work than is appropriate for the level of work.

The Chinese Herbs

Horses on the Chinese herbs were considerably more alert and eager. The Chinese herbs also alleviated wheezing sounds in the lungs and were the only products to help horses that had respiratory distress triggered by exercise, suggesting they may indeed have a bronchial dilating effect.

The most dramatic product responses we saw were to Breathe Ease and Jet Breathe, similar formulas utilizing traditional Chinese herbs that have proven immune-modulating properties and help thin and stimulate the removal of mucus.

The inclusion of one herb, dan shen (sage), is a bit of a mystery, however, as this is traditionally used as a focusing or mental-enhancing ingredient—and is even mildly hallucinogenic in strong extracts. In any event, the horses on full doses of these products not only breathed much more easily but were "on their toes" and alert. They weren't nervous or unmanageable but showed a much higher energy level than without it.

Your veterinarian usually can confirm the diagnosis with a chest exam. It also helps to have the horse scoped to see how much mucus is in the lungs, if they look inflamed, and to see if there are changes that would warrant a culture to check for infection. Antioxidants and immune-stimulator or modulator products often help, but they may not give you good control of mucus and bronchial irritation. This is where we found the herbal blends really come into play.

Breathe was found by the Nutraceutical Alliance to reduce the effort of breathing and reduce the respiratory rate of horses with allergic lung disease, and we found it to be a good choice for stable cough and mild lung problems, including early heaves or COPD.

We also observed obvious improvement with the other western herbal blends we tested, as well as Hilton Freeway, even though the mixtures of herbs these products employ are often quite different.

The toughest test of effectiveness, though, was in horses that had decreased exercise tolerance and abnormal recoveries from exercise. In these horses, Jet Breathe and Breathe Ease produced superior results.

Chronic Infections

Any horse receiving treatment for a respiratory problem is likely to get antibiotics somewhere along the line, even if it is only "just in case." Chronic coughs in young horses typically start after a viral infection and are usually characterized by lymphoid hyperplasia in the throat, which is the equivalent of chronic tonsillitis in children.

This may or may not include an element of chronic infection. Gutteral-pouch infections, bacterial or fungal, are a common cause of chronic nasal discharge and throat irritation. With lung infections, it is often hard to tell if it's the chicken or the egg. Low-grade infections make the lungs more sensitive to irritation and allergic reactions, and vice versa.

Lymphoid hyperplasia following an upper-respiratory tract infection is a common cause of chronic cough in young horses. Long courses of antibiotics usually fail, probably because bacteria aren't involved. We had excellent results using the immune-stimulating products with this condition, alone or in combination with additional antioxidants in tough cases. Coughs cleared in a maximum of 10 days.

Chronic gutteral-pouch infections may also be at the root of persistent coughs or nasal discharge, and sometimes also of decreased exercise tolerance. To make this diagnosis, the horse needs to be scoped. If your veterinarian determines an infection is at the root of your problem or is complicating an allergic process, use the drug he or she prescribes.

We suggest you also support the horse's immune system and ability to clear these infections by using Equinacea, Herbal-Plex, or Herbal-Mune Plus at the same time. The antioxidants in these products will help with symptom control. These are also excellent products to keep on hand for use before shipping or before competitions for horses with allergic respiratory problems. An allergy, like any type of inflammation, can make the horse more vulnerable to infections.

Good Old Vitamin C

Everyone knows to take vitamin C for colds, but taking vitamin C for prevention of allergy symptoms is an even better idea. Frankly, you would be hard pressed to find a "natural" treatment for any disease with more solid scientific literature to support its use. The ability of vitamin C and vitamin E to protect the lungs and upper-respiratory linings from allergic reactions is well documented. It can even prevent wheezing and reduce the risk of permanent lung damage when used long term.

A paper presented at the 1997 American Association of Equine Practitioners meeting reported similar improvement of symptoms in six horses with symptoms of COPD/"heaves" when supplemented with calcium ascorbate (Ester-C) in an amount equivalent to 20 to 30 grams of vitamin C a day. Our stable cough, runny nose, and mildly heavy/bronchitis horses also responded well to supplements providing them with either a minimum of 7 grams/day of plain vitamin C or lower doses of mixed antioxidant compounds. Contact: Pure C, Uckele, 800-248-0330; Ester-C, Select the Best 800-648-0950.

Lung Bleeding (EIPH)

Lung bleeding, technically known as exercise induced pulmonary hemorrhage (EIPH), is a potential problem for any horse that performs at high speeds.

Studies have repeatedly shown that at least low-level evidence of pulmonary bleeding can be found in over 95% of horses performing at speed. Some bleeders actually do show blood draining from the nostrils, but many horses are believed to bleed in the lungs, which goes virtually undetected until they're scoped and diagnosed by a veterinarian.

Bleeding certainly does influence performance. At what point performance decreases is difficult to quantify, especially since one commonly cited study found a high percentage of bleeders among racehorses that had won their races.

However, two other studies reported only about half as many bleeder horses as nonbleeders do well racing. Common sense alone would tell you that areas of the lungs that are blood-filled aren't taking up oxygen and getting rid of carbon dioxide.

There are long-term consequences as well. The presence of blood in the lung causes a significant inflammatory reaction, which thickens lung tissues, and decreases efficiency and can render tissues totally nonfunctional in terms of gas exchange. In addition, the horse with free blood in his lungs is at high risk of developing a variety of infections.

Mechanisms

In a nutshell, anything that leads to abnormally high pressures along the capillaries of the lung can cause bleeding. A significant factor in lung bleeding is the high pressure that develops in the vessels of the horse's lung during exercise, especially the tiny capillaries, where walls are thinnest and where gas exchange occurs.

Furosemide (Lasix or Salix) is the only drug that reliably reduces the amount of lung bleeding, although it doesn't completely prevent it. This is because furosemide lowers the high vascular pressures. However, studies have also shown that there is no significant difference between intravascular pressures during exercise in horses that bleed versus horses that don't, so there must be other causes operating here.

Many experts think the real answers as to why horses bleed have to do with factors that involve the lung tissue itself and pressures in the airways. In fact, a Kansas State study concluded that changes in pulmonary artery pressure could only account for 20% of the variability in levels of EIPH seen in racing horses.

The documented ability of Flair Nasal Strips, which hold the nasal passages in an open position at a critical narrowing spot, to at least reduce symptoms of lung bleeding is an example. By lowering resistance to air flow, bleeding is reduced. Anything that interferes with the ability of the horse to breath easily, from anatomical problems to allergies, can increase the risk of bleeding.

Products Designed to Help Bleeders

Category	Mechanism	Indications	Product Choices
Mechanical aids	Reduce resistance to airflow at the level of the nostrils.	May help reduce EIPH in any bleeder. Check with local authorities and disciplines regarding legality of use.	**Flair Nasal Strips**, CNS, www.flairstrips.com 888-683-5247, not reusable, about $10/strip. **Breathe E-Z**, Protecto, 586-754-4820, www.protectohorse.com, re-usable, $29.95.
Bioflavonoids/anti-oxidants. These include vitamin C, hesperidin, quercetin, pycnogenols, vitamin E, selenium, and other trace minerals	Improve capillary strength and integrity, help combat allergic and inflammatory reactions.	Any bleeder, especially when an allergic or irritative component is also suspected.	**Hesperidin Bioplex**, Uckele, 800-248-0330, www.uckele.com, $29.95/2 lbs. **Bio-Quench**, Uckele, $22.95/2 lbs. **Hemo Cease**, Peak Performance, 800-944-1984, www.peakperformancenutrients.com, $37.95/2 lbs.
Western herbs, including mullein, lungwort, yarrow, marshmallow, borage, coltsfoot, fenugreek, ginger, capsicum, horehound, myrrh, yerba santa	Many of these herbs have not been evaluated for their pharmacological actions, and their use is based primarily on folklore. Some have inherent high-antioxidant capacity, others are chosen for either their astringent (drying) or emollient (soothing) characteristics.	Horses with evidence of respiratory tract irritation, especially when cough is present.	**Lungwort Compound**, Equilite, 800-942-5483, www.Equilite.com, $85/5 lbs. **Breathe**, Herbs for Horses, 888-423-7777, www.horseherbs.com, $45/2.2 lbs. **Respiration**, Wendals Herbs, 800-981-0320 www.wendals.com, $37.50/2.2 lbs.
Aromatic oils, including camphor, eucalyptus, orange, mints	Have both mild bronchodilating and mucus-thinning effects.	May help ease breathing in any horse, especially indicated when upper respiratory and/or lung irritation/inflammation is present.	**Wind Aid**, Hawthorne, 765-768-6585, www.hawthorne-products.com, $14/32 oz. **Resprun**, Uckele, 800-248-0330, www.uckele.com, $4.95/tube. **Air Power**, Finish Line, 800-762-4242, www.finishlinehorse.com, $22/liter.
Chinese herbs, including Bei Sha Shen, Dan Shen, Gui Zhi, Huang Qi, Jie Geng, Kun Bu, Nan Sha Shen, Wu Jiao Shen	Bronchodilating, anti-allergy and mucus-loosening effects.	All bleeders.	**Breathe Ease**, Equine Gold, 800-870-5949, www.equinegold.com, $57.95/lb. **Jet Breath**, Just Win, 800-227-2987, www.justwin.net, $150/3 lbs.

Bottom Line

Obviously, no single drug, device, or supplement can eliminate the risk of lung bleeding. How well anything works depends on the risk factors operating in the individual horse, so we can't give you a blanket recommendation, beyond furosemide, which is a prescription drug. Nasal strips do at least reduce air resistance, but they may not be legal under your competition's rules. Be sure you check.

Your best bets on the supplement front are products that work to improve the strength and integrity of capillaries, minimize or help eliminate mucus, and control allergic or irritative reactions in the airways and the lungs. We've listed good choices in the accompanying chart. Pay attention to the indications to make the best selection for your horse. Please note

Diet and Lung Allergy Symptoms

Despite your aggressive efforts to keep feed irritants from making their way up the horse's nose, some horses just don't show improvement. The triggers may be unrelated factors such as pollution, arena dust, barn mold and dust, plant or tree allergens, or permanent lung damage. Perhaps it's time to adjust the horse's medications or supplements. However, your horse might also be reacting to allergens he absorbs through his intestinal tract.

A variety of peptides (small proteins) and complex carbohydrates in grains, seeds, nuts, or legumes (like alfalfa and soy) have been known to worsen asthma symptoms in some people and experimental animals. This could also occur with your horse.

You can switch to a feed that doesn't contain potential problematic ingredients in your current feed, including:

- Soy
- Wheat mids
- Alfalfa
- Seed meals
- Distiller's dried grains

However, finding a commercial feed that doesn't contain one or more of these ingredients can be difficult to impossible. You may want to start with a strict simple diet of one ingredient, such as triple cleaned plain whole oats. If that helps, then try adding things back in one at a time. Allow two weeks after each change to judge effects. Do not change medications or supplements during this time, and pick a time of year when you know your horse's symptoms are typically fairly constant.

these products primarily address possible lung problems contributing to elevated pressures across capillary beds.

Don't waste your money on products that don't disclose their ingredients or supposedly are "natural" alternatives to diuretics or furosemide. Some herbal and natural diuretics are potentially toxic. Vitamin K, a nutrient essential for normal clotting, is a common ingredient in supplements for bleeding, but we can find no evidence to suggest vitamin K deficiency is ever involved. 🐎

Skin and Coat Supplements

The quality of your horse's coat, hooves, and skin is a good indicator of your horse's general health and the adequacy of his diet. Your horse needs to receive a variety of nutrients to produce a sleek, high-gloss coat, and we've listed these target nutrients in the accompanying chart (see page 262).

When problems with coat quality arise, it's usually because there's insufficient intake of a key nutrient or not enough is being made available to the skin and coat, possibly due to an illness, the demands of growth, or parasitism.

While you can simply throw extra fat at the horse and increase "grease" of the coat, so that the coat is shiny, the result isn't the same as a healthy coat. Despite what you might hear, you're simply not going to find one magical ingredient that can fix all coat and skin problems. You must get to the root of the problem and fix it.

If you're considering using a supplement that claims to be designed to enhance your horse's coat, be sure that you first:

- Rule out an underlying medical problem as the cause, especially if the skin or coat problem was not there before on an identical diet.

- Do an evaluation of your horse's diet and correct any problems with mineral balances, vitamin deficiencies, and protein intake first. In most cases, these dietary adjustments will solve the problem.

- Use our section on common problems that may show up in poor skin or coat quality, and choose your supplement according to what your horse's diet lacks.

Simplify Your Shopping

Beware of advertising that draws you to the product but offers no ingredients or scientific basis for the claims being made, or lists useless generalities. Claims like "balanced blend of fats" are usually meaningless.

Remember that not all oils are made the same. Only raw, unprocessed oils are likely to contain any significant amount of the omega-3 and omega-6 essential fatty acids you want to be sure are adequate in the horse's diet, which is why basic grocery-store corn oil provides little more than fat calories (that faux shine we talked about earlier).

If you're considering a liquid supplement, be sure you note how it must be stored. Raw flax oil, which is high in needed omega-3 fatty acids, must be refrigerated. Although raw soy or rice-bran oil, which are high in omega-6 fatty acids, are a bit more stable, we still recommend you refrigerate them after opening.

Oils that are stable at room temperatures are either highly processed or contain preservatives—not what we recommend you use to boost your horse's nutritional intake and get that natural gleam.

Dry products aren't necessarily the answer either. Look for the term "stabilized" if you need a dry product to supply good levels of omega-3 and/or omega-6 fatty acids. This will allow for easier, longer storage while still ensuring solid levels of the omega fatty acids. All the products in our chart contain stabilized forms of flax or rice bran.

While we're all for saving money with larger containers, we aren't going to try it with high-fat supplements. For the best results with supplements containing moderate (10 to 20%) or high (20% and over) fat, don't buy more than a 30-day supply

A gleaming coat is the hallmark of a well conditioned, properly fed horse.

No amount of expensive shampoos can produce the glow that good nutrition provides.

Dietary Factors in Various Diet Types

Diet Type	Possible Problem Areas
Pasture	Mineral deficiencies or imbalances (zinc, iodine, selenium).
Hay and no grain or less than 5 lbs./day of a fortified grain	Omega-3 fatty acids, methionine, biotin, zinc, iodine, elenium.
Hay and 5 lbs. or more/day of a fortified grain or a protein/vitamin/mineral supplement	Omega-3 fatty acids, biotin. Mineral deficiencies are still possible if the hay has a very unbalanced mineral profile.
Complete feed	Omega-3 fatty acids, biotin.

at one time. Be sure you protect the product from heat and sun and reseal it carefully after use to prevent rancidity.

Finally, be sure you look for an expiration date on the container. While all nutrients have a shelf life, these types of products are especially vulnerable.

Problems That May Show in Your Horse's Coat

- **Intestinal Parasites.** Significant parasite burdens may be present in individual horses even after routine paste dewormings and negative fecals. This is particularly true with older horses, young horses, and horses either on crowded turnout or those rotated through high-traffic paddocks. If the horse's diet is good and well-balanced, consult your vet about tapeworm-specific treatments and larvicidal deworming.

- **Chronic Illness.** Undiagnosed chronic illnesses, especially chronic infections (e.g. internal abscess, Lyme disease), hormonal problems like Cushing's disease, and malignancies can cause a poor coat. Suspect an illness, especially if you're seeing changes in appetite, weight, personality, etc. and get a veterinary work-up.

- **Protein Quality/Quantity.** Although many people worry about the amount of protein in their horses' diets, protein deficiency in quality or quantity isn't a common problem unless the horse is on a diet of only low-quality hay, with protein under 8%, and eating less than 20 pounds per day of hay.

With protein malnutrition, the horse will be in poor shape in general, showing poor muscling and likely to be underweight if the hay isn't supplying sufficient calories. Absolute protein deficiencies will show up in the coat but are most likely in growing or pregnant or nursing horses and those receiving a diet of primarily low-protein hays.

Deficiencies of key amino acids—the building blocks of protein molecules—are more common, particularly if the horse receives only one type of hay and a grain mix that is not fortified with lysine and methionine. Feeding a variety of hay types is a good way to improve amino acid profiles in the diet, or choose a coat supplement that has this feature.

- **Minerals.** The effect of trace-mineral imbalances or deficiencies on coat quality is often overlooked, yet this is one of the most common causes of both a poor coat and skin problems, including poor shine and "bleaching." Virtually any significant mineral deficiency or imbalance will show up in the coat because minerals are required for every body process. Trace-mineral problems of low copper and zinc compared to high iron and manganese are especially common deficiencies.

Sulfur and silica are commonly recommended for people with skin- or hair-quality problems but aren't likely to be deficient in an equine diet, except for sulfur-containing amino acids, which are addressed by correcting any protein problems in the diet.

Ask your veterinarian or an equine nutritionist to evaluate your horse's diet and correct any problems along these lines first, then look at coat-specific supplements that may address the problem.

- **Vitamins.** Vitamin A is important for skin health, but it's not likely to be deficient in most diets. However, inadequate vitamin E is a common problem and contributes to dry skin and coat, allergic or hypersensitive reactions, and poor resistance to skin infections. Deficiencies of B

We recommend using a gentle equine shampoo for bathing.

Key Nutrients for Skin and Coat Health

Nutrient	Symptoms of Deficiency	Feeding Solution
Fat	Dry, brittle coats. There may be some skin flaking/dryness as well. A deficiency of omega-6 fatty acids may predispose to skin infections, and omega-3 deficiency can lead to overly sensitive, itchy, and inflamed skin.	A little vegetable/corn oil may improve the situation if your horse's diet is just too low in fat, but it's much better to approach it from the direction of supplying essential fatty acids at the same time. Best option for that is stabilized rice bran and whole ground flax.
Protein	Dull coat that's slow to grow and shed out	A base of rice bran and flax is a good idea, since they contain generous levels of both protein and esential fatty acids. Soy-based supplements will also have good protein levels, including lysine, as long as they haven't been overly processed.
B Vitamins	Skin rash/scaling, and thin hair or balding patches are the usual signs of biotin deficiency.	Yeasts, grain products, brans, and seed meals (flax or soy) are good natural sources of Bs. Consult with your vet about the likelihood of a biotin or B vitamin problem being major in your horse before you base a supplement selection on higher levels of Bs.
Minerals	Brittle hair, dull color, reddish discoloration of dark coats or black manes and tails. The skin may be less resistant to infections, more prone to exaggerated inflammatory reactions and allergies.	Mineral supplements should be based on the mineral levels in the grains and hays. Don't guess or try to patch up isolated problems with one or two minerals given blindly. Many coat/skin supplements contain at least some added zinc, but this is unlikely to fully correct mineral-related problems.

vitamins severe enough to cause coat problems are probably rare. Suspect B vitamin shortages in horses that are older or have chronic intestinal problems.

Biotin (a B vitamin) would be most likely involved and deficient, and slow hoof growth will be present. Biotin is essential to the horse's healthy skin and coat and strong hooves. In fact, all the B vitamins play a role in maintaining the skin, with B6 (pyridoxine) also being a major player because of its role in protein metabolism. However, the B vitamins work together and should be supplemented together.

A true biotin deficiency probably doesn't occur in horses, although estimates of dietary requirements may be too low. A skin problem related only to biotin or B vitamin intakes is also unlikely. B vitamin inadequacies may be particularly likely in heavily exercising, stressed, or ill horses; older horses; horses with a history of intestinal-tract upsets; and horses eating primarily hay or poor-quality forage.

- **Fatty acids.** Deficiency of fat per se is highly unlikely unless the horse is getting only old, dry, low-quality hay. However, even horses on good-quality hays and grains are receiving a different profile of fats compared to a horse on grass. Both omega-6 and omega-3 fatty acids must be provided by the diet.

  Grains and all vegetable oils, except for flaxseed/linseed oil, are high in omega-6 and low in omega-3, while fresh pasture is exactly the opposite—extremely high in omega-3 and low in omega-6.

  This makes whole ground stabilized flax or cold-pressed flaxseed oil ideal fatty-acid supplements for horses. Horses that are receiving hay and no or little grain may benefit from a supplement with a blend of omega-6 and omega-3 fatty acid sources, but we recommend always choosing one higher in omega-3.

Bottom Line

For supplements that will give a moderate fat boost with a balanced profile of omega-6 and -3, we'd suggest Uckele's Equi Omega Complex, Grand Meadows Grand Coat, Med Vet's Omegas, or Gleam & Gain from Adeptus. All of these products also contain good supplemental protein levels. The Equi Omega Complex offers the greatest variety of amino acids because of the blend of different protein sources.

For horses with poor coats and a tendency toward itchy or inflammatory skin conditions, we recommend a supplement that is richer in omega-3 fatty acids, because the omega-3 fatty acids are anti-inflammatory and help quiet allergies. Horses receiving whole grains are getting omega-6 from this source and are most likely to benefit from a flax-only fat and protein supplement. Omega Horseshine is the most concentrated source of quality omega-3 essential fatty acids we've found and is our first pick. However, for horses likely to have inadequate B vitamins

Allergies can make your horse so itchy he spends all day trying to get some relief.

and/or trace minerals complicating the picture, we think Horse Tech's Glanzen 3 is the way to go.

If your horse has any dietary shortfalls, they're likely to surface as a dull coat, often in combination with poor hooves. The end of grazing season deprives your horse of quality protein, essential fatty acids, and vitamins in their optimal form. If they are not replaced in the diet, the coat and hooves will be the first to show it.

A horse's natural diet, grass, is very low in fat but does provide a constant source of the omega-3 and omega-6 fatty acids. These are the only fats that the horse can't manufacture for himself. Hays, grains, and processed oils have little or no essential-fatty-acid content left in them. Even storage of whole grains reduces the level of fatty acids.

To make matters worse, grass is rich in omega-3 anti-inflammatory fatty acids, which are more fragile than the omega-6 fats, and everything else we usually include in the base diet, like grain products, is high in omega-6. Adequate essential fatty acid intake is also important for hoof quality and immune function. The solution is to feed flaxseed. Flaxseed contains both omega-3 and omega-6 fatty acids, in a ratio close to grass.

Most horses have adequate total protein in their diet but could easily be lacking key amino acids because of insufficient variety of foods. Every plant, seed, and grain has its own distinctive amino acid pattern. None are perfect, so feeding a variety helps guarantee all bases are covered. Feeding mixed hay is a good place to start, but if you can't feed it on a consistent basis, you can look into purchasing hay pellets or cubes to substitute for some of your regular loose hay.

Prevention of sun "bleaching" and red ends on dark manes and tails requires adequate intake of zinc and copper.

Specifics

Zinc is a common mineral deficiency that can manifest itself as poor quality hooves, dry skin with low resistance to infections, and a dull coat. Many of the B vitamins play critical roles in hoof, skin, and coat health as well. The horse's main source of B vitamins is from the teeming microorganisms that live in a healthy digestive tract, but they are present in fresh feedstuffs as well. Estimates of B-vitamin requirements are for levels needed to avoid full-blown deficiency states, but may not be the same as those required for optimal health, including hoof and skin condition. Supplementing Bs, especially biotin and pyridoxine, may help most horses that have skin and hoof problems, especially older horses or those with digestive-tract problems.

Vitamin C is another vitamin in abundant supply in fresh food that is rapidly destroyed by drying and storage. Horses can make their own vitamin C when the diet is lacking it, and it's still not really clear if C supplementation is helpful. Consider adding C in winter for horses that are working hard, have lung problems of any type, or are prone to infections. C can upset the gut in large amounts, so feed no more than 5 grams per day.

Although vitamin A is critical to maintaining healthy skin, hays contain abundant vitamin A, and grains and supplements are heavily fortified with it. If your hay is over six months old and you're not feeding at least 5 lbs. a day of commercial grain or a high-A supplement, add a few carrots a day to boost vitamin A. 🐎

Supplements Targeting Coats

Product	Price	Comments	Best Suited For
Clovite Fort Dodge Labs, www.fortdodge.com, 800-685-5656	$44.95/ 27 lbs.	Soy meal and flour base with moderate amounts of vitamins A, D, and B12, also multiple Bs and E in unspecified amounts.	Horses eating very old hay low in protein and vitamin A. Soy is also a good source of the essential amino acid lysine.
Command Coat Brookside Equine Supplements, www.brooksideequine.com, 800-419-9524	$24.95/ 5 lbs.	Stabilized ground flax base with low doses of amino acids and biotin (less than 1 mg), moderate chelated zinc, and low chelated copper (about a third of estimated daily requirement).	Horses on hay or poor-quality pasture, with or without grain, where protein quality is likely poor.
Dapples Horse Health Products, division of www.farnam.com, 800-234-2269	$14/ 6.5 lbs.	Low-protein, moderate-fat supplement with base of grain products and alfalfa, containing soy and wheat germ oils, moderate levels of zinc, animal fat, biotin (amount unspecified), natural preservatives.	Horses on low/no grain with hay or poor quality pasture but dietary protein adequate. Poor source of omega-3 fatty acids.
Equi-Omega Complex Uckele Health and Nutrition, www.uckele.com, 800-248-0330	$14.95/ 7.5 lbs.	19% protein blend of stabilized ground flax seed, rice bran, cocosoya oil, in a base of distiller's grains and beet pulp	Horses on a diet of predominantly hay. Excellent choice for dieters and horses that are insulin resistant. High palatability a plus for picky eaters.
Gen-A Coat Nickers International, www.nickint.com, 800-642-5377	$28.95/ 4 lbs.	Active ingredients are ground stabilized flax and biotin (15 mg/oz).	Horses showing problems with dry, flaking skin and dull coat as well as dry, cracking hooves. Doses higher than the 1-oz. serving recommended may be needed due to the low level of essential fatty acids.
Glanzen 3 HorseTech, www.horsetech.com, 800-831-3309	$36.95/ 12 lbs.	Very high biotin (30 mg) and very high omega-3 content from stabilized ground flax, high methionine (6,500 mg), generous levels of chelated trace minerals and all B vitamins. Amounts are all per 6-oz. serving.	Itchy and inflammatory skin and coat problems, horses on unsupplemented grain mixes and hay or poor-quality pasture.
Gleam & Gain Adeptus, www.adeptusnutrition.com, 866-233-7887	$40 / 10 lbs.	Very high fat (41%), moderate protein supplement with vegetable oil, stabilized flax, and rice bran (higher omega-3), in base of distiller's dried grains and yeast. Balanced calcium:phosphorus.	Thin horses on low/no grain with hay or poor-quality pasture likely to lack sufficient fat and protein.
Grand Coat, Grand Meadows, www.grandmeadows.com, 800-255-2962	$23.95/ 5 lbs.	Moderate protein (19%), high fat (31%), stabilized flax and rice-bran based, with low levels of essential amino acids (less than 1 gram/serving of lysine, methionine, leucine), higher omega-3 compared to omega-6, good zinc, low copper (about ¼ of daily minimum requirement), 1 mg. biotin/2 oz. serving. Expiration dated.	Horses on low/no grain with hay or poor-quality pasture.
Mirra Coat PetAg, www.petag.com, 800-323-6878	$18/ 5 lbs.	Soy and vegetable (type not specified) oil, soy-flour-based product, sugar added, with moderate zinc and vitamin A, low vitamin E, B6, and biotin.	Horses on low/no grain with low- or poor-quality protein from poor-quality hay or pasture. Does not address omega-3 needs.
Nu-Image Richdel, Select The Best, www.selectthebest.com, 800-648-0950	$18.87/ 5 lbs.	High protein and moderate fat (primarily omega-6, soy) with moderate zinc and some biotin (less than 1 mg/oz.), riboflavin and folic acid.	Horses receiving little or no grain with hay or poor-quality pasture. Does not address omega-3 needs.
Omega Horseshine Enreco flax, www.omegafields.com, 877-663-4203	$18.99/ 4.5 lbs.	Very high potency omega-3, stabilized ground flax-based supplement, with modest levels of supplemental trace minerals and B vitamins in addition to those naturally occurring in the flax and yeast base.	Itchy and inflammatory skin and coat problems, horses on diets that do not include fresh grass.

Product	Price	Comments	Best Suited For
Omegas Med Vet Pharmaceutical, www. unitedvetequine.com, 800-328-6652	$23.35/ 4 lbs.	Moderate protein and fat (higher in omega-3s) from blend of soy, flax, wheat germ, and coconut oil.	Horses on grain with hay or poor-quality pasture diets.
Shed N Shine Equine America, www. equineamerica.com, 800-838-7524	$24/ gallon	Liquid. Soy, wheat germ, and cod liver oils with added omega-6, anise flavoring. zinc, vitamins A, E, D (amounts not specified). 98% fat.	Horses with inadequate fat intake, on diets of highly processed grains or no/low grain and poor-quality hay or pasture. Does not address omega-3 needs.
Super 14 Farnam, www.farnam.com, 800-234-2269	$16.49/ 3 lbs.	High protein (soy flour) (27%) and moderate fat (corn and soy oils) (18%), dextrose for flavoring (sugar), with low levels of methionine (198 mg/oz), zinc (10 to 15% of estimated daily requirement), B6, and vitamins A and E.	Horses on low/no grain or low protein from poor-quality hay or pasture. Does not address omega-3 needs.
Super Coat 17 Med Vet Pharmaceutical, www. unitedvetequine.com, 800-328-6652	$13.25/ 3.5 lbs.	Corn, soy oils, soy flour, added sugar, low levels of all important trace minerals and multiple B vitamins, vitamin E.	Horses on low/no grain with low or poor-quality protein from poor-quality hay or pasture. Does not address omega-3 needs.

Weight-Gain Strategies

The first thing you need to ask yourself is whether or not your horse really needs a weight-gain product. Lately, especially with young sales horses and show horses, the body weight many horsemen seem to consider ideal is actually too fat. This trend is compounded by the fact that many recreational horses, especially ponies and easy-keeper breeds, are overweight due to a lack of regular work and/or overfeeding. We've ended up in a situation where the ideal body image of what a horse is supposed to look like is distorted in many people's minds. A horse that's actually a bit overweight begins to appear normal. The worst part is that our horses pay for it in terms of their health.

Any horse carrying around a body-condition score of over 5 (see sidebar, page 270) is at increased risk of tendon, ligament, and muscle injury from the excess weight, as well as arthritis, foot problems, decreased exercise tolerance, and significant metabolic disorders, such as insulin resistance and consequent laminitis. Reproductive health might also be affected.

Before you put your horse on a weight-gain product, be sure you compare him to genuinely fit horses to see what a truly healthy weight looks like. Cartoon Thelwell ponies are cute, but real ponies aren't supposed to look like balloons floating over New York City on Thanksgiving.

You should be able to feel your horse's ribs. Note we said *feel* your horse's ribs; you shouldn't be able to see them, however.

Remember that there's a difference between roundness

from muscling and roundness from fat. Fat feels soft to the touch, while muscle feels more like touching a steak. Fit horses can have flat muscling, such as racehorses and endurance horses. Fit horses can also have a more round look, as you see in dressage horses, working Quarter Horses, and draft horses. While it's easy to note when a racehorse looks fat, it can be tougher with a breed that's naturally more round. Note where the excesses appear on the horse. A round gut, bulging flanks, or thick crest is likely fat. A truly fit horse has evenly distributed muscling.

Management First

If your horse truly is too thin, he may indeed need a weight-gain product, which is a better solution than throwing him a ton of concentrates. Too much grain can cause ulcers, colic, and excess energy. However, before we increase our horse's calorie intake, we'd also be certain to:

- Check teeth for floating and any other necessary dental work, to ensure you're not really dealing with a chewing problem.

- Be certain the horse consumes at least 2% of his body weight in feed per day. That's 20 pounds per 1,000 pounds of bodyweight. This is the minimum amount you should be feeding before considering a weight-gain product. If you're not feeding him this amount, you're probably underfeeding him. We recommend you feed this as all hay for inactive horses, skipping grain, while 30% of that 20 pounds can come from grain for horses in work. Horses in moderate to heavy work may need to consume 2.5 to 3.0% of their body weight.

- Feed hay free-choice. Allowing horses to gain needed weight by consuming additional hay is your first-line strategy and by far the most healthful.

- If his appetite for grain is poor, consider whether he could be battling ulcers. A horse with ulcers tends to go for his hay before his grain or may pick at his grain.

Body-Condition Scoring

1 Poor.
Extremely emaciated; spinal processes, ribs, tailhead, hips, and back projecting prominently, no fatty tissue can be seen.

2 Very Thin.
Emaciated; slight fatty covering over base of spinal processes; transverse processes of lumbar vertebrae feel rounded; spinal processes, ribs, tailhead, hips, and back prominent; withers, shoulders, and neck structure faintly discernible.

3 Thin.
Fat buildup about halfway on spinal processes; slight fat covering over ribs; spinal processes and ribs easily discernible; tailhead prominent, but individual vertebrae can't be identified visually; hips appear rounded but easily discernible; withers, shoulders, and neck are accentuated.

4 Moderately Thin.
Slight ridge along back; faint outline of ribs discernible; tailhead prominence depends on conformation—fat can be felt around it; hips not discernible; withers, shoulders, and neck not obviously thin.

5 Moderate.
Back is flat (no crease or ridge); ribs not visually distinguishable. Fat easily felt around tailhead and area beginning to feel spongy; withers appear rounded over spinal processes; shoulders and neck blend smoothly into body.

6 Moderately Fleshy.
May have slight crease down back; fat over ribs spongy; fat around tailhead soft; fat beginning

How fat is your horse? Very thin and very fat are pretty easy, but what about a horse who appears fit? This horse looks "show fat" but is really a 6 to a 7. A little weight loss is in order.

to be deposited along the side of withers, behind shoulders, and along sides of neck.

7 Fleshy.
May have crease down back; individual ribs can be felt, but noticeable filling between ribs with fat; fat around tailhead soft; fat deposited along withers, behind shoulders, and along neck.

8 Fat.
Crease down back; difficult to feel ribs; fat around tailhead soft; area along withers filled with fat; area behind shoulder filled with fat; noticeable thickening of neck; fat deposited along inner thighs.

9 Extremely Fat.
Obvious crease down back; patchy fat appearing over ribs; bulging fat around tailhead, along withers, behind shoulders, and along neck; fat along inner thighs may rub together, flank filled with fat.

- Do a fecal-egg count check regardless of your current deworming program and consider treating for tapeworms, as these are difficult to find on a fecal. Do a larvicidal deworming with a five-day double-dose of fenbendazole for immature, non-egg-laying parasites.

- If undigested grain is present in the manure, try a pelleted feed instead of whole grains.

Although weight gain products invariably rely on fat as a concentrated calorie source, we're not keen on overdoing a horse's fat intake. Fat is not a quick-energy fuel. Horses don't use recently ingested fat as an energy source. The fats that muscle cells use during exercise are tryglycerides that are released from body stores. However, fat is good for weight gain.

Even horses in the grueling sport of endurance racing can maintain muscle mass and a healthy body weight when fed properly.

We define a high-fat diet as one that contains more than 10% fat. However, some horses need additional calories, and fat is an understandable way to pack the most caloric punch per ounce.

Before reaching for more grain and adding fat to the horse's diet, however, try optimizing the efficiency of fiber digestion. Too much grain or fat can be detrimental to fiber digestion, meaning you lose some of the benefit of the horse's natural calorie source, grass and hay. In addition, because fat can affect protein absorption, be sure your horse's overall protein level in the diet does not fall below 12%.

Magnesium absorption can also be negatively impacted by fat.

The addition of beet pulp, a readily fermented fiber that supports fiber-fermenting organisms (a prebiotic), can help the horse get more out of the fiber he's ingesting. A pound of dry beet pulp has about the same calories as a pound of oats. Feeding a 50:50 blend of beet pulp and plain oats gives you the best of both worlds (fiber and concentrate) with no sacrifice in calories and is also naturally mineral balanced for major minerals.

We also find the regular use of 1.5 to 2 oz. of psyllium (3 to 4 oz. if you're using a volume scoop) is also a good way to support fiber-fermenting bacteria and protozoa.

For details on probiotics and intestinal organisms, see chapter 9. Basically, less-than-optimal microorganism numbers in the large colon will rob your horse of valuable calories.

A good place to start in ensuring adequate "gut bugs" is Ration Plus (www.cytozyme.com, 801-533-9208), a liquid pre-biotic product that provides the growth factors these organisms need to thrive. This will help ensure your horse makes maximal use of everything he consumes.

Oils for Fat

Seeds can be incorporated into your weight gain program. At about 30% protein and 30% fat, they contain half the starch of grains.

Focusing on a healthy weight and implementing our management suggestions should cure weight issues for most horses. However, a few horses are genuine hard keepers. Others can't eat enough grain or hay to maintain their weight and need special help. Gradually introduce any fat product to your horse. Sudden, large amounts of fat can cause bloating and flatulence.

The route chosen by most people, at least initially, is to add oil to the diet. Calories in the form of oils are readily absorbed and processed and may be more likely to end up as body fat. The classic choice is corn oil.

Corn oil off your grocery-store shelf definitely packs a significant calorie punch, to the tune of at least three times the calories of grains on a weight basis. It's readily available and will get the job done, but you can get added nutritional benefits by using unprocessed oils.

Store oils are heavily processed to remove much of the natural flavor and all "solids," including some beneficial antioxidant compounds found in natural oils. Stabilization, which is done to ensure a long shelf life, may also alter the structure of the fats and essentially destroys fragile essential fatty acids like the anti-inflammatory omega-3s.

Cold-pressed, unfiltered, and unbleached oils have many health benefits and are far more likely to be well-accepted. All oils contain about the same number of calories. To achieve weight gain from added oil, you will need to feed a minimum of 2 oz. a day, usually more. Start low and allow at least a week to gauge the effects. If you try to feed over 8 oz. of oil a day, you may cause the horse to back off feeding.

Uckele's Cocosoya is a palatable blend of unprocessed coconut and soy oils with an aroma and color reminiscent of caramel. It's a good source of omega-6 fatty acids, triglycerides for energy, vitamin E, and other natural antioxidants. Fatty acids will benefit your horse's coat, skin, and hooves. They also help enhance his immune function.

Farnam's Weight Builder Liquid, an excellent blend of canola, soybean, and flaxseed oils, is guaranteed to contain 10% omega-3 and 30% omega-6 fatty acids, stabilized by vitamin C and vitamin E (meaning no preservatives), and provides a generous 800 IU of vitamin E per ounce.

Wheat-germ oil is generally well-accepted and a good source of vitamin E. It also contains some omega-6 fatty acids. Select the Best's Wheat Germ Oil is cold-pressed, but they don't guarantee the levels of essential fatty acids and it includes a chemical preservative.

Unprocessed soy and rice-bran oils are also available for horses, with high omega-6 fatty acids and vitamin E content. They're a fine choice, if your horse finds them palatable.

Rapid weight loss unexplained by change in diet or activity level is a red flag to get a thorough veterinary examination rather than just reaching for a weight-gain product.

Solid Fat Sources

Solid weight-gain products usually have a base of stabilized rice bran and/or flaxseed. Plain rice bran alone has little to offer over grain in terms of calorie density, but the weight-gain products based on rice bran contain added fat to boost calorie content. Again, we prefer to stay as unprocessed as possible to reap maximum health and nutrition benefits. Remember, processing leaves the calories but destroys some of the other potential beneficial nutrients.

We found many powdered and pelleted weight-gain products, and prices were highly competitive. However, we prefer products that are free of animal fat, as the long-term health effects on horses are still unknown. This narrows the choices down to Gleam & Gain, Farnam Weight Builder, Fat-Cat, and LinPro.

Weight and High-Performance

Supplemental fat has been suggested as the ideal way to keep weight on any horse, but we find high fat can have detrimental effects on horses that perform at speed. Unless the horse has a proven problem with tying-up related to polysaccharide storage myopathy, we prefer to support the high-performance horse with simple, easily absorbed carbohydrate sources instead. This includes glycogen-enhancing products, like Vapco's Fat-Cat. If the horse is having trouble holding muscle mass rather than fat, you need to consider a nutritional anabolic, although horses supported with dextrose/maltodextrin supplementation also often show improved muscle mass. Remember fat builds fat, not muscle.

Non-Grain Weight-Gain Options

Unfortunately, the horses most likely to be hard keepers, like Thoroughbreds, are also the ones most likely to become too full of energy when fed significant amounts of grain. It's often suggested that high fat be used instead, as the horses tend to be calmer on high-fat diets. While this routine will work, we'd first try to:

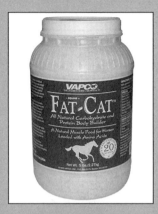

- Maximize hay intake, at least 2% of the body weight/day and keep it available free-choice.

Try one of the following as your grain substitute:

- 50:50 mix of beet pulp and plain oats.
- Plain beet pulp with 2 to 3 oz. of rice bran per pound of beet pulp.
- Plain beet pulp with 3 to 4 oz of wheat bran per pound of beet pulp.
- Calcium-added rice bran (naturally about 13% fat).

Each option provides the same or more calories per pound as plain grain.

We like the formulation of LinPro, plus the natural preservatives, but its calorie density is about the same as plain oats. It's really more suitable as a protein/mineral/fatty acid supplement than a weight-gain product.

With Fat-Cat, the overall amount of fat is less than what we want to add as calories.

Bottom Line

Your choice of a liquid or solid largely depends upon your horse's current diet and tastes. Liquids can be sprinkled on hay, while solids require a mixer, like a little grain or, better yet, beet pulp. In addition, some horses don't find oils palatable, and most have a limit as to how much they like. However, oils do pack the biggest calorie punch for your dollar. If you go with a dry product, the calorie density will be proportional to the percentage of fat.

In the liquids, if you're hooked on grocery-store corn oil because of its convenience and price, it will get the job done in terms of calories. Just know you're sacrificing other benefits. We think Cocosoya, our best buy, and Farnam's Weight Builder Liquid are better choices.

In the solids, we're torn between Gleam & Gain and Farnam's Weight Builder Granules. They're nearly the same in price, analysis, and ingredients. Both are excellent choices. Let convenience and your horse's taste be your guide. 🐎

Products That Promote Weight Gain

Product	Price	Ingredients/Analysis	Form and Dose/Day
Cocosoya Uckele www.uckele.com 800-248-0330	$9.95/128 oz.	Blend of unprocessed coconut and soybean oils. No chemical preservatives. 98+% fat.	Liquid 2 to 8 oz.
Fat-Cat Vapco www.vapco.com 800-523-5614	$11.95/2 lbs.	Vegetable proteins, dextrose, calcium, phosphorus, digestive enzymes, probiotics, corn oil, B complex, vitamin A, BHA/BHT. Protein 24%, fat 3%, calcium 1%, phosphorus 0.59%, magnesium 0.13%, biotin 3 mg/lb., L-lysine 8,700 mg/lb., DL-methionine 250 mg/lb.	Dry 3 to 4.5 oz.
Gleam & Gain Adeptus www.adeptusnutrition.com 866-233-7887	$33.99/10 lbs.	Ground stabilized flax and rice brans, vegetable fat, distiller's grains, natural preservatives and BHA, yeast cultures, calcium. Protein 10%, fat 41%, calcium 1%, phosphorus 0.4%, alpha-linolenic 2,100 mg/2 oz., linoleic 550 mg/2 oz.	Dry 4+ oz.
Hard Keeper Solution Vita-Flex www.vita-flex.com 800-848-2359	$18.50/6 lbs.	Animal fat, grains, flaxseed meal, live probiotics, digestive enzymes, BHA/BHT chemical preservatives. 15% protein, 40% fat, calcium 1.25%, phosphorus 0.5%.	Dry 4 oz.
LinPro Foxden Equine www.foxdenequine.com 540-337-5450	$25/5 lbs.	Whole flaxseed, soy protein, legume proteins, wheat mids, yeast, chelated trace minerals, selenium yeast, iodine, cobalt, vitamins A/D/E, folic acid, biotin, natural preservatives. Protein 23.9%, lysine .97%, threonine .26%, methionine 350 mg/oz., calcium 0.42%, phosphorus 0.194%, magnesium 4.3%, iodine 2.045 ppm, copper 714.27 ppm, zinc 2,944.7 ppm, selenium 2.5 ppm, biotin 560 mg of 2% biotin/oz., folic acid 78 mg/oz., vitamin A 59,980 IU/kg, vitamin D 5,998.02 IU/kg, vitamin E 1,250 IU/kg.	Dry 2 to 6 oz.
NuWeight Select the Best www.selectthebest.com 800-648-0950	$39.95/10 lbs.	Animal fat, whey, whole extruded soy, tertiary butyl hydroquinone (chemical preservative), yeast, bacterial fermentation products. Fat 59%, protein 10%, calcium 1.2%, phosphorus 0.8%.	Dry 4 to 8 oz.
Radiance HorseTech www.horsetech.com 800-831-3309	$59.95/20 lbs.	Whole ground stabilized flax (50%), distillers dried grains, yeast, hydrogenated and chemically preserved animal fat, vitamin E, L-lysine, calcium. Protein 14%, fat 40%.	Dry 4 to 8 oz.
Rice Bran Oil McCauley Bros. www.mccauleybros. com 800-222-8635	$18.50/128 oz.	Rice bran oil, 95% fat, vitamin E 200 IU/lb., gamma-oryzanol 2%, free fatty acids 7%.	Liquid 2 to 8 oz.
Rice Bran Oil Triple Crown www.triplecrownnutrition.com 800-451-9916	$33.98/128 oz.	Rice bran oil, flaxseed oil, corn oil, fat 98%, total fatty acids 90%, free fatty acids 1%.	Liquid 2 to 8 oz.
Silky Coat Show Gloss Royal Mile Inc. 952-469-3492	$13.35/5 lbs.	Whey, whey protein concentrate, animal fat preserved with BHT, lecithin, sodium silico aluminate. Protein 7%, fat 60%.	Dry 4 to 8 oz.
Weight Builder Solid Farnam www.farnamhorse.com 800-234-2269	$25/8 lbs.	Dehydrated corn distiller's grains with solubles, vegetable fat, heat-stabilized flax, calcium, BHA/BHT chemical preservatives. Protein 14%, fat 40%, calcium 1%, phosphorus 0.5%.	Dry 4 to 8 oz.
Weight Builder Liquid Farnam www.farnamhorse.com 800-234-2269	$17.99/64 oz.	100% vegetable fats from canola, soybean, and flaxseed oils, vitamin E and mixed tocopherols, vitamin C, rosemary extract and natural flavors. Fat minimum 93%, alpha-linolenic (omega-3) 10%, linoleic (omega-6) 30%, oleic (omega-9) 30%, vitamin E 800 IU/oz.	Liquid 2 to 8 oz.
Wheat Germ Oil Blend, Select the Best www.selectthebest.com 800-648-0950	$13.95/128 oz.	Blend of wheat germ and cold-pressed soy oil with tertiary butyl hydroquinone (chemical preservative). Protein 1%, fat 98%, essential fatty acid content not guaranteed or specified.	Liquid 2 to 4 oz.

Index

A

AAFCO (Association of American Feed
  Control Officials), ix–x

Absorbine Flex (joints), 168

Actimune (immune system), 158, 160

adaptogens. *See also* herbs, 73, 231

Adeptus supplements

  Ally (antacid), 96

  Gleam & Gain, 263, 266, 273,
    275, 276

age

  and anemia, 38

  calcium, phosphorus & calorie
    requirements, 48

  feeding foals and weanlings, 125–32

  feeding seniors, 136–44

Air Power (respiratory), 239, 243, 256

allergies, 161–63

  allergens in diet, 257

  food allergies, 80, 165, 241

  and recurrent airway obstruction,
    237–38

  vitamin C for, 254

amino acids. *See also* BCAAs (branched
  chain amino acids)

  coat quality, 261

  Cushing's disease, 73–74

  hoof/skin quality, 145–46, 147

  lysine, 118, 119, 123, 126

  stress reduction, 52

anemia. *See also* blood, building, 38, 151

  and illness, 38, 41

  supplements for, 40

antacids, 96

anti-inflammatories, xi, 17–21

  caution with, 17–19

  herbs, 19

  products, xi, 20–21

antioxidants, 22–29

  affect on blood clotting, 18

  blood building, 37, 39, 42

  chronic infections, 253

  immune-system support, 154,
    157, 160

  minerals, 8

  muscle support, 199–200, 213

pain relief, 19

performance support, 230

stable cough/RAO, 241–42

supplements, 28–29

APF (performance), 233, 234

appetite. *See also* diet, 30–36

and illness, 34

picky eaters, 30–31

in seniors, 144

signs of ulcers, 93, 100

taste tempters, 35–36

apple juice, 35

arginine. *See also* BCAAs, 199

Arthrigen (joints), 177, 181

arthritis. *See also* joint support

antioxidants for, 25

chondroitin for, 174

Artri Matrix (joints), 177, 181

aspergillus. *See also* probiotics, 90, 91

asthma, 163

At-Ease (stress), 55, 59, 60

B

BCAAs (branched chain amino acids). *See also* amino acids, 199, 202, 231

muscle support/performance trials, 203, 204, 206–7, 208–12

products with creatine, 205

bedding, 240

beet pulp. *See also* diet, 32, 57, 195–96, 271

calorie/energy content, 228

holding weight, 33, 35

and HYPP, 216

and insulin resistance, 191, 192

for seniors, 141–42, 143

treating stable cough/RAO, 241

when ill, 34

beta-carotene, 3

bicarbonate ion, 105

bioflavonoids. *See also* nutraceuticals, x, 18, 19

antioxidant capacity, 23

Bio-Flax 20 (hoof), 146

biotin. *See also* B vitamins, 2, 4, 6

and coat quality, 262

Blitz (performance), 233, 235

blood, building, 37–44

blood counts and immune system, 151

iron deficiency, 43

nutrients for, 39, 42

supplements for, 40

B-L Solution and Paste (pain), 20, 21

body-condition score, 268, 270

bones, strengthening, 8, 45–48

calcium, phosphorus, calories requirements, 48

minerals in hay, 46–47

boswellia, 19

Breathe Ease (respiratory), 239, 249, 250, 252, 253, 256

breeding stallion, calorie needs for, 224

breeds. *See also* specific breeds

and biting midges, 164

diet requirements of, vii

insulin resistance of, 192

broodmares. *See also* mares, 116–24

calorie needs, 48, 224

lysine, 118–19

mineral needs, 48, 119–20, 121, 134–35

nutritional/supplement requirements, 122–24, 126

protein needs, 116–18, 122

Buckeye supplements

Grass Plus, 120

Gro N' Win, 124, 132

Perform N' Win, 109, 111

bute. *See* phenylbutazone (bute)

B vitamins

    antioxidant capacity, 23, 26

    blood-building, 39, 42

    coat quality, 261–63, 264

    hoof/skin quality, 145, 147

    requirements for, 4, 5

    for seniors, 138

    stress reduction, 50, 51, 53–54, 56, 59

    synthesis of, 2

    toxicity of, 3

C

calcium, ix, 8, 12, 105

    broodmare requirements, 122, 123, 126, 135

    in hay, 119

    and magnesium, 95, 97

    and nervous-system function, 50

    and phosphorus, 45–46

    requirements by age/class, 48

calorie needs. *See also* diet

    by age/class, 48

    average, 224

    broodmares, 126

    for muscle support, 198–99

    for performance, 231

Carbo Charge (performance), 233, 235

carbohydrates. *See also* diet, ix, 231

    and glycogen, 236

    in sports drink trials, 206, 207, 208, 209, 210, 211, 212

carrot juice, 32, 35

cat's claw, 19

chamomile, 19, 51

chloride. *See also* salt, ix, 105, 106

Chondrogen EQ (joints), 168

chondroitin. *See also* joint support, x, 166, 167, 174, 175

chromium, 232

chronic obstructive pulmonary disease (COPD), 163, 237, 238–40, 247

clove, 83

coat condition, 258–67

    deficiencies affecting, 260–63

    supplements for, 259–60, 263–64, 266–67

cobalt, 12

    hoof/skin quality, 147

    requirements for, 37–38

Coffman, J. R., 187, 188

colic. *See also* digestive tract, 75–77

    probiotics for, 89

    and water consumption, 78–79

Conquer gel (joints), 166, 176, 182

copper, ix, 12, 105

    antioxidant capacity, 23, 26

    bone strength, 46

    broodmare requirements, 123, 126, 135

    and DOD, 134

    hoof/skin quality, 145, 147

    and iron levels, 37, 39, 42

    ratios with other minerals, 9

    for seniors, 140–41

Corta-Flx (joints), 166, 175, 182

Cosequin (joints), 166

coughs. *See* respiratory system; stable cough

creatine. *See also* BCAAs; muscle support, 202, 204, 205–6, 232

    trials with, 206, 208, 209, 210, 211, 212

Culicoides, 164

curcumin, 18, 19

Cushing's disease, 63–74

    herbs for, 63–64, 72

    and insulin resistance, 72, 187, 188,
        190, 195

D

DeFelice, Stephen, x

dehydration. *See also* electrolytes, 78,
    114, 115

dental work, 136, 269

    and holding weight, 33

developmental orthopedic disease
    (DOD), 134

devil's claw, xi, 17–18, 19

    products containing, 20, 21

dewormers, 79–84, 271

    diatomaceous earth, 80–82

    and older horses, 136

diarrhea, 97, 101, 104

diatomaceous earth (DE), 80–82

diet. *See also* supplements

    allergens in, 247–48, 257

    antioxidants in, 24

    broodmares, 116–24

    coat quality, 259–60, 264

    colic, 76–77

    Cushing's disease, 72–74

    deficiencies in types of, 260

    electrolytes in, 105, 106, 107

    essential nutrients in, ix

    evolution of, vii, 1

    foals/weanlings, 125–32

    food allergies, 80, 81, 165

    holding weight, 33, 35

    hoof/skin quality, 145–46, 147

    and illness, 34

    immune-system support, 153

    importance of, vii–ix

    improving taste, 35–36

    inflammatory bowel disease, 102–3

    insulin resistance, 190–91, 192,
        193–97

    meal size and starch in, 77–78

    minerals in, 8–19, 47, 48

    muscle support, 198–99

    and nervousness, 57

    overfeeding, 30

    performance, 230, 231

    picky eaters, 30–31

    Quarter Horses, 213–14

    for seniors, 136–37, 139, 141–44

    treating stable cough/RAO, 240–41

    and ulcers, 93

    vitamins in, 1–8

    water consumption, 78–79, 114

    weight gain, 269–75

    weight loss, 220–24

digestive tract, 75–104

    and B vitamins, 2

    colic, 75–77, 78

    dewormers, 79–84

    diarrhea, 97, 101, 104

    electrolyte abnormalities/
        dehydration, 115

    gastric ulcers, 92–97

    inflammatory bowel disease, 102–3

    prebiotics and probiotics, 84–92

    in seniors, 136–37, 143

    undigested starch in, 77–78

    and water consumption, 78–79

diseases. *See* illnesses; specific diseases

DMG (dimethylglycine), 232

drugs, viii

    and blood clotting, 18

    dewormers, 83–84

insulin resistance, 197
lung bleeding, 255
pain relievers, 17
pergolide, 72, 73
stable cough (RAO), 242

E
echinacea, 159, 160
electrolytes. *See also* minerals, 105–15
 checking for dehydration, 114
 and exercise, 107–8, 113
 low potassium levels, 110
 salt, 105, 106, 107
 supplements, 109–10, 111, 112
EquiAide Product's Body Builder (muscles), 57, 202, 203, 218
Equi-Bac (probiotic), 86, 92
Equilite's Equine Relax Blend, 55, 56, 61
Equinacea (immune system), 253
Equine Generator (probiotic), 33, 84, 87, 92
equine polysaccharide storage myopathy (EPSSM), 213, 214, 216–17
Equi-Pro (muscles), 210, 212
Equitussin (coughs), 239, 243
EquuSea (joints), 170, 171, 179
essential fatty acids (EFAs), 142
 and age, 138, 140
 coat quality, 259, 263
 hoof/skin quality, 146, 147
 immune-system support, 154
Ester-C. *See also* vitamin C, xi, 24
exercise
 building muscles, 200, 213
 and Cushing's disease, 69
 and digestive-tract health, 76, 77, 92–93, 94
 electrolyte losses during, 107–8

exercise-induced cough, 248, 250
exercise induced pulmonary hemorrhage (EIPH), 238, 254–57
 in heat, 111, 113
 immune system stress, 154
 increasing appetite, 33
 and insulin resistance, 189, 190
 lactate levels after, 215
 and ulcers, 92–93, 94
 and weight loss, 223, 226
Ex-Stress, 55, 59, 60
eyes, irritated, 162–63

F
Farnam supplements
 Ascend Hoof Gel, 147, 149
 Platform Mare and Foal (feed), 121, 128, 129
 probiotics, 87, 92
 Red-Cell (anemia), 40
 Weight Builder Liquid, 273, 275, 276
Farrier's Formula (hoof), 147, 149
fats. *See also* essential fatty acids; diet, ix, 57
 and coat condition, 258, 259, 262, 263
 metabolism of, 231
 for weight gain, 271, 272–73
feeds. *See also* diet; supplements
 allergens & mold in, 246, 247–48, 257
 calorie/energy content of, 227, 228
 dietary deficiencies in, 260
 for foals/weanlings, 127–29
 glycemic index of, 195–96
 for insulin resistance, 191, 193–94
 lysine content, 118–19
 minerals in, 119
 protein/mineral comparison of, 121

regulation of, ix–x

for seniors, 139, 142–43

Feisty Mare (stress), 58

fiber, and age. *See also* diet, 137, 143

fibrotic myopathy, 217–18

Flair Nasal Strips (respiratory), 255, 256

flunixin (Banamine), 17

fly mask, 162

Foal-Bac (probiotic), 86, 92

foals and weanlings, 124–34

    calcium, phosphorus, calorie

        requirements, 48

    diet for, 125–33

    DOD in, 134

    OCD in, 133

    probiotics for, 85, 88

    signs of deficiencies, 133

folic acid. *See also* B vitamins, 4, 6

food allergies, 80, 81, 165

Foxden supplements

    anemia supplement, 40

    Foxden Flex (joints), 175, 183

    LinPro (weight gain), 273, 274, 276

Frank, Nicholas, 188

free radicals. *See* antioxidants

furosemide, 255

Futurity Blend 30 (broodmares), 124

G

gamma oryzanol, 201–2

garlic, 82

gastric ulcers, 92–97

    B12 deficiency, 39, 42

    loss of appetite, 31

    and pain relievers, 18

    products for, 96, 98–99, 171

    symptoms and treatment guidelines,

        93–94, 100

Gateway supplements

    Su-Per HMB (muscles), 202, 219

    Su-Per Lytes (electrolytes), 109,

        111, 112

ginseng, 231

glucosamine. *See also* joint support, x, 166,

    167, 170, 173, 174–75

    sulfate or chloride, 169

glucose, 198–99

glycogen, 198, 233, 236

Glycogen Loader (performance),

    233, 235

grains. *See also* diet

    calories in, 117, 222, 224, 225,

        226, 228

    digestibility of, 77, 78, 81

    and DOD, 135

    for foals/weanlings, 126–27, 130

    holding weight, 33, 35

    and nervousness, 57

    for seniors, 141

Grand Meadows supplements

    Grand Coat (coat), 263, 266

    Grand Flex (joints), 166, 175

grass. *See* hay; pasture (grass)

grazing muzzle, 223, 228

H

hay. *See also* diet

    allergens & mold in, 237, 247–48

    calories in, 221, 225, 228

    dietary deficiencies in, 260

    for foals/weanlings, 130–31

    holding weight, 33

    and insulin resistance, 189, 191,

        194, 196–97

    minerals in, 10–16, 46–47, 105,

        107, 119–20

index

potassium in, 105, 110

healthcare, natural. *See also* diet;
    supplements, vii–ix

heat
    and exercise, 111, 113
    and salt loss, 106

heaves. *See also* respiratory system, 163,
    238–39, 247

Herbal-Mune Plus (immune system), 253

HerbalPlex (immune system), 253

herbs. *See also* supplements; specific herbs
    coughs/respiratory problems, 249,
        252–53
    Cushing's disease, 63–64, 72, 73
    dewormers, 79
    immune-system support, 153, 155,
        156, 158–60
    improving taste, 35
    lung bleeding, 256–57
    pain relief, xi, 18, 19
    stress reduction, 51, 52, 54–55,
        56, 59

hesperidin, 23

Hilton Freeway (respiratory), 239, 243,
    249, 252

Hooflex, 147, 149

hoof quality, 145–50
    and biotin, 2, 145, 146
    non-nutritional factors, 150

Hormonise, 58, 59, 61, 72
    and Cushing's disease, 63–64,
        65, 72

Horses Prefer DFM-EQ powder (probiotic),
    86, 92

Horse Tech supplements
    immune-system support, 154, 156
    Preox (antioxidant), 25, 29
    Quench (electrolyte), 110, 111

hyaluronic acid (HA). *See also* joint support,
    x, 166, 167–68, 172, 175, 177

hyperkalemic periodic paralysis (HYPP),
    214, 216

I

Icelandic ponies, 164

illnesses
    and appetite, 34
    and blood count, 38, 41
    chronic infections, 253
    and coat quality, 260
    Cushing's disease, 63–74
    developmental orthopedic disease
        (DOD), 134
    diarrhea, 97, 101, 104
    gastric ulcers, 92–97
    heaves/COPD, 238–40
    inflammatory bowel disease (IBD),
        102–3
    insulin resistance (IR), 187–97
    osteochondrosis (OCD),
        133, 168
    stable cough, 237–38, 239

immune system, 151–65
    allergies, 161–63, 165
    and antioxidants, 22
    and blood counts, 151
    field trials, 155–60
    supplements for, 153–55, 156
    symptoms of weak, 152

infections, chronic, 253

inflammatory bowel disease (IBD),
    102–3

In Motion (joints), 168, 178

inosine, 232

insulin resistance (IR), 187–97
    and Cushing's disease, 72

index

diagnosing, 189–90

and laminitis, 187–88

and obesity, 188–89

and OCD, 133

treating, 190–97

iodine, 8, 12

broodmare requirement, 123, 126

iron, ix, 8, 12, 37, 41, 42, 105

in body tissues, 38

checking for deficiency, 43

and copper, 39

isoleucine. *See also* BCAAs, 199, 205

J

Jet Breathe (respiratory), 249, 250, 252, 253, 256

jiaogulan (Gynostemma pentaphyllum), 73, 242, 244

Johnson, Philip, 187

Joint Renew (joints), 175, 184

Joint Saver (joints), 171, 179

joint support, 166–86

choosing a supplement, 169, 172, 173, 177

Conquer gel, 176

dosage recommendations, 175

glucosamine & chondroitin, 174–75

liquids or powders, 177, 179–80

specialty products, 170–71

supplements for, 178–79, 181–86

trials with hyaluronic acid, 166–68, 172

K

kava kava, 51, 52, 54–55

Kentucky Equine Research's supplements, 109, 110, 111

L

lactic acid (lactate), 215, 232

laminitis

and black walnut, 79

and insulin resistance, 187–88, 189, 195

leucine. *See also* BCAAs, 199

Lube All Plus (joints), 175, 178

lungs. *See* respiratory system

lysine. *See also* amino acids, 118, 119, 123, 126, 199

M

magnesium, ix, 12, 105

bone strength, 46

breathing disorders, 242

and calcium, 9, 95, 97

laminitis/insulin resistance, 187, 193

stress reduction, 50, 51, 53, 55, 56

manganese, ix, 12, 105

antioxidant capacity, 23, 26

broodmare needs, 123, 126, 135

and copper, 9

and DOD, 134

mares. *See also* broodmares

and Cushing's disease, 63–64

fertility of, 122

insulin resistant, 197

stress supplements, 58, 59

Master Hoof Blend, 147, 148

Matrix 4 (joints), 168, 178, 185

meadowsweet, 19

Med-Vet supplements

Anti-Ox, 25, 29

Omegas (coat), 267

midges, biting, 164

minerals. *See also* specific minerals; supplements, 8–16, 105 antioxidant capacity, 23

blood-building, 39

bone strengthening, 45–47

for broodmares, 119–20, 123,
    134–35

coat quality, 261, 262

electrolytes, 105–15

for foals/weanlings, 131–32

in hay, 10–16, 46–47, 107

hoof/skin quality, 145, 147

and insulin resistance, 190, 191

major or trace, 12

muscle support, 200, 201

nervous-system function, 50

performance enhancing, 230

ratios of, 9

for seniors, 138, 140–41, 142

toxicity of, 8, 9

Mobile Milling's Exer-Lyte (electrolyte),
    109, 111, 112

molds, and RAO, 237–38

MSM. *See also* joint support, xi, 170, 172

muscle support, 198–219, 231

    action plan, 203

    creatine for, 202, 205–6

    and electrolytes/dehydration, 115

    exercise for, 200

    fat or muscle, 200

    and lactic acid, 215

    products for, 201–2, 218–19

    for Quarter Horse, 212–14,
        216–18

    trials with sports drinks, 203–4,
        206–12

muzzle, grazing, 223, 228

N

Natural Plan Stomach Soother, 97, 98

nervousness. *See* stress, calming

niacin. *See also* B vitamins, 2, 4, 6

NSAIDs (non-steroidal anti-inflammatory
    drugs), 18

Nu-Hoof Accelerator, 147

nutraceuticals. *See also* joint support;
    supplements, viii, x–xi

    cough remedies, 249

    hyaluronic acid, 172

    joint supplements, 166, 167, 170–77,
        178–79, 181–86

    for pain, 18

Nutrena feeds, 120, 121

Nutrena Life Design Junior, 118,
    128, 129

nutrition. *See* diet; supplements; vitamins;
    minerals

O

oats. *See also* diet; grains

    allergens in, 247

    calorie/energy content, 228

    for food allergies, 79, 80, 81

    for seniors, 141

    starch in, 78

obesity, 195, 220–29

    diet for, 220–24

    and insulin resistance, 188–89, 195

    serious problems, 227–29

    temporary problems, 224–27

oils, 272–73

Omega Field's Horseshine (immune
    system/coat), 154, 156, 263, 266

Ontario Dehy Balanced Timothy Cubes,
    191, 193

osteochondrosis (OCD), 133, 168

Oxy-Equine (muscles), 201, 219

P

pain. *See also* anti-inflammatories
  decreased appetite, 32–33
  local therapies for, 18
  severe pain, 18
  as warning signal, 17
PalaMountains Equine (muscles), 201
pantothenic acid. *See also* B vitamins, 2,
    4, 6
parasites. *See also* dewormers, 260
pasture (grass). *See also* diet; hay
  antioxidants in, 24
  dietary deficiencies in, 260
  digestibility of, 34, 88
  fatty acids in, 264
  for foals/weanlings, 130–31
  grass juice recipe, 36
  minerals in, 10
  protein in, 117
  for sick horse, 34
  vitamins in, 1
  water content of, 76
  and weight gain, 192, 222–23
Peak Performance supplements
  BCAA Complex (muscles/
      performance), 202, 233, 235
  Natural Balance Electrolite,
      109, 111
  Nutrients' Pro VM, 40, 44
performance, 230–35
  electrolyte problems, 115
  glycogen loading, 236
  sports drinks for, 203–4, 206
  supplements for, 234–35
  and weight, 274
  what to avoid, 232
pergolide, 72, 73
Perna mussel, x, 166

phenylbutazone (bute), 17, 18, 170
phobias. *See* stress, calming
phosphorus, ix, 12, 105
  broodmare requirements, 123, 126
  and calcium, 9, 45–46
  in hay, 119
  requirement by age/class, 48
  for seniors, 138, 140
plants. *See also* herbs
  and anemia, 40
  antioxidants in, 23
  salicylates in, 19
ponies, vii
  calorie restrictions for, 221
  insulin resistance in, 187, 190, 192
potassium, ix
  daily requirement of, 105
  low levels of, 110
Poulin Carb Safe (feed), 193
Power Pak (performance), 233, 235
prebiotics. *See also* probiotics, 87
probiotics. *See also* diet; supplements, 73,
    77, 84–92
  bacteria-based, 90–91
  dosage of, 88–89
  fiber digestion, 33
  products, 86–87
  for seniors, 137, 144
  yeast-based, 91
protein. *See also* diet; supplements, ix, 75
  broodmare requirements, 116–18,
      123, 126
  coat quality, 260–61, 262
  Cushing's horses, 73
  and DOD, 134
  foal/weanling needs, 132
  hoof/skin quality, 145–46, 147
  muscle support, 199, 202

senior needs, 137–38

whey protein, 154, 156, 157

pumpkin seeds, 83

Purina feeds, 121, 128–29

pyridoxine. *See also* B vitamins, 2, 4, 6

pyruvate, 232

Q

Quarter Horses, muscle support for,
212–14, 216–18

quercetin, 23

R

Ralston, Sarah, 138

Rapid Response (joints/ulcers), 97, 98,
170–71, 177, 179, 185

Ration Plus (probiotic), 57, 87, 90, 91,
101, 272

diarrhea recovery, 101

fiber digestion, 33, 137

holding weight, 89

Recovery (joints), 170, 171, 179

recurrent airway obstruction (RAO).
See also respiratory system, 237–38

Relax Her (stress), 58, 59

respiratory system, 237–57

chronic infections, 253

cough remedies, 243, 249

exercise-induced cough, 248

heaves/COPD, 238–40

herbs for bronchospasm, 242,
244–47

lung bleeding (EIPH), 254–57

lung conditions, 251–53

nasal discharge, 250–51

stable cough, 237–38, 239

treating stable cough/RAO, 239,
240–42

vitamin C and allergies, 254

resveratrol, 23

riboflavin. *See also* B vitamins, 2, 4, 6

rice bran. *See also* feeds; grains,
228, 273

Richdel's Select Stress-Pak, 109, 112

rutin, 23

S

saccharomyces yeast, 91, 92

salt. *See also* electrolytes, 105, 106, 107,
198

seeds, 272

pumpkin seeds, 83

selenium, ix, 8, 12, 120

antioxidant capacity, 23, 25, 26

for broodmares, 123, 126

muscle support, 199–200, 214

for seniors, 141

Senior Flex (joints), 175, 178, 185

Seniorglo (feed), 139, 142

Shoer's Friend, 147, 149

skin problems. *See also* coat condition,
163, 164

Skode's Horse Treats, 36

sodium. *See also* salt, ix, 105, 106

Spillers Happy Hoof, 193

spirulina platensis, 155, 156, 162, 163

for breathing disorders, 242, 244,
245–47

Sport Horse (muscles), 201, 219

stable cough. *See also* respiratory system,
237–38, 239

stallion. *See* breeding stallion

Sterett Brothers Low Carb Complete
Feed, 193

straw, 222, 228

molds in, 237, 240

stress, calming, 49–62
    feeds and nervousness, 57
    herbs for, 51, 52
    in mares, 58
    supplements for, 60–62
    and trailering, 53
Superior Seniors (feed), 139, 143
supplements. *See also* herbs; nutraceuticals,
    viii, ix–xi
    antioxidants, 25, 28–29
    blood building, 39–40, 44
    broodmares, 118, 120, 124
    coat quality, 259–60, 263–64,
        266–67
    cough/breathing, 239, 241–42,
        243, 249
    Cushing's disease, 63–64, 72, 73
    dehydration, 114
    electrolytes, 109–10, 111, 112
    hoof support, 148–49, 150
    immune system, 153–55, 156
    joint support, 170–71, 178–79,
        181–86
    lung bleeding, 256–57
    making palatable, 32
    and minerals, 10
    muscle support, 201–2, 218–19
    pain relief, 20–21
    performance enhancing, 234–35
    probiotics, 86–87
    seniors, 137–38, 140
    sports drinks (muscles/performance),
        203–4, 205, 206–12
    stress reduction, 50–55, 59–62
    ulcers, 96, 98–99
    vitamins, 6–7
    weight gain, 273–76

T
taurine, 51, 52
thiamine. *See also* B vitamins, 2, 4, 6
    and stress reduction, 50, 51, 53–54,
        55, 59
Thoroughbreds, vii, 3
    holding weight, 33
    obesity and insulin resistance
        in, 188
trailering, and stress, 53
Triple Crown supplements
    feeds, 118, 124, 128, 129, 132
    low-carb feeds, 193
    senior feeds, 139, 143
    vitamin/mineral lines, 7, 124, 132,
        153–54, 156
trytophan, 51, 52, 54, 56, 59
turmeric, 19
tying-up (muscle condition), 214

U
Uckele supplements
    anemia, 40
    antioxidants, 25, 26, 27, 29
    appetite stimulators, 35
    Carbo Load, 233, 235
    coat quality, 66, 263, 266
    Equi-Hoof Complex, 147, 149
    joint support, 175, 178, 183, 184,
        185, 186
    Liquid E-50 (immune system),
        154, 156
    Liqui-Fuel (dehydration), 114
    muscle support, 202, 203, 205, 212,
        217, 218, 219
    pain relief, 20, 21
    probiotics, 86, 87

protein, 73, 74

respiratory conditions, 239, 243, 249, 251, 256

stress reducing, 55, 60

ulcers, 97, 98

weight gain, 273, 275, 276

U-Gard Solution (antacid), 96, 97

ulcers. See gastric ulcers

V

valerian, 51, 52, 54–55, 56, 59

valine. See also BCAAs, 199

Vapco's Fat Cat (muscles), 202, 203, 219, 273, 274, 276

Vicks VapoRub, 239, 242, 243

Vintage Senior (feed), 139, 143

Vita-Key's Antioxidant Concentrate, 25, 29, 44, 154, 156

vitamin A, 3, 6

broodmare requirements, 123, 126

coat quality, 265

vitamin C, 3, 6

for allergies, 254

antioxidant capacity, 23, 25, 26

coat quality, 265

Ester-C, 24

requirements for, 5

for seniors, 138

vitamin D, 3, 6

vitamin E, x, 2, 3, 6

antioxidant capacity, 23, 25, 26, 27

broodmare requirements, 120, 123, 126

coat quality, 261

immune-system support, 154

muscle support, 199, 214

supplements for, 5, 8

vitamin K, 3, 6, 257

vitamins. See also specific vitamins; supplements, 1–8

antioxidant capacity, 23

coat quality, 261–63, 265

estimated daily B requirements, 4

and muscles, 200, 201

and nervous-system function, 50

and performance, 230

supplementing, 3, 5, 6–7

synthesis of B vitamins, 2

toxicity of, 3

vitamin E deficiencies, 2, 3

Vitex agnus castus (chasteberry), 59, 63, 64–65, 71

W

water, drinking, 76, 78–79, 106, 198

checking for dehydration, 114

Watts, Katy, 196

weanlings. See foals and weanlings

Weese, Scott, 88

weight. See also obesity

and age, 144

and body-condition score, 268, 270

gaining, 268–76

holding, 35–36

and insulin resistance, 188–89

wheat-germ oil, 273

white willow, xi, 19

Wind Air (respiratory), 239, 243, 256

Witcheylady Creations & Potions, 36

work. See also exercise; performance

antioxidant needs, 24

calorie needs, 224

hay requirements, 33

salt needs, 106

vitamin needs, 6, 199

wormwood (Artemisia). *See also* herbs, 82–83

Y

yeasts. *See also* probiotics, 91

yucca, 19

Z

zinc, ix, 12, 105

    antioxidant capacity, 23, 26

    bone strength, 46

    broodmare requirements, 123, 126, 135

    coat quality, 265

    and copper, 9

    and DOD, 134

    hoof/skin quality, 145, 147

About the Author

Dr. Eleanor Kellon has been the veterinary editor of *Horse Journal* since 1995. *Horse Journal* is the horse owner's version of *Consumer Reports*. The magazine publishes informative care articles, as well as extensive product reviews. No advertising is accepted. Because of this independence from advertising dollars, a positive review from *Horse Journal* is highly prized and will often be cited by manufacturers. Dr. Kellon's articles in *Horse Journal* over the years have run the gamut from basic feeding advice for all classes of horses to nutritional strategies for addressing specific problems such as tying-up, hoof problems, weight issues, allergies, and more.

Dr. Kellon has written hundreds of articles for horse magazines over her career. She is also the veterinary editor and a contributing author for *John Lyons Perfect Horse* and has had articles appear in *Equus, Practical Horseman, Hoofbeats,* and the *Chronicle of the Horse.* She has written five books, including *Equine Supplements and Nutraceuticals* (Breakthrough Publications, currently in revision). She was invited to the 2006 Equine Health and Nutrition Congress in Ghent, Belgium, to speak on the topic of nutraceuticals and also to deliver a presentation on iron overload in insulin-resistant horses. Dr. Kellon was interviewed on the "If Your Horse Could Talk" radio show on the topic of diet and balancing minerals. She authored the chapter on medical causes of laminitis and its dietary treatment in the textbook *Equine Podiatry.* She also coauthored an article on the feeding of insulin-resistant horses that appeared in the February 2004 issue of *Compendium of Continuing Education for the Practicing Veterinarian*.

Dr. Kellon has a strong interest in an integrative approach to health and treatment of disease, which relies heavily on provision of optimal nutrition to allow the horse's body to build, protect, and repair itself as efficiently as possible. She is currently very active in the design of unique herbal and nutritional support for horses with insulin resistance, laminitis, and degenerative tendon and ligament problems, as well as allergies. She is the co-owner of the nearly 5,000-member Yahoo group, Equine Cushing's and Laminitis, and very active in the group DSLD-Equine (Degenerative Suspensory Ligament Desmitis). She is also very involved in both consulting and hands-on application of optimal nutrition for breeding, growth, development, and performance. She and Andy, her husband of 24 years, breed, raise, train, and race Standardbreds.

Dr. Kellon is a 1976 *magna cum laude* graduate of the University of Pennsylvania Veterinary School and completed a three-year internship and residency in large animal medicine at New Bolton Center. 🐎